MITCHELL
BEAZLEY
WINE
GUIDES

WINES OF
Bordeaux

Introduction by Hugh Johnson

DAVID PEPPERCORN

Wines of Bordeaux
by David Peppercorn

First published in Great Britain in 1986 as *David Peppercorn's Pocket Guide
to The Wines of Bordeaux*. This edition, revised, updated and expanded,
published in 2004 by Octopus Publishing Group Ltd., 2–4 Heron Quays,
London E14 4JP.

A CIP catalogue record for this book is available from the British Library.

ISBN 1 84000 862 8

The author and publishers will be grateful for any information that will assist
them in keeping future editions up to date. Although all reasonable care has
been taken in the preparation of this book, neither the publishers nor the
author can accept responsibility for any consequences arising from the use
thereof or from the information contained therein.

Commissioning Editor: Hilary Lumsden
Executive Art Editor: Yasia Williams
Editor: Emma Rice
Designers: Colin Goody, Peter Gerrish
Index: Hilary Bird
Production: Gary Hayes

Typeset in Versailles
Printed and bound in China

Contents

Introduction

Access to the personal files of a top professional is surely the most that any serious amateur of wine could ask. The new generation of wine books represented by David Peppercorn's guide to the wines of Bordeaux amounts almost to such a privileged snoop.

The situation reports and critical opinions that form the basis of buying decisions are normally classified information. But wine literature has moved with quite startling speed from the phase of enthusiastic generalization to that of precise wine-by-wine commentary. In this book it drops at least its sixth, if not its seventh, veil. Now we are allowed to know as much as the most experienced professionals.

David Peppercorn is one of the most perceptive and respected of that ancient aristocracy of Anglo-Saxon merchants whose specialty is the wine of Bordeaux. He inherited both skill and passion from his father, one of the great "claret men" of the previous generation. Indirectly, one might say, he inherited them from a long line of predecessors stretching right back to the *negotiator brittanicus* who was identified on the waterfront of Burdigala, Roman Bordeaux, 18 centuries ago.

Accumulated experience is a serious merchant's vital stock-in-trade. It allows him to watch the passing show with a sense of historical perspective, to interpret as well as to observe. But to keep up with such a complex scene as Bordeaux demands, above all, perpetual tastings and almost daily communication with the marketplace. Thousands of properties vary from one vintage to another in their relative success or failure, while their older wines develop – not always in predictable ways.

David Peppercorn combines these two essential elements – a background of experience and a fund of knowledge constantly kept up to date – as well as any merchant-turned-author has ever done. It is a remarkable privilege to be able, as it were, to look over his shoulder at the enthralling pageant of Bordeaux.

Hugh Johnson

How to Use this Book

This book has three main sections: first, an introductory one giving a general picture of the Bordeaux wine region and how it works; second, a series of château profiles arranged by appellation with a short briefing on each appellation; and third, an alphabetical listing of châteaux that do not feature in the profiles section, but whose product makes them worthy of a brief mention at least. Out of the 4,000 or so châteaux in the region, a careful selection has been made of some 1,000 properties, ranging from the most illustrious growths to many lesser-known *crus* that are worth seeking out. These include not only châteaux but also some domaines and cooperatives.

To look up a name, find the page reference in the full alphabetical index at the back of the book. If the reference leads to the "Additional Châteaux" section, the entry there will be followed by brief factual details such as appellation, ownership, vineyard area and production figures. A star beside one of these entries indicates that, although not profiled, the wine is above-average in its class. If the château merits a profile, the index will refer you to the appropriate page in the body of the book: "Château Profiles by Appellation". If the name is that of a second or other label, the index entry appears in italic and the page number refers to that of the parent château.

To save space, a number of abbreviations have been used. Vineyard areas are expressed in hectares (shortened to ha), and yields are given in hectolitres per hectare (hl/ha).

Where a company owns a property, the company name may be preceded by the following abbreviations. These indicate types of company as follows:

Éts	Établissement	**SARL**	Société à Responsibilité Limité
GAEC	Groupement Agricole d'Exploitation en Commun	**SC**	Société Civile
		SCA	Société Civile Agricole
GFA	Groupement Foncier Agricole	**SCEA**	Société Civile d'Exploitation Agricole
SA	Société Anonyme	**SCI**	Société Civile Immobilière

The following abbreviations are used for grape varieties:

CF	Cabernet Franc	**Musc**	Muscadelle
Col	Colombard	**PV**	Petit Verdot
CS	Cabernet Sauvignon	**Sauv**	Sauvignon Blanc
Mal	Malbec	**Sém**	Sémillon
Mer	Merlot		

The following rating system is applied to the châteaux entries

★	very good in context of AC	→	improving
★★	excellent	V	recommended as
★★★	outstanding		particularly good value
(☆	white wines)		

The Region and its Wines

Bordeaux occupies a pre-eminent place among the world's wine regions. Its special geographical situation enables it to produce more fine wines with more regularity than any other part of France, or any other country.

Nowhere else are the greatest wines made in such quantity (only Ausone and Pétrus are in really short supply). And if worldwide acclaim has driven the prices of the first growths beyond the reach of most of us, there are a number of excellent wines at far more reasonable prices that can often rival them, especially when young. For if Bordeaux can claim nine *premiers crus* (eight red and one white), how many other remarkable and exceptional wines does it make? Tot up the best of the classified Médocs (and some of the unclassified ones) and the best of the Graves and St-Émilion classified growths, to say nothing of the best Pomerols, and you arrive at a figure of around 100 growths that can or do produce great bottles of wine. An impressive roll-call. This covers only red wines, but there are also great sweet white wines and good dry whites.

Of course, this small elite is only the tip of the iceberg. The Bordeaux bible, *Bordeaux et Ses Vins*, by Edition Féret, lists over 4,800 property names in its 1995 edition, while just over 13,500 growers made wine in the *département* of Gironde in 1995 (this includes *vin de table*) and over 112,000 hectares of vineyards were dedicated to the growing of vines with the right to an *appellation contrôlée*. Bordeaux wines are indeed within the reach of all today and its most modest wines have never been better made.

Geography

Physically, Bordeaux lies in the southwest of France, on the 45° latitude, with the often stormy waters of the Atlantic Ocean in the Bay of Biscay only a few miles to the west. Its vineyards spread out along the rivers Gironde, Garonne and Dordogne. Here the warming influence of the Gulf Stream is crucial; bear in mind that, on the other side of the Atlantic, the same latitude goes through Nova Scotia and Maine. The Gulf Stream and the Atlantic provide Bordeaux with hot summers, long, mild autumns often extending to the end of October, relatively mild but wet winters, and mild springs. The consistency of the weather is emphasized by the way in which years of bitter cold (1709, 1740, 1820, 1956, 1985) or years of excessive rain (1930–2, 1965, 1968, and 1992) stand out.

The geology of the region is also important – not so much, it is now thought, for what the soils contain as for the drainage they provide. Going south from the Pointe de Grave and the ocean, the riverside land to the west of the Gironde and Garonne is basically gravel, that to the east predominantly sand, limestone and clay, in constantly changing patterns and proportions. There are exceptions, such as the gravel found in parts of Pomerol and the part of St-Émilion that adjoins it, and the limestone and clay that lies under the gravel which gives Sauternes its special character. The flat, gravelly ridges of the Médoc and Graves are protected from Atlantic gales by the thick pine forests bordering the ocean; they also buffer the rainfall. The hills and rivers in the Premières Côtes and Entre-Deux-Mers also provide important differences in microclimate between those vineyards to the west of the Gironde and Garonne (Médoc and Graves) and those to the east of the Dordogne (the Libournais). The distances involved are also significant. From the Pointe de Grave in the north to Langon in the south is 148 kilometres (92 miles); from the city of Bordeaux eastwards to Ste-Foy-la-Grande is 70 kilometres (44 miles), so important climatic variations are hardly surprising.

Historical Background

Three centuries of allegiance to the English crown (1152–1453) gave Bordeaux a sense of unity as a region set apart from the rest of France, and helped to orient it firmly towards the Atlantic and its associated seafaring trade routes.

During these centuries, the relative strengths and weaknesses of the sides ebbed and flowed. In the long term, the development of sea trade was to have the most far-reaching consequences of all. The evolution of the city of Bordeaux, both as the commercial centre of the region and as its principal port, was natural enough in view of its position. But the development of Libourne as the main port on the Dordogne resulted from a deliberate act of policy by the English to expand trade by creating, in 1270, an entirely new town and port.

After the inevitable trading setback caused by the severance of the political ties between Bordeaux and England, it took some time for the region to recover, but as it did, the value of the sea routes and the trading links built up through them became clear. Not only was trade with England, and soon Scotland and Ireland, restored on a lesser scale, but trade with other maritime powers, such as Holland and the Hanseatic ports, was developed. Sea links were also important in establishing trade with Brittany, Normandy and Dunkirk. It was also logical that the lucrative West Indies business should have been built up and carried on through the port of Bordeaux. This brought considerable wealth to the city in the 18th century.

The 18th century also saw significant developments in the pattern of land ownership. The movement to build up important estates in the Médoc had begun in the previous century, but now it really began to take shape. This consolidation of land holdings in the hands of the so-called *noblesse de robe* (the legal and political aristocracy of Bordeaux) has had a vital influence in creating the château system that gives the Bordeaux vineyards their unique character. At the same time, a new and prosperous merchant class began to assert itself, first as *courtiers* (brokers) and *négociants*, and later as proprietors.

This gave Bordeaux as a region a structure that was durable and resilient enough to withstand the vast social and political upheavals of the French revolutionary period (1789–96). Of course, there were many important changes in ownership. One British general even acquired a château and gave it his name, Palmer, after the final defeat of Napoleon in 1815. But many châteaux changed ownership in name only, having been bought by relatives of exiles whose absence abroad led to their lands being forfeited, and the eventual return of these exiles, in many cases, saw a restoration of the status quo.

In the post-Napoleonic era the importance of the new merchant class, often enriched by commerce with the West Indies, greatly increased. Families such as Barton, Guestier, and Johnston became château proprietors as well as *négociants*. The growing success of the Médoc was crowned by the Paris Exhibition of 1855 for which the famous classification was

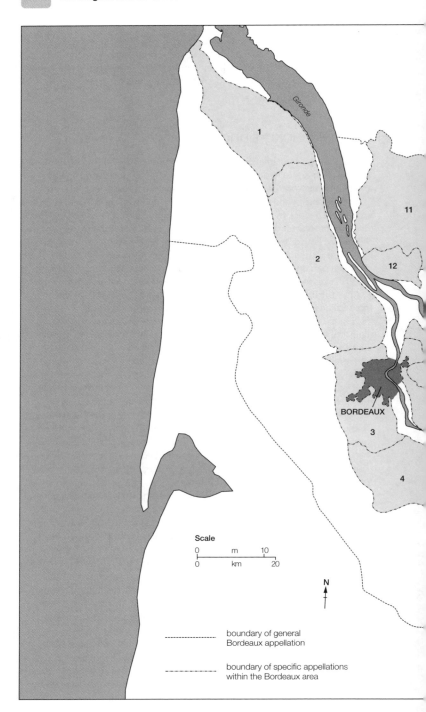

Scale

0   m   10
0   km   20

N

boundary of general
Bordeaux appellation

boundary of specific appellations
within the Bordeaux area

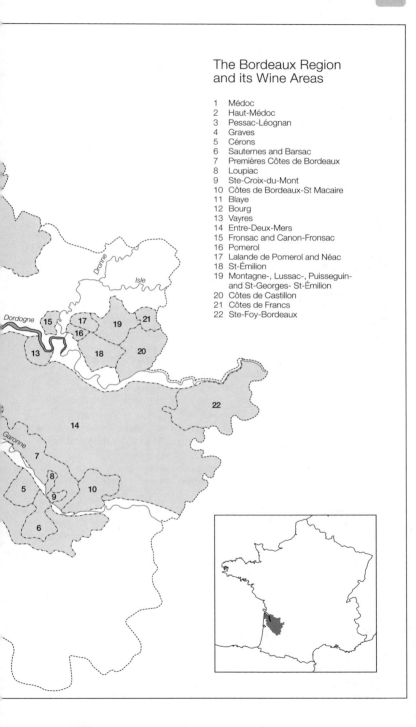

The Bordeaux Region and its Wine Areas

1   Médoc
2   Haut-Médoc
3   Pessac-Léognan
4   Graves
5   Cérons
6   Sauternes and Barsac
7   Premières Côtes de Bordeaux
8   Loupiac
9   Ste-Croix-du-Mont
10 Côtes de Bordeaux-St Macaire
11 Blaye
12 Bourg
13 Vayres
14 Entre-Deux-Mers
15 Fronsac and Canon-Fronsac
16 Pomerol
17 Lalande de Pomerol and Néac
18 St-Émilion
19 Montagne-, Lussac-, Puisseguin- and St-Georges- St-Émilion
20 Côtes de Castillon
21 Côtes de Francs
22 Ste-Foy-Bordeaux

prepared, covering the red wines of the Médoc (with the addition of Haut-Brion) and the great sweet wines of Sauternes and Barsac.

In 1853, the Paris–Bordeaux railway was opened. This was to have a vital impact on the opening of much of the French market to Bordeaux wines at a period of increasing prosperity. It was especially important for the development of St-Émilion, which had lagged behind the Médoc until this time. Napoleon III had ushered in the Second Empire in 1851, and a period of new buoyancy enabled France increasingly to share in the fruits of the industrial revolution, which had been launched in Britain.

Parisian bankers such as the Rothschilds (Lafite and Mouton) and the Péreires (Palmer) invested in properties in the Médoc. Even more important in the long run, the Libournais (St-Émilion, Pomerol, and Fronsac) began to emerge from their long obscurity and make their mark. But just as the whole region seemed set on the greatest period of expansion and prosperity in its history, disaster struck. The period often called the *Grande Belle Époque* was effectively ended in 1878 by the devastations of phylloxera. Not until 1893 was there a large vintage of fine quality again.

It said much for the resources built up during the previous years, as well as the energy and determination of the large landowners who led the way in combating the disease, that Bordeaux recovered in the way it did. Once it was discovered that grafting the original French vines onto disease-resistant American rootstock was the only sure remedy, the reconstitution of the vineyards began. Yet an undertaking of this magnitude could not be accomplished overnight, nor without a great deal of cost and experimentation.

The picture of what actually happened during these years is a complex one. The need to produce large quantities of serviceable wines quickly was met by planting on marginal lands not previously used for vines and on the *palus* (riverside plain), where treatment by flooding and the sandy soil inhibited the spread of the disease. At the same time, the owners of quality vineyards fought, with a good deal of success, to preserve their ungrafted vines, realizing that fine wines needed mature vines. That is why many of the great vineyards of the Médoc, as well as some in St-Émilion and Pomerol such as Cheval-Blanc, Figeac, and La Conseillante, were able to continue making great wines during the years of transition.

But a new *Belle Époque* was not yet in sight. After two great years in 1899 and 1900, there was to be no outstanding vintage again until 1920. Economically, the years leading up to the First World War were depressed in Europe as a whole, and the Bordeaux trade did not experience the same degree of prosperity it had known in the 1850s, 1860s and 1870s. Although the 1920s produced some splendid vintages, economic conditions became steadily worse. The price of the 1926 vintage collapsed, and the world slump soon followed. Poor vintages and a disastrous economic climate spelled ruin for many growers and merchants during the 1930s.

Bordeaux Since 1945

It was against this background that Bordeaux celebrated peace in 1945 with a series of wonderful vintages, but it took some time for the region to repair the years of neglect and begin to rebuild its prosperity. It was not until the late 1950s that one could say with confidence that a new age was dawning. Prices, and with them investment in vineyards and buildings, began to rise. The real prosperity of the 1960s culminated in the speculation and spiralling prices of 1971–3, which ended in disaster precipitated by the oil crisis of 1974 and was exacerbated by a thoroughly unhealthy market situation in Bordeaux itself. But after only two years of disorder, the Bordeaux market recovered, and progress, prosperity, and good vintages were the region's hallmarks until the combination of the world recession, high stocks following the exceptional and plentiful vintages of the 1980s, and the difficult vintages of '91 and '92 led to a sharp fall in prices. The '88 vintage marked the peak of prices in the 1980s: they did not attain this level again until '95. The *primeur* campaigns for '95, '96, and '97 saw a spiralling of prices similar to that of '70/'71, taking them to a new level for the leading *crus*. The prices for '97 were perceived as unjustified in relation to the quality and were largely rejected by merchants and consumers alike. By 2002, many of the star wines could be bought deeply discounted by between thirty and fifty per cent. Prices then eased but the much heralded 2000s reached new levels, before prices for 2001, and especially 2002, eased back again.

The revival of prosperity, especially in the Médoc, owed not a little to the enterprise and hard work of an important group of newcomers, colloquially known as *pieds noirs*. These were Frenchmen who had owned estates in Algeria prior to 1960. Many of them bought properties in the northern Médoc, where prices were low and much of the land was lying fallow.

Technical Progress and Innovation

The 1960s and 1970s were years of enormous technical progress. In the vineyards, the success of sprays in preventing rot have meant that a Bordeaux vintage has not been harvested in an unhealthy condition since 1968. The vinification of these healthy grapes has also seen important improvements. The temperature at which wine is fermented is now so carefully controlled that even in hot years, such as 1982, 1983, 1985, 1989, and 1990, few wines become acetic, whereas in 1947 this misfortune was commonplace. The quality of dry white wines has improved almost beyond recognition now that fermentation is carried out at around 18°C (64°F) and the wine is aged in steel rather than wooden barrels. But in recent years, there has been a widespread return to cask-fermentation for quality wines.

Great improvements have been made among top growths, especially in the Médoc where the properties are large, by taking much more care over the selection of grapes before the final *assemblage* for the *grand vin*. This has been one of Professor Émile Peynaud's many contributions to the improvements in quality which have been so widely achieved over the past 30 years.

Bordeaux tends to be rather ambivalent about modernization, so not everyone would hail the introduction of mechanical harvesters as an improvement. Nowhere in France has their use spread more rapidly, and today more machines are employed in the Gironde than in any other *vignoble* of France: 1,050 were in use by 1983 and 1,500 by 1986, harvesting more than half the area under vine. Today the figure is nearer two-thirds. The large estates in the Médoc and Entre-Deux-Mers are especially well adapted to their use as the land is rather flat and the *cuviers*, where the wine is vinified, are usually adjacent to the vineyards. The major advantage of mechanical harvesting is its speed, enabling a much more precise decision to be made as to when the picking should take place, permitting all the grapes to be harvested when perfectly ripe and minimizing the risk of part of the harvest being overripe or the weather breaking mid-harvest.

Many of the *crus classés* are still resisting the introduction of machines on the grounds that it would be detrimental to quality. One suspects that they are also concerned about the image created by the machine in the context of an expensive, high-quality product.

The present indications are that, with the progress that has been made in adapting these machines to French vineyards, excellent results can be obtained. For white wines, the cylindrical presses now in use in the winery – the horizontal screw press and, especially in recent years, the pneumatic press – can press the white grapes. Machines also leave unripe grapes unpicked, and in this respect make a better selection "on the vine" than would most pickers. In recent vintages, the use of the *vendange vert*, a severe cutting off of grapes in July, has become widespread in the best vineyards in an effort to control excessive yields, and so improve quality.

The Appellations

The concept of appellations, developed in France immediately after the First World War, and the final legislation giving effect to the system we now know, was enacted in 1935. It meant that any wine of more than purely local fame was given the designation *Appellation d'Origine Contrôlée* (AOC), usually shortened to *Appellation Contrôlée* (AC). The original purpose was to protect the famous wine names of France from cheap imitations at a time of surplus production and low prices. It also spearheaded an important campaign to remove hybrid vines from appellation vineyards. These are crosses between European vines and phylloxera-resistant American vines, as distinct from grafted vines or crosses between different European vines (such as Müller-Thurgau). These hybrids, which often carry over something of the odd "foxy" flavour to be found in American vines, were planted in many vineyards after the phylloxera epidemic as an alternative to grafting.

The principal functions of an appellation regulation are:

1   to define the area entitled to a name (eg. Médoc);
2   to list what grape varieties may be planted;
3   to specify the density per hectare of vines to be planted, and how they shall be pruned;
4   to set maximum yields per hectare;
5   to set minimum degrees of alcohol (and sometimes for white wines, maximum degrees) and regulate chaptalization (addition of sugar to must to increase alcoholic degree in years of deficient ripeness);
6   since 1974, to insist on analyses and tastings before finished wines may receive their appellation documents; and,
7   to require growers to make a declaration of their production after each vintage, and a declaration of stocks held as at August 31 each year.

To administer this system and liaise with the syndicates of growers in each appellation, the *Institut National des Appellations d'Origine* (INAO) was formed, and remains the key body for monitoring and reforming the system.

In the Bordeaux region, the definition of a particular area entitled to an appellation of its own caused fewer problems than in some other parts of France. But in the Libournais, there was much local controversy as to the use of the name St-Émilion. In the 19th century, its use was widespread, as old copies of Cocks & Féret's *Bordeaux et ses Vins* bear witness. St-Émilion at this time included not only Pomerol and the communes to the north but also the area to the east now known as the Côtes de Castillon. In 1921, the situation was finally resolved when the Tribunal of Libourne judged that the name of St-Émilion should refer only to those parishes contained within the ancient jurisdiction of the Jurade de St-Émilion. But in 1936, the communes that had been refused the right to sell their wines as St-Émilion were permitted to add the name to their own, thus Montagne-St-Émilion, etc. These are now known as the St-Émilion Satellites.

In the Médoc, the area north of St-Estèphe known as Bas-Médoc received the AC Médoc, while the best part southwards as far as Blanquefort was made Haut-Médoc. However, within the Haut-Médoc, the growers of the most renowned villages sought, and eventually received, their own appellations. A similar situation arose in Graves, where the growers in the best northern parts sought to use Pessac and Léognan instead of Graves. A compromise was agreed in 1984, with each château concerned adding one of the two names to that of Graves. In 1987, however, after a long campaign, the new appellation Pessac-Léognan was granted. A rather odd anomaly exists in Sauternes, where the commune of Barsac, one of five within the appellation, also has its own AC, and growers may choose to call their wines either Barsac or Sauternes.

The control of what grape varieties may be planted ensures that the traditional character of each wine is preserved and prevents the use of inferior, and possibly higher-yielding, varieties. At the same time, of course, it prevents experimentation, not that this is something much sought after in Bordeaux.

The significance of the density with which vines are planted may not at first be obvious. However, it has been shown that if vines are planted more widely apart than is traditional in Bordeaux, they produce higher yields, and the character and quality of the wine changes. A decree in 1974 fixed 2,000 vines per hectare for the Bordeaux AC, as opposed to 5,000 to 10,000 for the Médoc ACs. Traditionally, between 8,000 and 9,000 vines are planted per hectare in the Médoc, the figure being closer to 6,000 per hectare in St-Émilion.

The relationship between quantity and quality has long been a vexed one. While it is clear that high yields normally lead to lower quality, at what stage this occurs is not always easy to determine. Several points need to be made. The more effective control of disease, more extensive use of fertilizers, and the cloning of the most successful vines have all produced higher yields. The vintage of '53 produced an average yield of 40.8 hectolitres per hectare, and '55 yielded 41.1, compared to 24 in '49 and 25.7 in '61. But '70 produced 52.6, and '73 achieved 55.3, which seemed remarkable by all historic standards. However, '79 saw a figure of 62.9 hectolitres per hectare reached, and the great '82 vintage yielded 60, as did '89. With its disastrous flowering of the Merlot, '84 achieved only 36.9, but that should be compared with the figure of 17 in '56 after the infamous frost, while the spring frost of '91 reduced the figure to 24.

It is clear, then, that the red grape varieties planted in Bordeaux are capable of producing fine wines from relatively high yields – certainly much higher than would have been thought possible a few years ago. In Burgundy, by contrast, the Pinot Noir's quality falls significantly when yields rise over 50 hectolitres per hectare in hillside vineyards. There were many examples of this in '82. But in the same vintage in Bordeaux, both the Merlot and Cabernet Sauvignon produced magnificent wines of real concentration at this level of yield and higher. White wines are less susceptible to loss of quality from high yields, and in Bordeaux the best growths for dry wines tend to combine the more dependable Sémillon and the more irregular Sauvignon.

The minimum of degrees of alcohol are supposed to provide some guarantee of quality and, unless they are achieved, chaptalization (the addition of sugar) is illegal. But it is interesting to note that the great clarets of the past were low in alcohol, often between nine and ten per cent by volume, and many have lasted superbly. Even as recently as the 1940s some great wines scarcely reached 11 per cent. Certainly, there is no call for a Médoc to be more than 12 per cent if it has to be chaptalized, or for a St-Émilion to be more than 12.5 per cent. In exceptional vintages it is, of course, possible to produce wines of over 13 per cent quite naturally in St-Émilion.

Bordeaux was the first major wine region in France to institute tastings before the granting of an appellation. St-Émilion had made this part of its new classification system, in itself the first classification to be tied to AC regulations, in 1955. In the Médoc, tasting was introduced on a voluntary basis. After the major overhaul of the whole AC system in 1974, tastings became compulsory throughout the whole of France in the awarding of appellations. There is a certain cynicism about the tastings because it is said that wines are rarely turned down. The panels consist of growers, *courtiers* (brokers) and *négociants* (merchants). The cask or vat samples must represent an *assemblage* of all wines at a given property (including *vin de presse* and second-label wines) for which the appellation is required. So the quality of a sample is usually inferior to that of the wine that will go out under the château label, especially at the larger properties. Proprietors are often requested to resubmit samples because, in the early stages, wines often show minor faults that subsequently disappear. My own experience of these tastings is that they are serious affairs.

The declaration of stocks, another stipulation of the AC system, is more or less self-explanatory. It enables the authorities and the trade to know precisely how last year's sales have gone and so what there is to sell in the coming year. By adding together the stocks at August 31 with the declarations for the new vintage, the amount available for the coming sales campaign becomes clear. A comparison of the level of stocks from year to year also provides a valuable barometer of the health of the market and has an influence on price levels.

The overhaul of the AC system in 1974 did much to remove the inflexibility of the old system and its insensitivity towards vintage variations. The new system revolves around three concepts:

rendement de base (basic permitted yield). This corresponds to the old maximum yields, which had changed little since being established in 1935. For Bordeaux they were revised in 1984 (backdated to apply to the '83 vintage), and most appellations were given higher allowances, sometimes by as much as five hectolitres per hectare. But under the new system, this simply represents a norm and has less significance than previously.

rendement annuel (annual yield). Each year the growers in each appellation, through their syndicate, make a proposal to the INAO as to what normal production levels should be, bearing in mind the actual conditions of the year. This figure may be above or below the *rendement de base*.

plafond limité de classement (PLC). This is a fixed proportion (usually 20 per cent) given in the decrees governing each appellation which, when applied to the *rendement annuel*, gives the maximum permitted yield for that year. If the *rendement annuel* allows a flexibility for the conditions of a particular year, the PLC allows flexibility between different vineyards and growers. To apply for this extra allowance, all the property's wines must be offered for tasting: anything over this limit has to be used for distillation.

Grape Varieties

Today, five grape varieties, three red and two white, dominate the vineyards of Bordeaux, but it was not always so. At the end of the 18th century, nine red and four white varieties were recorded in the Médoc, but this was nothing compared with the 34 red and 29 white varieties in the Libournais. The process of selection made rapid progress in the 19th century, and its completion was finally precipitated by the phylloxera crisis which, over a period of years, led to the replanting of all vineyards. Today, the most important varieties are as follows.

RED

Cabernet Sauvignon This is the most important variety in Médoc and Graves, especially for the *grands crus*. It produces wine with a deep, brilliant colour, a marked bouquet, often reminiscent of blackcurrants, and a flavour that is markedly tannic when young but which develops great finesse and complexity. This is a hardy variety and it is notably resistant to *coulure* at flowering and to grey rot before the harvest. It has a thick skin and is a late ripener. It does best on gravelly soils and has a relatively low yield.

Cabernet Franc This is an important secondary variety in both St-Émilion and the Médoc. In St-Émilion it is known generally as Bouchet. It produces perfumed wines with less colour and tannin than Cabernet Sauvignon, but in other respects it is similar.

Merlot The most important variety in St-Émilion and Pomerol, but also important in the Médoc and Graves since it harmonizes so well with Cabernet Sauvignon. It produces wines that are deep in colour, less tannic and higher in alcohol than Cabernet Sauvignon, supple, and full-flavoured. It does well in the presence of clay – precisely where the Cabernet Sauvignon does less well. It is an early ripener and generous yielder, but it is susceptible to *coulure* during the flowering and to rot in wet weather. However, new sprays have helped to overcome this last deficiency. Once fully ripe, Merlot grapes must be speedily picked, or they become too alcoholic and rather flat.

Malbec Also known as Pressac in the Libournais and as Cot in Cahors. This variety used to be particularly important in Fronsac, Pomerol and the Côtes de Bourg, as well as having a minor role in most Médoc vineyards. Today, because of its flowering problems, its importance has seriously declined, and only in Bourg and Blaye does it remain a significant element, although many châteaux in the Médoc, St-Émilion and Pomerol still have a few old Malbec vines left. This is a high-yielding, early ripening variety, producing soft, delicate wines with good colour.

Petit Verdot Used in small quantities in the Médoc, especially on the lighter soils
of Margaux, it is declining. Late in ripening, producing highly coloured wines,
high in alcohol and tannin, adding complexity to wines for long ageing.

WHITE

Sémillon The most distinctively Bordelais of the white varieties. It has suffered
as a result of the popularity of the Sauvignon, but it is now making
something of a comeback. It is the most important component of all the
great sweet wines, and provides complexity and ageing potential in dry
Graves. Its distinctive and complex bouquet requires bottle-age to develop
in dry wines, and becomes richer and more honeyed. The wine is taut and
firm, before becoming increasingly full-flavoured and complex with ageing.
It blends well with Sauvignon. Its susceptibility to *pourriture noble* (noble
rot) is responsible for its success in making great dessert wines.

Sauvignon Blanc This has been planted traditionally as a minor partner to the
Sémillon in the sweet-wine areas and as an equal component of the dry wines.
In recent years it has been increasingly used on its own, especially in Entre-
Deux-Mers, to produce wines sold as Bordeaux Blanc Sauvignon. This variety,
also widely planted in other parts of France, tends when unblended to have a
character so strong that it obliterates regional characteristics, especially when
complete ripeness is not obtained. However, in Bordeaux it can produce wines
high in natural sugar and therefore in alcohol, with more finesse and style,
especially when aged in oak. The Pavillon Blanc of Château Margaux is an
outstanding example of this. Sauvignon tends to be a lower and more erratic
yielder than Sémillon, so that where a vineyard is planted half-and-half with
Sémillon, there will always be more Sémillon in the resulting blend. It has
recently been shown that the extraction of its distinctive flavours from the skins
during fermentation is an essential element in acheiving varietal character.

Muscadelle An extremely perfumed and aromatic grape variety that can be useful
in small doses. It is particularly favoured in the Premières Côtes for producing
sweet wines for early drinking, and as an adjunct to Sémillon and Sauvignon.

The essence of winemaking in Bordeaux is to mix the different varieties in
the right proportions for the soil in each particular vineyard and the style of
wine the proprietor is trying to make. The small but important variations
between châteaux, with soil and microclimatic differences, are what give
Bordeaux wines their remarkable variations and individuality. Thus, in the
Médoc, where Cabernet Sauvignon dominates, some proprietors use Merlot
as their second variety, with little Cabernet Franc; others use less Merlot and
more Cabernet Franc. In St-Émilion and Pomerol, where Merlot is dominant,
some proprietors have 80 per cent Merlot, while others plant it half-and-half
with Cabernet Franc or mix it with Cabernet Franc and Cabernet Sauvignon –
in fact, you can find every conceivable variation in the proportions.

Châteaux

The château system has been a crucial factor in building and maintaining the
prestige of the great Bordeaux wines. In the Médoc in the 18th century, many
small farms came together to form large estates capable of producing

sufficient quantities of wine to create a wide reputation on many markets. The first growths led the way in England in the early years of the 18th century; the other wines followed, creating a unique image of excellence for Bordeaux.

In the Médoc, the château names have in effect become *marques*, whose proprietors can increase the size of their vineyards at will, provided they remain in the same appellation. Nobody controls the extent of an individual vineyard now. Only the reputation of the wine and its consistent quality counts.

In St-Émilion, however, where the 1954 classification system is under the control of the INAO, vineyards of classified wines cannot be expanded at will, and when Beau-Séjour-Bécot took over two other properties and incorporated their production into its *premier grand cru classé* wine, it lost its status in the 1985 revision of the classification. It worked its passage back, however, and was reinstated in the 1995 version.

The success of the château system, however, has produced its own problems. It is difficult for the consumer to remember the names of more than a handful of châteaux, let alone the thousands that exist in the whole region. But because the consumer knows that good Bordeaux wines come from châteaux, it is hard to create successful brands which cannot, of their nature, have a château name. It is not without significance that the most successful brand of claret by far is Mouton Cadet, precisely because many consumers believe, erroneously, that the wine is directly connected with the famous Château Mouton-Rothschild. Even the *caves coopératives* now sell many of their wines under château names.

Cooperatives

Co-ops are of increasing importance in Bordeaux, and their role is changing. Today, 76 *caves* produce nearly 25 per cent of the production of AC wines.

Initially, much of the wine sold by cooperatives went to *négociants* for their generic blends and brands. Increasingly, however, they are vinifying the wines of their best members separately and marketing them under their château labels, on which they have the right to put *mis à la propriété*. In addition, cooperatives are creating their own brands and selling these and some of their château wines directly to wholesalers in France and to importers in foreign markets, rather than selling them through the traditional Bordeaux trade, although the latter remains a significant part of their business.

The most important co-op in the Médoc is at Bégadan, with 170 members producing some 25,000 hectolitres of Médoc AC. In St-Émilion, the Union des Producteurs has 360 members producing some 45,000 hectolitres, including over 16,000 hectolitres of St-Émilion *grand cru*, the best of it aged in casks.

Négociants

Traditionally, the Bordeaux trade has been carried out by the *négociants*. In Bordeaux itself, this used to centre on the Quai des Chartrons, conveniently placed for the docks. *Négociants* not only distributed Bordeaux wines in France and on export markets, they also effectively acted as bankers for the château proprietors, buying their wines when they were a few months old, then either taking them into their own cellars, where they would be looked after until ready for bottling, or keeping them at the châteaux for châteaux-bottling. They also kept substantial bottle stocks and could always supply mature wines ready for drinking or old vintages for special occasions.

Inflation and high interest rates, however, have provided a challenge to which the *négociants* have found no answer. None has been able to achieve the size and financial muscle to meet the new problems while retaining its traditional role, which has inevitably contracted. Far more wines are now château-bottled, and far more stock is now held and financed at the property than ever before. Many firms now work on minimum stocks or act purely as brokers, not buying wines until they have sold them, which puts them at the mercy of the notoriously volatile Bordeaux market. The *courtiers* themselves still have an important role as the link between the growers and the *négociants*, largely because there are so many growers – the bigger merchants simply could not select from the huge range of wines.

The following list describes today's leading *négociant* houses.

Jean-Baptiste Audy A traditional Libourne family firm that has revived in the 1990s. They run a number of properties including Clos du Clocher (Pomerol) and have a group of exclusives, mostly in the Libournais, Bourg, and Blaye.

GAM Audy Based at Château Jonqueyres, with Jean-Michel Arcaute as technical adviser until his tragic death in 2001. The firm distributes Châteaux Sansonnet, Beau-Soleil (Pomerol), La Croix-du-Casse, and Jonqueyres, and is very active in the Far East. It is also involved in Château Pajzos in Tokaj, as well as wineries in South Africa and Argentina.

Baron Philippe de Rothschild (formerly La Bergerie and then La Baronnie) After the legendary Baron's death in 1987, it was decided to perpetuate his name in this, the commercial arm of his enterprise. Apart from selling its property wines, d'Armailhac and Clerc-Milon, the principal business is Mouton Cadet and brands. (Mouton-Rothschild is sold via the Bordeaux market, and not exclusively through this house.) Eighty per cent of the business is export.

Barrière Frères Since 1988, this *négociant* operation has been part of the Group Grands Millésimes de France, which is jointly owned by GMF (the Civil Servants' Pension Fund) and the Japanese firm Suntory. The group also owns Château Beychevelle and Château Beaumont. The company owns a very modern warehouse at Ludon-Médoc, which has storage for five million bottles.

Barton & Guestier This famous old concern is part of Diageo and is only a pale reflection of the firm it used to be, largely concentrating on brands sold on the US market. In 1995, it sold its bottling and warehousing operation to Cordier and entered into a contract to bottle its requirements. Nevertheless, the quality of the wines remains good, but only half the business is now Bordeaux.

Borie-Manoux A dynamic family firm with some important properties which include Châteaux Batailley, Trottevieille and Beau-Site as a basis for its quality business. Its wines are well distributed on export markets as well as in France.

Calvet Since 1997, this famous old firm has been reinvented by the dynamic Jack Drounau as a purveyor of quality branded wines. Calvet Réserve, red and white, is the cornerstone of the business, with a strong presence in Japan.

Cheval Quancard A family firm which has grown considerably in the past twenty-five years. It owns several properties, including Château Terrefort, and offers a wide range of *petits châteaux* and brands.

Compagnie Médocaine des Grands Crus (CMGC) Since 2001, a wholly owned subsidiary of AXA-Millésimes' Châteaux & Associés company, based in

Blanquefort. Apart from distributing AXA's properties (Pichon-Longueville-Baron, Cantenac-Brown, Pibran, Suduiraut, and Petit Village) on a non-exclusive basis, it specializes in quality wines strongly focused on exports.

Cordier One of the leading firms in Bordeaux, which owns 500ha of vineyards, including Meyney, Lafaurie-Peyraguey, and Clos-des-Jacobins. The Cordier family sold control of the company in 1984. Since 1997, it has been part of the Val d'Orbieu Group. The Cordier properties are sold on an exclusive basis and not through the market, so it specializes in selling a limited range of its own exclusivities and brands. 65 per cent of its business is export.

Crus & Domaines Subsidiary of Pernod-Ricard, owning Cruse and Alexis Lichine.

CVBG (Compagnie des Vins de Bordeaux et de la Gironde) Dourthe Kressman
The wines from this group are marketed under the old company names Dourthe and Kressman. In 1983, the families sold to a Dutch firm, but since 1998 it belongs to its managers. These companies have a good reputation and sell a wide range of wines, many on an exclusive basis, including Château Le Boscq, Château La Garde and Château Tronquoy-Lalande.

Dulong Frères & Fils A family firm situated at Floirac just across the bridge from Bordeaux. It enjoys a good reputation for its *petits châteaux* and *crus bourgeois* exported to the UK and the US. Fifty per cent of its business is export.

Ginestet Now part of the Bernard Taillan Group, this is one of the leading Bordeaux merchants, with a large portfolio of managed and exclusive properties as well as developing brands. Over 40 per cent of its turnover is in exports.

GVG (Grands Vins de Gironde) Formerly owned by Rémy-Cointreau, but subject to a management buy-out in 1999. It now includes De Luze, De Rivoyre & Diprovin, SDVF and Chantecaille. Combined, it now forms the region's largest group, commercializing some ten per cent of the region's production, with 32 per cent going to exports.

Joanne Run by members of the Castéja family, this remains one of the traditional houses. It has maintained and consolidated its position as a specialist for the *grands crus*. It also owns Doisy-Védrines. Seventy-five per cent of the business is export.

Nathaniel Johnston Formed in 1734, it is still run by the same family. Even if it no longer owns great châteaux such as Ducru-Beaucaillou, it still specializes in selling a wide range of Bordeaux's leading growths, with 50 per cent exported.

Mähler-Besse A family firm still firmly rooted in its Dutch origins. Part-owner of Château Palmer, as well as owning properties in Médoc and St-Emilion they hold extensive stocks of the *grands crus*.

Yvon Mau & Fils A family firm specializing in middle-price-range wines, situated near La Réole in Entre-Deux-Mers. It is now one of the leading exporters.

Mestrezat & Domaines A house specializing in a wide range of wines, mostly château-bottled. It manages Grand-Puy-Ducasse and Rayne-Vigneau, as well as several lesser *crus*. Since 2000 owned by Val d'Orbieu Group – *see* Cordier.

J.P. Moueix Founded in 1937 by Jean-Pierre Moueix, who became a legend in his own lifetime as he established the worldwide reputation of the great wines of the Libournais. He died in his 90th year in 2003. Now Christian, his son, is there to carry on the tradition, and the old Bordeaux house of Duclot, under his other son, Jean-François Moueix, complements this, with a classic range of Médocs, Graves, and Sauternes to accompany the St-Émilions and Pomerols. This firm has the ownership or exclusive distribution of many châteaux, headed by Pétrus, Trotanoy, La Fleur-Pétrus, Hosanna and Magdelaine.

André Quancard André There is now no connection between this firm and

Cheval Quancard. It has a wide range of *petits châteaux* and ranks among the ten leading *négociants*. Twenty-one per cent goes for export.

Schröder & Schÿler This famous old business was founded in 1739; there are still Schÿlers working in the company. The main markets are Scandinavia and Holland. Owns Château Kirwan.

Maison Sichel Following the death of Peter Sichel in 1998, his son Allan is the new president and managing director, three of his brothers share the responsibilities for exports, while son Benjamin runs the family property at d'Angludet. In 1992, Peter A. Sichel acquired the business of Édmond Coste at Langon. In France, Coste's wines continue to be sold from the Langon office, but the Peter A Sichel company looks after all the export business for Coste's selections. Seventy-nine per cent of the business is export.

Vintex Founded in 1982 by the former directors of Delor, Bill Blatch and his colleagues run a dynamic and very focused business concentrating on a range of carefully selected *petits châteaux* and *crus bourgeois*, and also specializing in the great Sauternes. Ninety-nine per cent of the business goes to exports.

Understanding a Bordeaux Label

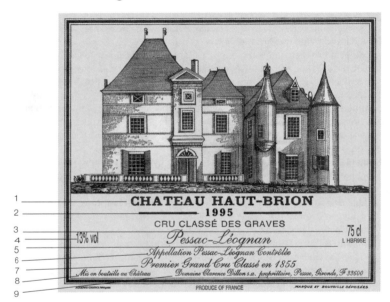

1   Most Bordeaux wines are sold under a château name. In addition, many wines that are sent to be vinified at *caves coopératives,* but kept separate and allowed to use the name of their property on the label.

2   Year of vintage.

3   This is the standard bottle-size in the EU.

4   Alcohol by volume.

5   Lot number specific to Château Haut-Brion's bottling line.

6   It is a legal requirement that the appellation be indicated, the name

shown between the words "Appellation" and "Contrôlée".

7 Classification. The wines of the Médoc were classified in 1855 at the same time as those of Sauternes and Barsac. More recently, there have been classifications for St-Émilion and Graves.

8 "Bottled at the château". Until the 1970s, the majority of Bordeaux wines were bottled either in the Bordeaux cellars of *négociants* or abroad in such places as London and Brussels. Château-bottling became obligatory for all *crus classés* in the early 1970s. The words *mis en bouteille à la propriété* indicate that the wine has been bottled by the *cave coopérative* where it was made.

9 Name and address of producer.

Classifications

1855 CLASSIFICATION OF THE MÉDOC

The Médoc first growths had emerged as such in the 18th century; by the early 19th century, classifications were being made covering a range of Médocs and some Graves. They were essentially based on market prices and were produced by *courtiers* and *négociants* as guides for their customers.

When the newly fledged Second Empire was preparing its answer to London's Great Exhibition of 1851, it was decided to show a range of Bordeaux wines, and the question arose as to which châteaux should represent the region. A commission of *courtiers* was given the task, and the result was the Classification of 1855 encompassing the red wines of the Médoc plus Château Haut-Brion and the great sweet wines of Sauternes. It was rather an accident of history that this particular list should have become enshrined as an immutable and permanent order of merit, something its authors certainly never intended. When, in 1867, a group of St-Émilions was shown at a subsequent Paris Exhibition, no such permanent value was accorded to the list.

There have been various attempts to update the 1855 classification, but the vested interests opposed to it seem more powerful than those who would like to see change. I have indicated under the individual entries which growths I consider to be superior or otherwise to their classifications. The only official change was the elevation of Mouton-Rothschild to the status of first growth in 1973, recognizing a position it had in reality long held.

It is important to remember that there is no control over the vineyards of any of the listed châteaux. Some have remained virtually unchanged since 1855, while others have expanded or contracted.

The list that follows is essentially the original 1855 list. Apart from the promotion of Mouton-Rothschild to *premier cru* in 1973 there have been no fundamental changes, except that certain *crus* have disappeared and others have been divided or changed their names. The list encompasses the great red wines of the Médoc, the sole exception being the inclusion of Haut-Brion in the Graves.

1855 Classification of the Médoc

The château name is followed by that of the commune.

Premiers Crus

Lafite-Rothschild	Pauillac
Margaux	Margaux
Latour	Pauillac
Haut-Brion	Pessac (Graves)
Mouton-Rothschild	Pauillac

Deuxièmes Crus

Rauzan-Ségla	Margaux
Rauzan-Gassies	Margaux
Léoville-Las-Cases	St-Julien
Léoville-Poyferré	St-Julien
Léoville-Barton	St-Julien
Durfort-Vivens	Margaux
Gruaud-Larose	St-Julien
Lascombes	Margaux
Brane-Cantenac	Cantenac
Pichon-Longueville Baron	Pauillac
Pichon-Longueville Comtesse	Pauillac
Ducru-Beaucaillou	St-Julien
Cos d'Estournel	St-Estèphe
Montrose	St-Estèphe

Troisièmes Crus

Kirwan	Cantenac
d'Issan	Cantenac
Lagrange	St-Julien
Langoa-Barton	St-Julien
Giscours	Labarde
Malescot-St-Exupéry	Margaux
Boyd-Cantenac	Cantenac
Cantenac-Brown	Cantenac
Palmer	Cantenac
La Lagune	Ludon
Desmirail	Margaux
Calon-Ségur	St-Estèphe
Ferrière	Margaux
Marquis-d'Alesme-Becker	Margaux

Quatrièmes Crus

St-Pierre	St-Julien
Talbot	St-Julien
Branaire-Ducru	St-Julien
Duhart-Milon	Pauillac
Pouget	Cantenac
La Tour-Carnet	St-Laurent
Lafon-Rochet	St-Estèphe
Beychevelle	St-Julien
Prieuré-Lichine	Cantenac
Marquis-de-Terme	Margaux

Cinquièmes Crus

Pontet-Canet	Pauillac
Batailley	Pauillac
Haut-Batailley	Pauillac
Grand-Puy-Lacoste	Pauillac
Grand-Puy-Ducasse	Pauillac
Lynch-Bages	Pauillac
Lynch-Moussas	Pauillac
Dauzac	Labarde
d'Armailhac	Pauillac
du Tertre	Arsac
Haut-Bages-Libéral	Pauillac
Pédesclaux	Pauillac
Belgrave	St-Laurent
de Camensac	St-Laurent
Cos Labory	St-Estèphe
Clerc-Milon	Pauillac
Croizet-Bages	Pauillac
Cantemerle	Macau

1855 Classification of Sauternes

Again, the original list, apart from divisions and changes of name. The château name is followed by that of the commune.

Premier Grand Cru

d'Yquem	Sauternes

Premiers Crus

La Tour-Blanche	Bommes
Lafaurie-Peyraguey	Bommes
Clos Haut-Peyraguey	Bommes
Rayne-Vigneau	Bommes
Suduiraut	Preignac
Coutet	Barsac
Climens	Barsac
Guiraud	Sauternes
Rieussec	Fargues
Rabaud-Promis	Bommes
Sigalas-Rabaud	Bommes

Deuxièmes Crus

de Myrat	Barsac
Doisy-Daëne	Barsac
Doisy-Dubroca	Barsac
Doisy-Védrines	Barsac
d'Arche	Sauternes
Filhot	Sauternes
Broustet	Barsac
Nairac	Barsac
Caillou	Barsac
Suau	Barsac
de Malle	Preignac
Romer-du-Hayot	Fargues
Lamothe	Sauternes
Lamothe-Guignard	Sauternes

CLASSED GROWTHS OF GRAVES

After World War II, interest in classification revived, and both Graves and St-Émilion began to negotiate with the INAO for their own. The Graves classification, which was a great deal simpler to agree, emerged first in 1953, encompassing only red wines. It was revised in 1959 to include whites. In 2003, it was announced that a revision of this classification has been requested and a committee set up to undertake it. With such a small number of wines actually classified, there is, not surprisingly, no attempt to place the wines in different categories, with the result that the wines vary in quality considerably, from Haut-Brion with its *premier cru* status to wines that sell at prices of Médoc fifth growths, or top *crus bourgeois*. Again, I have assessed the standing of each wine under its individual entry.

Red Wines

Bouscaut	Cadaujac
Haut-Bailly	Léognan
Carbonnieux	Léognan
Domaine de Chevalier	Léognan
Fieuzal	Léognan
Olivier	Léognan
Malartic-Lagravière	Léognan
La Tour-Martillac	Martillac
Smith-Haut-Lafitte	Martillac
Haut-Brion	Pessac
La Mission-Haut-Brion	Talence
Pape-Clément	Pessac
La Tour-Haut-Brion	Talence

White Wines

Bouscaut	Cadaujac
Carbonnieux	Léognan
Domaine de Chevalier	Léognan
Olivier	Léognan
Malartic-Lagravière	Léognan
La Tour-Martillac	Martillac
Laville-Haut-Brion	Talence
Couhins	Villenave d'Ornon

THE 1996 ST-ÉMILION CLASSIFICATION

St-Émilion had long been in a chaotic state, posing special problems for the consumer. Many *crus* described themselves as *premiers*, and the properties, mostly small and many with similar names, change more often than elsewhere. Although there are over 5,000 hectares under vine in the appellation, only 14 domaines are of more than 25 hectares, and only 34 properties have between 12 and 25 hectares, the total area of these covering 589 hectares. The classification divides the châteaux into two categories, *premiers grands crus classés* and *grands crus classés*, with the *premiers* Ausone and Cheval Blanc singled out as category A, the rest as B.

The first list, published in 1955, comprised 12 *premiers grands crus* and 63 *grands crus*. At the first revision (1969), the *grands crus* were increased to 71; a second (1985) reduced the *premiers crus* to 11 and the *grands crus* to 62. A third (1996) increased the *premiers crus* to 13 and reduced the *grands crus* to 55, its smallest numbers yet. Three *crus* demoted in 1985 were restored, while Laroque was classified for the first time.

The 1996 St-Émilion Classification

Premiers Grands Crus Classés

(A)   Ausone
      Cheval Blanc
(B)   L'Angélus
      Beauséjour (Duffau-
         Lagarosse)
      Beau-Séjour-Bécot
      Belair
      Canon
      Clos Fourtet
      Figeac
      La Gaffelière
      Magdelaine
      Pavie
      Trottevieille

Grands Crus Classés

L'Arrosée
Balestard-la-Tonnelle
Bellevue
Bergat
Berliquet
Cadet-Bon
Cadet-Piola
Canon-la-Gaffelière
Cap-de-Mourlin
Chauvin
Clos des Jacobins
Clos de l'Oratoire
Clos St-Martin
La Clotte

La Clusière
Corbin
Corbin-Michotte
La Couspaude
Couvent-des-Jacobins
Curé-Bon
Dassault
La Dominique
Faurie-de-Souchard
Fonplégade
Fonroque
Franc-Mayne
Grand-Mayne
Grand-Pontet
Guadet-St-Julien
Grandes Murailles
Haut-Corbin
Haut-Sarpe
Lamarzelle
Laniote
Larcis-Ducasse
Larmande
Laroque
Laroze
Matras
Moulin du Cadet
Pavie-Decesse
Pavie-Macquin
Petit-Faurie-de-Soutard
Le Prieuré
Ripeau

St-Georges-Côte-Pavie
La Serre
Soutard
Tertre-Daugay
La Tour-du-Pin-Figeac
  (Giraud-Bélivier)

La Tour-du-Pin-Figeac
  (Moueix)
La Tour-Figeac
Troplong-Mondot
Villemaurine
Yon-Figeac

THE CRUS BOURGEOIS OF THE MÉDOC

In 1932, the first official recognition for this ancient term came when 444 properties were officially listed and classified. In 1962, the Federation for the Crus Bourgeois was created. European labelling laws of 1979 put a stop to giving legal authority to a new classification made by the Federation in 1978. Then, in 2000, new legislation opened the way for a new official classification of the 419 properties in this category. They represent 50 per cent of the Médoc's production, with almost 7,500 hectares of vines producing some 55 million bottles per annum.

The new classification was finally unveiled in time for VinExpo in June 2003. It proved to be a stricter selection than had been expected, which can only add weight to its standing as a serious piece of work by a highly qualified and respected panel of experts. Of the 490 *crus* that applied for classification only 247 were successful. This is made up of nine *crus bourgeois exceptionnels*, 87 *crus bourgeois supérieurs* and 151 *crus bourgeois*. Château Sociando-Mallet, which now regularly sells at prices – both *en primeur* and on the secondary market – above some *crus classés* and well above any *cru bourgeois*, did not apply to be included. Under the new rules, all *crus* not included in this new classification cannot in future call themselves *crus bourgeois*. These new ratings will first feature on the labels of the 2003 vintage. The classification will be revised every 12 years.

The 2003 Crus Bourgeois Classification

Crus Bourgeois Exceptionnels	
Chasse-Spleen	Moulis-en-Médoc
Phélan-Ségur	Saint-Estèphe
Haut-Marbuzet	Saint-Estèphe
Potensac	Médoc

Crus Bourgeois Supérieurs	
d'Agassac	Haut-Médoc
d'Angludet	Margaux
Anthonic	Moulis-en-Médoc
d'Arche	Haut-Médoc
Arnauld	Haut-Médoc
d'Arsac	Margaux
Beaumont	Haut-Médoc
Beau-Site	Saint-Estèphe

Labégorce Zédé	Margaux
Poujeaux	Moulis-en-Médoc
Les-Ormes-de-Pez	Saint-Estèphe
Siran	Margaux
de Pez	Saint-Estèphe

Biston-Brillette	Moulis-en-Médoc
Le Boscq	Saint-Estèphe
Bournac	Médoc
Brillette	Moulis-en-Médoc
Cambon-La-Pelouse	Haut-Médoc
Cap Léon Veyrin	Listrac-Médoc
La Cardonne	Médoc

Caronne-Sainte-Gemme	Haut-Médoc
Castéra	Médoc
Chambert-Marbuzet	Saint-Estèphe
Charmail	Haut-Médoc
Cissac	Haut-Médoc
Citran	Haut-Médoc
Clarke	Listrac-Médoc
Clauzet	Saint-Estèphe
Clément-Pichon	Haut-Médoc
Colombier-Monpelou	Pauillac
Coufran	Haut-Médoc
Le Crock	Saint-Estèphe
Dutruch-Grand-Poujeaux	Moulis-en-Médoc
d'Escurac	Médoc
Fonbadet	Pauillac
Fonréaud	Listrac-Médoc
Fourcas-Dupré	Listrac-Médoc
Fourcas-Hosten	Listrac-Médoc
Fourcas-Loubaney	Listrac-Médoc
du Glana	Saint-Julien
Les Grands Chênes	Médoc
Gressier-Grand-Poujeaux	Moulis-en-Médoc
Greysac	Médoc
La Gurgue	Margaux
Hanteillan	Haut-Médoc
Haut-Bages Monpelou	Pauillac
La Haye	Saint-Estèphe
Labégorce	Margaux
Lachesnaye	Haut-Médoc
de Lamarque	Haut-Médoc
Lamothe-Bergeron	Haut-Médoc
Lanessan	Haut-Médoc
Larose-Trintaudon	Haut-Médoc
Lestage	Listrac-Médoc
Lestage-Simon	Haut-Médoc
Lilian Ladouys	Saint-Estèphe
Liversan	Haut-Médoc
Loudenne	Médoc
Malescasse	Haut-Médoc
de Malleret	Haut-Médoc
Maucaillou	Moulis-en-Médoc
Maucamps	Haut-Médoc
Mayne-Lalande	Listrac-Médoc

Meyney	Saint-Estèphe
Monbrison	Margaux
Moulin à Vent	Moulis-en-Médoc
Moulin de la Rose	Saint-Julien
Les Ormes Sorbet	Médoc
Paloumey	Haut-Médoc
Patache d'Aux	Médoc
Paveil-de-Luze	Margaux
Petit Bocq	Saint-Estèphe
Pibran	Pauillac
Ramage La Batisse	Haut-Médoc
Reysson	Haut-Médoc
Rollan de By	Médoc
Saransot-Dupré	Listrac-Médoc
Ségur	Haut-Médoc
Sénéjac	Haut-Médoc
Soudars	Haut-Médoc
du Taillan	Haut-Médoc
Terrey-Gros-Cailloux	Saint-Julien
La Tour de By	Médoc
Tour de Marbuzet	Saint-Estèphe
La Tour-de-Mons	Margaux
Tour de Pez	Saint-Estèphe
Tour du Haut Moulin	Haut-Médoc
Tour-Haut-Caussan	Médoc
Tronquoy-Lalande	Saint-Estèphe
Verdignan	Haut-Médoc
Vieux Robin	Médoc
Villegeorge (de)	Haut-Médoc

Crus Bourgeois

Andron-Blanquet	Saint-Estèphe
Aney	Haut-Médoc
d'Arcins	Haut-Médoc
L'Argenteyre	Médoc
d'Aurilhac	Haut-Médoc
Balac	Haut-Médoc
Barateau	Haut-Médoc
Bardis	Haut-Médoc
Barreyres	Haut-Médoc
Baudan	Listrac-Médoc
Beau-Site-Haut-Vignoble	Saint-Estèphe
Bégadanet	Médoc
Bel Air	Saint-Estèphe
Bel Air	Haut-Médoc

Bel-Orme-Tronquoy-de-Lalande	Haut-Médoc
Bel-Air-Lagrave	Moulis-en-Médoc
des Belles Graves	Médoc
Bessan Ségur	Médoc
Bibian	Listrac-Médoc
Blaignan	Médoc
Le Boscq	Médoc
Le Bourdieu	Médoc
Le Bourdieu Vertheuil	Haut-Médoc
de Braude	Haut-Médoc
du Breuil	Haut-Médoc
La Bridane	Saint-Julien
des Brousteras	Médoc
des Cabans	Médoc
Cap de Haut	Haut-Médoc
Capbern-Gasqueton	Saint-Estèphe
Chantelys	Médoc
La Clare	Médoc
La Commanderie	Saint-Estèphe
Le Coteau	Margaux
Coutelin-Merville	Saint-Estèphe
de la Croix	Médoc
Dasvin-Bel-Air	Haut-Médoc
David	Médoc
Devise d'Ardilley	Haut-Médoc
Deyrem-Valentin	Margaux
Dillon	Haut-Médoc
Domeyne	Saint-Estèphe
Donissan	Listrac-Médoc
Ducluzeau	Listrac-Médoc
Duplessis	Moulis-en-Médoc
Duplessis-Fabre	Moulis-en-Médoc
Duthil	Haut-Médoc
L'Ermitage	Listrac-Médoc
d'Escot	Médoc
La Fleur Milon	Pauillac
La Fleur Peyrabon	Pauillac
La Fon du Berger	Haut-Médoc
Fontesteau	Haut-Médoc
Fontis	Médoc
La Galiane	Margaux
de Gironville	Haut-Médoc
La Gorce	Médoc
La Gorre	Médoc
Grand Clapeau Olivier	Haut-Médoc
Grandis	Haut-Médoc
Granins-Grand Poujeaux	Moulis-en-Médoc
Grivière	Médoc
Haut-Beauséjour	Saint-Estèphe
Haut-Bellevue	Haut-Médoc
Haut Breton Larigaudière	Margaux
Haut-Canteloup	Médoc
Haut-Madrac	Haut-Médoc
Haut-Maurac	Médoc
Houissant	Saint-Estèphe
Hourbanon	Médoc
Hourtin-Ducasse	Haut-Médoc
Labadie	Médoc
Ladouys	Saint-Estèphe
Laffitte-Carcasset	Saint-Estèphe
Laffitte Laujac	Médoc
Lafon	Médoc
Lalande	Listrac-Médoc
Lalande	Saint-Julien
Lamothe-Cissac	Haut-Médoc
Larose Perganson	Haut-Médoc
Larrivaux	Haut-Médoc
Larruau	Margaux
Laujac	Médoc
La Lauzette-Declercq	Listrac-Médoc
Leyssac	Saint-Estèphe
Lieujean	Haut-Médoc
Liouner	Listrac-Médoc
Lousteauneuf	Médoc
Magnol	Haut-Médoc
de Marbuzet	Saint-Estèphe
Marsac-Séguineau	Margaux
Martinens	Margaux
Maurac	Haut-Médoc
Mazails	Médoc
Le Meynieu	Haut-Médoc
Meyre	Haut-Médoc
Les Moines	Médoc
Mongravey	Margaux
Le Monteil d'Arsac	Haut-Médoc
Morin	Saint-Estèphe
du Moulin Rouge	Haut-Médoc
La Mouline	Moulis-en-Médoc

Muret	Haut-Médoc	Saint Estèphe	Saint-Estèphe
Noaillac	Médoc	Saint-Hilaire	Médoc
du Perier	Médoc	Saint-Paul	Haut-Médoc
Le Pey	Médoc	Segue Longue	Médoc
Peyrabon	Haut-Médoc	Ségur de Cabanac	Saint-Estèphe
Peyredon	Listrac-	Sémeillan Mazeau	Listrac-Médoc
Lagravette	Médoc	Senilhac	Haut-Médoc
Peyre-Lebade	Haut-Médoc	Sipian	Médoc
Picard	Saint-Estèphe	Tayac	Margaux
Plantey	Pauillac	Le Temple	Médoc
Poitevin	Médoc	Teynac	Saint-Julien
Pomys	Saint-Estèphe	La Tonnelle	Haut-Médoc
Pontac-Lynch	Margaux	Tour Blanche	Médoc
Pontey	Médoc	La Tour-de-Bessan	Margaux
Pontoise-		Tour-des-Termes	Saint-Estèphe
Cabarrus	Haut-Médoc	Tour-du-Roc	Haut-Médoc
Puy Castéra	Haut-Médoc	Tour Prignac	Médoc
Ramafort	Médoc	Tour-Saint-Bonnet	Médoc
du Raux	Haut-Médoc	Tour Saint-Fort	Saint-Estèphe
La Raze Beauvallet	Médoc	Tour Saint-Joseph	Haut-Médoc
du Retout	Haut-Médoc	Trois Moulins	Haut-Médoc
Reverdi	Listrac-Médoc	Les Tuileries	Médoc
Roquegrave	Médoc	Vernous	Médoc
Saint Ahon	Haut-Médoc	Vieux Château	
Saint Aubin	Médoc	Landon	Médoc
Saint-Christophe	Médoc	de Villambis	Haut-Médoc

What Happens in the Vineyard

Good wine begins with good grapes, and good grapes, in turn, depend on good viticulture and the weather. After the enormous progress made in winemaking in the past 30 years, some say there is little more to be done in this respect, but there are certainly still improvements possible in viticulture.

Starting with a new vine, the first decision concerns what American rootstock to use and which clone of the European vine to select. Different varieties perform better in different soils. Much work has been done by the Station de Recherches Viticoles du Sud-Ouest to discover rootstocks that are resistant to chlorosis in limestone soils. Some varieties do better than others in poorly drained, humid soils as opposed to dry, well-drained ones. Less work has been done on the cloning of vines here than in Burgundy, to say nothing of Germany. Dissatisfaction with the excessive production of many vines has led many properties to return to making selections from within their own vineyards – a process known as *sélection masal*. Recently, there has been a steady move in favour of more natural methods, reducing sprays and looking to natural predators to counter pests such as red spider.

The yearly pattern in the vineyards proceeds along the following lines.

January The work of the *taille* (pruning), begun in December, continues. New stakes are put in place and secured, and the pruned canes are attached to the vines.

February The pruning continues, together with the clearing of the vineyard, gathering of the bundled canes and so on. The vines are given their first treatment against excoriose (a fungus which attacks the wood), esca (another fungus, also called black measles), and red and yellow spider (which later attack the young leaves).

March The first buds normally break in late March, between the 20th and 30th of the month. The first ploughing removes the earth from around the foot of the vine in order to aerate it after the winter.

April Spring begins. Any dead vines are replaced and the first hoeing takes place. The vines may be dusted with sulphur against oidium and sprayed with a copper sulphate solution against mildew.

May The work begun in April continues according to weather conditions, as do the treatments against disease. The first pinching back of the young shoots is carried out at this stage to limit the growth of the vine and direct it towards the production of grapes. Stray shoots from the base of the vine are cut back.

June This is classically the month of the flowering. Most typically it happens between the second and tenth of the month. This gives the approximate timing for the vintage, which normally occurs 100 to 110 days after the flowering. Ploughing continues, the new shoots are tied up, and the length of the new growth permits it to be trained between the second and third row of wires, though not attached to them.

July The soil is now ploughed away from the vines again so there is a mound of soil running between each row of vines, and weeds are hoed. Treatment continues according to the conditions. The *véraison* (the changing of the colour of the grapes, the most important indication of ripening between the flowering and the vintage) can begin in late July. If the potential crop looks too large, this is the usual time to thin out (*vendange vert*).

August A quiet period when many *vignerons* go on holiday, this can nevertheless be a crucial time for treating the vines, especially against premature rot if the weather is damp and humid. If the *véraison* has not occurred in July, it usually happens in the first week of August. Leaf thinning at this time can assist the ripening process.

September The preferred month for beginning the harvest. From '85 to '96 all vintages began in this month. In the weeks before the harvest, the last preventative treatments are carried out, but at this time the *vigneron* hopes to be able to concentrate his efforts on preparing for the vintage in the *cuvier*.

October The month of the harvest (vintage, or *récolte*) and hence the key month in the viticultural calendar. Even if the vintage began in September, much of it will take place and be completed in October. Sometimes the vintage in Sauternes will go on until the end of the month, or beyond.

November The harvest is over and the plough returns to the vineyard to earth up the vines for the winter. The manuring also takes place.

December The pruning begins. First the foliage is cut back to make the work of pruning easier. The cuttings are bundled up and burnt. Any vines that have been damaged or have died during the year are noted for replacement next year. The work goes on.

Making Wine

RED WINE

Forty years ago it was almost true to say that, in most years, the great red Bordeaux made themselves. They are still not complicated wines to make, but the art has been refined, at least at most properties.

The process is as follows.

1   When the grapes arrive in the press-house, they are, increasingly, inspected on a sorting table or conveyor belt to remove leaves and damaged and unripe grapes. Then they are de-stemmed and lightly broken – "crushed" is too strong a term for today's more gentle process – before being pumped into the fermentation vats. Mechanically harvested grapes will already have been de-stemmed, but here the sorting table can be even more important.

2   The traditional Bordeaux fermentation *cuve* (vat) is wooden, and the top is often reached by a wooden gallery. Many of these old *cuves* are still in use, but they are steadily being replaced by vats of stainless steel, metal lined with enamel, or concrete lined with enamel.

    The advantages of the new *cuves* are that (a) they are easier to clean; (b) the temperature at which fermentation takes place is easier to control; and (c) they are often of smaller size to assist selection and temperature control. But recent research suggests that the advantages are not all in one direction and that wooden *cuves* may produce better results. Fermentation usually lasts from five to ten days, and the object is to ferment at 28–30°C (82–86°F), instead of allowing the temperature to rise to 34°C (93°F) as formerly.

3   After the fermentation has been in progress for a few hours, the solid matter, mostly skins, rises to the top of the vat to form what is known as the cap. At regular intervals the fermenting must is pumped over the top of the cap to keep it moist, keep its temperature down, and extract colour. A variation on this classic system is that in which the cap is submerged. In this method, the cap is prevented by a mesh from rising to the top of the *cuve*.

4   In Bordeaux, natural yeasts are usually allowed to bring about and sustain the fermentation. Normally there is an abundance of them, and the results they give usually prove satisfactory. Only when the grapes are unhealthy (affected by rot) can problems arise with this approach, and this is now rare.

5   The temperature is controlled by a variety of means. The most traditional in Bordeaux is a contraption that looks like a milk cooler. The must passes through a coil while cold water runs over the outside. With stainless-steel vats, either the cold water runs down their exterior sides, or interior cooling coils are used, as they can be for other types of vat. All this is a long way from throwing blocks of ice into vats, a system that was still in use in many cellars in 1961. Many of the most recent installations have computer-controlled cooling systems.

6   Chaptalization (the addition of sugar to fermenting must to increase its potential alcohol) is now much more common in Bordeaux where, prior

---

Recent steps in the vineyard to improve quality by limiting production and obtaining better ripeness
- Looking for less productive vines: massal selection instead of clones
- Removing buds prior to flowering
- Bunch thinning in July, prior to the *véraison*
- Leaf thinning in July/August to give more exposure to the bunches to assist ripening
- Improving vineyard drainage

---

to 1962, it was almost unknown and illegal. Most Médocs are now chaptalized to 12 per cent and St-Émilions and Pomerols to 12·5 per cent, except in the best years when the natural degrees are quite sufficient. The sugar is normally added at the beginning of fermentation after the composition of the must has been carefully checked.

7   The progress of the fermentation, the fall in density and the temperature are normally shown in chart form on each vat and checked every few hours. When no sugar remains, the wine (as it has now become) is either drawn off or left to macerate for some days with the skins. In the past this often continued for several weeks, but now the view is that most of the colour extraction takes place during fermentation, owing to the high temperatures, and that afterwards any improvement in the colour is minimal but tannins are still extracted, and these may not always be desirable. Bacterial infections may also be caused by prolonged skin contact and many winemakers like to draw the wine off immediately when it has finished fermenting in order to avoid this.

8   After the new wine has been drawn off, the remaining solid matter (mostly that which was contained in the cap) is removed from the vat and pressed. The result is what is known as *vin de presse*. The first *vin de presse* is usually of superior quality and will later be put back into the finished wine at the *assemblage*, or blending stage. The result of the second pressing is not normally of sufficiently high quality to be included. These two *vins de presse* between them account for about 15 per cent of the wine produced. While *vin de presse* is not usually a desirable element in ordinary wines made for early consumption, it is richer in all its elements than the free-run wine, except in alcoholic degree, and so adds an important element in fine wines intended for long maturation and keeping.

9   The next stage is known as malolactic fermentation. Ideally, this should follow immediately after the alcoholic fermentation. It is the process by which the astringent malic acid is converted into the more supple lactic acid, and in the process the total acidity is also diminished. Some winemakers like this to take place in the *cuve*, others put the wine straight into cask. This secondary fermentation occurs most easily at 20–25°C (68–77°F), so much emphasis is placed on completing it before the weather turns too cold as the large *cuviers* of Bordeaux are hard to heat, particularly in comparison with the small cellars of Burgundy. If vats are equipped with an internal cooling system, this can also be used, if necessary, for warming, thus facilitating the onset of malolactic

fermentation. Until this process is finished, the wine is not truly stable and it is also vulnerable to bacterial infections. In the past it was often observed that the wine would begin "working" in the spring, at the time when the vine began to push out its first buds; this was, in reality, carbon dioxide released when the malolactic fermentation began again, the warm weather permitting the bacteria to become active once more. It is preferable, however, to finish the process in the autumn rather than leaving the wine unstable through the winter.

10   Most, but not all, properties leave the new wine in *cuve* until the final selection or *assemblage* (blending) has been completed. This usually happens in January, sometimes later, depending on the year. All the *cuves* are tasted and decisions taken as to what will go into the *grand vin* (the main château label) and what should be eliminated in order to maintain the quality and reputation of the château wine. Increasingly there is a second label (such as Pavillon Rouge of Château Margaux, Réserve de la Comtesse of Pichon-Lalande, Clos du Marquis of Léoville-Las-Cases), but most of the rejected wine is usually sold under a simple generic label. This applies mostly to large properties and therefore mostly to the Médoc.

One of the less publicized but important decisions taken at this time is the addition of *vin de presse*. This gives the wine more tannin and extracts, and provides an important element in wines of quality that are intended for ageing.

11   The best Bordeaux châteaux mature their wines in 225-litre oak casks, the finest using 100 per cent new casks each year. But the wine has to have the power and composition to withstand such handling and, apart from the first growths, most *crus classés* use around one-third new wood each year. Wooden barrels are important in giving complexity and "finish" to a wine, but they must be in good condition and not more than about five years old.

In the past, many lesser *crus*, not being able to afford to buy new casks regularly, spoiled their wines by keeping them in old casks; these can easily taint the wine, making it seem mouldy or just not clean. It is better to keep the wine in vat rather than do this, and this is the policy of many lesser *crus* today, with resulting benefits to the wine. Bottling dates vary according to style and quality. The old system for the first growths was to bottle only after the third winter in cask, that is, in the spring of the third year. Now most are bottled either after the vintage in the second year (at the latest) or several months earlier in the late spring or (most commonly) in the summer of the second year.

DRY WHITE WINES

Over the past few years in Bordeaux, the preparation of these has changed much more radically than winemaking techniques for the reds. The use of stainless-steel horizontal presses, pneumatic presses, and low-temperature fermentation has revolutionized the style and quality of dry wines. In the past, Bordeaux made a few superb white Graves, but much of its white wine production was over-sulphured, heavy, and dull. Now the wines are fruity and perfumed, fresh, and clean.

RECENT INNOVATIONS

Malolactic fermentations in barrel

With the tendency to use more new oak, it has been found that by putting the wine warm from the vat into barrel and then encouraging the malolactic fermentation, a better marriage between wood and wine is achieved. Châteaux using 100 per cent new oak are increasingly turning to this method, as the wines are then more flattering to taste at the time of the *en primeur* tastings. Whether the effect is permanent is still a matter of discussion.

Bubbling oxygen through the wine in cask as a substitute for racking

This allows the wine to stay on its lees. Practitioners of this method do not fine the wine until just prior to bottling. The object is to preserve the fruit to a greater degree. Some very good results have recently been obtained but the proof will be in the ageing.

The basic process is as follows.

1 The grapes are fed into a horizontal or pneumatic press as they come from the vineyard. The pressing must be gentle, and the *marc* (solid cake or pomace of skins and other solid matter left after pressing) is continuously broken up by chains inside the horizontal presses, which rotate at the same time as the grapes are squeezed.

2 Juice runs from the press and is collected in a stainless-steel *cuve*. This is often chilled nowadays and held as grape juice over a period of 12–24 hours in order to precipitate its solids. This process is known as *débourbage*. An increasing number of Graves *vignerons*, and even some in Entre-Deux-Mers have now reverted to barrel fermentation in place of stainless steel. In this case, the must is run straight into new or used barrels, which are often kept in an air-conditioned *chai*. The must is lightly sulphured to guard against oxidation.

3 Fermentation then takes place once the must has been racked off its solids after the *débourbage*, either into another *cuve* or into barrel. Fermentation is now usually controlled at 15–20°C (59–68°F).

4 As with reds, white wines in Bordeaux normally undergo a malolactic fermentation.

5 As soon as the second fermentation is finished, the wine is clarified to prevent it from picking up any undesirable odours. This is usually done by filtration, or in large cellars by centrifuge. Some producers are now keeping their wines on the lees in barrel and stirring them, as in Burgundy, to increase the aromatic qualities of the wine.

6 Since the object nowadays is to prevent oxidation, wines spend much less time in pre-bottle maturation. Only the finest Graves spend more than a few months in cask; most wines are kept in *cuve* and bottled in the spring, some six months after the vintage, to conserve their freshness and fruit.

SWEET WHITE WINES

Because of the state of grapes affected by *pourriture noble* (noble rot or *Botrytis cinerea*, to give the scientific name), both the harvesting and vinifying of grapes for sweet wines pose special problems. The grapes cannot be picked as for dry wines, because the infection by *Botrytis cinerea* does not occur uniformly, either in the vineyard or even in single bunches. This means that the workers must go through a vineyard several times (four to six times at the best properties) selecting the best grapes from each bunch, a method requiring a certain amount of skill. Such grapes obviously cannot be mechanically harvested.

Botrytis cinerea itself is a fungus which, when it attacks overripe grapes, dehydrates them, thus concentrating their sugar content. Mild, humid conditions, typical of a Bordeaux autumn, are required for this infection to thrive. If conditions are too dry, the fungus will not attack even ripe grapes. This happened in 1978. On the other hand, if it rains at the wrong moment the vintage can be ruined, or only a small part of it will be useable. For these reasons there are far fewer successful vintages in Sauternes than in neighbouring Graves.

The process of vinification is as follows.

1   Because of the condition of the grapes, they are not crushed in a separate operation but go straight into the press. The pressing is difficult because the grapes are so rich in sugar (20–25° Baumé, 360–450 grams per litre) and the juice so viscous. Three pressings are usual for Sauternes.

2   A *débourbage* is not usual because of the danger of sulphur dioxide binding the yeast cells and thus inhibiting their activity, and because a must so rich in sugar and bacteria is susceptible to oxidation at this stage. The best method of clarification is to centrifuge and then chill the must before beginning the fermentation, which can still be in barrel, but is now more usually and safely effected in *cuve*.

3   The fermentation is slow and often continues for many weeks. It must be controlled carefully in order to obtain a balanced wine. Thus, a wine with 12.5 per cent alcohol is well-balanced with 30–35 grams of sugar per litre but not with 50. This sort of result would be typical of wines made in the Premières Côtes. A wine with 14 per cent alcohol, however, needs 60 to 70 grams to be balanced. Although the yeast becomes tired and "blocked" when the level of alcohol rises to around 14 per cent, the wine will still not be permanently stable, and must therefore be stabilized by the addition of sulphur dioxide. Stabilization is often assisted by filtration and chilling. Wines with less sugar must, in any case, be stopped from further fermentation in this way in order to ensure a balance.

4   The *élevage* (literally "raising" the wine, as one would children or livestock) then proceeds in much the same way as for dry wines, except that the best sweet wines seem to benefit from maturing in cask, and the process is more lengthy, as much as two to 2.5 years before bottling takes place. Selection between *cuves* and even casks is also important when seeking to obtain really fine Sauternes, or indeed Loupiac or Ste-Croix-du-Mont.

Vintages

In temperate climates, vintages are always important. Although there are fewer poor vintages than there used to be in Bordeaux, it is still important to know how the vintages vary, because this can tell you broadly which wines should be laid down and which can be drunk early. But each year has its distinctive character. Indeed, the finer the year, the stronger the vintage character, and the more pronounced the character of each *cru*.

2002

Weather and General Assessment The first significant feature to record is the dryness of the winter between 1 October and 31 March. The rainfall was the lowest since '88/'89 at only 311mm for the six month period. The previous winter had registered 1004mm while 556mm was the average for the previous 20 years. The next major factor was the poor flowering, caused by cold, wet conditions. This resulted in serious *coulure* and *millerandage*, especially but not exclusively affecting the Merlot. It is important to note that the worst casualties were among old vine, Right Bank Merlots. The extensive, but less damaging, *millerandage* mostly affected the Cabernet Franc and Cabernet Sauvignon. After this, the summer was drier than usual, but cool. The beginning of September was dangerously warm and showery and rot was now a real threat. The change came on 9 September, when a high pressure system suddenly arrived and stayed. Only a storm and some hail on 20 September caused any problems. The resulting wines are of very mixed quality, with the Cabernet Sauvignons of the Left Bank doing best. The autumn weather enabled the small crop to ripen well and the wind, sun and dryness of the soil concentrated the grapes to an exceptional degree, especially in the northern part of the Médoc. With less time available for the earlier ripening Merlots and so much already lost, this variety produced less quality. Very good results were obtained from the Petit Verdot and Cabernet Franc on the Right Bank. The dry whites were again zesty and fresh with lots of fruit. It was another excellent year for Sauternes, if not up to 2001.

Médoc and Graves Unlike other parts of the region, all the front line communes did well. Exceptional wines were made in St. Julien, Pauillac, and St-Estèphe, with record tannin levels. Margaux is consistently fine, if less remarkable, as is Pessac-Léognan. But the westerly communes and those in the northern Médoc are very mixed. It was a year for the "*grands terroirs*".

St-Émilion and Pomerol Although some fine wines were made, and those with good proportions of Cabernet Franc did best, it was a case of doing well in unfavourable circumstances. In general, there are a few very good wines and many moderate ones.

Dry Whites Consistently fine aromatic, fruity wines in Pessac-Léognan, with rather better acidity levels than in 2001.

Sauternes Another highly successful year: if not quite up to the exceptional level of 2001, then to be compared with '99 or '96. The level of quality among the best *crus* is consistently high.

2001

Weather and General Assessment After an exceptionally wet winter, double the average, and even more than a normal year's rainfall, warm weather in May and June ensured a rapid, even flowering across the region. But July was wet until the last ten days, as was August. The first half of September was cool but dryish, with the warmest weather coming in October. Acidities were noticeably higher than usual in the Cabernets. In comparison with 2000, the quality across the region was markedly more uneven. However, the most successful wines had more fullness and concentration than in '99, less power than in 2000 but real elegance and style. With high tannin levels, great care was necessary during the fermentation and overextracted wines are disappointing. Sauternes made up for the disappointment of 2000 with an exceptional vintage.

Médoc and Graves The best wines have real charm and fine aromatic fruit character. There are very good wines in all parts of Médoc and Graves, but also some disappointments. The wines showed a very good evolution in cask; one must now wait to see how they settle down in bottle.

St-Émilion and Pomerol The best Pomerols have rich, succulent, well-textured, aromatic fruit. Most St-Émilions do not quite reach the same level, although there are some delicious wines.

Dry Whites Consistently high quality with lovely fresh, aromatic fruit.

Sauternes A great vintage, the best since 1990. The wines have great richness and concentration as well as balance.

2000

Weather and General Assessment A warm, wet spring caused serious problems in the vineyards, only brought under control by rapid treatments and a spell of dry, warm weather in June. Fortunately, the flowering passed off well at the end of May and beginning of June, indicating a vintage slightly later than '99. The quality of the vintage was only assured by the exceptional weather from 29 July to 10 October. Temperatures were above average, with very little rain. The Merlots had very thick skins and were high in alcohol. Cabernet Franc gave exceptional results in St-Émilion and Pomerol. The Cabernet Sauvignons, harvested at the beginning of October with optimum ripeness, are of exceptional quality, with elements of the length and purity of '96 and the massive, spicy tannins of '86.

In general, there are outstanding wines at every level and in all districts. The best wines have a striking individuality and originality, intense fruit flavours, an exceptional aromatic quality, lots of glycerol, and sweet fruit, all balancing a massive tannic structure, producing beautifully rich textures. The first tastings in bottle have confirmed the exceptional quality and consistency of the wines. The dry whites are excellent, but only a small quantity of very fine, sweet wines was made, due to the wet weather in October.

Médoc and Graves Clearly the best vintage here since 1990, but more classic and concentrated. There are elements of '86 in the powerful tannins but much more suppleness and sweet fruit. Every appellation in the Médoc did well. All the first growths are exceptional, and one sees the difference between the greatest terroirs and the less good more clearly than usual. There seem to be fewer highlights in Pessac-Léognan.

St-Émilion and Pomerol Those properties with an important element of Cabernet Franc are especially favoured and tend to have produced the most complex wines. But the Merlots have produced rich, aromatic wines of the highest quality as well.

Dry Whites Very fresh, aromatic, fruity wines.

Sauternes Very rich concentrated wines but yields varied from about one-third of a crop to only a few barrels.

'99

Weather and General Assessment The weather pattern was unusual, with heavy outbreaks of rain from April onwards, combined with average temperatures above those for the last 30 years. Accelerated ripening and high sugar levels resulted. A hailstorm struck St-Émilion on 5 September, affecting ten per cent of the appellation. Then the rain returned just as the Merlots were ripe and ready to be harvested. In the Médoc, the Cabernets were picked mostly when the weather was dry. This was a record crop for both red wines and for AC wines as a whole and much depended on the work and vigilance of each producer over the growing season in managing to arrive at harvest with ripe, healthy grapes. There is a wide range of qualities, but the best wines have charm and style which, being lighter than the luscious '98s, provide attractive wines for medium-term drinking. This was another great Sauternes vintage, the fourth in a row.

Médoc and Graves Many producers claimed that their '99s were better than their '98s. They were certainly fruitier and more immediately accessible, while lacking the structure of the preceding year. And in part, this claim was a reaction against premature press comments belittling '98 Médocs. There was a wide variation of quality in Pessac-Léognan, while in the Médoc, there were more good wines in Margaux, St-Julien, and Pauillac than elsewhere. While there are attractively fruity wines, there are also dilute and over-extracted ones.

St-Émilion and Pomerol Here the Cabernet Franc generally did less well than in '98, so some wines lacked the depth and complexity of the '98s. But the strike rate both in St-Émilion and Pomerol is high, with many supple, rich wines which should be ready to drink earlier than the more profound '98s.

Dry Whites At the lower level, many wines are dilute. In Pessac-Léognan, the heat at harvest time resulted in a loss of aromatic character and acidity in the Sauvignons, with high alcohol, but the Sémillons went some way to compensate for this.

Sauternes The wines have a fine, concentrated, botrytis style and good acidity and richness. In style they seem close to the marvellous '98s and '96s.

'98

Weather and General Assessment The special character of this vintage is due to the exceptional heat of August, after a good flowering and cool weather in June and July. This meant that when rain came in September, just before the harvest, and then more seriously at the end of the month, the effect was much less than expected. Although the chance to make a great vintage may have slipped by, some great wines were undoubtedly made. The wines have exceptional colour and powerful, rich tannins. Initially heralded as a Merlot year, the evaluation of the Cabernets has surprised many tasters. The dry whites and sweet wines are excellent.

Médoc and Graves The favourable evolution of the Cabernets, together with the outstanding Merlots, have surprised many early pessimists. Great wines have been made on the great terroirs. Pessac-Léognan is especially successful, St-Estèphe perhaps less so than the communes to the south. Even the good *crus bourgeois* will need keeping for at least another year or two.

St-Émilion and Pomerol This is undoubtedly a great year for Pomerol but St-Émilion is more mixed. There are dense, textured, opulent wines, but some St-Émilions seem over-extracted. The best now seem superior to '95.

Dry whites These are lovely wines of intense fruit, reminiscent of '96, but with less acidity.

Sauternes Very rich, concentrated wines which seem to resemble the '96s but have less elegance than '97.

'97

Weather and General Assessment A year marked by a most unusual weather pattern. A warm spring resulted in a flowering that began in early May, but which then continued throughout the month as the weather turned cold. This resulted in an unevenness of maturity of the grapes, which continued through to the vintage. Four weeks of hot, humid weather from 25 July to 28 August, followed by a week's stormy weather, led into September, when from the second to the fifth of October no rain fell. Vintaging was very spread out and difficult. At their best, the wines have elegance and charm, but are less concentrated than '95 and '96.

Médoc and Graves The more careful growers have produced delicious, early-drinking wines in all areas, but the public perception was damaged by the excessive *primeur* prices. They have breed and style.

St-Émilion and Pomerol Many wines developed much better than at first seemed likely. In some cases the wines rival the rather variable '96s.

Dry whites While quantities are small due to problems at the time of harvesting, the top properties made delightful wines.

Sauternes This was the one region to produce indisputably great wines of remarkable elegance and style during this year, although the wines were less rich than the '96s, or '98 and '99.

'96

Weather and General Assessment The unusual weather pattern produced wines of marked character. Often above-average temperatures in June and July, but those of August were below average and there was more rain than usual. Then came three weeks of dry, sunny weather, but less heat than expected in early September. This surprisingly caused a rapid rise in sugar levels while the cold nights left acidity levels high. The result was exceptional Cabernet Sauvignon, higher in sugar content than in '89 or '82; Merlot higher than '85 but lower than '89; exceptional dry white wines and sweet wines.

Médoc and Graves The best wines are in St-Julien and points north, where they have exceptional length and depth of flavour and great breed and finesse. In Margaux, southern Médoc and Graves, where there was more rain, the wines are similar to '85 and elegant.

St-Émilion and Pomerol The quality is not as uniformly high as in '95, and some wines are noticeably lighter, but the best are still rich and fine.

Dry Whites With the richness of '89 and '90 but an exceptional acidity balance, the wines are extremely good with the top Pessac-Léognan reaching heights seldom seen.

Sauternes Undoubtedly a great year. The wines have the richness of '89 but the higher acidities give them the elegance of '88.

'95

Weather and General Assessment At last: the vintage Bordeaux was waiting for after the disappointment of '94 and '93. The growing season was dry and hot and the vines were as forward as they had been in '94 and '93. But this time, the usual September rainfall was much less serious, and perfect weather from September 20 until October enabled ripe grapes to be harvested without the anxieties of '94. The feature of the year is the regularity of the quality at all levels.

Médoc and Graves These powerfully structured wines have in general not evolved as well as expected. They tend to be rather chunky and graceless and are evolving more slowly than the '96s. The exception is Pessac-Léognan, where the wines have more ripeness and breed.

St-Émilion and Pomerol A superb vintage. The wines have richness and beauty of flavour. Some great wines were made.

Dry Whites Well-balanced, fruity and elegant wines.

Sauternes The best vintage since '90. Perfumed wines with good botrytis concentration and fruit. A fine if not a great year, but '96–'99 were better and more consistent.

'94

Weather and General Assessment Once more, a great vintage was dashed from our lips at the last moment. An early flowering coupled with excellent growing and ripening conditions had produced grapes which, in the first week in September, were in line with '82 and '90. But heavy rain between 14 and 17 September, followed by intermittent showers, which were often heavy, until the end of the month, detracted from the quality of the vintage. However, both the ripeness and excellent condition of the grapes promised significantly better wines than in '93. The top *crus* were able to produce firm, fine wines with style and richness. But yields were generally down – as much as 20 per cent below those of '93 in many vineyards. However, their evolution has been disappointing.

Médoc and Graves The best wines came from vineyards with the earliest-ripening Cabernet Sauvignon, which was of excellent quality. The AC Médoc and those Haut-Médocs farthest from the river did less well. Pessac-Léognan was uniformly good, and St-Julien of a high overall standard. They have evolved very slowly.

St-Émilion and Pomerol A good overall level of quality, with juicy, ripe wines that show generous fruit and good structure. Again, have evolved more slowly than expected.

Dry Whites Mostly gathered in before the rains; fruity, well-balanced, stylish wines were made.

Sauternes Another traumatic vintage for producers. The weather changed at the beginning of October but there was little left to save. A handful of decent wines were made in tiny quantities. Yquem proved an exception.

'93

Weather and General Assessment A much better growing and ripening season: conditions were almost a re-run of '92, much to the frustration of producers. The yields were a little below the record of the previous year, but still high, and while the rain seemed more intermittent, this was still a wet September. Only the top *crus* succeeded in making significantly better wines than in '92.

Médoc and Graves After a dull patch, most wines are now drinking well. Pessac-Léognan, St-Julien, Pauillac and St-Estèphe produced the best results, with a handful of really good attractive wines.

St-Émilion and Pomerol The Merlot did much better than '92, but Cabernet Franc still had problems. The wines are less dilute, and plenty of pleasing examples were the result.

Dry Whites Because most of the grapes were brought in before the rain affected them, this is a good year for Entre-Deux-Mers and Graves, with fruity, stylish wines.

Sauternes These are only marginally less awful than in '92, with a handful of usable wines.

'92

Weather and General Assessment These were probably the most difficult weather conditions for *vignerons* since '74. The growing season was exceptionally wet, with the August rainfall three times its normal level, while temperatures fluctuated between warm (during May, July and August) and cool (in June and first three weeks of September). To crown it all, it rained right through the harvest. As far as volume is concerned, this was the largest crop of AC wines recorded. Well-run properties were able to make severe selections resulting in pleasant commercial wines for early drinking for the red – but the whites are generally more successful.

Médoc and Graves Rather dilute Cabernets result in a wide variation in quality. Strict selection was vital. The best wines are light, fruity and charming now.

St-Émilion and Pomerol Merlots did well but Cabernet Franc posed problems at many properties. The best wines show attractive, supple fruit. Drink up!

Dry Whites Some fine Graves and plenty of attractive wines from Entre-Deux-Mers, but a wide range of qualities.

Sauternes A vintage to forget!

'91

Weather and General Assessment The frost on the night of 20–1 April was the most serious to strike Bordeaux since that of 1945. Then cold weather hampered the development of secondary shoots, resulting in big ripening differences at harvest time. Poor weather in September and rain during the vintage dashed any hopes of reasonable quality. Only a few exceptional sites, mostly in the Médoc, were able to make wines solely from first-generation grapes – and only the first-generation grapes produced any real quality.

Médoc and Graves A few vineyards close to the Gironde were spared the worst of the frost, and châteaux such as La Tour de By, Sociando-Mallet, Montrose, Cos d'Estournel, Latour and Léoville-Las-Cases produced surprisingly attractive, supple wines of real substance. However, in general, the wines are pretty but insubstantial.

St-Émilion and Pomerol The story here is bleak. Only part of the Côte de Pavie escaped the full ravages of the frost, and then the poor weather conditions were not kind to the remaining second-generation Merlots.

Dry Whites The smallest crop recorded in Bordeaux! Yields in Pessac-Léognan were only 12.9 hl/ha. But the wines that were made are fruity and attractive.

Sauternes Disastrous yields between ten and 11 hectolitres per hectare but one or two good selections resulted in tiny quantities of wine which are finer and richer than the '92s and '93s.

'90

> *Weather and General Assessment* The pattern of '89 was followed to a degree that is rare. The flowering was in May, and but for a combination of heat and drought in July, which simply stopped the vines in their tracks, the vintage would have been even earlier than in '89. As it was, the vintage for the Merlots began around 10 September, while the Cabernet Sauvignons in the Médoc needed to wait until the beginning of October. The wines have outstanding fruit and good structure, in the mould of '82 and '89. The crop was marginally larger than '89, but with slightly lower yields.

> *Médoc and Graves* The more northerly regions of the Médoc, with their heavier soils, did especially well. There are many outstanding successes among the *crus bourgeois*, and many exceptional wines in St-Estèphe, Pauillac and St-Julien, but Margaux is more varied. Graves are often opulent but also have elegance and great individuality.

> *St-Émilion and Pomerol* St-Émilions are characterized by an attractive combination of rich, luscious fruit and good structure, while Pomerols are notable for the concentration of the wines. They now look consistently more impressive than the '89s.

> *Dry Whites* Outstandingly aromatic fruit. Many producers achieved better balance and acidity than they did with the '89.

> *Sauternes* The *annus mirabilis* for Sauternes, with the richest wines seen since '29, even surpassing the wonderful '89s. The wines are remarkably exotic in character.

'89

> *Weather and General Assessment* The warmest, sunniest and driest summer, on average, in 30 years, with a flowering that began on 20 May, and the earliest vintage since 1893, beginning on 28 August. The wines are high in alcohol, with luscious fruit and soft, ripe tannins reminiscent of '82. The yields for red AC wines set a new record, surpassing that of the '86 vintage by over 350,000 hectolitres.

> *Médoc and Graves* The St-Juliens are a stunning group, but there are lovely wines in all the main communes. Selection of the best fruit, due to high yields, has meant that the leading growths have done correspondingly better than the lesser *crus*. In general, they now show more concentration and power than the '90s, and are more backward. There are some gloriously rich, fruity wines. The Graves are lighter and more elegant in structure.

> *St-Émilion and Pomerol* Amazingly dense-textured and forceful wines, with exceptional structure to add to the opulence of a great Merlot vintage, but many lack the flavour of '90.

> *Dry Whites* Big, fat, fruity wines, but many suffer from shortage of acidity and could, with advantage, have been harvested even earlier. For drinking now.

> *Sauternes* This is an exceptional year, comparable with '47 but with more of everything. The '89 and '90 must be the greatest pair of Sauternes since '28 and '29, coming at the end of a decade of fine vintages.

'88

> *Weather and General Assessment* A wet winter and spring were followed by a drier-than-average summer and a warm October. The resulting variations in maturity between the grape varieties were significant, as were those between the same variety at different sites, and this caused

noticeable variations in quality. In style, the wines began life as forbiddingly tannic, in the mould of '86, but have become classically elegant and fine.

Médoc and Graves Classically structured wines that seem finer, but have less power, than the '86s. They are long-lived and harmonious, with fine concentration and breed. Now drinking well.

St-Émilion and Pomerol The St-Émilions are exceptionally rich and concentrated, usually superior to the '86s, while the Pomerols are really opulent, with a great depth of flavour.

Dry Whites The wines have pronounced fruit, with the best Graves having complexity and elegance.

Sauternes Another classic botrytis year to set beside '83 and '86. The wines have character and great breed, they are well-balanced and the top wines are consistent.

'87

Weather and General Assessment After above-average temperatures in July, August and September, heavy rain during the vintage. Wines are soft, fruity and easy to drink young.

Médoc and Graves The Cabernets were caught by the rain, so the Merlots are of more than usual importance. The wines have plenty of fruit and charm, if light in body and rather short. Pleasing, early drinking wines. Should be drunk up now.

St-Émilion and Pomerol With their high proportion of Merlot, these regions did better than the Médoc and Graves. The wines are supple and fruity and have developed quickly. To drink up.

Dry Whites Well-balanced, with pleasing fruit character.

Sauternes Where strict selections were made, good wines have resulted.

'86

Weather and General Assessment There was successful flowering and a good summer but heavy rain, especially around Bordeaux, in late September. Exceptionally dry conditions during the harvest. The red-wine crop beat the '85 record. The quality of the best wines is excellent, with some classic wines for long keeping. The most tannic year since '75, and a complete contrast to '85.

Médoc and Graves A Cabernet year: many vats of Merlot remained unused. Wines have great power, depth and promise but still need patience.

St-Émilion and Pomerol Here there was less rain, and the Merlot did much better. The Pomerols are powerful and tannic, the St-Émilions have more charm but are generally less powerful.

Dry Whites Perfumed and attractive, sometimes better-balanced than the '85s.

Sauternes Another great Sauternes vintage. The onset of botrytis was more general and rapid than in '85, the quality more consistent than '83.

'85

Weather and General Assessment In spite of rain, there was an excellent setting of the fruit. This was the driest September on record, with sustained heat, and a warm and dry October, resulting in the largest crop of AC reds. Overall quality is high, the wines have charm and breed, classic in the style of '53, but they are more outstanding across the board. The bargain vintage among mature wines.

Médoc and Graves Outstanding in Margaux and Graves, more rigorous selection necessary in Pauillac, St-Julien and the Médoc: yields were high. Properties that delayed picking their Cabernets until the second week of October did best. Wines are rich in fruit and tannin and harmonious. Delicious drinking now.

St-Émilion and Pomerol Sugar levels in the Merlot were higher than in '82, and the general level among the leading growths is more uniform than usual. There were lower yields than in '82.

Dry Whites Extremely perfumed, fruity wines, but with low acidity.

Sauternes The few properties that prolonged picking have made excellent wines with great elegance, if less luscious than in '83.

'84

Weather and General Assessment A cold, wet May led to the worst Merlot in living memory as flowers failed to set. Late September experienced rain and storms, but a perfect October followed. There are few successes, and in general the wines appear rather mean.

Médoc and Graves Average yields produced wines that have not lived up to early expectations. Few pleasant surprises.

St-Émilion and Pomerol A small crop of rather average wine which lacks character and appears mean.

Dry Whites Excellent quality, normal yield. The wines have more delicacy and are lighter than the '83s, with pronounced character, and have aged well.

Sauternes Some fine wines were made.

'83

Weather and General Assessment A wet spring, good flowering in June. Early September brought more rain, but the weather was ideal for the vintage. A fine year, producing classic wines, mostly now at their best, with style and character.

Médoc and Graves Another large vintage. The quality is not as regular as in '82, but fine at *cru classé* level, with some stylish wines. Most wines are now at their best.

St-Émilion and Pomerol A high yield. Some outstanding wines but more variation than in '82. Most drinking well now.

Dry Whites Good wines with more acidity and style than the '82s.

Sauternes A great year, probably the best since '76. Luscious wines, but well-balanced and long-lived.

'82

Weather and General Assessment A classic hot year, with a large yield and perfect ripeness – certainly the outstanding vintage since '61. The wines have a special vintage character.

Médoc and Graves Wines of exceptional concentration and power, with plenty of fruit to cover the high tannin levels. Some wines now betray a lack of selection. An exceptional year, the most individual since '61.

St-Émilion and Pomerol Wines of exceptional opulence and power, reminiscent of '47. As in '47, some of the top wines proved remarkable for early drinking, but are now at their best.

Dry Whites These wines have charm but are short of acidity. Most should have been drunk.

Sauternes The dry, hot weather delayed the noble rot; the rain in October started too early, resulting in medium-weight wines that are no more than acceptable for early drinking. Yquem is the exception.

'81

Weather and General Assessment Good weather right through the growing
period, but some rain during the vintage. Wines have more breed but less
body than in '79.

Sauternes The best are luscious, better than the '82s and are still attractive.

'80

Weather and General Assessment The coldest June since '46 caused
prolonged flowering and widespread *coulure*. A cold summer and very
late harvest. Stylish wines that should have been drunk.

Médoc and Graves Attractive wines, but showing their age.

St-Émilion and Pomerol More variable than Médoc but, since Merlot ripened
better than Cabernet Sauvignon, these areas produced many supple,
fruity wines. Should have been drunk.

Dry Whites Light, pleasant wines that should have been drunk.

Sauternes The wines are rather light, but the best have a pleasant fruitiness
and charm without real lusciousness.

'79

Weather and General Assessment Late flowering and excellent setting; a
cold and wet August, but better conditions in September yielded a large
crop. Wines have great depth of fruit, vigour and lots of charm, but lack
backbone and breed.

Médoc and Graves Wines have a marked vintage character and are rich and
dense in texture. They have developed slowly, and lack the finesse of '78.
To drink now.

St-Émilion and Pomerol The Merlot's exceptional ripeness produced more
luscious, dense and opulent wines than in '78. This kind of year brings out
the best in these districts.

Dry Whites Stylish wines with fruit and breed.

Sauternes Vies with '81 as the best vintage between '76 and '83. Luscious,
fruity wines.

'78

Weather and General Assessment The wettest March since 1870
was followed by an exceptionally dry July, August, and September.
The average-sized vintage was harvested late but in ideal conditions,
and classic wines with harmonious balance were the result. They
have developed more quickly than expected and are ideal for
drinking now.

Médoc and Graves Wines of great character and finesse. Their considerable
tannin, well blended with fruit and richness, has given them a long
development. They are now at their best.

St-Émilion and Pomerol These wines have developed attractively. Some are
rather lean, but most are decidedly stylish. Not such typical wines as the '79s.

Dry Whites A fine year. To drink.

Sauternes A freak year, with perfect ripeness but almost no noble rot,
leaving the wines lacking in classic character.

'77

Weather and General Assessment A small harvest of very light wines.
Should have been drunk.

'76

Weather and General Assessment This year offered dry, hot weather from
April to the end of August. The vintage began 13 September, but rain

diluted the musts. This mixture of tannin and concentrated fruit, diluted with rainwater, produced diverse wines. Some are deeply coloured, rich and fruity. In others, tannin and fruit seem to have separated. It has also affected the development cycle of the wines, which has been relatively rapid.

Médoc and Graves The best wines are supple, powerful and attractive, but there are also disappointments. They have developed well and are by now at their best. To drink rather than to keep.

St-Émilion and Pomerol Overripeness and diluted colours are a feature here. Many wines suffer from low acidity and have aged rapidly. A few have more structure and are delicious now.

Dry Whites Wines low in acidity that needed drinking early. Some top Graves are rich and fine.

Sauternes A great vintage, with luscious wines that are more elegant and stylish than the '75s.

'75

Weather and General Assessment Excellent flowering, then a dry, hot summer. Some rain in September was just what was needed. A year of moderate yields, good alcoholic degrees, and thick skins resulted in tannic wines that are slow to develop. They lack the balance and charm of the '61s which some optimists believed them to resemble at an early stage.

Médoc and Graves At some châteaux, this year now looks like the best vintage of the decade, with the tannins peeling away to reveal rich, concentrated, classic wines possessed of both power and fruit. Elsewhere, the tannins can seem too dry.

St-Émilion and Pomerol As often happens in a tannic year, the best wines seem better balanced than in the Médoc. The emphasis is on ripeness and opulence: there are many successful wines.

Dry Whites The best Graves are concentrated and powerful but lack the elegance of the '76s.

Sauternes Many wines have too much botrytis and are too alcoholic: clumsy, tarry wines that are ageing rapidly (Yquem, Climens, Coutet and Doisy-Daëne are notable exceptions).

'74

Weather and General Assessment Good flowering ensured a large vintage. A fine summer promised good quality but a cold, wet September changed all that. Austere, charmless wines for the most part, which lack any real appellation or *cru* character.

'73

Weather and General Assessment Good flowering conditions ensured a large crop, but the summer alternated between hot and sunny and wet. The vintage was gathered in good conditions in October. Most wines are now past their best.

Médoc and Graves Attractive, early developing wines. Most should have been drunk, but some are holding up surprisingly well.

St-Émilion and Pomerol These are rather overblown wines which had great charm but were short-lived, with a few notable exceptions.

Dry Whites Some stylish Graves have lasted well, but most should have been drunk some time ago.

Sauternes Pleasant but moderate wines, on the light side.

'72

Weather and General Assessment A cold spring, a poor summer with rain in August and a late harvest of unripe grapes. A year of high prices and mean, dull wines that are best forgotten.

'71

Weather and General Assessment A cold, wet spring caused a poor flowering and a correspondingly small crop. Then the summer turned warm and sunny with just the right amount of rain. A complete contrast to the previous vintage.

Médoc and Graves Flattering, charming wines that developed quickly and have been at their peak since the late 1970s. With their low acidities, they now need drinking, and many have already turned the corner.

St-Émilion and Pomerol Some great successes here, with rich, luscious but rather overblown wines. They should be drunk up, except for a few Pomerols.

Dry Whites Perfumed, elegant Graves at the top level are lasting well.

Sauternes A great, classic Sauternes year, combining richness with elegance, usually better than '70.

'70

Weather and General Assessment Ideal growing conditions produced the rare combination of quantity and perfect ripeness. The new plantings of the 1960s yielded quality wines, and 1970 marked the beginning of the great switch from white to red wines and heralded the large yields of the 1970s and 1980s. This was the largest quality year since '34. A fine vintage: slow to develop but generally worth waiting for.

Médoc and Graves These wines have taken much longer to develop than expected, due perhaps to a lack of maturity in parts of the vineyards at this period. Nevertheless, these are classic long-distance wines, well-structured, with breed and fruit to match the tannin. They are now becoming enjoyable to drink, especially the Margaux, St-Juliens and Graves, but there are some disappointments.

St-Émilion and Pomerol These have also been slow to evolve, but they have more charm than many Médocs and are drinking well. The power and the structure of these wines promise a long life.

Dry Whites The best Graves are rich and solid and holding well.

Sauternes Big, luscious wines, with less style for the most part than in '71. Long-lasting wines.

OLDER VINTAGES STILL DRINKING WELL

'66 A classic vintage with old-fashioned, concentrated wines, the best of the decade after '61.

'64 The Pomerols and St-Emilions are still superb, in many cases the best of the decade. The Médocs are in decline.

'62 Although without the concentration of '66, there are fine, classic wines ageing gracefully.

'61 These outstanding wines continue to delight and astonish. They have no rivals today until '82.

'59 Wines have a roasted character. Some rival '61 but most lack their harmony.

'55 Some still remarkably fresh, solid, and more interesting than they were a few years ago.

What Makes Great Bordeaux

RED

Vineyard
Well-drained, relatively poor soil, high in gravel (Médoc and Graves), limestone (St-Émilion côtes), gravel, sand and clay (St-Émilion, Graves) or gravel and clay (Pomerol).

Grape varieties
Cabernet Sauvignon, Cabernet Franc and Merlot.

Mature, healthy grapes
The right balance of sugar and acidity; no rot.

Careful vinification
No extraction of acids from the stalks. Fermentation at 28–30°C (82–86°F).

Careful selection
Rejection of any substandard cuves (grapes from young vines, an inferior part of the vineyard, or cuves affected by rain or rot).

Addition of vin de presse (see page 31).
This adds colour and extracts and so provides additional elements to assist ageing.

Use of new barrels
The percentage of new barrels should be correct for the weight of the wine; it ranges from 30–100 per cent.

Bottling at the right time
After 18–24 months, depending on the wine's tannin and power.

SWEET WHITE

Vineyard
Well-drained, poor soil, characterized by the presence of clay with gravel and limestone.

Grape varieties
Sémillon and Sauvignon.

Overripe grapes affected by noble rot
This must be carefully controlled by selection. Too little botrytis and the wine lacks character; too much, and the wine becomes clumsy.

Selection in the vineyard
The pickers must go through the vineyard from three to six times to select overripe and botrytized grapes.

Slow and long fermentation in cask
The ideal temperature is normally about 20°C (68°F). Because of this and the high concentration of sugar, the fermentation usually lasts two to five weeks.

Cask-ageing
The best crus still keep their wines in cask for two to three years. A proportion of the casks are new.

Selection for bottling
Selection is made between pressings (the third is usually the best), and between casks.

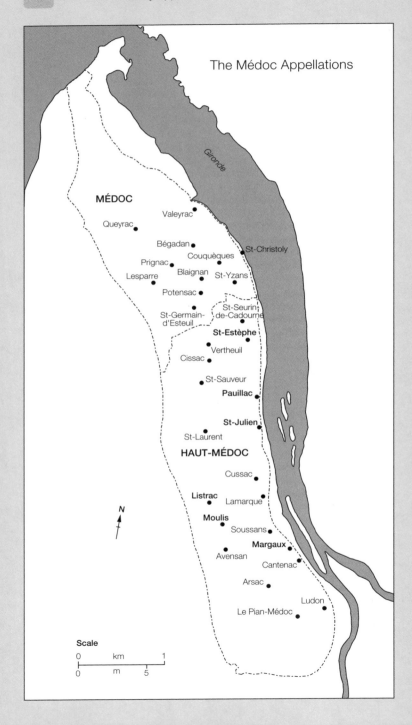

The Médoc Appellations

Gironde

MÉDOC

Valeyrac

Queyrac

Bégadan
Couquèques   St-Christoly
Prignac
Lesparre   Blaignan   St-Yzans
Potensac
St-Seurin-
de-Cadourne
St-Germain-
d'Esteuil   **St-Estèphe**
Vertheuil
Cissac
St-Sauveur
Pauillac
St-Julien
St-Laurent
HAUT-MÉDOC
Cussac
Listrac   Lamarque
Moulis
Soussans
Margaux
Avensan   Cantenac
Arsac   Ludon
Le Pian-Médoc

N

Scale

| 0 | km | 1 |
| 0 | m | 5 |

Château Profiles by Appellation

This section focuses on properties that merit special consideration. It includes not only the great names of Bordeaux but also many less well-known producers whose wines deserve recognition. The entries are arranged by appellation; each appellation is introduced with a description of its general character. In the Médoc, which encompasses many important appellations, there is also a general introduction to the region.

After the name of the property, each entry begins with the following details, where obtainable and relevant: classification, owner, administrator, number of hectares planted with vines, number of cases produced annually, grape varieties and respective percentages present in the vineyard, and any secondary or other labels. *See* page 5 for a key to the abbreviations.

The Médoc Appellations

The Médoc has been the great ambassador for the red wines of Bordeaux the world over. From the early 18th century, when wealthy and discerning Englishmen first paid a premium to obtain better wines, until the beginning of the 21st century the fame of the region has centred on the treasure trove of the Médoc.

With its proximity to the city of Bordeaux, the commercial and political centre of the Gironde, it was natural that the Médoc should be developed earlier and more thoroughly than any other part of the region. In the 17th and 18th centuries, the great wine estates there were put together in much the same form as they exist today. Because of the poor, gravelly soil, mixed subsistence farming easily gave way to specialized viticulture. A glance at the map opposite shows the Médoc to be a narrow but lengthy strip of land running along the estuary of the Gironde from just outside the modern suburbs of northern Bordeaux, at Blanquefort and Le Taillan, to St-Vivien, 70 kilometres (44 miles) to the north. In few places do the vineyards extend more than ten kilometres (six miles) inland from the river, and most lie to the east of the main Bordeaux–Lesparre–Soulac road. This is where the ridges of gravel are at their deepest and purest. As you go north, the soils get heavier and the gravel more interspersed with clay or sand, while to the west, the land becomes sandy and the pine forests of Les Landes begin.

Viticulturally, the Médoc is divided into two distinct areas: the Haut-Médoc in the south and the Bas-Médoc (called simply Médoc for appellation purposes) in the north. Within the Haut-Médoc, six communal appellations have been carved out. In addition, the name Haut-Médoc itself constitutes a seventh appellation, encompassing wines not covered by the communal appellations. The latter correspond to the area where the great majority of the finest vineyards lie. This is vividly illustrated by the following figures showing the proportion of the area under vine in the five appellations occupied by the *crus classés* (the remaining two contain no *crus classés*): Haut-Médoc – 5.5 per cent, Margaux – 68 per cent, St-Julien – 75 per cent, Pauillac – 72.5 per cent, St-Estèphe – 19.5 per cent.

Although more and more of the *crus bourgeois* now bottle at least a proportion of their wines at the château, many smaller vineyards find it makes economic sense to join cooperatives where the methods of vinification have been modernized, rather than face the large capital cost of modernizing their own *cuviers*. Members of cooperatives account for the following proportions of the areas under vine in these appellations: Médoc – 42.5 per cent, Haut-Médoc – 17.5 per cent, Pauillac – 18 per cent, St-Estèphe – 26 per cent, – Listrac 24 per cent, Moulis – 6.5 per cent. Standards in cooperatives have improved considerably in the past few years and they are now undoubtedly a positive influence on quality.

The dominance of the Cabernet Sauvignon grape in all the vineyards of the Médoc ensures a certain family resemblance, a crispness of definition on nose and palate, and a tendency for the tannin to be dominant in the first year or so in bottle. The development of bouquet, combined with delicacy and character of flavour, comes with bottle-ageing. Médoc wines all need to be aged, and even quite modest *crus* keep and improve well.

MARGAUX

Margaux is the only one of the six commune appellations that is not restricted to the area bearing its name. Also included under this appellation are most of the commune of Arsac and all of Cantenac, Labarde, and Soussans. The area under vine increased by ten per cent between 1990 and 2000.

The outstanding characteristics of the appellation's wines are finesse and breed, the results of deep, gravelly ridges and a high proportion of Cabernet Sauvignon. But the variations of emphasis are considerable. Labarde wines tend to have more body and richness, the Cantenacs are more elegant and often lighter, as is du Tertre, the sole *cru classé* of Arsac. Many Margaux wines have more tannin and are slower to evolve.

Château d'Angludet ★ V →

Cru Bourgeois Supérieur. Owners: Sichel family. 32ha. 14,000 cases. CS 55%, Mer 35%, PV 7%, CF 3%. Second label: La Ferme d'Angludet.

Angludet was unfortunate not to be classified in 1855. At that time, it was divided and had much declined in importance since the 18th century, when it had been ranked with the leading growths. First under Peter Sichel's devoted care, then under his son Benjamin's, the wines are becoming steadily better as the vineyard matures. Benjamin is now responsible for the winemaking. The excellent vineyard, situated on the plateau of Cantenac, produces wines that are finely perfumed and combine great finesse with elegance and vigour. Since the excellent '78, the wines have been consistently impressive. I would single out the '82, '85, '86, '89, '90, '95, '96, '98, '99, and 2000, all of which are fine examples of these vintages.

Château d'Arsac →

Cru Bourgeois Supérieur. Owner: Philippe Raoux. 112ha. 65,000 cases. CS 60%, Mer 40%. Château Le Monteil d'Arsac AC Haut-Médoc. Second label: Ribon Bleu de Château d'Arsac.

From 1995, 42 hectares of this property's vineyards have been classified as AC Margaux, the remainder being AC Haut-Médoc, under the Le Monteil d'Arsac label. This *cru* was always something of a curiosity, since it was the only major one in Arsac not to benefit from the Margaux AC until recently: when the AC was being established, there were no vines planted and the proprietor did not bother to apply for recognition. A start was made in reconstructing the vineyard when it changed hands in 1959, but the real change came when the present dynamic owner arrived in 1986.

Since then the massive *chai* has been restored, the *cuvier* modernized and the vineyard increased from only 11.5 hectares to its present 112 hectares. The new vinification facilities were operational for the '88 vintage. The amount of oak-ageing has been increased, and 25 per cent new oak is now being used.

Château Bel-Air-Marquis-d'Aligre

Owner: Pierre Boyer. 17ha. 4,500 cases. Mer 35%, CS 30%, CF 20%, PV 15%.
Second label: Château Bel-Air-Marquis-de-Pomereu.

Confusingly, this is one of the three Margaux properties sporting the name "Marquis" in its title, and the only one not classified. It lies at the back of Margaux, with part of the vineyard in the adjoining commune Soussans.

Pierre Boyer is a perfectionist who makes his wines with great care from low yields. Only organic fertilizers are used in the vineyards. The wine has real finesse and a certain unctuousness combined with delicacy and freshness.

Château Boyd-Cantenac

3e Cru Classé. Owner: Pierre Guillemet. 18ha. 7,500 cases.
CS 67%, Mer 20%, CF 7%, PV 6%.

This property has a chequered history. It lost many of its vineyards to Cantenac-Brown in 1860, disappeared as a name for 45 years before reappearing again in 1920, then lost its buildings to Château Margaux.

Until 1982, the wine was made at Château Pouget, Pierre Guillemet's neighbouring property, but now the wines are separately made. I feel that the wines here have been rather sidelined by all the improvements of the '90s. They lack the style and finesse expected of a *cru classé*.

Château Brane-Cantenac ★★ →

2e Cru Classé. Owner: Henri Lurton. 90ha. 36,500 cases. CS 70%, Mer 20%, CF 10%.
Second label: Le Baron de Brane.

Brane-Cantenac owed its name and pre-eminence in 1855 to Baron de Brane, famed as a viticulturist and responsible for the rise of Mouton. Now it belongs to another family of viticulturalists, the Lurtons. In 1992, Lucien Lurton handed this property to his son, Henri, as part of his family plan to pass on specific vineyards to his children. He made the important decision to re-introduce wooden fermentation vats.

With vineyards enjoying a prime position on the plateau of Cantenac, this property produces a wine noted for its delicacy, finesse, and breeding (quintessential Margaux qualities) and this in spite of its high proportion of Cabernet Sauvignon: a sure indication of the influence of soil on grape varieties. Like many Margaux wines, it can often be drunk young with enjoyment, but lasts well, as demonstrated by its lovely '66.

Good wines were made in '78, '79, and '81; the '82 is outstanding; '85 has the breed of the year; '86 less tannic than some, '88, '89, and '90 combine concentration with great finesse, and '94, '95, '96, '98, '99, and 2000 are among the successes of the appellation. A wine on the way up.

Château Cantenac-Brown ★ →

3e Cru Classé. Owner: AXA-Millésimes. Administrator: Christian Seely. 32ha.
12,500 cases. CS 65%, Mer 25%, CF 10%.
Second labels: Château Canuet (Margaux), Lamartine (Bordeaux Supérieur).

The English name "Brown" is from John Lewis Brown, a Bordeaux merchant of English origin and an artist famous for his animal pictures. He was responsible for this unusual château, described as *Renaissance Anglaise* in style. It now belongs to AXA-Millésimes, which also owns Pichon-Baron.

Cantenac-Brown today does not enjoy the reputation (or sell for the price) it once did. The wine is more tannic, with less finesse than the best Cantenacs, and has a certain coarseness. Efforts being made by the new owners to improve matters started to show dividends in '95.

Château Dauzac V →

5e Cru Classé. Owner: Société Fermière d'Exploitation. 40ha. 29,000 cases. CS 58%, Mer 37%, CF 5%. Second labels: Châteaux Labarde, La Bastide.

Until recently, this property in Labarde had suffered a long period of neglect. In 1993, the management of the estate was reorganized as a cooperative, and a substantial shareholding was allotted to the SCEA Les Vignobles André Lurton, which took over responsibility for the future management of the property.

The Lurton team is now turning its attention to the vineyard, much of which is planted on unsuitable rootstocks, and this should complete the long process of rehabilitation for this *cru*. The '96 vintage showed a big advance in terms of finesse and breed, and this improvement has been maintained.

Château Desmirail

3e Cru Classé. Owner: Denis Lurton. 28ha. 5,000 cases. CS 70%, Mer 25%, CF 5%. Second label: Château Fontarney.

This famous old growth was resurrected by Lucien Lurton, vineyard owner extraordinary of Margaux (*see* Brane-Cantenac, Durfort-Vivens, etc). In 1992, Lucien handed over this *cru* to his son, Denis.

The wines are perfumed, soft, and elegant in spite of the high proportion of Cabernet Sauvignon. Some outstanding wines were produced from '83 onwards. This is a *cru* with an increasing reputation.

Château Deyrem-Valentin

Cru Bourgeois. Owner: Jean Sorge. 13ha. 7,000 cases. CS 51%, Mer 45%, PV 2%, Mal 2%.

This small property is situated in the best part of Soussans, and neighbours include Lascombes, Malescot, and the two Labégorces. It has belonged to the present family since 1928; Jean Sorge is very much a working resident proprietor. The '96 had fine, scented fruit, was rich and solid but a bit coarse.

Château Durfort-Vivens ★ V →

2e Cru Classé. Owner: Gonzague Lurton. 30ha. 5,000 cases. CS 70%, CF 15%, Mer 15%. Second label: Second de Durfort.

The names come from the Comtes Durfort de Duras, who were the proprietors from the 15th century until the Revolution of 1789; Vivens was added in 1824. As is often the way in Bordeaux, the Vivens and the Durfort families were actually related. From 1937 until 1961 it was under the same ownership as Château Margaux; it was then sold to its present owner. The contrast between Durfort and Brane-Cantenac is always an interesting one. Durfort is always firmer and more tannic but usually has less finesse and charm. In recent vintages, however, the wines have had more richness and fruit to match their tannin. Gonzague took over from his father in 1992, and the wines now show more elegance and finesse than in the '80s. '94, '95, '96, '97, '98, '99, and 2000 are all excellent examples of these vintages.

Château Ferrière ★ V →

3e Cru Classé. Owner: Claire Villars. 8ha. 4,000 cases. CS 75%, Mer 20%, PV 5%. Second label: Les Remparts de Ferrière.

This small growth was farmed by Château Lascombes from 1960. In 1992, the Villars family (*see* Chasse-Spleen, Haut-Bages-Libéral and La Gurgue) bought the vineyard and has already brought its experience to bear. The family's first vintage (of that year) suggested that wines worthy of the property's status would once more be made here, as has proved to be the case.

Château Giscours ★ →

3e Cru Classé. Owner: GFA du Château Giscours. Administrator: Eric Albada-Jelgersma. 80ha. 20,000 cases of Grand Vin. CS 53%, Mer 42%, CF & PV 5%. Second label: La Sirène de Giscours.

After its acquisition by the Tari family in 1952, much time and money was invested in this property to restore it to its former glory. Now it is one of the largest and most important Margaux properties. In 1995, problems in the Tari family led to control passing to new Dutch owners.

The wines of Giscours are deeply coloured with a pronounced bouquet combining richness and fruit, while the wine itself is fruity, vigorous and full-bodied. If not as stylish as the wines of Cantenac and Margaux, the wine clearly has breed. In the 1980s, the wines became more powerful, obscuring the finesse of previous years, but from 1996 the new owner has produced notable improvements, culminating in the excellent 2000.

Château La Gurgue V

Cru Bourgeois Supérieur. Owner: SC du Château La Gurgue.
Administrator: Claire Villars. 10ha. 5,000 cases. CS 70%, Mer 30%.

A well-placed vineyard, together with Desmirail it is the closest neighbour to Château Margaux on its western boundary. There was a change of ownership in 1978, and the new investment, together with the undoubted flair of Bernadette Villars (*see* Chasse-Spleen and Haut-Bages-Libéral), resulted in a marked improvement in the wines. Fine wines were produced throughout the '80s. Since her mother's tragic death, Claire Villars has proved herself equally talented. This is a delicate, perfumed type of Margaux, with style and breed, nice fruit, not a lot of body but plenty of flavour and refinement. Certainly a wine to follow.

Château d'Issan ★ →

3e Cru Classé. Owner: Mme Emmanuel Cruse. 30ha. 12,500 cases. CS 70%, Mer 30%. Second label: Blason d'Issan.

Regum mensis arisque deorum ("for the tables of kings and the high altars of the gods") says the inscription over the gateway at d'Issan. This is one of the oldest properties and the most splendid château in the whole Médoc, with a beautiful early 17th-century château sitting within the moat of its medieval predecessor.

After a long period of neglect, d'Issan was bought by the Cruse family in 1945 and both château and vineyard have been painstakingly restored to their former glory. Formerly this was a Cruse (négociant) exclusivity; now it is sold on the market, and there have been steady improvements in the wine in recent years. This is a wine of great individuality, combining a power and richness rare in Cantenac with great breed and a lovely perfume. There was some inconsistency in the '80s, then in '94, Emmanuel Cruse, grandson of the owner, took over and a clear improvement has been apparent.

Château Kirwan ★ →

3e Cru Classé. Owner: Family Schÿler. Administrator: Jean-Henri Schÿler. 35ha. 17,800 cases. CS 40%, Mer 30%, CF 20%, PV 10%. Second label: Les Charmes de Kirwan.

Château Kirwan is named after an Irishman from Galway who lost his head in the French Revolution. It now belongs to the Bordeaux firm of Schröder & Schÿler, which bottled the wines in its Bordeaux cellars until 1966, '67 being the first vintage to be château-bottled.

A great deal of work and investment has gone into improving the quality of Kirwan. New wood was used in the barrel-ageing for the first time in '78. Recent vintages are deeply coloured, powerful, concentrated wines which are beginning to attract favourable comments. The '89 and '90 marked a real step up, with more fruit and succulence. The second wine was first produced in '93 as part of the new consultant Michel Rolland's programme for improving quality. From '95 onwards, much better wines have been made, with the quality of the tannins markedly finer.

Château Labégorce ★ →

Cru Bourgeois Supérieur. Owner: Hubert Perrodo. 34ha. 17,000 cases.
CS 60%, Mer 34%, CF 5%, PV 1%.

This is certainly one of the best unclassified wines of Margaux, together with its close neighbour, Labégorce Zédé. The vineyards are well placed in Margaux and Soussans and the château has nothing bourgeois about it. The wines have Margaux finesse combined with richness. The property changed hands in 1989, when it was sold to an oil tycoon who is also a wine-lover. He has already made a marked improvement.

Château Labégorce Zédé ★

Cru Bourgeois Exceptionnel. Owner: Luc Thienpont. Administrator: Luc Thienpont.
27ha. 17,000 cases. CS 50%, Mer 35%, CF 10%, PV 5%.
Second Label: Château de l'Amiral.

For some years, the wines of Labégorce Zédé took second place to those of its neighbour, Labégorce. Luc Thienpont took over in 1979, standards have improved, and fine wines are now being made. The emphasis is on finesse and breeding: the wine begins with a superbly perfumed bouquet, but initially, it can be quite tannic. This is one of the best unclassified wines of the appellation.

Château Lascombes ★

2e Cru Classé. Owner: Colony. Administrator: Dominique Befve
83ha. 41,500 cases. CS 55%, Mer 40%, PV 5%.
Second label: Château Segonnes. Second wine: Chevalier de Lascombes.

Lascombes was a small property until its purchase in 1951 by Alexis Lichine and an American syndicate, which subsequently sold to the giant UK brewery group Bass-Charrington in 1971. Since 1951, its vineyards and production have been greatly increased. In March 2001 it was bought by the US Pension Fund Group, Colony, with Dr. Alain Reynaud and Michel Rolland acting as consultants.

The basic problem at Lascombes has been that the vineyard area was enlarged with scant regard to quality. Under René Vannetelle's stewardship this fact was recognized. Only 50 hectares are capable of producing wines of *cru classé* quality: the rest is now sold under the Segonnes label and for making rosé. The result was a marked improvement in the second half of the 1980s. Then, a second wine was introduced in '97 to improve the selection for the *grand vin*. 2002 showed that the new team are further improving quality.

Château Malescot-St-Exupéry ★ V →

3e Cru Classé. Owner: Roger Zuger. Administrator: Jean-Luc Zuger
23.5ha. 14,000 cases. CS 50%, Mer 35%, CF 10%, PV 5%.
Second labels: Château Loyac, La Dame de Malescot.

Since acquiring the property in 1955 from the English firm of WH Chaplin, the Zuger family has done much to rebuild this *cru* which had greatly declined in size and standing. The charming château, now restored and lived in again, stands in the centre of the village of Margaux, while the vineyards are in Margaux (adjoining Château Margaux) and Soussans.

In spite of a fine bouquet, I used to find the wines rather edgy with a certain harshness; there was a marked improvement in the 1980s, however, especially from '83 onwards. The '86, '88, '89, '90, '95, '96, '97, '98, '99, and 2000 have a degree of finesse allied to concentration that was lacking before. Since Jean-Luc Zuger took over from his father in the '90s, there have been many innovations and improvements. Since the '98 vintage, wines have been kept on their lees with only two rackings. The results so far are impressive.

Château Margaux ★ ★ ★ V

1er Cru Classé. Owner: SC du Château Margaux (Corinne Mentzelopoulos).
Administrator: Paul Pontallier. 93ha. Red (81ha): 33,000 cases. CS 75%,
Mer 20%, PV and CF 5%. White (12ha): 3,300 cases. Sauv 100%.
Second label: Pavillon Rouge du Château Margaux.

This château has had its ups and downs, but new heights of quality and consistency have been achieved since the Mentzelopoulos family acquired the property in 1977. A new underground cellar has been built, the château and gardens restored to their former glory, and much work has been done to improve the vineyard.

At its best, Château Margaux is one of the most sumptuous and sensual of Médoc wines, with all the perfume and finesse of a fine Margaux as found in its neighbours, but allied to more body, remarkable character, and individuality. After some great vintages in '45, '47, '49, '50, and '53, its wines became less outstanding and less consistent, although the '66 stands out in this lean period. Then, from '78–'90, Château Margaux consistently produced wines that were among the finest examples of their respective vintages. The '93 and '94 are fine wines in the context of the difficult vintages, and magnificent wines were made in '95, '96, '98, '99, and 2000. The '97 is a fine example of the year. A second wine, Pavillon Rouge du Château Margaux, is made as a result of the stricter selection now practised. The first vintage was '79. The wines are lighter than the *grand vin*, but have breed and charm and are ready to drink much earlier.

Pavillon Blanc du Château Margaux, an excellent white wine made from low-yielding Sauvignon vines in Soussans, has real distinction. Its bouquet and breed are remarkable – but so, unfortunately, is the price!

Château Marquis-d'Alesme-Becker

3e Cru Classé. Owner: Jean-Claude Zuger. 15.5ha. 9,600 cases.
CS 30%, Mer 45%, CF 15%, PV 10%. Second label: Marquise d'Alesme.

This small and little-known *cru classé* was owned by the English firm of W. H. Chaplin and run partly with Malescot. The present proprietor is the brother of Roger Zuger at Malescot, and the château is the original building of Château Desmirail. The vineyards are in Soussans and Margaux. With its small production and history of obscurity, unfortunately it remains a wine that is hard to find. I have found it possessed of elegant, stylish fruit with a firm backbone. It needs time to develop.

Château Marquis-de-Terme ★ →

4e Cru Classé. Owner: Sénéclauze family. 38ha. 16,000 cases.
CS 55%, Mer 35%, CF 3%, PV 7%. Second label: Terme des Goudats.

A good proportion of this wine is sold direct on the French market, with the result that it is not as widely known on export markets as its size might suggest.

Much work has recently been done to make good deficiencies in the *chai,* now modernized and well equipped. The vineyard is well kept, but yields are high.

I have found this wine to have charm and a certain easy appeal, without being among the best of Margaux in terms of finesse or originality. Since the 1980s, there has been a clear advance in quality.

Château Marsac-Séguineau

Cru Bourgeois. Owner: SC du Château Marsac-Séguineau. Administrator: Jean-Pierre Angliviel de la Beaudelle. 10ha. 4,000 cases. Mer 60%, CS 28%, CF 12%. Second label: Château Gravières-de-Marsac.

This is a full-flavoured, supple wine which nevertheless lasts well. The vineyard is in Soussans. The wines are exclusively distributed by the négociant Mestrezat, which is also in effect the owner, and which has done much to reorganize the vineyards. There was a return to hand-picking in '92.

Château Martinens

Cru Bourgeois. Owners: Simone Dulos and Jean-Pierre Seynat-Dulos. 30ha. 11,700 cases. Mer 40%, CS 30%, CF 20%, PV 10%. Second label: Château Guiney, Château Bois du Monteil and Le Cadet de Martinens.

The pleasing château at Martinens was built in 1767 by three sisters from London: Ann, Jane, and Mary White. But they sold after only nine years. The present owners have run the property since 1945. It lies in Cantenac and enjoys a reputation for stylish, attractive wines.

Château Monbrison ★ V

Cru Bourgeois Supérieur. Owner: Van der Heyden family. 20.6ha. 11,000 cases. CS 50%, Mer 30%, CF 15%, PV 5%. Second label: Château Cordat.

The property was bought in 1921 by Robert Meacham-Davis, an American commissioner in the Red Cross; the present proprietors are his grandchildren. Jean-Luc Van der Heyden made this one of the most sought-after *crus bourgeois* of the 1980s, and especially from '85 onwards, the price and quality challenged some of the lesser *crus classés* of Margaux. Tragically, Jean-Luc died in 1992 and now his brother, Laurent, is determined to maintain the legacy left to him.

I have found the wine most attractive, well-structured with plenty of fruit and balancing tannin.

Château Palmer ★★

3e Cru Classé. Owner: SC du Château Palmer. Administrator: B Bouteiller. 52ha. 12,000 cases. CS 47%, Mer 47%, PV 6%. Second label: Alto Ego.

Named after a British general who fought under Wellington, Palmer is now owned by French, Dutch, and British proprietors (Bouteiller, Mähler-Besse, and Sichel). It lies in the hamlet of Issan, and most of its vineyards were once part of Château d'Issan's domaine. The charming château, with its four towers, was built in the years 1857–60, when it was owned by the Péreire family. The reputation of Palmer has soared in the past 40 years. This was one of the first of the "Super Seconds", a reputation which effectively dates from the superlative '61. Philippe Delfon took over as *régisseur* in the mid-'90s from the Chardon family who had worked at Palmer for three generations and had become an institution here.

The wine is characterized by an opulence and richness that are almost Burgundian in the best years, yet this is combined with real finesse and breeding. They are famed for their consistency. The '82, decried at the time, now looks more stylish than the rather one-dimensional '83. In 1995, wooden vats were replaced by stainless steel. The '98 marked an important development with the introduction of a new second wine, Alto Ego, and much stricter selection. Previously, 90 per cent of the production often went into the *grand vin,* and the old second wine, Réserve du Général, was produced intermittently. Alto Ego represents approximately 35 per cent of the crop.

Château Paveil-de-Luze V

Cru Bourgeois Supérieur. Owner: GFA du Château Paveil. Administrator: Baron Geoffroy de Luze. 32ha. 17,000 cases. CS 65%, CF 5%, Mer 30%.
Second labels: Château de la Coste, Enclos du Banneret.
A fine vineyard on deep, well-drained gravel in Soussans with a charming *chartreuse*-style château, Paveil has belonged to the de Luze family for over a century. Now it has parted from the firm that bears its name and the wine is château-bottled and has improved. At its best, this is a wine of some style and distinction: lots of charm and breed rather than body.

Château Pontac-Lynch

Cru Bourgeois. Owner: GFA du Château Pontac-Lynch. Administrator: Marie-Christine Bondon. 10ha. 6,000 cases. CS 30%, CF 20%, Mer 45%, PV 5%. Second label: Château Pontac-Phenix.
A little-known *cru* bearing two famous names, Pontac-Lynch apparently sold for higher prices in the mid-18th century than its famous neighbours. The wines have been winning medals recently, and should be worth looking out for.

Château Pouget

4e Cru Classé. Owner: GFA des Châteaux Boyd-Cantenac et Pouget.
Administrator: Pierre Guillemet. 10ha. 4,400 cases. CS 66%, Mer 30%, CF 4%.
Under the same ownership as Château Boyd-Cantenac. Until the '82 vintage, both wines were made here and Pouget was treated as the second wine of Boyd-Cantenac; since '83, however, the wines have had quite separate facilities. Since the 1980s, the wines have become more tannic, but coarser in style, and seem to have been rather sidelined among all the improvements in the appellation during the '90s.

Château Prieuré-Lichine ★ V →

4e Cru Classé. Owner: Ballande family. Administrator: Patrick Bongard. 70ha. 38,000 cases. CS 56%, Mer 34%, PV 10%. Second label: Le Cloître du Château Prieuré-Lichine.
The property has been restored and the vineyard enlarged and reconstructed since it was bought by Alexis Lichine in 1952. This charming château in Cantenac, formerly the priory, was Alexis Lichine's European home until his death in 1989. His son, Sacha, then ran the property until he sold it in 1999. The Ballande family brought in Michel Rolland and Stéphane Derencourt to oversee the improvements in the vineyards and vinification. The quality and reputation of this *cru* have deservedly grown in recent years. The wines are full-bodied and rich, and a consistent standard is maintained and is now being improved upon.

Château Rauzan-Ségla ★★ →

2e Cru Classé. Owner: Chanel. Administrator: John Kolasa.
51ha. 23,000 cases. CS 61%, Mer 35%, CF 2%, PV 2%. Second label: Ségla.
This is one of the oldest and most famous *crus* in Margaux, but unfortunately, its wines for some years failed to match their high classification. Having belonged to the Cruse family for several generations, the property was bought by the Liverpool firm of John Holt (now part of Lonrho) in 1960, and managed by négociant Louis Eschenauer.

In 1989, Eschenauer and the château were sold to Brent Walker, who in 1994 resold to Chanel. David Orr, until recently director at Château Latour, was brought in to manage Rauzan on Chanel's behalf. Extensive improvements have been made in both château and *chais*. The new owner has also reverted to the original spelling of Rauzan with a "z".

In theory, this is a long-lasting wine which develops great finesse; in practice, too many vintages in the past were austere and charmless. The '82 vintage marked the beginning of a substantial improvement, with the '85 even better. The '86, '88, '89, and '90 vintages have proved to be outstanding, challenging Palmer's reputation as the best wines in the appellation after Margaux. The new management has made further improvements that have helped to make '94, '95, '96 , '98 , '99, and 2000 all outstanding examples of those vintages.

Château Rauzan-Gassies V →

2e Cru Classé. Owner: J-M Quié. 28ha. 13,300 cases. CS 65%, Mer 25%, CF 10%. Second label: Enclos de Moncabon.

Until the French Revolution of 1789, this was part of the same property as Rauzan-Ségla. There is no château. Since 1943, it has belonged to the Quié family, and in the past some great wines were made. In recent years, however, the wines have been consistent but not top flight. The style of the wine is more powerful and richer than many Margaux, more in the character of Cantenac, with delicacy and charm developing in bottle. In 1994 Jean-Louis Camp, formerly of Château Loudenne, was brought in here, and at Croizet-Bages and Bel-Orme. He has a clear idea of what needs to be done, and the '96 showed a marked improvement, while '98 is the finest wine for many years, with 2000 at least as good.

Château Siran →

Cru Bourgeois Exceptionnel. Owner: William-Alain B Miailhe. Administrator: Brigitte Miailhe. 24ha. 14,000 cases. CS 50%, Mer 30%, PV 12%, CF 8%. Second labels: Châteaux Bellegarde, St-Jacques.

This is something of a showplace for a *cru bourgeois*, but then the proprietor Alain Miailhe is convinced that it should be a *cru classé* and is eloquent on this topic. There is a heliport here, an anti-nuclear shelter well stocked with the best vintages, and a park famous for the property's cyclamen.

The wines have a charming bouquet and have become noticeably richer and fuller in flavour since around 1970. There is some point of comparison with nearby Giscours. Michel Rolland has advised since 1995, and it shows.

Château Tayac

Cru Bourgeois. Owner: André Flavin. 37ha. 22,000 cases. CS 65%, Mer 30%, PV 3%, CF 2%.

Lying in Soussans, this is the largest Margaux *cru bourgeois*. Its good reputation is the work of André and Nadine Flavin, who inherited the property in 1960, and of Guy Portet, who succeeded them in '99. Wines are perfumed and robust, with something agreeably rustic in their make-up.

Château du Tertre V →

5e Cru Classé. Owner: Eric Albada-Jelgersma. 50ha. 15,000 cases of Grand Vin. CS 40%, CF 20%, Mer 35%, CF & PV 25%. Second label: Les Hauts du Tertre.

The word *tertre* means a knoll, a piece of high ground, and Château du Tertre is a splendidly situated vineyard on the highest ground in the Margaux appellation. The soil is classically pebbly. After taking over the property in 1961, Philippe Gasqueton (of Château Calon-Ségur) steadily restored the vineyard. In 1998, the owner of neighbouring Giscours bought the property.

I believe that this is one of the most underrated of the *crus classés*. The wines have beautifully vivid fruit and considerable finesse, breeding and charm. While good wines were made before, quality has moved up a gear since '98.

Château La Tour-de-Bessan

Cru Bourgeois. Owner: Marie-Laure Lurton-Roux. 17ha. 8,300 cases.
CS 80%, Mer 20%.

The *tour* is a ruined 15th century watchtower built during the last years of English rule. The Soussans vineyard, the humblest part of the Lurton's Margaux empire, produces light, supple wines of breed and charm: Lurton Margaux at a more modest price.

Château La Tour-de-Mons

Cru Bourgeois Supérieur. Owner: Credit Agricole and others.
Administrator: Henri Corbel. 40ha. 25,000 cases. CS 38%, Mer 48%, CF 6%, PV 8%.
Second label: Château Rucheterre.

An old property in Soussans with a long-standing reputation, and yet another to pass from family to institutional ownership. Since the change in '95, important improvements in vineyard practice together with a new *cuvière* and air-conditioned storage promise a rise in standards. The excellent '98 bodes well for the future.

MOULIS

This is the smallest of the six communal appellations, but there are more outstanding *crus bourgeois* here than in Listrac. The area under vine has increased in the last 20 years, but it is still under 600 hectares. The vineyards lie northwest of Margaux and directly west of Arcins. The wines are powerful and rich, the best having fruit and finesse as well; they are long-keeping and very attractive.

Château Anthonic

Cru Bourgeois Supérieur. Owner: Jean-Baptiste Cordonnier. 23ha. 13,000 cases.
CS 48%, Mer 48%, CF 2%, PV 2%.

This *cru* has carried its present name only since 1922. The château is on the outskirts of the village of Moulis, and the vineyards are some of the oldest in the commune.After some reconstruction of the vineyards, with an increase in the Merlot at the expense of the Cabernet Sauvignon, the wines are riper and finer. The '90 and '96 are fine examples of what this *cru* can produce.

Château Bel-Air-Lagrave

Cru Bourgeois. Owner: Jeanne Bacquey. 9ha. 4,500 cases. CS 60%, Mer 35%, PV 5%.

This vineyard is on the gravelly ridges of Grand Poujeaux, certainly the best sector of the Moulis vineyards. It has been in the same family for 150 years. The owners believe in hard-pruning and low yields to produce the best quality. The wines are clearly carefully made. Their charm and fruit is emphasized, and they are softer and more refined than many from this appellation, with individuality and a definite finesse and balance that firmly removes them from any suggestion of the rustic. Definitely some wines to watch.

Château Biston-Brillette

Cru Bourgeois Supérieur. Owner: Michel Barbarin. 22ha. 13,000 cases.
CS 55%, Mer 40%, PV 3%, Mal 2%.

An old-fashioned and rather rustic label hardly does justice to the excellent wine now being made here. Typically Moulis with its dense texture, there is also a hint of complexity about its spicy, concentrated fruit, which lifts it from the general run of wines from this appellation. The emphasis on fruit and balance makes this a wine that can be enjoyed young, but its keeping qualities remain uncompromised.

Château Bouqueyran V →
Leased by Philippe Porcheron. 13ha. 3,300 cases. CS 41%,
Mer 57%, PV 2%. Second label: Les Tourelles de Bouqueyran.

With the arrival of a new proprietor, impressively rich, dense-textured wines are now being made here, beginning with '95. Sixty per cent new oak is used. In 2000, a *cuvée* of 600 cases was made by the team from Valandraud called La Fleur de Bouqueyran. Watch this space!

Château Branas-Grand-Poujeaux
Owner: Jacques de Pourquéry. 6ha. 3,300 cases. CS 50%, Mer 45%, PV 5%.
Second label: Clos des Demoiselles.

A small property with a well-placed vineyard and a most enthusiastic owner determined to make fine wines. In a blind tasting of '81 Moulis wines held in 1984, I placed this wine on the same level as some *crus bourgeois exceptionnels*. At this stage the wine had charm, a fine middle flavour and richness, with real style and breed. All the wine is aged in casks, of which one-third are new each year. A wine to watch – if you can find it!

Château Brillette V
Cru Bourgeois Supérieur. Owner: Jean-Louis Flageul. Administrator: Jean-Louis Flageul. 34ha. 20,000 cases. CS 40%, Mer 48%, PV 3%, CF 9%.

When Raymond Berthault bought this property in 1976, it had declined badly and there was much work to be done. At the time, he was the owner of Viniprix and Euromarché, and Brillette was to be a hobby. One-third new wood is used each year. Now his son-in-law continues along the lines already laid down. This was always a good solid Moulis; now it it has some flair. Look out for 2001.

Château Chasse-Spleen ★ V
Cru Bourgeois Exceptionnel. Owner: SC du Château Chasse-Spleen.
Administrator: Claire Villars-Lurton. 80ha. 41,000 cases. CS 73%, Mer 20%, PV 7%.
Second labels: L'Ermitage de Chasse-Spleen, l'Oratoire de Chasse-Spleen.

Chasse-Spleen has long been recognized as not only the leading *cru* of Moulis, but as deserving of *cru classé* status. Its present owners include a bank, but the most important partner is the Société Bernard Taillan, whose director is the dynamic Jacques Merlaut. Claire Villars succeeded her gifted and much-lamented mother, and shows a sure touch. With her marriage now to Gonzague Lurton of Durfort-Vivens, two remarkable Médoc dynasties have been united. The curious name "Chasse-Spleen" is attributed to a quip of Lord Byron's to the effect that the wine chased away "spleen" (ill-humour or melancholy).

I have felt that there was a shade too much new oak here, which tended to make the wines seem lean, but this has now been reduced to 40 per cent, and there is more Cabernet Sauvignon. As a result, the wines have more fruit while remaining more classically Médoc than Poujeaux. The '93, '94, '95, '96, '97, '98, '99, and 2000 are good examples of their vintages. This wine does not take as long to mature as you might think – it keeps well and seldom disappoints.

Château La Closerie-Grand-Poujeaux
Owner: GFA Le Grand Poujeaux. Administrator: Jean-Paul Bacquey. 8ha. 4,000 cases. CS 60%, Mer 35%, PV 5%.

This small vineyard was the creation of a former *régisseur* of Chasse-Spleen. Everything is done in a traditional way; long-lived, solid wines are the result, with the emphasis on body and richness, rather in the same style as Dutruch.

Château Duplessis (Hauchecorne)
Cru Bourgeois. Owner: SC des Grands Crus Réunis. Administrator: Marie-Laure Lurton. 18ha. 8,900 cases. Mer 61%, CS 25%, CF 12%, PV 2%.

The wine of this château has for some time been labelled simply as Duplessis. It is now proposed that the word *Hauchecorne* be added to the label in smaller letters to avoid confusion with the nearby Duplessis-Fabre. The wines here are rich and supple and are made for reasonably early drinking. Since Lucien Lurton took over management in 1983, there have been some impressive wines with a more marked character. In 1992, Lucien handed over to his daughter Marie-Laure Lurton.

Château Dutruch-Grand-Poujeaux V

Cru Bourgeois Supérieur. Owner: François Cordonnier. 26ha. 14,000 cases. CS 45%, Mer 50%, PV 5%.

The wines of Dutruch have long enjoyed a deserved reputation for quality and consistency. The present owner, a relative of previous owner M. Lambert, took over in 1967. I noted then that the wines here were characterized by their body and richness, and this is still the case today. These wines repay keeping.

Château Gressier-Grand-Poujeaux

Cru Bourgeois Supérieur. Owner: Héritiers de St-Affrique. Administrator: Bertrand de Marcellus. 22ha. 12,000 cases. CS 50%, Mer 30%, PV 10%, CF 10%.

This fine old property has been in the hands of the same family since 1724, and the family arms of the St-Affriques give the label a distinctive look. Improvements and modernizations have been made in recent years, and new oak is now used in the maturation process. The wines have always had more fruit and finesse than those of many neighbouring properties, and have maintained a consistent standard over many years.

Château Malmaison Baronne Nadine de Rothschild

Owner: Baronne Nadine de Rothschild. Administrator: Eric Fabre. 24ha. 11,000 cases. Mer 80%, CS 20%.

The vineyard, contiguous with Château Clarke in Listrac, was purchased by Baron Edmond de Rothschild in 1973. The vineyard at this time had been more or less abandoned, with less than a hectare of vines remaining. The vineyard was reconstituted between 1974 and 1978.

The high level of Merlot makes for a more generous, fruity wine than Clarke, and now that Eric Fabre has arrived from Château La Cardonne, where he did such good work, and Michel Rolland has cast his eye over the property, things can only get better.

Château Maucaillou V

Cru Bourgeois Supérieur. Owner: Dourthe family. 68ha. 44,000 cases. CS 55%, Mer 36%, CF 2%, PV 7%. Second labels: Cap de Haut (Cru Bourgeois), Franc-Caillou.

Maucaillou is the pride of the Dourthe family. It no longer controls the négociant firm which bears its name, but it has kept this château, where the business started. Three-quarters of the vintage is aged in new oak (unusual for a non-classified growth), and there is a modern stainless-steel installation for the fermentation.

In a blind tasting of '79 Moulis wines held in 1984, I placed Maucaillou first. The '82, '83, '85, '88, '89, '90, '94, '95, '96, '98, '99, and 2000 are also successful vintages. The wines combine the power of Moulis with a beautiful flavour, real breed, and charm. This *cru* often competes well with the *crus classés* in blind tastings.

Château Mauvesin

Owners: Vicomte et Vicomtesse de Baritault de Carpia. Managers: SCA Viticoles de France. 60ha. 36,000 cases. CS 45%, Mer 40%, CF 10%, PV 5%. (7ha under AC Haut-Médoc producing 3,780 cases.)

Lying in the south of the appellation, this is the largest property in Moulis. Records show that it belonged to the de Foix family – who also owned Château d'Issan – until 1647, when it was bought by Pierre Le Blanc, *conseiller du roi* at the Parlement de Bordeaux. The Le Blanc family built the large Victorian château that stands on the property today. The wines of Mauvesin are light, soft, and quite elegant, their easy fruit encouraging early drinking.

Château Moulin à Vent V

Cru Bourgeois Supérieur. Owner: Dominique Hessel. 25ha. 12,000 cases. CS 60%, Mer 35%, PV 5%. Second label: Moulin-de-St-Vincent. 5,000 cases.

Moulin à Vent – "windmill" – may seem an odd name for a Bordeaux château, but in the Middle Ages, mixed agriculture was the norm in the Médoc, and many ruined mills can still be found. Since buying the property in 1977, Dominique Hessel has made a number of improvements, including the enlargement of the vineyard, and matures the wine in casks instead of vats.

The wines have a fine flavour and are rich and vigorous, developing a complex bouquet with bottle-age. This property now deserves to be numbered with the leading *crus* of Moulis. Moulin-de-St-Vincent, the second label, used to be an exclusivity of Ginestet. Under the present management a deliciously fruity, early maturing wine is being produced.

Château Moulis

Owner: Alain Darricarrère. 17ha. 11,000 cases. CS 58%, Mer 40%, CF 2%.

In the last century, this was a vast estate with around 100 hectares. Now, it is a modest one with vineyards grouped around the château just outside the village of Moulis. There is a modern stainless-steel installation for vinification, and the wines are matured in wood. All the wine is château-bottled.

Château Poujeaux ★ V

Cru Bourgeois Exceptionnel. Owners: François and Philippe Theil. 53ha. 30,000 cases. CS 50%, Mer 40%, CF 5%, PV 5%.

Second label: Château La Salle-de-Poujeaux.

Though Moulis is the name of the appellation, the commune of Poujeaux is where most of the best *crus* are, and there is none better than Château Poujeaux itself. The wines are deeply coloured with an arresting bouquet – sometimes there are overtones of tobacco and a flavour that is stylish and fine, although tannic and powerful. This is a long-lived wine that deserves long maturing in the best vintages (one-third is put in new oak) and is certainly always one of the best wines in the appellation.

In comparison with its rival, Chasse-Spleen, Poujeaux tends to be more fleshy and fruity, but is equally deserving of *cru classé* status. The 1980s were an impressive period. Then, in the difficult vintages of the early 1990s, the skills of the winemaking here really came to the fore, producing a highly recommendable '92 and fine examples in '93 and '94; '95, '96, '97,'98, '99, and 2000 were all excellent examples of their vintages.

Château Ruat

Owner: Pierre Goffre-Viaud. 16ha. 8,500 cases. Mer 50%, CS 35%, CF 15%. Second label: Château Jean Viaud.

Petit Poujeaux is a hamlet just outside Moulis and well away from Grand Poujeaux. Ruat was the name of a pre-Revolution property, whose ownership was dispersed during the Revolution but patiently pieced together again after the present proprietor's great-grandfather bought it in 1871. Recently, Petit-

Poujeaux has been dropped from the name. The wines have charm, fruit, and typical Moulis richness and solidity, with a tendency to evolve more quickly than many wines of this appellation. This is good, middle-of-the-road wine.

LISTRAC

Listrac and its neighbour, Moulis, differ in important respects from the other four communal appellations. They contain no *crus classés*, and do not border the river where the best *crus* are, but are on a plateau inland. Yet both produce excellent wines whose characteristics are increasingly appreciated.

The area under vine here increased by 45 per cent between 1972 and 1986, but has been static since. The wines were often considered to be tough and astringent, but in recent vintages I have been impressed by the number of châteaux producing powerful, fruity wines.

Château Cap Léon Veyrin

Cru Bourgeois Supérieur. Owner: Alain Meyre. 23.6ha. 14,000 cases.
Mer 62%, CS 35%, PV 3%.

This is an amalgamation dating from 1908 of two vineyards. The wines are matured in cask, including 25 per cent new oak. They are powerful, long-lived, and repay keeping, yet can also be enjoyed young. Also, as the notices on the Bordeaux–Lesparre road point out, the property offers farm holidays, so that visitors can actually stay on the domaine and enjoy traditional Médocain hospitality.

Château Clarke

Cru Bourgeois Supérieur. Owner: Baron Benjamin de Rothschild. Red: 51ha. 22,000 cases. CS 40%, Mer 60%. Second label: Les Granges des Domaines de Rothschild. White: 2ha. 900 cases. Le Merle de Clarke Sauv 50%, Sém 30%, Musc 20%.

Baron Edmond de Rothschild developed this large vineyard virtually from scratch between 1973 and 1978, making it one of the showplaces of the Médoc. Prior to the '82 vintage, I found the wines rather lean, austere, and marked by new wood. The '82 indicated an improvement, but then rather reverted to type; since then the wines seemed to be ageing rather quickly; the '96 marks a big step forward and is the best yet. Now Michel Rolland is involved, and Eric Fabre, formerly at Château La Cardonne in the Médoc, is now the manager, so further improvements can be hoped for. A small quantity of white wine began to be produced from '93. An attractive rosé is also made here. There are good facilities for receiving visitors between June and September.

Château Ducluzeau

Cru Bourgeois. Owner: Mme Jean-Eugène Borie. Administrator: François Xavier Borie. 4.9ha. 2,600 cases. Mer 90%, CS 10%.

In 1850, Charles Cocks listed this château as the second *cru* of Listrac. Since then, it has decreased in size and importance, but nevertheless produces some fine wines uncharacteristic of the region in that they come from vineyards planted with 90 per cent Merlot. They are matured in cask for six months and château-bottled. Ideal luncheon wines, perfumed, with plenty of fruit.

Château Fonréaud

Cru Bourgeois Supérieur. Owner: Chanfreau Family. Administrator: Jean Chanfreau. 34ha. 18,000 cases. CS 55%, Mer 42%, PV 3%. Second label: La Tourelle de Château Fonréaud. Blanc Le Cygne, Blanc de Fonréaud, 1.8 ha. Sauv 60%, Sém 20%, Musc 20%.

The château is something of a landmark on the main Lesparre road south of Listrac. The wines are now aged in cask, with one-third being new. The wines tend to be elegant, attractive, fruity, and easy to drink when young, and are consistent. Very fruity, attractive white wines are now being made here. They mature well too; the '96 was still fresh and delicious in 2002.

Château Fourcas-Dupré V

Cru Bourgeois Supérieur. Owner: SC du Château Fourcas-Dupré. Administrator: Patrice Pagès. 44ha. 20,000 cases. CS 44%, Mer 44%, CF 10%, PV 2%.

Guy Pagès lived at and managed this château from 1967 until his untimely death in 1985. During this time, he established high standards and made many improvements. He was succeeded by his son, Patrice, who was already well-versed in the affairs of the property. There are both stainless-steel and concrete vats for fermentation, and casks from leading *crus classés* are used for ageing, and 33 per cent are now new.

The wines of Fourcas-Dupré are perfumed, quite tannic and powerful in the best years but supple and attractive in lesser ones. The 2000 may be their best wine so far. Comparison with the neighbouring Fourcas-Hosten is interesting, especially as Patrice Pagès has assisted in the running of the latter for some years. The Hosten wines have more depth and richness.

Château Fourcas-Hosten V

Cru Bourgeois Supérieur. Owner: SC du Château Fourcas-Hosten. Administrators: Bertrand de Rivoyre, Patrice Pagès, Peter M Sichel. 46.7ha. 26,000 cases. CS 45%, Mer 45%, CF 10%.

Until 1972, this château belonged to the St-Affriques of Gressier, and the wines were made and kept there. It now belongs to a French, Danish and American syndicate. The *chai* and *cuvier* have been reconstructed. Thirty-three per cent new wood is now used for ageing, and the vineyard has been gradually enlarged. The wines of Fourcas-Hosten have exceptional colour and are notable for their power and richness, with an assertive character but more fruit combined with tannin than the other *crus* of Listrac. This is a consistent wine. The '85 is exceptional; '86 concentrated; '89 and '90 outstanding; the '93 above-average for the year, and '94, '95, '96, '98, '99, and 2000 are fine wines.

Château Fourcas-Loubaney

Cru Bourgeois Supérieur. Owner: Altus Finances and Château Moulin de Laborde. 48ha. 16,500 cases. CS 60%, Mer 30%, PV 10%. Second labels: La Closerie Fourcas-Loubaney, Château La Bécade, Château La Fleur-Bécade, Château Moulin de Laborde.

Fourcas-Loubaney's production from low-yielding vines is now of a standard that is creating quite a reputation. Quality has increased recently, and up to 50 per cent new-oak casks are used for maturation. Recently acquired by a branch of Crédit Lyonnais, some delicious wines are now being made, with the 2000 the best yet.

Cave Coopérative Grand Listrac

Owner: Coopérative. 165ha. 94,000 cases. Mer 60%, CS 35%, PV 5%.

This co-op has long enjoyed an excellent reputation, especially in France, where Grand Listrac was for many years the best buy on the French Railways. Today, there are 70 members. Seven Listrac properties are sold under their château names, including Capdet and Vieux Moulin, as is one Moulis wine: Guitignan.

Château Lafon

Owner: Jean-Pierre Théron. 14.8ha. 9,500 cases. CS 55%, Mer 45%. Other label: Château les Hauts-Marcieux.

When he bought the estate in the late 1960s, M Thérou found no more than a dilapidated ruin. Everything had to be restored and the vineyard reconstructed and enlarged. The quality here has evolved, with 75 per cent being aged in cask and only 25 per cent in vat. These are pleasant, commercial wines.

Château La Lauzette-Declercq

Cru Bourgeois. Owner: Jean-Louis Declercq.15ha. 8,000 cases. CS 48%, Mer 46%, PV 4%, CF 2%. Second label: Les Galets de la Lauzette.

When the present Belgian owner bought this property in 1980, it was called Bellegrave, but following a dispute with a litigious neighbour, the present more distinctive name was adopted. I have found the wines well-balanced, with attractive fruit and ripe tannins, and rather stylish.

Château Lestage

Cru Bourgeois Supérieur. Owner: Héritiers Chanfreau. Administrator: Jean Chanfreau. 42ha. 22,000 cases. Mer 52%, CS 46%, PV 2%.

The château, under the same ownership and management as Fonréaud, is a large, ornate 19th-century mansion. One-third of the wine is aged in new oak, and is supple and early-maturing. It needs bottle-age in better years.

Château Liouner

Cru Bourgeois. Owners: Pierre, Lucette and Pascal Bosq. 26ha. CS 55%, Mer 45%, PV 5%. Second wine: Château Cantegric.

Commendable wines are now being made here. The '96 has enjoyable, juicy middle fruit and good structure for drinking in the medium term.

Château Mayne-Lalande

Cru Bourgeois. Owner: Bernard Lartigue. 18ha. 8,000 cases. Mer 45%, CS 45%, PV 5%, CF 5%.

One of the up-and-coming vineyards of Listrac. Fifty per cent new oak is now used. The '96 shows stylish, ripe fruit with elegance and medium depth.

Château Peyredon Lagravette

Cru Bourgeois. Owner: Paul Hostein. 6.8ha. 4000 cases. CS 65%, Mer 35%. Second label: Château Cazeau Vieil.

Deeds of the property dated 26 November 1546 still survive, and it has remained in the same family since that time. Yet there is nothing old-fashioned about the deliciously fruity, early drinking wines now made here.

Château Reverdi

Cru Bourgeois. Owner: Christian Thomas. 15ha. 9,000 cases. Mer 50%, CS 50%. Second label: Château Croix de Laborde.

The owner's father bought this property in 1953, and he succeeded him in 1981. Twenty-five per cent new oak is used, ten per cent in *cuves*. The result is polished tannins, attractive fruit, and a certain mellowness.

Château Rose-Ste-Croix

Cru Bourgeois. Owner: Philippe Porcheron. 12ha. 6,000 cases. CS 55%, Mer 44%, PV 1%. Second label: Pontet Salanon.

The picturesque name has an unusual story behind it. Jean Buroleau acquired a veneration for the symbol of the rose and the cross while serving with Napoleon's armies. He was rewarded by the grant of some land in the parish of Donnisan, where, of course, he grew vines and roses. So it was that when his great-great-grandson decided to sell his wines in bottle in 1926, he registered this name.

The present owners took over in 1987, and later bought Château Bouqueyran, in neighbouring Moulis. I found the '95 strong-flavoured, with plenty of fruit and rich tannins. In 2000, as at Bouqueyran, the Thunevins of Valandraud made a small *cuvée* from equal proportions of Cabernet Sauvignon and Merlot which was lighter in body than its Moulis cousin, but with very good fruit and stylish tannins demonstrating the differences between Listrac and Moulis.

Château Saransot-Dupré

Cru Bourgeois Supérieur. Owner: Yves Raymond.
Red: 14ha. 6,400 cases. Mer 57%, CS 24%, CF 15%, PV 3%.
White: 2.3ha, 1,000 cases. Sém 55%, Musc 10%, Sauv 35%.

Yves Raymond is the third generation of his family to own this *cru,* although the family has lived in Listrac for 300 years. Saransot-Dupré is a 225-hectare property that includes woods and pasture. A flock of sheep is kept to provide all the manure necessary for the vineyard. The '96 has charming fruit, on the light side for early drinking. A small quantity of white AC Bordeaux is also made.

ST-JULIEN

This commune has the highest proportion of *crus classés*. The area under vine increased by under 15 per cent between 1985–95, and has been stable since. The soils have more clay than Margaux, and there is quite a difference between the vineyards near the Gironde and those further inland, where more fleshy wines are made. These wines, of great character and originality, with more body and vivid fruit than those of Margaux, match the best Pauillacs for longevity.

Château Beychevelle ★

4e Cru Classé. Owner: Grands Millésimes de France. Administrator: Philippe Blanc.
90ha. 55,000 cases. CS 60%, Mer 28%, CF 8%, PV 4%. Second label: L'Amiral de Beychevelle. Other label: Les Brulières de Beychevelle (AC Haut-Médoc).

This is one of the most beautiful châteaux in the Médoc, and in the summer months it is set off by a superb bank of flowers at its roadside entrance. When it belonged to the Duc d'Épernon, who was an admiral of France at the end of the 16th century, ships passing by on the Gironde were required to lower their sails as a salute. Thus, *Beychevelle* is a corruption of *baisse voile,* meaning "lower sail". In 1984, the Achille Fould family, then the proprietors, sold part of this holding to the GMF, the French Civil Servants' Pension Fund. The GMF subsequently bought the remainder of the shares, later selling 40 per cent to Suntory (*see* Château Lagrange). All this has resulted in some much-needed investment.

At its best, Beychevelle is a glorious example of everything that makes the wines of St-Julien so attractive: a bouquet of great elegance and immediate impact, together with a ripe, fresh flavour that asks to be drunk from an early age, although the harmony of the wine also ensures good keeping. In spite of the improvements since '84, I still feel the full potential here is not being realized, due, I suspect, to high yields and not enough selection. A degree of dilution has been noticeable in some excellent years. The '90 is a good example. Les Brulières de Beychevelle comes from a vineyard in Cussac without the St-Julien appellation, and so is sold separately.

Château Branaire-Ducru ★ →

4e Cru Classé. Owner: SA du Château Branaire-Ducru. Administrator: Patrick Maroteaux. 50ha. 25,000 cases. CS 70%, Mer 22%, CF 5%, PV 3%.
Second label: Château Duluc.

The simple, classical façade of the château here faces Beychevelle but can easily be missed, as it stands well back from the road. It would be a pity to miss the wine, however. Most of the vineyards lie further inland than those of Beychevelle and Ducru-Beaucaillou, and the wines have less finesse but more body and are not without breeding. Jean-Michel Tapie ran the property, which his father bought in 1952, until he sold his 50 per cent holding to La Sucrière de Toury, a leading French sugar refinery, in 1988. Soon afterwards Patrick Maroteaux gained control when he bought some Tari shares for La Sucrière, and the new owners have been investing heavily, renewing the *cuvier* and *chai*.

The wines have a marked character that often comes through in blind tastings. The bouquet is noticeably powerful, with an almost Pauillac assertiveness and a distinct chocolate character in the fat years. The wine has a good deal of body and fruit and is extremely supple: it is often possible to enjoy a Branaire when other wines are still not ready. This is a consistent wine, and excellent examples were made in '85, '86, '88, '89, and '90, while '93, '94, '95, '96, '97, '98, '99, and 2000 are charming examples of the vintages. Certainly this is a wine to follow in terms of value for money. It is not yet an "investment" wine, but is one of exceptional attractiveness. Clear improvements in the wines are now discernible since the change in ownership.

Château La Bridane

Cru Bourgeois. Owner: Pierre Saintout. 15ha. 4,200 cases. CS 35%, CF 25%, Mer 38%, PV 2%.

La Bridane is one of the relatively new *crus bourgeois* in St-Julien, though it has long enjoyed a good reputation. Much of the wine is exported. The wines have attractive fruit and some depth of flavour. This is good, attractive St-Julien at an accessible price.

Château Ducru-Beaucaillou ★★ →

2e Cru Classé. Owner: Borie family. Administrator: Bruno Borie. 50ha. 19,000 cases. CS 65%, Mer 25%, CF 5%, PV 5%. Second label: Château La Croix V.

This château acquired its name and reputation in the first part of the 19th century, when it belonged to the Ducru family. *Beaucaillou* referred to the name of the vineyard itself. The distinctive château, with its massive Victorian towers and simple, classical façade between them, has been made familiar by the distinctive yellow-brown label.

The reputation of the *cru* today is the work of Jean-Eugène Borie, a resident proprietor who was one of the most widely respected winemakers in the Médoc. On Jean-Eugene Borie's death in '98, François-Xavier stepped into his shoes. A new *chai* was completed in '99. Following the reorganization of family interests in 2003, Bruno Borie took over from his brother.

Ducru-Beaucaillou was the first of the Médoc *crus classés* on the open market to break away from the pack and establish a higher price for itself than the other second growths, thus creating the "Super Seconds" (Palmer had achieved a higher price earlier, but was available only through the two négociant owners, Mähler-Besse and Sichel).

The wines here have long had elegance, lightness, and breed (Jean-Eugène Borie's first great vintage was '53). In recent years they have acquired a little more firmness and richness, especially in the best vintages; beauty of flavour and finesse are still the hallmarks, rather than the power one finds in Léoville-Las-Cases. The years '78, '81, '82, '83, '85, and '86 all produced classic wines, while '94, '95, '96, '98, '99, and 2000 are outstanding examples of those vintages.

Château du Glana V

Cru Bourgeois Supérieur. Owner: Gabriel Meffre.
43ha. 27,500 cases. CS 65%, Mer 30%, CF 5%. Second label: Château Sirène.

Château du Glana is not one of the Médoc's more romantic wines. Strictly speaking, it has no château, and the ugly little red-brick villa that appears on the label is now not part of the property. More obvious is the massive, functional *chai* sitting amidst the vineyards nearby, close to Gloria and Ducru-Beaucaillou. This and Gloria are the two largest *crus bourgeois* of St-Julien.

The reputation of du Glana has been rather mixed. I can speak only about recent vintages, and have found the wine well-made, with charm. Glana is commercial in the good sense: it provides just the sort of wine, with the character of the appellation, that the wine-lover of today looks for and can enjoy without long keeping. Watch for the wines labelled *Vieilles Vignes*.

Château Gloria

Cru Bourgeois. Owner: Henri Martin. 50ha. 25,000 cases. CS 65%, Mer 25%, CF 5%, PV 5%. Second labels: Châteaux Haut-Beychevelle-Gloria and Peymartin.
Gloria is the life's work of Henri Martin, one of the great figures of the Médoc. As *grand maître* of the Commanderie du Bontemps, he did much to promote the Médoc in general over many years. His son-in-law, Jean-Louis Triaud, who has succeeded him, had already in effect been running the property for some time. The vineyard has been put together in one generation from bits and pieces of *cru classé* vineyards only. For this reason, it has not joined the Syndicat des Crus Bourgeois and sells for the same price as some fifth growths.

The wine is generous and supple, with fullness and richness of flavour. It is noted for its consistency. The problem is that it is certainly not as good as the classified growths of St-Julien, although it is superior to some lesser Margaux and Pauillac classifieds, and it is more expensive than most *crus bourgeois*.

Château Gruaud-Larose ★★ →

2e Cru Classé. Owner: Group Bernard Taillan. Administrator: Georges Pauli. 82ha. 51,000 cases. CS 57%, Mer 30%, CF 8%, Mal 2%, PV 3%.
Second label: Sarget du Gruaud-Larose V.
Léoville-Las-Cases and Ducru-Beaucaillou are the archetypical St-Juliens of the riverside vineyards; Gruaud-Larose is the classic example of a St-Julien from the plateau that lies between the riverside properties and St-Laurent. This large estate was created in the 18th century, divided in the 19th and then reunited by the Cordiers in 1934. In 1992, Jean Cordier sold to the Cordier firm which sold on the following year to Alcatel while retaining responsibility for winemaking and sales. In 1997, the Group Bernard Taillan bought the property but Georges Pauli, who supervised the running of the property for many years, remains to provide continuity. In 1995, a new *cuvier* with 14 wooden vats replaced the stainless steel.

As with some other *crus classés* sold as *négoce* exclusives, Gruaud sold at a more modest price than it would have on the open market. Now it is on the open market and with stricter selection is producing wines of "Super-Second" quality, with prices rising accordingly.

The wines here have great concentration and richness and have been decidedly tannic in the past few years, but with maturity they acquire a soft, velvety texture with great breed and charm. Very fine wines were made in '82, '83, '85, '86, '88, '89, and '90. The '93 is one of the best St-Juliens of the vintage, and '94, '95, '96, '97, '98, '99, and 2000 are all excellent. The second wine is well worth looking out for. It is packed with fruit, and can be drunk earlier than the *grand vin*, but still has plenty of structure.

Château Lagrange ★ V

3e Cru Classé. Owner: Château Lagrange. Administrator: Marcel Ducasse. 109ha. 66,000 cases. CS 66%, Mer 27%, PV 7%. Second label: Les Fiefs-de-Lagrange V.

In 1983, Lagrange was sold to the giant firm of distillers and wine merchants, Suntory, and so became the first Bordeaux *cru classé* to be bought by a Japanese company. The vineyard is well placed on the plateau of St-Julien behind Gruaud-Larose. One of the attractions for its new owners was the considerable potential for increasing the vineyard area. Expansions and improvements complete, this has now increased from 49–109 hectares.

The buildings, including the château, have been completely overhauled, the 19th-century *chai* restored and two new ones built to cope with the increase in production. After many years of tough, coarse wines, there had been some improvement just prior to the sale, after which Marcel Ducasse was brought in by the new owners to manage the property.

The '82, made by the previous owners but sold by the new ones, is an excellent example, with a scent of prunes and great depth of flavour and fruit, tannin, and complexity. For the delicious '85, the crop was split 60:40 between the *grand vin* and Les Fiefs. Impressive wines followed in '86, even '87, '88, '89, and '90 Les Fiefs is proving a particularly attractive and stylish wine. Good wines were made in '93, '94, '95, '96, '97, '98, '99, and 2000.

Château Lalande-Borie V

Cru Bourgeois Supérieur. Owner: Borie family. 18ha. 8,000 cases. CS 65%, Mer 25%, CF 10%.

This *cru* was created by Jean-Eugène Borie, owner of Ducru-Beaucaillou, from a vineyard that was part of Lagrange. The new vineyard was planted only in 1970 but is now making stylish, elegant, medium-weight wines that have charming fruit. The first important vintage was the '79, and the wines have been improving since then. Even the difficult '92 was good here. This wine offers an excellent opportunity for assessing the Borie family's deft hand with St-Julien at a modest price – an opportunity not so easy to come by nowadays.

Château Langoa-Barton ★ V

3e Cru Classé. Owner: Antony Barton. 17ha. 7,000 cases. CS 74%, Mer 20%, CF 6%.

This château has belonged to the same family since 1821, longer than any other *cru classé*. When Hugh Barton acquired the property it was known as Pontet-Langlois. The 18th century château is one of the finest in the Médoc, not as well-placed as Beychevelle but not far behind in pure architectural terms. The wines of Langoa and the Barton portion of Léoville were not château-bottled until 1969, but were removed to Barton & Guestier's Bordeaux cellars for bottling.

The wines of Langoa accurately reflect their classification. Usually ready to drink earlier than those of Léoville-Barton, they have a classic St-Julien character but are generally lighter in texture, less tannic but have lots of elegance, fruit, and charm – and real breeding. Every now and then Langoa produces something surprising, as with the unusually good '74 or the '71 which seems even better than the Léoville. The two seem to have a relationship not dissimilar to that between Gruaud-Larose and Talbot. The vintages here follow those of Léoville-Barton closely, with marvellous wines in '81, '82, '83, '85, '86, '88, '89, and '90. Better-than-average wines were made in '91, '92, and '93, while '94, '95, '96, '97, '98, '99, and 2000 are excellent.

Château Léoville-Barton ★★ V →

2e Cru Classé. Owner: Antony Barton. 47ha. 20,000 cases. CS 72%, Mer 20%, CF 8%. Second label: La Reserve Léoville-Barton.

Like its neighbour, Poyferré, Léoville-Barton was a part of the enormous estate of the Marquis de Las-Cases until the 1820s. In 1826, Hugh Barton, who had bought Langoa only five years before, acquired what was then a quarter share of the original Las-Cases estate and used the cellars of Langoa for making and housing the produce of his new acquisition. One hundred and seventy five years later, the Barton family still owns the property, with Antony Barton having taken on the burden of management from his uncle Ronald, who lived in the château until his death in 1986.

Léoville-Barton, under Ronald Barton's long stewardship, remained a traditionally made wine: finely perfumed, powerful, and rich in tannin at first, then developing that beautiful fruit and richness of flavour that are hallmarks of the best St-Juliens. The style tends towards more richness than Poyferré, but with a shade less elegance. There were some inconsistencies in the 1970s, but with stricter selection now evident, outstanding wines were made in '81, '82, '83, '85, '86, '88, '89, and '90. The '93, '94, '95, '96, '97, '98, '99, and 2000 are fine examples of the vintages. Recent vintages suggest that the wines are moving towards the "Super Second" category.

With the marked improvement that has characterized Léoville-Poyferré in the '80s and '90s, it is going to be interesting to draw comparisons between the three Léovilles again.

Château Léoville-Las-Cases ★★★

2e Cru Classé. Owner: SC du Château Léoville-Las-Cases. Administrator: Jean-Hubert Delon. 97ha. 47,000 cases.CS 65%, Mer 20%, CF 12%, PV 3%.
Second label: Clos-du-Marquis V. Third label: Domaine de Bigarnon.

The label of this wine states *Grand Vin de Léoville du Marquis de Las-Cases* (no mention of château) and serves as a reminder that this is the residue of what was, in the 18th century, the most important estate not only in St-Julien but also in the Médoc. With its magnificent *clos* adjoining Latour on a gravel ridge within sight of the Gironde, Las-Cases represents half the original estate. The original château, standing at the southern entrance to the village, is actually divided between Las-Cases and Poyferré, with the Las-Cases portion on the left.

The modern reputation of Las-Cases was established during the stewardship of Michel Delon from 1976 to 1996, when he handed over to his son, Jean-Hubert. Jean-Hubert is the third generation of Delons descended from Théophile Skawinski, manager until 1930. Las-Cases now produces wines to rival the first growths. In style, it is firmer and slower to mature than other St-Juliens. Recently, the wines seem to have filled out and are now not only elegant but also concentrated and powerful. The bouquet is especially characteristic, reserved at first but slowly evolving to become elegant and firm.

Great wines were made in '82, '83, '85, '86, '88, '89, and '90: all true *vins de garde*. In 1991, the Grand Clos was one of the few vineyards to escape the great frost, and the resulting wine is outstanding for the vintage, together with that of its neighbour Latour. The '92, '94, and '97 are fine examples of these vintages, and '95, '96, '98, '99, and 2000 are outstanding. The Clos-du-Marquis is one of the best and most consistent of the second wines.

Château Léoville-Poyferré ★★ V →

2e Cru Classé. Owner: Cuvelier family. Administrator: Didier Cuvelier. 80ha. 44,000 cases. CS 65%, Mer 25%, PV 8%, CF 2%. Second label: Château Moulin-Riche.

Like Léoville-Barton, Léoville-Poyferré originally represented a quarter portion of the Las-Cases estate, acquired by the Baron de Poyferré by marriage to a Las-Cases. Unlike the other two Léovilles, Poyferré has not had the same continuity of ownership since that time, and its fortunes have been more varied. At its best, it has produced wines as fine as Las-Cases, as in '28 and '29. But at that time, although under different ownerships, both were managed by Théophile Skawinski.

Now, after a period of inconsistency, a member of the younger generation of the Cuvelier family has assumed responsibility, and the results show. First of all, the *cuvier* was completely modernized in 1980, then more new wood was introduced and a capable new *maître de chai*, with the reassuringly Médocain name of Dourthe, took over.

The '82 is a glorious example of this exceptional year, a great bottle, while the '83 has length, concentration and harmony. The '85 is a beauty, '86 is more powerful and tannic, while '88, '89, and '90 are outstanding. Good wines were made in '93, '94 and '97; excellent ones in '95, '96, '98, '99, and 2000. Although good wines were made before this, the *cru* was certainly not reaching the heights of which it is capable. Now the future is exciting.

Château St-Pierre ★ V

4e Cru Classé. Owner: Domaines Martin. 17ha. 8,000 cases.
CS 70%, Mer 20%, CF 10%.

This property has certainly had a chequered history. The name derives from a Monsieur St-Pierre who acquired the estate in 1767. Then, in 1832, it was divided between different branches of the family, and the suffixes Bontemps-Dubarry and Sevaistre appeared. Although reunited by its Belgian owners after World War II, parts of the vineyard had been sold off, notably to Gloria and du Glana. Then, in 1982, Henri Martin of Gloria bought the château (now beautifully restored) and most of the vineyard. St-Pierre is now housed in the same *chai* as Gloria, itself originally the St-Pierre-Bontemps *chai*.

St-Pierre produced elegant, perfumed, stylish, and typically St-Julien wines for some years, but Henri Martin and his son-in-law Jean-Louis Triaud (now in charge since Henri Martin's death in 1991) lifted it to higher plains. From '82 onwards, lovely wines of great breed have been made, clearly superior to those of Gloria, yet somehow the wine seems forgotten, and ignored by the market.

Château Talbot ★★ V

4e Cru Classé. Owners: Rustmann-Cordier, Bignon-Cordier. 102ha. Red: 54,000
cases. CS 66%, Mer 26%, PV 5%, CF 3%. White: 6ha Sauv 84%, Sém 16%. 3,000
cases. Second labels: Connétable Talbot, Caillou Blanc du Château Talbot.

It is Talbot's misfortune that it was always obliged to stand in the shadow of Gruaud-Larose. The name commemorates the Earl of Shrewsbury, who was killed commanding the English forces at Castillon-la-Bataille in 1453, yet it seems doubtful that he ever owned the estate. In 1992, Jean Cordier exchanged his holding in Gruaud-Larose for the Company's shares in Talbot, and thus once more became sole proprietor of what had always been his favourite base in the Médoc. On his death in 1994, the estate passed to his daughters.

Talbot has long been noted for its consistency. The wines generally have less tannin and concentration than those of Gruaud-Larose, and are ready to be drunk sooner, but they also keep well. The charm of Talbot is its harmony: no St-Julien is more seductive. The wines are beautifully perfumed and have great St-Julien refinement in their fruit. There is a fine '75 which evolved beautifully, and the '81 has developed well and has great finesse. Not surprisingly, '82 and '83 are superb. The opulent, rich '85 contrasts strongly with the dense, tannic '86, and '88, '89, and '90 are a great trio. Good wines were made in '93, '94, and '97; '95, '96, '98, '99, and 2000 are excellent.

Since the change of ownership in 1994, Talbot has been sold on the Bordeaux market. Because of the large production, it is excellent value. The second wine, Connétable Talbot, is really delightful, ideal for early drinking, with lots of vivid St-Julien fruit. The white wine is pleasant, fresh, and clean and becoming really impressive.

Château Terrey-Gros-Cailloux

Cru Bourgeois Supérieur. Owners: Annie Fort and Henri Pradère. 14ha. 8,000 cases. CS 70%, Mer 25%, PV 5%.

Ever since I came across this *cru* for the first time – it was the '66 vintage – I have been greatly impressed by the real breed and finesse of the wine. Certainly it is one of the best of the *cru bourgeois* in St-Julien. The vineyard is in several parcels, the most important of which is behind the village of Beychevelle – where the *chai* is – and adjoining Talbot and Léoville-Barton. Another is next to Gruaud-Larose, and yet another adjoins Beychevelle and Ducru-Beaucaillou. At their best, the wines have ripe fruit and good richness. Certainly this is a wine to look for if you enjoy St-Julien but do not want to pay *cru classé* prices all the time.

PAUILLAC

The name of Pauillac is assured from the reflected glory of its three first growths: Lafite-Rothschild, Mouton-Rothschild, and Latour. The area covered by the *crus classés* here is greater than in any other appellation, even though the village has only 18 compared with 21 in Margaux. The area under vine increased by 18 per cent in the years 1985–95, but has been static since. Cabernet Sauvignon achieves its most characteristic results here, producing that marked blackcurrant style for which it is justly famous. The wines are the most powerful, in terms of bouquet, body, and flavour, of all Médocs. The best *crus* combine this with a finesse that develops with ageing, although some lesser *crus* have a certain coarseness.

Château d'Armailhac ★ V

5e Cru Classé. Owner: GFA Baronne Philippine de Rothschild. 50ha. 17,000 cases. CS 50%, Mer 25%, CF 23%, PV 2%.

No leading Bordeaux château has undergone so many changes of name. Acquired by the late Baron in 1933, it retained the original "Mouton d'Armailhac" until 1956 when it became Mouton Baron Philippe, then in 1975 "Baron" changed to "Baronne" to commemorate Baron Philippe's second wife. In 1991, his daughter, Philippine de Rothschild, decided that the names Mouton Rothschild, Mouton Cadet, and the company name Baron Philippe de Rothschild were confusing, and that this property deserved a distinctive personality of its own. So we shall now have to get used to Château d'Armailhac, which first appeared with the lovely '89 vintage.

Situated just a few hundred yards from the front gate of Mouton-Rothschild, this château is a curious unfinished building, its classical portico sliced down the middle as if it were a piece of cake. Although only a stone's throw away from the great Mouton, it is run entirely separately but with equal care.

The wines are true Pauillacs, though less rich and opulent than those of their big brother. In the best years, they have a good concentration, but in lesser ones they can be slightly mean and dull. As one would expect, they are nearer in style to their other neighbour, Pontet-Canet, than to the great *premier cru*, although recent vintages seem more charming and accessible.

Château Batailley ★ V

5e Cru Classé. Owner: Castéja family. 60ha. 33,000 cases. CS 70%, Mer 25%, CF 5%.
Second label: Château Haut-Bages Monpelou, Cru Bourgeois Supérieur.

The early reputation and classification of Batailley date from the period of Guestier's ownership. Now another négociant, Philippe Castéja of Borie-Manoux, is in charge. There is sometimes a tendency to undervalue châteaux that are not sold through the Bordeaux market, especially if, in their pricing policy, they are more concerned with offering continuity to their customers than with what their neighbours are doing. Batailley's real worth should not be underrated on account of its relatively modest price.

All the present vineyard is on land that was classified in 1855, and it is situated at the back of Pauillac on the St-Laurent road. Wines are consistent, solid, and dependable. In the past Batailley occasionally produced memorable wines (such as the '53, '61, and '64), otherwise, they were sound but unexciting. Now they consistently have more fruit and concentration, as well as being more stylish. Years to look out for are '82, '85, '88, '89, '96, '98, '99, and 2000.

Château Clerc-Milon ★ V

5e Cru Classé. Owner: Baron Philippe de Rothschild. 30ha. 13,000 cases.
CS 70%, Mer 20%, CF 10%.

This rather neglected property was bought by Baron Philippe de Rothschild in 1970. The vineyard is well-placed between the road and the river, north of Pauillac, close to Mouton and Lafite. Milon is the small village where the property lies, and Clerc the name of the owner during the 1855 classification.

There was much to be done in the vineyard, and for this reason it took time to turn the quality of the wine around. The turning point came with the '81 vintage, when, for the first time, the wine surpassed Mouton Baronne Philippe (*see* Château d'Armailhac) in breed and harmonious fruit. After this, the most successful years have been '82, '85, '86, '89, '90, '94, '95, '96, '98, '99, and 2000. The higher proportion of Cabernet Sauvignon compared to that of d'Armailhac now sets Clerc-Milon firmly apart.

Château Colombier-Monpelou

Cru Bourgeois Supérieur. Owner: Nadette Jugla. 24ha. 15,400 cases. CS 55%,
Mer 35%, CF 5%, PV 5%. Second label: Grand Canyon.

For many years this was the best wine to emerge from the Pauillac cooperative. Then, in 1970, it was bought by Bernard Jugla, proprietor of the adjoining Château Pédesclaux. Because Colombier parted company with its château and *chai* in 1939 (these now serve as the headquarters of La Baronnie, négociant company of Baron Philippe de Rothschild), a completely new installation had to be built. The wines are fermented in metal vats and aged in casks, of which 40 per cent are new each year. This is good, honest, robust Pauillac that has a certain elegance and suppleness and pleasing fruit.

Château Croizet-Bages V →

5e Cru Classé. Owner: Jean-Michel Quié. Administrator: Jean-Louis Camp. 28ha.
15,500 cases. CS 40%, Mer 45%, CF 15%. Second label: Enclos de Moncabon.

This *cru* was created by the brothers Croizet in the 18th century. Its *chai* and *cuvier* are in the hamlet of Bages, close to its more famous neighbour, Lynch-Bages, on high ground in the south of Pauillac. It has belonged to the Quié family since 1930. There is no château. The wines are attractively robust and full-flavoured, and mellow fairly quickly, yet in my experience they keep well. Following a mediocre period, an improvement was noticeable in '95 and '96, after Jean-Louis Camp assumed responsibility. The '98 marked another leap forward, '99 is a delicious, forward wine, and 2000 is very promising.

Château Duhart-Milon-Rothschild ★ →

4e Cru Classé. Owner: Domaines Baron de Rothschild. 64ha. 17,000 cases. CS 57%, Mer 21%, CF 20%, PV 2%. Second label: Moulin-de-Duhart.

When the Rothschilds of Lafite bought the neighbouring vineyard of Duhart-Milon in 1962, it was in a sorry state: only 16 hectares of vineyards in production and a high proportion of Petit Verdot. The wines were often undistinguished. It takes a long time to see the results when a vineyard has to be almost entirely reconstituted, but good results are now emerging, and Duhart is again taking its place as a leading Pauillac.

The vineyard lies mostly on the plateau of the Carruades, and the *chai* and *cuvier* are in Pauillac. There is no château. The '86 has extra concentration and opulence. There was still a degree of coarseness until Charles Chevalier, who took over in 1994, moved the wine into a new mode in '96, with 2001 even finer.

Château La Fleur Milon

Cru Bourgeois. Owner: Héritiers Gimenez. Administrator: Claude Mirande. 12.5ha. 8,000 cases. CS 65%, Mer 25%, PV 5%, CF 5%.

The vineyards of this *cru* are indeed well placed. Its *chai* is in the village of Le Pouyalet (there is no château), and the various small plots of vineyard adjoin Mouton-Rothschild, Lafite-Rothschild, Duhart-Milon, and Pontet-Canet. Until recently, the wines were decidedly rustic, but the judicious use of new oak and better winemaking are resulting in polished tannins and mellow fruit.

Château Fonbadet V

Cru Bourgeois Supérieur. Owner: Pascale Peyronie. 20ha. 8,500 cases. CS 60%, Mer 20%, CF 15%, PV 5%. Second labels: Châteaux Haut-Pauillac, Padarnac, Tour-du-Roc-Milon, Montgrand-Milon.

This charming 18th century château lies south of the village of St-Lambert, just past the two Pichons as you drive from Bordeaux. The trees in its park stand oasis-like in a sea of vines. The present owner is very much the working, resident proprietor. Thirty per cent new casks are used. This is a sound, classic Pauillac from old vines, made with meticulous care. It often does well in blind tastings and fully deserves its excellent reputation.

Château Grand-Puy-Ducasse →

5e Cru Classé. Owner: SC du Château. Administrator: Alain Duhau. 40ha. 11,000 cases. CS 60%, Mer 40%. Second label: Château Artigues Arnaud.

Until the present proprietors bought it in 1971, Grand-Puy-Ducasse was a small vineyard of only ten hectares, adjoining Mouton and Pontet-Canet. The new owners bought two additional vineyards, one adjoining Batailley and Grand-Puy-Lacoste on the plateau behind Pauillac, the other adjoining the two Pichons, so that it now has vineyards in all three main sectors of Pauillac. The château is a pleasing neo-classical building on the quayside near the centre of the village of Pauillac. For many years it also served as the *maison du vin*.

The new regime has produced mixed results. The wines at their best are classic Cabernet Sauvignon, blackcurrant Pauillacs, and the structure supple, rich, and harmonious. The '75, for instance, was splendid. Since then, the best years have been '82, '85, '88, and '89. However, too many wines in the 1990s have been marred by tough, astringent tannins, but '96 saw a marked improvement that has been maintained.

Château Grand-Puy-Lacoste ★★

5e Cru Classé. Owner: Borie family. Administrator: François Xavier Borie.
50ha. 16,700 cases. CS 75%, Mer 25%. Second label: Lacoste-Borie V.

This *cru* has long had an excellent reputation for producing typically robust and fine Pauillacs. Raymond Dupin was owner until extreme old age caused him to sell to the Borie family in 1978. If some things had begun to slip in his last few years, this should not detract from his achievements. The Bories decided to replace the old *cuvier* with stainless steel after the '80 vintage, and the previously dilapidated château has been tastefully renovated.

Most of the vineyard is in one piece in front of the château on the Bages plateau, and is of the highest quality. The consistency and excellence of the wines reflect this. These wines are powerful and often rather tannic and tough at first. The Bories are still making concentrated wines, but are trying to emphasize the fruit a little more. With the '81, the wines seemed to acquire an extra dimension; '82, '83, '85 (exceptional), '86, '88, '89, and '90 all produced fine wines and in the difficult vintages of '92, '93, '94, and '97, excellent wines were made. The '95, '96, '98, '99, and 2000 are outstanding. This is now among the finest wines in Paulliac, after the Pichons.

Château Haut-Bages-Libéral ★

5e Cru Classé. Owner: SC du Château. Administrator: Claire Villars. 27ha. 13,300 cases. CS 80%, Mer 20%. Second label: Chapelle de Bages.

This *cru* has had a chequered history. When it was bought by the Cruses in 1960, it lost part of its vineyard to Pontet-Canet, and its wines were bottled in the Cruses' cellars. With the introduction of compulsory château-bottling for the *crus classés* in 1972 and the sale of Pontet-Canet, the Cruses were obliged to build a new installation for handling the wines. In 1983, they sold to the company that also runs Chasse-Spleen and La Gurgue, and that company has made investments to bring the property and vineyards up to standard.

The vineyard is on the plateau of Bages and adjoins Latour, Lynch-Bages and Pichon-Longueville Baron. The Libéral has no political connotations, but was the name of the 19th-century owner at the time of the classification. In the last years of the Cruse management, there were improvements: the wine was rich and fruity – the '76 and '82 were particularly attractive. But Mme Villars soon made her mark. The '85 was good; '86 even better; '88 and '89 equally impressive; '94, '95, '96, '97, '98, '99, and 2000 were all good wines. As from '97, the malolactic fermentation has been done in cask.

Château Haut-Batailley ★ V

5e Cru Classé. Owner: Mme de Brest-Borie. Administrator: François-Xavier Borie.
22ha. 10,000 cases.CS 65%, Mer 25%, CF 10%.
Second label: Château La Tour-d'Aspic.

When the Borie family bought Batailley in 1942, it was divided between the two brothers: négociant Marcel and François, who bought Ducru-Beaucaillou. Haut-Batailley is much the smaller part. Its vineyard had to be replanted and took time to mature. There is no château, as the house stayed with the main part of the property, and the wine is vinified at La Couronne.

There is a marked contrast in style between Haut-Batailley and Batailley, the former producing wines of less weight but real elegance. Comparing Haut-Batailley with Grand-Puy-Lacoste shows the same sort of contrast. Grand-Puy and Batailley are more assertively – even aggressively – Pauillac. Haut-Batailley is consistent, the beautifully balanced fruit and mature tannins making it drinkable relatively young, but still able to age attractively.

Château Lafite-Rothschild ★★★ →

1er Cru Classé. Owner: Domaine Rothschild. 100ha. 55,000 cases. CS 70%,
Mer 25%, CF 3%, PV 2%. Second label: Carruades de Lafite-Rothschild V.

Lafite has experienced something of a renaissance in recent years. In the
1960s and early 1970s, there were far too many disappointments for a wine
of Lafite's standing. In 1974, a new era began with the appointment of a
younger generation of the family, Baron Eric de Rothschild, as the member
responsible for Lafite. In 1975, Professor Peynaud was called in to advise
and Jean Crété was subsequently appointed *régisseur*, with his invaluable
experience at Léoville-Las-Cases behind him. The combination of these
changes was most beneficial for Lafite and showed up vividly in the glass.
Jean Crété retired in 1983 and was followed by Gilbert Rokvam.

Since 1985, there has been much stricter selection, with more wine
being set aside for the Carruades label, which, as a result, is much improved.
Further changes occurred, and the practice of keeping the wine in cask
for three years, irrespective of the character of the vintage, was abandoned.
In 1987, a new second-year cask cellar in an innovative circular design was
finished, and in the following year a new *cuvier* of stainless-steel vats was
introduced to supplement the traditional oak ones. The features one notices
about Lafite vintages of this era are their depth of colour, richness, and
concentration of flavour. The most outstanding vintages were '82, '85, '86, '88,
'89, and '90.

On Gilbert Rokvam's retirement in 1994, he was succeeded by Charles
Chevalier, who has made such a success of Rieussec. His first vintages –
'94, '95, and '96 – confirmed that he is a winemaker with green fingers and
a touch of magic. The '97, '98, '99, and 2000 are outstanding examples of
these vintages. Lafite's great potential is now being fully realized.

The second wine, Carruades, is also much improved, some consolation for
those who find Lafite priced out of reach. To drink a bottle of Lafite should be
one of the ultimate experiences for any wine-lover, and it is good to know that
in future there should be no disappointments.

Château Latour ★★★

1er Cru Classé. Owner: François Pinault. Administrator: Frédéric Engerer.
65ha. 36,700 cases. CS 75%, Mer 20%, CF 4%, PV 1%.
Second label: Les Forts de Latour V. 10,000 cases.

In 1963, the Pearson group bought a majority shareholding in Latour, with
Harveys of Bristol taking a 25-per-cent holding. Harveys later became part
of Allied-Lyons, which, in 1989, also acquired Pearson's share of the
property. Jean-Paul Gardère as administrator was the dominant influence
on the wines of Latour from his appointment in 1963 until his retirement in
1987. In 1993, Allied-Lyons, having bought at the top of the market in 1989,
sold out at the bottom to François Pinault, who, like André Mentzelopoulos
before him, has made his money through retailing in France. In 1999,
Christian Le Sommer left after ten years of excellent winemaking. Frédéric
Engerer is the president, with F. Ardouin as technical director.

Latour has produced monumental wines for generations. The modernization
of the *cuvier* and improvements in the vineyard have simply tended to make
the wines more accessible. But retrospective tastings show that Latour has lost
none of its legendary characteristics: its great depth of colour, classic Cabernet
nose, and remarkable concentration of fruit and tannin. Admirers of Latour
often used to bemoan the fact that they doubted they would live long enough

to enjoy the most recent vintages. After the legendary '61, the great vintages were '62 and '66, with '64 and '67 above average for these years. In the 1970s, the outstanding wine is '75, followed in quality by '70 and '78, with an exceptional '73 and a good '76. Of the 1980s, the '81 is probably one of the best wines of its year, the '82 is a great classic, '86, '88, '89, and '90 are outstanding and long-maturing, while '85 is lovely and more quickly maturing. In 1991, the vineyard escaped the worst of the frost and one of the best wines of the vintage resulted. After one of the best '92s, '93, and '94 showed the advantages of a terroir which allows the Cabernet Sauvignon to ripen earlier than it does in neighbouring properties and produced outstanding wines in each vintage. The '95, '96, '98, '99, and 2000 are great years here.

Les Forts de Latour is produced partly from vineyards whose produce does not go into the *grand vin* and partly from the younger vines of Latour. There is a shorter fermentation, and the wine has the characteristics of Latour but with less concentration, so it develops more quickly. The wine used not to be placed on the market until it was ready to drink, but from the '90 vintage it has been offered *en primeur*.

Château Lynch-Bages ★★

5e Cru Classé. Owner: Cazes family. Administrator: Jean-Michel Cazes. 90ha. 35,000 cases. CS 75%, Mer 15%, CF 10%.
Second label: Château Haut-Bages-Averous (7,000 cases) V.
White: Blanc de Lynch-Bages. 4.5ha. Sauv 40%, Sém 40%, Musc 20%.

Lynch-Bages arouses markedly varying opinions among claret-lovers. Some admire it unreservedly; others call it the poor man's Mouton or claim that it lacks finesse and breed.

From an objective point of view, this is a marvellously attractive, almost plummy, Pauillac with a really concentrated, blackcurrant bouquet and flavour. At the same time, it is less tannic and aggressive than many Pauillacs, with an emphasis on fruit and suppleness. This *cru* also has a fine record for making good wines in lesser vintages.

The château, which is the home of Jean-Michel Cazes, who now runs Lynch-Bages, stands on the edge of the plateau of Bages, commanding views across the Gironde with the vineyards behind it. In recent years, there has been an impressive programme of enlarging and modernizing both *cuvier* and *chai*. Certainly standards have never been higher than they are today. Recent outstanding years have been '82, '83, '85, '86, '88, '89, and '90. Honourable wines were made in the difficult vintages of '92, '93, '94, and '97 and very good wines were made in '96, '98, '99, and 2000.

Haut-Bages-Averous is something of a cross-breed. There are five hectares of good *cru bourgeois*, the produce of which is assembled with those vats of Lynch-Bages that have been eliminated from the *grand vin*. The result is a light, deliciously fruity, and easy-to-drink wine.

Château Lynch-Moussas →

5e Cru Classé. Owner: Castéja family. 35ha. 17,000 cases. CS 75%, Mer 25%.

This *cru* has belonged to the Castéja family for many years, and there were many members of the family involved, until Émile Castéja was able to buy out the others in 1969. At that time the production had fallen to less than 2,000 cases and the property was in a run-down condition. Émile Castéja, who is also responsible for all Borie-Manoux's properties, has had to rebuild and re-equip the *cuvier* and *chai* and replant the vineyard, which adjoins Batailley and is the most westerly of all Pauillac *crus*. Part of it lies near the hamlet of

Moussas, the rest near Duhart-Milon and Lafite to the north and near Pichon and Latour to the south.

Before the restoration, this was a pleasant but rather light wine, without much distinction. The wines are now more stylish without being big and have charm and breed. After good wines in '94 and '95, Lynch-Moussas excelled in '96 with probably the best wine produced here.

Château Mouton-Baronne-Philippe

See Château d'Armailhac.

Château Mouton-Rothschild ★★★

1er Cru Classé 1973. Owner: GFA Baronne Philippine de Rothschild.
75ha. 23,000 cases. CS 80%, CF 10%, Mer 8%, PV 2%.
White: Aile d'Argent (Bordeaux Blanc Sec) 4ha. Sauv 38%, Sém 48%, Musc 14%.
1,200 cases. Second labels: Le Second Vin ('93 only), Le Petit Mouton.

The Mouton-Rothschild we know today is the life's work of one man: Baron Philippe, who, from the day he took charge in 1923 until his death in 1988, set about making something special. He was the first to introduce compulsory château-bottling, along with the other first growths, though at this time Mouton itself was not a first. He hit upon the idea of having an artist design an original work for each year's label, something that has happened every year since 1945. Finally, he cut through the petty jealousies of Bordeaux to see Mouton proclaimed an official *premier cru classé* in 1973. In his last years he persuaded his only child, Philippine, to become involved, and she now ably continues her father's work.

Mouton wines are quintessential Pauillacs, curiously closer in style to Latour, on the other side of the commune, than to its near neighbour and long-time rival, Lafite. There is a similar concentrated, blackcurrant bouquet and flavour combined with a richness and opulence that disguise the tannin more than at Latour. Recent great vintages have been '82, '83, '85, '86, '88, '89, '90, '95, '96, '98, '99, and 2000. In 1985, Patrick Léon took over as technical director with a sure touch. The second wine was introduced in '93. Aile d'Argent's first vintage was '91. Initially, it was 100 per cent Sauvignon but fermented in new oak, and needs two to three years in bottle to show its class.

Château Pédesclaux

5e Cru Classé. Owner: Jugla family. Administrator: Bernard Jugla.
12ha. 5,800 cases. CS 50%, Mer 45%, CF 5%.

This is one of the more obscure *crus classés*. Its vineyards and *chai* are just to the north of the village of Pauillac, near to Pontet-Canet. The name comes from a *courtier* (wine broker) who was proprietor at the time of the 1855 classification. It was bought by the Jugla family in 1950, and the facilities have been improved and the production increased under their management. Belgium is the principal export market. The reputation of Pédesclaux is for making solid, honourable Pauillacs rather than exciting ones – but I find the wines too rustic for their status. However, 2000 showed a marked improvement.

Château Pibran →

Cru Bourgeois Supérieur. Owner: AXA-Millésimes. Administrator: Christian Seely.
18ha. 6,000 cases CS 60%, Mer 25%, CF 10%, PV 5%.
Second label: Château La Tour Pibran.

This *cru* lies just outside Pauillac to the northwest of and adjoining Pontet-Canet. It belonged to the Billa family from 1941 to 1987 and the wine established a good reputation. Now, as part of the AXA empire, attractively fruity, assertive wines are being made. The 2000 may be the best yet. In 2002, the adjoining La Tour Pibran was acquired. The name is now used for the second wine, with the best parcels of the two vineyards providing the *cuvée* for the Pibran label.

Château Pichon-Longueville Baron ★★ →

2e Cru Classé. Owner: AXA-Millésimes. Administrator: Christian Seely.
50ha. 20,000 cases. CS 75%, Mer 25%. Second label: Les Tourelles de Pichon.
The château here is a notable landmark on the *route des châteaux*, its slender turrets and high-pitched roof giving it a fairy-tale look. In 1855, the property was undivided and, apart from Mouton (now elevated to *premier cru* status), was the only Pauillac in the *deuxième cru* category. The vineyard is superbly situated, adjoining Latour. The new owners have restored the château, which has been little more than a shell since the war, and have also built a new *chai* and *cuvier*, whose size and extent are rather too dominating for their surroundings.

There was a time when Pichon-Baron (as it is usually called to distinguish it from the neighbouring Comtesse) was normally the better of the two wines, but the 1960s and especially the 1970s were disappointing times under the previous management. Since AXA-Millésimes bought the property in 1987, Jean-Michel Cazes has quickly turned things round again and produced classic wines in '88, '89, and '90. In the early 1990s, the wines seemed over-oaked for these rain-troubled vintages, but returned to form with the '95, '96, '98, '99, and especially 2000 vintages. This is quintessential Pauillac, compared to the more feminine character of Comtesse across the road.

Château Pichon-Longueville Comtesse-de-Lalande ★★

2e Cru Classé. Owner: May Elaine de Lencquesaing. 85ha. 50,000 cases.
CS 45%, Mer 35%, CF 12%, PV 8%. Second label: Réserve de la Comtesse.
Unlike its neighbour, the Baron, Pichon-Comtesse has a charming château which is now lived in for much of the time by the present administrator and owner, Mme de Lencquesaing. It was her father, Edouard Miailhe, who acquired the property in 1926. But it is really since Mme de Lencquesaing took over in 1978 that the reputation of Pichon-Comtesse has soared into the top category of second growths. A new *cuvier* was ready for the reception of the '80 vintage, further extensions have been made to the *chai*, and the facilities for receiving guests and providing tastings have been much improved.

The wines here have always had great finesse and breed. The fact that part of the vineyard lies in St-Julien helps to give the wine a special character, more opulent and feminine than a Pauillac, yet richer than a St-Julien. The introduction of the Réserve de la Comtesse has led to a more rigorous selection and a corresponding rise in quality. Outstanding wines have been made in '78, '79, '81, '82, '83, '85, '86, '88, '89, '90, '94, '95, '96, '98, and 2000, while '80, '84, '87, '92, '93, and '97 produced wines above the years' general levels. This is one of the most prized wines in the Médoc after the firsts.

Château Plantey

Cru Bourgeois. Owner: Gabriel Meffre. 26ha. 16,000 cases. CS 50%, Mer 45%, CF 5%.
This good *cru bourgeois* is well-placed between Château d'Armailhac and Château Pontet-Canet. Gabriel Meffre, who owns extensive vineyards in the Rhône, also owns du Glana in neighbouring St-Julien. Good, rich, robust, traditional wines are made here, and quality was very consistent in the '90s.

Château Pontet-Canet ★ V →

5e Cru Classé. Owner: Tesseron Family. Administrator: Alfred Tesseron. 80ha.
50,000 cases. CS 62%, Mer 32%, CF 6%. Second label: Les Hauts de Pontet.

This large property lies north of Pauillac and adjoins Mouton-Rothschild. For
many years it was the pride of the Cruse family, who sold it in 1975 to Guy
Tesseron, member of a well-known Cognac family who married a Cruse. The
château, fine *chai* and underground cellar (a feature in few Médoc properties)
are impressive. Unfortunately, during the latter years of the Cruse regime,
the reputation of Pontet-Canet declined. The wine was bottled in their
Bordeaux cellars and not at the château. Now all the wine is château-bottled.

Under the new ownership, the fortunes of Pontet-Canet might have been
expected to improve, but progress was slow. The introduction of the new
second label in 1982 has resulted in a stricter selection, yet the austere
quality of the tannins still came through. Finally, Alfred Tesseron called
on Michel Rolland. The wines made a real breakthrough in '94 and '95,
replacing dry tannins with ripe fruit and much better balance. The '96 was
outstanding, and after a delicious '97 came a great '98, a very attractive, fine
'99, and an outstanding 2000.

Cave Coopérative La Rose Pauillac

Owner: Groupement des Propriétaires-Viticulteurs de Pauillac. 70ha. 45,000 cases.
CS 55%, Mer 40%, PV 2%, CF 3%.

This cooperative, founded during the crisis year of 1933, marked the beginning
of the cooperative movement in the Médoc. There were 52 members initially,
rising to 125 in the mid-1980s, but today, membership is in decline, with
individuals leaving to make their own wines. Most of the wine is sold under the
label of La Rose Pauillac, but Château Haut-Milon and Château Haut de la
Bécade make their own declaration. The co-op enjoys a reputation for
producing good, solid Pauillacs which are fruity and not too tannic.

ST-ESTÈPHE

In many ways this is a transitional area between the two parts of Médoc. The
wines exhibit a wide range of qualities, from the breeding and power of
the leading *cru*, Cos d'Estournel, to some rather lean, austere wines with a
distinct *goût de terroir*. But improved methods of vinification have rendered
many wines less rustic than they were. There has been little change in the
area under vine, which has increased only slightly in the past 15 years.

Château Andron-Blanquet

Cru Bourgeois. Owner: Domaine Audoy. Administrator: Bernard Audoy.
16ha. 10,000 cases. CS 40%, Mer 35%, CF 25%.
Second label: Château St-Roch.

Since 1971, Andron-Blanquet has been under the same ownership and
direction as Cos Labory, whose vineyards it adjoins at some points. This wine
has that strong *goût de terroir* found in some St-Estèphes, especially when
young, but it is matched by sufficient fruit and richness to become a pleasing
wine with quite a strong flavour. A wine of character – if you like the character!

Château Beau-Site V

Cru Bourgeois Supérieur. Owner: Héritiers Castéja.
32ha. 20,000 cases. CS 70%, Mer 30%.

The name means "beautiful spot", and the view from the small courtyard
in front of the château and *chai* explains why it was chosen. The village of

St-Corbian, where it is situated, is on high ground and there is a splendid prospect across the vineyards of Calon-Ségur and towards the Gironde. The property is owned by the Castéja family and the wines are distributed exclusively by the Bordeaux négociants Borie-Manoux. Fifty per cent new oak is now used. The wines, like many St-Estèphes, have quite a strong flavour at first, but soon develop the richness to produce harmonious and pleasing wines. There can be a touch of austerity about the finish, but this usually rounds off with ageing. It is very consistent.

Château Beau-Site-Haut-Vignoble

Cru Bourgeois. Owner: Jean-Louis Braquessac. 18ha. 10,000 cases. CS 69%, Mer 22%, PV 5%, CF 4%.

Beau-Site-Haut-Vignoble is in St-Corbian, the same village as Beau-Site. This wine is distinctly more *artisanal*, and though carefully made, it is not in the same class as its neighbour. A lack of richness combined with toughness gives a certain leanness and other features characteristic of many lesser St-Estèphes. This is nevertheless an honourable wine, typical of its region.

Château Le Boscq V →

Cru Bourgeois Supérieur. Owner: Dourthe-Kressman. 16ha. 8,400 cases. Mer 51%, CS 42%, PV 7%.

This property is in the north of St-Estèphe on gravelly ridges overlooking the Gironde. I remember an excellent '53 bottled by Calvet, but in recent years the wine was little heard of until the present owners took over at harvest time in 1995. This is a very new, oak-influenced style of wine, but the '96 shows delicious fruit and remains sweet at the finish.

Château Calon-Ségur ★★ →

3e Cru Classé. Owners: Capbern-Gasqueton and Peyrelongue families. Administrator: Mme Gasqueton. 58ha. 20,000 cases. CS 50%, Mer 25%, CF 10%, PV 5%. Second label: Marquis de Ségur.

This is the oldest of the leading St-Estèphe *crus*. In the 12th century, it was given to a bishop of Portiers, Monseigneur de Calon, while in the 18th century it belonged to the famous Marquis de Ségur, who was proprietor of Lafite and Latour. He is supposed to have said that, although he made his wine at Lafite, his heart was at Calon – hence the heart-shaped device seen on the label and in many places at the property.

After the death of his uncle in 1962, Philippe Gasqueton ran the property and maintained the wine's reputation for consistency. In 1984, a large, new underground cellar was completed. It is L-shaped and runs along two sides of the *chai*, 60 metres long on one side and 50 metres (about 197ft x 189ft) on the other. The beautiful old wooden *cuvier* is still preserved but has not been used since 1973. The new stainless steel *cuves* are of 100 hectolitres each – this size representing half-a-day's picking – enabling control and selection. Since Philippe Gasqueton's death in 1995, Mme. Gasqueton has been in charge.

This is a wine that seldom comes top in comparative tastings of cask samples of *cru classé* St-Estèphes, but then often does better in bottle. The wines are noticeably softer and fruitier, and more generous than Cos or Montrose, but less fine perhaps. Undoubtedly it has gone through a lean patch and there has been a lack of consistency but at the end of the eighties, '88, '89, and '90 are classic Calons. Then excellent wines were made in '95, '96, '98, and 2000. Calon was always a great favourite in England, but in recent years, its reputation has been rather eclipsed. Now a recovery seems underway.

Château Capbern-Gasqueton

Cru Bourgeois. Owner: Capbern-Gasqueton family. Administrator: Mme Gasqueton.
35ha. 10,000 cases. CS 50%, Mer 35%, CF 15%. Second label: Le Grand Village
Capbern (exclusively distributed by Dourthe).

The château, a solid mansion in the centre of St-Estèphe, is the home of the
Gasqueton family and has been for many generations. The vineyard is in
two parts, one adjoining Calon-Ségur, the other near Meyney. All the wine is
matured in casks but 30 per cent new wood is used. As at Calon-Ségur, the
fruit is emphasized to avoid the harshness often associated with St-Estèphe.

Château Chambert-Marbuzet

Cru Bourgeois Supérieur. Owner: SC du Château (H Duboscq & Fils).
7ha. 3,900 cases. CS 70%, Mer 30%.

Another outpost of the Duboscq empire around Marbuzet (*see* Haut-
Marbuzet). The wine is well-made and most attractive, even when young,
yet clearly has the ability to age well. I have found it scented and packed
with fruit, well supported by ripe tannin, with an attractive flavour.

Château la Commanderie

Cru Bourgeois. Owner: Gabriel Meffre. 8.5ha. 5,000 cases. CS 55%, Mer 40%, CF 5%.

This is a northerly outpost of Gabriel Meffre's empire. At one time all the
wines were made at du Glana; now they have their own *chai*. The name goes
back to the Middle Ages when this was a commanderie of the Knights
Templar. Château la Commanderie is situated in the southern part of the
commune, between Marbuzet and Leyssac. The wine is exclusively
distributed by Dourthe and Kressmann.

Château Cos d'Estournel ★★ →

2e Cru Classé. Owner: Michel Reybier. Administrator: Jean-Guillaume Prats. 64ha.
28,000 cases. CS 58%, Mer 38%, CF 2%, PV 2%. Second label: Les Pagodes de Cos.

Cos is a landmark familiar to all who travel the *route des châteaux* on
account of its pagoda-like façade; it is strikingly placed on a hill overlooking
Lafite. This building is, in fact, the *chai*, for there is no château. From 1919
to 1998, it belonged to the Ginestet and then Prats families. Then after two
years as part of the Bernard Taillan Group, it was sold to its present owner.
But the management responsible for the now high standing of Cos came
from Bruno Prats (1971–'98), from whom his son Jean-Guillaume took over.
Cos has usually been considered as the leading *cru* of St-Estèphe and
certainly develops more finesse and breed in bottle than any other, as well
as being long-lived. There was a period in the 1960s when it was less
convincing, but after Bruno Prats assumed the direction, Cos has become
established as one of the leading *deuxièmes crus classés* once more.

When this wine is in cask it is always most impressive, concentrated and
tannic but finely balanced with great breed. There is often a dull patch in the
early years in bottle, but then the fruit, balance and breed come into their
own. This is a most rewarding wine to keep. Fine and often exceptional
wines were made in '82, '83, '85, '86, '88, '89, and '90, while in the challenging
1990s, the '91, '92, and '93 are all exceptional for the vintages. The '94 is fine,
while '95, '96, '98, '99, and 2000 are again outstanding.

Château Cos-Labory

5e Cru Classé. Owner: Domaine Audoy. Administrator: Bernard Audoy.
18ha. 10,000 cases. CS 60%, Mer 35%, CF 10%, PV 5%.

The style of the wines here is light and elegant, and they mature rather
quickly. There is certainly more refinement here than is usual in St-Estèphe,

but not the weight and character of the leading growths. The '86, however, marked the beginning of more concentrated and impressive wines, and, in spite of this, there is still not the consistency one would hope for.

Château Coutelin-Merville

Cru Bourgeois. Owner: Guy Estager et Fils. Administrator: Bernard Estager. 23ha. 14,000 cases. CS 25, CF 25%, Mer 46%, PV 4%.

Until 1972, this property was run with adjoining Château Hanteillan in Cissac, but inheritance problems forced the sale of the latter, so this *cru* now stands on its own. Wines are matured in cask and 25 per cent new oak is used. They have a scent of violets, power, good structure and length and require bottle-age to round off and give of their best.

Château Le Crock V →

Cru Bourgeois Supérieur. Owner: Cuvelier family. Administrator: Didier Cuvelier. 32ha. 17,500 cases. CS 58%, Mer 24%, CF 12%, PV 6%.

Since 1903, Le Crock has belonged to the Cuvelier family, which also now owns Léoville-Poyferré. This property is managed by the enthusiastic Didier Cuvelier, assisted by Francis Dourthe, the Poyferré *maître de chai*.

I do not know what the wines were like in the past, but recently they have been most impressive. They are scented, powerful, and complex on the nose, with a marked and agreeable personality; rich, with structure and depth on the palate. A wine to look out for, especially since its revitalized management took charge.

Château Haut-Beauséjour

Cru Bourgeois. Owner: Champagne Louis Roederer. 19ha. 9,000 cases. Mer 53%, CS 40%, PV 5%, Mal 3%.

Since its purchase by Roederer in 1992, steady progress has been made here. Very elegant, fruity wines are produced which drink well young.

Château Haut-Marbuzet ★

Cru Bourgeois Exceptionnel. Owner: SCV Duboscq. Administrator: Henri Duboscq. 58ha. 30,000 cases. CS 50%, Mer 40%, CF 10%. Second label: MacCarthy.

In the last 30 years or so, Henri Duboscq has built up a formidable reputation for his wines. Haut-Marbuzet, situated around the village of Marbuzet just to the south of Montrose, was his starting point. Now he has added MacCarthy, Chambert-Marbuzet and Tour de Marbuzet to his empire. One remarkable feature of this *cru bourgeois* is that all the wine is matured in new oak, something even most *cru classés* do not attempt. One might expect this to result in austere, tannic wines, especially in St-Estèphe, yet in my experience the wines are outstandingly attractive. The colours are deep and dense, the nose rich and concentrated, with fruit and well-married oak. The wine is well-balanced and stylish with an outstanding flavour. It can be drunk when relatively young yet is a good keeper. The consistency is also unusually good.

Château Laffitte-Carcasset

Cru Bourgeois. Owner: Vicomte Philippe de Padirac. 27ha. 16,500 cases. CS 70%, Mer 29%, PV 1%. Second label: Château La Vicomtesse.

The name is not an attempt to ape the *premier cru classé* but the name of an 18th century owner. The property is well placed, lying just past the *cave coopérative* as one travels north. The wines are carefully made, the emphasis being on finesse, although they also have plenty of body.

Château Lafon-Rochet ★ V →

4e Cru Classé. Owner: Tesseron family. Administration: Michel Tesseron. 40ha. 24,000 cases. CS 55%, Mer 40%, CF 5%. Second label: Les Pelerins de Lafon-Rochet.

Since Guy Tesseron (a Cognac négociant who married into the Cruse family) bought this *cru* in 1960, great efforts have been made to rebuild its reputation. There was much to be done in the vineyard as well as the *chai*, and an entirely new château was built, designed in a suitably traditional mould. It is clearly visible from the road just past Cos d'Estournel on the *route des châteaux*.

For many years, I criticized this *cru* for mean, dry tannins, especially at the finish. This was mainly a problem of too much Cabernet Sauvignon for the soil. The wine first came into balance in my judgment with the '90 – but that was an exceptional year. More impressive were the ripe fruit and fine harmony achieved in more demanding vintages such as '93 and '94. The '95, '96, '98, '99, and 2000 have raised this wine to new heights. On such form, Lafon-Rochet is one of the best buys in St-Estèphe.

Château Lavillotte V

Cru Bourgeois. Owner: Jacques Pedro. 12ha. 5,000 cases. CS 72%, Mer 25%, PV 3%. Second label: Château Aillan.

Jacques Pedro is a perfectionist, and this is reflected in his wines. They are matured in cask, with 30 per cent new oak, and not filtered, so decanting is essential. It tends to be heavily perfumed and rich, with distinctly minty overtones and real intensity. The flavour is fine and speaks of breed and complexity. I particularly like its attack and upfront fruit, yet there is also finesse, with slightly less body than expected.

Château Lilian Ladouys

Cru Bourgeois Supérieur. Owner: Château Lilian Ladouys. 40ha. 20,000 cases. CS 58%, Mer 37%, CF 5%.

When Christian and Lilian Thieblot bought this property in 1989, they transformed a rather run-down member of the cooperative into a *cru bourgeois* worthy of the name.

The vineyard was increased from 20 hectares to 50 by some judicious purchases from neighbours, and a new *cuvier* and *chai* were constructed around the charming *Directoire chartreuse* château, close to Cos. The first vintage to be bottled, '89, is impressively rich and spicy, with plenty of fruit and the character of the year. That and an equally delicious '90 suggest that this is a property of real potential. Unfortunately, the recession and the run of poor vintages in the early 1990s were too much for the new owners, who were obliged to surrender it to the Bank Natexis, which had financed the purchase. But with Georges Pauli (*see* Gruaud-Larose) now consulting here, good wines are still made.

Château de Marbuzet

Cru Bourgeois. Owner: Domaines Prats. 7ha. 3,900 cases. Mer 60%, CS 40%.

The handsome château here is the home of the Prats family, formerly of Cos-d'Estournel. The wine was treated as the second wine of Cos until the '94 vintage, when it became a wine in its own right again. The first vintages have been stylish and fine.

Cave Coopérative Marquis de St-Estèphe

Owner: Société de Vinification de St-Estèphe. 120ha. 77,000 cases. CS 65%, Mer 25%, PV 4%, CF 3%, Mal 3%.

The *cave* here was founded in 1934 by just 42 *viticulteurs*. Now there are 85 members, and this is one of the most up-to-date and best-run cooperatives in the Médoc, or indeed the Gironde. But in recent years it has been losing numbers, and its production has fallen as more *vignerons* decided to make and sell their own wines.

Only grapes from the St-Estèphe appellation are received here. Apart from the wine sold under its own *marque* of Marquis de St-Estèphe, the wines of a number of other important properties are kept separately and bottled *à la propriété* to be sold under their own names.

Château Meyney V

Cru Bourgeois Supérieur. Owner: Domaines Cordier. 51ha. 29,000 cases. CS 67%, Mer 25%, CF 5%, PV 3%. Second label: Prieur du Château Meyney.

St-Émilion abounds with old ecclesiastical buildings or their remains, but they are rare in Médoc, and Meyney certainly has the best-preserved example. The present buildings, finely situated on a ridge with views across the Gironde, date from 1662–6. The courtyard still has a rather monastic atmosphere. Until recently, the old name "Prieuré des Couleys" appeared on the label.

The wines balance fruit and tannin judiciously; they are quite dense in texture and strong but always juicy in flavour. I find that they are normally at their best when on the young side, and that although they seem to have the structure for ageing, if kept too long they dry up and acquire a bitter finish. But consistency has been the key here over many years. This is clearly one of the leading non-classified wines of St-Estèphe, in my judgment just behind de Pez and Phélan-Ségur as it lacks a little in breed.

Château Montrose ★★

2e Cru Classé. Owner: Jean-Louis Charmolüe. 68ha. 37,000 cases. CS 65%, Mer 25%, CF 10%. Second label: La Dame de Montrose V.

Disappointingly for the Scots, the name has no Scottish affiliation but refers to the old name for this vineyard, the "rose-coloured hill". This is the most recently planted of all the great *crus classés*, developed from completely uncultivated land, formerly part of Calon-Ségur, at the beginning of the 19th century. Like the neighbouring Meyney, it commands fine views of the Gironde from its ridge nearby. Montrose has belonged to the Charmolüe family since 1896 and is meticulously run. The present owner, Jean-Louis Charmolüe, is a resident working proprietor, like his much-respected mother before him. For the 2000 vintage, a new stainless-steel *cuvier* was used for the first time, but the old wooden vats have been preserved.

I have always admired Montrose in cask. Although it is less marked by Cabernet Sauvignon than it used to be, it has a lovely, clean, crisp, tannin flavour with new oak, tannin and fruit well matched. But this is not a wine to hurry over, and plenty of patience is required. As for vintages, the '81 is especially impressive, with its nice touch of sweetness over powerful tannins; '82 is fine but in no way outstanding, and '83 needs drinking. The benefits of a more severe selection after the high yields of '82 and '83 are evident, beginning with '84, which was exceptional for this vintage with its scented fruit and rich, supple flavour. The '85 is a beauty; '86 has a glorious cedar-like scent and beautiful flavour and balance; '88 is still closed; '89 less dense, with unctuous fruit and '90 even richer and finer with its lovely sweetness – one of the great wines of this great vintage. The '91 is one of the few outstanding wines of its year, thanks to a largely frost-free vineyard; '92, '93, '94, '95, '96, '98, '99, and 2000 are all among the leading wines of these vintages. Montrose has clearly moved up a notch in the last decade, and should now be regarded as one of the "Super Seconds".

Château Morin

Cru Bourgeois. Owners: Marguerite and Maxime Sidaine.
10ha. 6,000 cases. CS 48%, Mer 50%, PV 2%.

This *cru*, just outside St-Corbian in the appellation's northern sector, has been in the same family for several generations. It still uses a delightful old label, distinctly 19th century in appearance, and the property is run n traditional lines. The strongly flavoured wines are reasonably supple and of good repute.

Château Les-Ormes-de-Pez V

Cru Bourgeois Exceptionnel. Owner: Cazes family. Administrator: Jean Michel Cazes. 32ha. 15,000 cases. CS 55%, Mer 35%, CF 10%.

The great gift for winemaking that the Cazes family has brought to Lynch-Bages is also evident here. I have been agreeably surprised over the years by the consistently attractive wines. Even in difficult years they are usually supple and fruity, quite without the leanness or austerity of many St-Estèphes. In 1981, new stainless-steel fermentation vats were installed and a new ageing *chai* constructed. Previously the wines had been kept at Lynch-Bages.

The wines have plenty of concentration but are well-balanced, with suppleness, fruit, and plenty of character. Very good wines were made in '82 (especially rich), '83, '85, '86, '88, '89, '90, '96, '98, '99, and 2000. While Ormes-de-Pez sometimes lacks the breed of neighbouring de Pez, it seldom disappoints, which makes it one of the best and most reliable of St-Estèphe's *crus bourgeois*.

Château de Pez ★ V

Cru Bourgeois Exceptionnel. Owner: Champagne Louis Roederer. 24.1ha. 11,500 cases. CS 45%, CF 44%, Mer 8%, PV3%.

The grand, twin-turreted château of this old property is clearly visible from the *route des châteaux* as it winds its way throught the hamlet, just to the west of St-Estèphe. When Robert Dousson took over the management here for his aunt in 1955, the reputation of this *cru* grew, and it was regarded as the best non-classified *cru* in the commune. But then, in the late 1980s, things seemed to slip, and Phélan-Ségur overtook de Pez in reputation and consistency of quality. Then, in 1995, Louis Roederer bought the property, since when steady progress has restored Château de Pez to its position as a leading *cru* in the AC. The quality that de Pez has, and which is missing in most other *crus bourgeois* of the commune, is breed. This comes out clearly in blind tastings. There is an attractive spiciness on the nose, together with elegance, charm, and a lot of fruit, while the flavour has good concentration and richness, with breed and balance. Some years can be a little lean, but the balance is preserved. Under the new ownership there was a good '95, '96 is exceptional, then fine '98, '99, and 2000.

Château Phélan-Ségur ★ V

Cru Bourgeois Exceptionnel. Owner: Château Phélan-Ségur (President: Xavier Gardinier). 64ha. 40,000 cases. CS 60%, Mer 35%, CF 5%.
Second label: Franck Phélan. 8,330 cases.

As with neighbours Meyney and Montrose, this is a château you will not see from the *route des châteaux*. The handsome building is on the southern edge of St-Estèphe village, on high ground with a fine view across the river. There is a massive *chai*. In 1985, the Delon family, who had owned the property since 1924, sold to Xavier Gardinier, the former president director-general of Champagne Pommery.

At its best, this *cru* can make fine, long-lasting wines that are rich and supple, with complexity and breeding. In the latter days of the Delon ownership, some poor wines were produced. In 1987, Xavier Gardinier impressed Bordeaux by announcing that he would take back all the '83 vintage and was not going to sell the '84 or '85 under the château label. Then, starting work with a clean slate, the château proceeded to make an excellent '87 (in the context of that year), followed by impressive wines in '88, '89, and '90, while '92 and '93 are well above-average for these vintages. The '94 and '95 are good, the '96 excellent. Very good wines were made in '98 and 2000. Phélan is once again challenging as one of the best unclassified wines of St-Estèphe.

Château Picard

Cru Bourgeois. Owner: Mähler-Besse. 8ha. 5,000 cases. CS 85%, Mer 15%. Second label: Les Ailes de Picard.

This property was bought by Mähler-Besse in '97. Thirty per cent new oak is being used to make very attractive wines with nice, sweet fruit and richness.

Château Pomys

Cru Bourgeois. Owner: SARL Arnaud. 12ha. 8,000 cases. CS 50%, Mer 35%, CF 15%.

The picturesque château is now under separate ownership. The wines, however, often seen in England, are reliable, attractive and well-balanced.

Château Ségur de Cabanac →

Cru Bourgeois. Owner: Guy Delon. 7.1ha. 3,900 cases. CS 60%, Mer 30%, CF and PV 10%.

Guy Delon, whose family were the former owners of Phélan-Ségur, bought this property in 1985. It is made up of as many as 12 small parcels of vines with neighbours such as Calon-Ségur, Phélan-Ségur, and Meyney. The new *chai* and *cuvier* are down at the port of St-Estèphe. The '96 is a high-class wine with rich fruit and quality tannins in good harmony, while 2001 is one of the best wines in St-Estèphe.

Château Tour de Pez

Cru Bourgeois Supérieur. Owner: Tour de Pez. 30ha. 16,500 cases. CS 45%, Mer 40%, CF 10%, PV5%.

It seems likely that some parts of the vineyard were once part of Château de Pez. There are parcels in Leyssac and Aillan, as well as on gravelly slopes adjoining Calon-Ségur and Montrose. Since the present owners bought the property in 1989, there have been heavy investments. I found the '96 had sweet fruit, length and elegance, a wine of real quality. Definitely a name to look for.

Château Tour-des-Termes

Cru Bourgeois. Owner: Jean Anney. 15ha. 7,500 cases. CS 45%, Mer 50%, PV 5%.

A good-sized property situated near the village of St-Corbian in the north of the appellation. The wines I have come across are robust with plenty of character, but also supple and quite fine. They are aged in cask.

Château Tronquoy-Lalande →

Cru Bourgeois Supérieur. Owner: Arlette Castéja-Texier. 17ha. 10,000 cases. Mer 45%, CS 45%, PV 10%. Second label: Château Tronquoy de Ste-Anne.

I have always been attracted by the charming château with its two distinctive towers at each end of a *chartreuse*-style building. Lalande is the place, Tronquoy the name of an early 19th century owner. This is now a carefully managed property, for which Dourthe has exclusive distribution rights and provides technical assistance. The wines are matured partly in *cuve* and partly in wood, and were inclined to be tough and rustic when young, but since the '96, they are much more balanced and attractive.

HAUT-MÉDOC

The decline that this area suffered in the years of depression has been triumphantly reversed. The area under vine nearly doubled between 1973 and 1988, which is remarkable enough; between 1988 and 2000 there was a further 26 per cent increase. This is *par excellence* the area of the *crus bourgeois*, which here account for 62 per cent of the area in production and cover a greater area than in any other part of Médoc. Wines are produced in 15 diverse communes but in only ten of these are more than 100 hectares planted. The most important are St-Seurin, St-Laurent, Cussac, St-Sauveur, Cissac, and Vertheuil. The styles of wine vary considerably, with the largest-producing northern communes making robust, full-flavoured wines, and softer, lighter ones being made in the south.

Château d'Agassac ➜

Cru Bourgeois Supérieur. Owner: Groupama. 38ha. 20,000 cases. CS 47%, Mer 50%, CF 3%.

This is one of the few remaining examples of a genuine medieval fortress to survive in the Médoc. It is also the most important *cru* in Ludon, after La Lagune. After Philippe Gasqueton (*see* Calon-Ségur, Capbern, du Tertre) took over 30 years ago, marked improvements were made and the reputation of the wine was much enhanced. After his death it was sold to the present owners in 1996. The wine has marked and attractive individuality; it is vividly perfumed, with a special fruitiness and pronounced flavour. The '98 showed a marked improvement and 2000 is excellent, so watch this space.

Château Aney

Cru Bourgeois. Owner: Raimond family. 20ha. 13,000 cases. CS 55%, Mer 30%, CF 10%, PV 5%.

If you are driving through Cussac-Fort-Médoc, you cannot miss this *cru*, it is right on the road. The '96 has very solid, supple tannins and pleasing fruit and 2000 also shows lovely, spicy fruit.

Château d'Arche

Cru Bourgeois Supérieur. Owner: Mähler-Besse. 9ha. 5,500 cases. CS 45%, Mer 40%, CF 10%, PV 5%. Second label: Ch Egmont Lagrive.

The vineyard is in a single piece, adjoining La Lagune. Fifty per cent new oak. The wines are classically moulded Médocs with good fruit and some elegance.

Château d'Arcins

Cru Bourgeois. Owner: SC du Château d'Arcins. 97ha. 55,000 cases. CS 55%, Mer 40%, CF 5%. Second label: Tour de Mayne.

Castel Frères is the largest shareholder in the company running Château d'Arcins. It has in recent years invested much in the development of this property, which is the largest in its commune. The wines have many of the qualities that are also evident in the neighbouring growths of Margaux and Moulis, and are sold mostly in the north of France.

Château Arnauld

Cru Bourgeois Supérieur. Owners: M et Mme Maurice Roggy. 27ha. 11,000 cases. CS 60%, Mer 40%. Second label: Château Chambore.

Originally a priory, this property is the best in Arcins. It was bought by the Roggy family in 1956. The vineyards were replanted, and improvements in vinification followed the marriage of one of the Roggy daughters to François Theil of Château Poujeaux. The '97 is delicious, the '96 and '98 are rich and solid. A wine to look out for.

Château d'Arsac

See page 50.

Château d'Aurilhac

Cru Bourgeois. Owner: Erik Nieuwaal. 16ha. 11,000 cases. CS 56%, Mer 38%, CF 3%, PV 3%.

This is very much a newcomer. The vineyard, the most westerly of St-Seurin de Cadourne, was only planted in the late '80s. The '96 is very new-oak-influenced, the 50 per cent is probably too high for young vines, but with massively rich, ripe tannins, and more like Châteauneuf-du-Pape than Médoc with its amazing 13.5° alcohol. The '99 is fruity and delicious. It is very attractive in its new-wave way. Obviously this is another wine to watch.

Château Barreyres

Cru Bourgeois. Owner: SC du Château Barreyres. 109ha. 38,000 cases. CS 50%, Mer 50%. Second label: Tour Bellevue.

Castel Frères has, as at Château d'Arcins, invested much in this property, completing a new *cuvier* and *chai* in 1981 to enable improved vinification of this château's large output. The wines are attractive, with pleasant fruit character, but can be slightly coarse.

Château Beaumont V

Cru Bourgeois Supérieur. Owner: Grands Millésimes de France. Administrator: Philippe Blanc. 105ha. 66,700 cases. CS 60%, Mer 35%, CF 2%, PV 3%. Second labels: Châteaux Moulin d'Arvigny and Les Tours-de-Beaumont.

In marked contrast to those of their neighbour, Tour du Haut Moulin, the wines of Beaumont tend to be light, fruity, and ready to drink early. They are perfumed, with well-integrated new oak, tannin, and fruit, combining to make a harmonious whole, most attractively flavoured. The ownership here is the same as at Beychevelle (*see* page 66). The second wines, designed for early drinking, are a selection of about 25 per cent of the production, mostly from young vines.

Château Bel Air

Cru Bourgeois. Owner: Héritiers d'Henri Martin. 37ha. 20,000 cases. CS 65%, Mer 35%.

Henri Martin – owner of Château Gloria and one of the Médoc's greatest personalities until his death in 1991 – bought this property in 1980. It is now managed by the highly capable Jean-Louis Triaud, Martin's son-in-law, who coordinates Bel Air's three separate vineyards. These are dense-textured wines, with fruit and a good perfume. They are certainly wines to watch for.

Château Belgrave V →

5e Cru Classé. Owner: GFA. Administrator: Jacques Begarie. 57ha. 30,000 cases. CS 55%, Mer 32%, CF 12%, PV 1%. Second label: Diane de Belgrave.

Until the CVBG group (Dourthe-Kressman) bought this property in 1979, it had suffered from under-investment and neglect for decades. Consequently, the wine's reputation was negligible. The vineyard, however, was well situated on gravelly ridges behind Lagrange, and has good potential. The new owners carried out improvements to the *chai* and 40–60 per cent new casks are used for maturation. After extensive investment in the *chai* and *cuvier* a new phase began in '86 with Professor Alain Reynier in the vineyard and Michel Rolland as winemaker. The improvement in the wine is considerable; the coarse tannins have now been banished making for more friendly wines.

Château Bel-Orme-Tronquoy-de-Lalande →

Cru Bourgeois. Owner: Jean-Michel Quié. Administrator: Jean-Louis Camp.
28ha. 15,500 cases. Mer 55%, CS 35%, CF 10%.

Not to be confused with Tronquoy-Lalande in nearby St-Estèphe, this
property once belonged to the Tronquoy family. The words *bel orme* mean
"beautiful elm". The wines are powerful, solid and traditional, and they last
marvellously, as was proven by some bottles from the 1920s that I sampled.
The wines have benefited from Jean-Louis Camp's improvements and the
'96 is a big mouthful of wine with ripe tannins promising a long evolution.

Château Bernadotte V →

Owner: Mme May-Eliane de Lencquesaing. 30ha. 16,000 cases. CS 62%,
Mer 36%, CF/PV 2%. Second label: Château Fournas-Bernadotte.

This property straddles the boundary between Pauillac and St-Sauveur. When
the new owner, who also owns Château Pichon-Longueville Comtesse-de-
Lalande bought it in 1996, it was decided that only the Haut-Médoc portion of
the vineyard should carry the name of Bernadotte. The vineyard adjoins that
of Liversan. The wines have real quality, with rich tannins and expansive fruit.
The '96 was already impressive, while the '97 was above average for the year,
and the '98 has delicious fruit and harmony. A wine to watch and follow.

Château Le Bourdieu-Vertheuil

Cru Bourgeois. Owner: Richard family. 44ha. 19,000 cases. CS 60%, Mer 25%,
CF 10%, PV 5%. Second labels: Châteaux Victoria and Picourneau.

This is probably the best-reputed *cru* in Vertheuil today; the vineyards run from
the village of that name to the boundary with St-Estèphe. The wine is matured
in cask and well reflects the careful winemaking, the results of which combine
robustness with finesse. The style is typical of a good, lush St-Estèphe.

Château du Breuil

Cru Bourgeois. Owner: Vialard family. 25ha. 15,000 cases. Mer 34%,
CS 28%, CF 23%, PV 11%, Mal 4%. Second label: Château Moulin du Breuil.

The oldest recorded property in the Médoc, with records traceable through
the barony of Breuil back to the sixth century. The château is a medieval
fortress, inhabited until 1861 but now sadly deteriorated, though still majestic.
The current owners are the Vialard family (*see* Château Cissac), who
acquired the property in 1987; the *chai* and *cuvier* were in a run-down state
at this stage and needed much care and attention. Although some
respectable wines were made before this, under the Vialards the situation
has been transformed. Since '88 (the second vintage under the new
management), the wines have provided an interesting contrast to Cissac.

Château Cambon-la-Pelouse V →

Cru Bourgeois Supérieur. Owner: Jean-Pierre Marie. 60ha. 33,000 cases.
Mer 50%, CS 30%, CF 20%. Second label: Château Trois Moulins.

In 1996, Jean-Pierre Marie took over the lease from the Carrère family. The
wines now see wood with 30 per cent new oak and have been winning many
plaudits. The easy fruitiness is still there, but there is more body and substance.

Château de Camensac V

5e Cru Classé. Owner: Forner family. 75ha. 29,000 cases. CS 60%, Mer 40%.
Second label: La Closerie de Camensac.

Like the other *crus classés* of St-Laurent, Camensac had sunk into a state of
complete obscurity and neglect when it was rescued by the Forner brothers
in 1965. Of Spanish origins (they produce a fine Rioja) and new to Bordeaux,
they sought the help of Professor Émile Peynaud in rebuilding this *cru*.

Much of the vineyard had to be replanted, and the *chai* and *cuvier* completely modernized and re-equipped. In the 1980s, the wines seem to have a strong, coarse flavour, even when, as with the '82, there is a lot of richness and ripeness. Wines seem too extracted and heavily oaked for their weight. But '95 was an improvement: good wine made within its limitations.

Château Cantemerle ★ V

5e Cru Classé. Owner: Société Assurance Mutuelles du Bâtiment et Travaux Publics. Administrator: Philippe Dambrine. 87ha. 55,000 cases. Mer 40%, CS 50%, CF 5%, PV 5%. Second label: Villeneuve de Cantemerle.

This famous old property, after a period of decline, has now been rapidly restored to its former glory. It achieved a great and deserved reputation when Pierre Dubos was proprietor, a regime which lasted over 50 years and corresponded roughly with the first half of this century. Then came the division among a number of heirs – a constant problem in France – and the result was a lack of money and direction, so decline and decay set in.

The turning point for Cantemerle came in 1980 with the sale to a syndicate of which Domaines Cordier was part. The *cuvier* and *chai* were modernized, with stainless-steel fermentation vats taking the place of the old wooden ones. The style of Cantemerle leans towards lightness and elegance combined with good richness in the middle flavour. With the *cuvier* being rebuilt at the time, I found the first vintage of the new regime disappointing and dull. The '81 was better but not special, but then in '82, '83, and '85 superb wines were made, with an opulence and richness encountered only in exceptional years. Unfortunately, the '86 crop suffered from the effects of hail. Then, after a great and flattering '88, '89, and '90 are rich, opulent wines. Good wines were also made in '94, '95, '96, '98, '99, and 2000.

Canterayne

Owner: Cave Coopérative de St-Sauveur. 57ha. 35,000 cases.
CS 70%, Mer 25%, CF, Mal and PV 5%.

There are 69 members of this cooperative, which was founded in 1934. It produces wines that are well-made and express the firmness and solidity characteristic of the region.

Château Caronne-Ste-Gemme V

Cru Bourgeois Supérieur. Owners: Jean Nony-Borie. 45ha. 20,000 cases. CS 65%, Mer 33%, PV 2%. Second label: Château Labat.

This good *cru* is deservedly becoming much better known since the early 1980s. The family has owned the property since 1900. The vineyards are separated from Camensac and the rest of St-Laurent by the Jalle du Nord, which divides St-Julien from Cussac, and the nearest vineyard is Lanessan in Cussac, so their situation is rather special.

My overall impression of the wines here is that they are well-made, have more style and breed than most St-Laurent wines, with nothing rustic about them. But a strong assertive character comes through clearly, nicely balanced with fruit, and resulting in some complexity. The '96 has all these qualities. This is really a top *cru bourgeois*, with excellent keeping qualities, and consistency.

Château Charmail V →

Cru Bourgeois Supérieur. Owner: Olivier Sèze. 22ha. 14,000 cases. Mer 48%, CS 30%, CF 20%, PV 2%.

This property is excellently situated on the gravelly ridges of St-Seurin-de-Cadourne, near to the river. It was bought and restored in the 1970s by a Burgundian, Monsieur Laly. Roger Sèze, owner of Château Mayne-Vieil, took over in the early 1980s and the family is now producing rich, supple, and charming wines, likely to improve as the vineyards mature. The '96 was more concentrated, and consistently attractive and fruity wines have been made since. A wine with with a rising reputation.

Châtelleine

Owner: Cave Coopérative de Vertheuil. 66.7ha. 40,000 cases. CS 50%, Mer 50%.

The total annual output of the 70 members of this cooperative is 7,000 hectolitres. They are solid wines of good quality, some of which are marketed under their own château labels: Châteaux Ferré Portal and Julian.

Château Cissac

Cru Bourgeois Supérieur. Owner: Vialard family. 50ha. 30,000 cases.
CS 75%, Mer 20%, PV 5%. Second label: Reflets du Château Cissac.

Cissac has been inseparably linked for over a generation with Louis Vialard, who comes from an old Médocain family. The family has owned Cissac since 1885, and Louis Vialard has lived here since 1940. Extensive modernization has been carried out, and traditional methods – old vines, wooden fermenting vats and oak ageing casks (of which 50 per cent are normally new) – have been supplemented with new vats of stainless steel. There are no concessions to modern tastes here. The wines are still austere and the tannins unyielding. They certainly need to be kept a long time.

Château Citran

Cru Bourgeois Supérieur. Owner: Groupe Bernard Taillan. 90ha. 55,000 cases.
CS 58%, Mer 42%. Second label: Moulins de Citran.

This is the most important *cru* in Avensan. Part of the vineyard lies close to the village, but the oldest part is between the château and Paveil-de-Luze. When the Miailhe family bought the property in 1945, there was hardly any vineyard left. Jean Miailhe of Château Coufran ran the property until 1980. He expanded the vineyards and established a fine reputation for the wine. He then handed over to his sister and brother-in-law, who sold to the Japanese company Fujimoto in 1986. In 1997, Fujimoto sold to the present owners (*see* Chasse-Spleen, page 60).

The wines now have a good reputation and I have found them to have an excellent bouquet with pronounced fruit. They have a good flavour and balance with a certain earthiness. From 1979 until the sale in 1996, they were less consistent: dilute and dry in large vintages. But the first efforts under the new regime, '88, '89, and '90, together with an attractive new label, were most rewarding. Good wines were made in '94, '95, '96, '97, '98, and 2000.

Château Clément-Pichon

Cru Bourgeois Supérieur. Owner: Clément Fayat. 25ha. 13,000 cases. CS 50%,
CF 10%, Mer 40%.

Originally called Château Parempuyre, this property was owned by the Pichons until 1880. The subsequent owners built the flamboyant château that stands there today – similar in style to Châteaux Lanessan and Fonréaud, by the same architect. Clément Fayat (who changed the name) has invested in replanting and creating a new drainage system in the vineyards. The *chai* has been similarly modernized and new vats have been installed, enabling computer-controlled fermentation. The vineyards need more time to mature but the wines are already pleasant, if light.

Château Coufran V

Cru Bourgeois Supérieur. Owner: SC du Château. Administrator: Jean Miailhe.
75ha. 45,000 acres. Mer 85%, CS 15%. Second label: Château La Rose Maréchale.

The high proportion of Merlot here is unusual for the Médoc, even on these heavier soils. The result is an easy, supple, fruity wine for early drinking that does especially well in good years, but can be light in lesser ones. This is good commercial claret, however, and fulfils its declared purpose of producing easy-to-enjoy Médoc available at a reasonable price.

Château Dillon

Cru Bourgeois. Owner: Lycée Agricole de Bordeaux-Blanquefort. 35ha. 20,000 cases. Red: CS 50%, Mer 39%, CF 5%, PV 5%, Carmenère 1%. White: 25,000 cases. Sauv 80%, Sém 15%, Musc 5%. Second label: Château Linas (Bordeaux Blanc) 5ha.

This *cru* takes its name from an *émigré* Irishman who acquired the property in 1754. It has belonged to the Lycée Agricole since 1956, which has made improvements in the *cuvier* in order to carry out temperature-controlled fermentation. At their best, the wines produced here are light and elegantly flavoured, but there have been lapses in consistency. Some good wines were made in the 1970s. Since then an extension of the vineyard was added and little or no selection practised: the wines have therefore taken a step backwards in quality. The 2000 may mark an improvement.

Château Fontesteau

Cru Bourgeois. Owners: Christophe Barron and Dominique Fouin. 23ha. 13,000 cases. CS 45%, Mer 30%, CF 22%, PV 3%. Second label: Château Messine de Fontest.

The name comes from *fontaines d'eau*, because there are a number of old wells on this St-Sauveur property. The wines are made traditionally (fermentation in concrete vats, ageing in casks), and tend to be tough and tannic.

Château Grandis

Cru Bourgeois. Owner: GHF du Château Grandis. 9.6ha. 4,500 cases. CS 50%, Mer 40%, CF 10%. Second label: Aurac-Major.

Grandis was bought in 1857 by Armand Figerou and has remained in the family; today it is run by his descendant, François Vergez. The wines have the solidity typical of St-Seurin-de-Cadourne and are traditionally made. A ripe, powerful wine that repays keeping.

Château Hanteillan

Cru Bourgeois Supérieur. Owner: SARL du Château Hanteillan. Administrator: Catherine Blasco. 82ha. 50,000 cases. CS 50%, Mer 41%, CF 5%, PV 4%. Second label: Château Laborde.

In 1972, this property was bought by a group of partners connected to France's largest construction company. It used to share the same owners as Château Coutelin-Merville in St-Estèphe, and the vineyards adjoin one another. Despite Coutelin-Merville's superior appellation, I have found that Hanteillan today makes a more impressive wine. The high proportion of Merlot grown reflects the clay present in parts of the vineyard. This is a serious wine with some real breed and should be followed with interest as the vineyard matures.

Château Haut-Logat

Owner: Marcel and Christian Quancard. 16ha. 10,000 cases. CS 60%, Mer 30%, CF 10%. Second wine: Ch La Croix Margautot.

This good *cru* in Cissac is owned by the members of the family négociants Cheval Quancard, and is located close to their neighbouring property at Château Tour St-Joseph, which, however, has more Cabernet Sauvignon. I found the '96 to have fruit and charm, along with a distinct style and moderate body.

Château Haut-Madrac

Cru Bourgeois. Owner: Castéja family. 20ha. 12,000 cases. CS 75%, Mer 25%.
Bought by Émile Castéja's father in 1919, this St-Sauveur property adjoins the family's other property in Pauillac (Lynch-Moussas). It produces wines that are well-made, charming, and good for early drinking. Typically, these wines have light, fresh, and fruity characteristics.

Château La Lagune ★ V →

3e Cru Classé. Owner: SC Agricole. Administrator: Thierry Budin. 70ha.
38,900 cases. CS 60%, Mer 20%, CF 10%, PV 10%. Second label: Château
Ludon-Pomiès-Agassac (changing to Moulin de La Lagune for the '98).
The restoration of La Lagune began when it was bought by Georges Brunet in 1957. This dynamic man replanted the vineyard and reconstructed the *chai.* He installed a marvellous system of stainless-steel pipes to bring the new wine straight from the vats to the barrels and also to carry out racking mechanically and without contact with the air. It was a revolutionary system when installed over 30 years ago, but no one else has yet copied it at present.

Burnet undertook many costly improvements within a short time and as a result, ran short of money so had to sell in 1961, having made the mistake of selling that great year *sur souche* (on the vine, before the harvest). La Lagune was bought by Champagne Ayala for whom Thierry Budin is the administrator while Patrick Moulin is director, or *régisseur* to use the old terminology.

Now the vineyard has come of age, a series of splendid wines has given La Lagune an enviable reputation. It is extremely reliable and excellent value. This is a wine of great elegance; perfumed, usually rather marked by new wood at the start (100 per cent new wood was usual here but now reduced to 80 per cent) but this is soon absorbed to give a rich, supple flavour with great finesse. Since 1993, there has been more serious selection, with 25 per cent set aside for the second wine in '95 and '96, 30 per cent in '97, and around 50 per cent since the '98 vintage. As a result, the wines seem richer in cask and have better weight and harmony.

Château de Lamarque

Cru Bourgeois Supérieur. Owner: SC Gromand d'Évry. Administrator: Pierre-Gilles Gromand. 36ha. 16,000 cases. CS 46%, Mer 25%, CF 24%, PV 5%.
Second label: D de Lamarque.
The château here is the best-preserved and most impressive fortress in the Médoc of those that survive from the English period in Aquitaine. Although parts of it date from the 11th and 12th centuries, the main structure is 14th-century with some 17th century alterations. It lies between the *route des châteaux* and the ferry to Blaye, but is well-concealed amid the trees of its park.

Ownership of the château has passed through inheritance since 1841, when it was acquired by the Comte de Fumel, passing via a daughter to the present owner, Marie-Louise Burnet d'Évry, who married Roger Gromand, father of Pierre-Gilles. The wine is matured in casks, 33 per cent of which are new each year. In the 1970s, I found the wines light and agreeable in good vintages but without much personality. Then, in the 1980s and '90s, they filled out, becoming more powerful and much richer, albeit with a certain coarseness.

Château Lamothe-Bergeron

Cru Bourgeois Supérieur. Owner: SC Grand-Puy-Ducasse.
67ha. 17,500 cases. CS 44%, Mer 49%, CF 7%.
The name Lamothe-Bergeron comes from the word *motte* (a piece of high ground) and from the name of a previous owner of the château. This *cru* has

a reputation for producing well-made, reliable, and reasonably priced wines. Particularly attractive vintages were the '82, '85, '86, and '87; the '88 and '89 were even better.

Château Lamothe-Cissac V →

Cru Bourgeois. Owner: SC du Château Lamothe. Administrator: Vincent Fabre. 33ha. 18,000 cases. CS 70%, Mer 26%, PV 4%.

An old property: it was a *maison noble* in the 17th century and evidence of Roman occupation has also been found here. The château itself does not share this history and was built comparatively recently, in 1912. Lamothe-Cissac was bought by the Fabre family in 1964 in an extremely run-down state. Since then, a new *cuvier, chai,* and underground cellar have been built. Twenty per cent new oak is used each year for maturation, and as the vineyards develop, some impressive wines are emerging. The wines are stylish, with solidity and fruit. They are mostly sold direct, not via Bordeaux négociants.

Château Landat

Cru Bourgeois. Owners: Domaines Fabre. 20ha. 10,500 cases. CS 75%, Mer 20%, PV 5%. Second label: Château Laride.

Bought by the Fabre family of nearby Lamothe-Cissac in 1976, where they are now making rich, solid wines that also manage to emphasize the quality of the fruit, in a vintage such as 2000. Twenty per cent new oak is used and the quality is on a par with Lamothe-Cissac.

Château Lanessan ★ V

Cru Bourgeois Supérieur. Owner: Bouteiller family. Administrator: Hubert Bouteiller. 40ha. 17,700 cases. CS 75%, Mer 20%, PV 4%, CF 1%. Second label: Domaine de Ste-Gemme.

Since 1790, this property has been effectively in the same family, the Delbos, whose name still appears on the label alongside that of Bouteiller. It was handed from father to son until 1909, when the daughter of the last male Delbos inherited. She married Étienne Bouteiller. Hubert Bouteiller, the present member of the family in charge, has his home here. A feature of Lanessan unrelated to wine is the carriage museum, where the stables and harness room are displayed with a fine assortment of carriages.

The wines of Lanessan have a marked personality. There is a tendency to firmness at first, but in good years, the wines have marvellous fruit and richness and considerable breed. They are also consistent. There is a great capacity for ageing. I have tasted a number of old vintages going back to 1916, all of them well-preserved and many outstanding. Recently '81, '82, '85, '86, '87, '88, '89, '90, '95, '96, '98, and 2000 were all excellent examples. This is a wine for those who love fine Médocs for their own sake and are not slaves to labels.

Château Larose-Trintaudon

Cru Bourgeois Supérieur. Owner: Assurances Générales de France. Administrator: Jean Matouk. 175ha. 107,000 cases. CS 65%, Mer 30%, CF 5%. Second label: (since '90) Larose St-Laurent. Château Larose Perganson, Cru Bourgeois (for hand harvested old vines).

Bought and developed by the Forner family in the 1960s, this is now the largest vineyard in the Médoc. Élisée Forner continued as administrator until the autumn of 1988, when the new owner's management team took over. Franck Bijon came from Latour in April 1989 to become technical manager, with Mattheas von Campe joining as marketing manager in September. Mechanical harvesting is used, but all the wines are matured in casks, of which 30 per cent are new each year.

The new director is making clear improvements in the wines with more selection. The '90 is the best wine yet: its velvety texture fills the mouth and shows the potential of this *cru*. The Médoc's largest vineyard seems to have found its way. In 1996, between 12 and 15 per cent of the older vines were hand-harvested and sold as Larose Perganson. The contrast in quality is marked.

Château Lestage-Simon

Cru Bourgeois Supérieur. Owner: Charles Simon. 40ha. 26,000 cases. Mer 68%, CS 27%, CF 5%.

The wines here are typical of St-Seurin: fine, robust and solid, with the Merlot giving fruit and suppleness. I was once given a bottle of the '29 by a former proprietor, and I found it had kept splendidly. In the 1980s, wines were made for earlier drinking but were none the worse for that. They are widely distributed in good restaurants in France. There is an attractive, well-balanced '95. I found the very concentrated '96 oaky, but in '99 they got it right.

Château Liversan

Cru Bourgeois Supérieur. Owner: Domaines Lapalu. Administrator: Patrice Ricard. 40ha. 25,000 cases. CS 49%, Mer 38%, CF 10%, PV 3%.
Second label: Les Charmes de Liversan.

In 1983, Liversan was bought by the Polignacs, formerly the principal shareholders of Champagne Pommery, but following the death of Prince Guy de Polignac in 1996, the family sold to the owners of Patache d'Aux. The Polignacs' first move upon purchase was to install a new *cuvier* with stainless-steel fermentation vats.

The wines are now to be aged in oak with a good proportion of new wood. Excellent wines were made by the Polignacs following considerable investment. The sumptuous '96 is unfiltered, but since then, the wines have less richness and concentration.

Château Magnol

Cru Bourgeois. Owner: Barton & Guestier. 17ha. 7,200 cases. Mer 55%, CS 45%.
Most of the vineyards at this château were planted within the last 40 years. Vinification is carried out with much care, using modern temperature-controlled stainless steel vats and producing wines that are full-flavoured, rich and supple. Wines to be drunk young.

Château Malescasse V

Cru Bourgeois Supérieur. Owner: La Société Alcatel Alsthom. Administrator: Jean-Pierre Petroffe. 37ha. 22,000 cases. CS 55%, Mer 35%, CF 10%.
Second wine: La Closerie de Malescasse.

A charming, high-roofed château, dating from 1824, overlooks this property, which is on the gravelly ridges of the commune of Lamarque. Its vineyards are some of the best in the area between Margaux and St-Julien. During the inter-war recession, the area under vine had dwindled to only four hectares. A programme of replanting started in 1970 and was completed in 1992. In 1992, Alcatel bought the property from the Tesserons of Pontet-Canet.

The style and solidity of these wines is particularly impressive for a vineyard that is not yet fully mature; the recent vintages are all of a high standard, and sold at modest prices. A *cru* proving to be one of the appellation's best buys.

Château de Malleret V →

Cru Bourgeois Supérieur. Owner: SC du Château (Marquis du Vivier Family). 38ha. 20,800 cases. CS 65%, Mer 30%, CF 3%, PV 2%.
Second label: Châteaux Barthez and de Nexon, Domaine de l'Ermitage Lamouroux.
These wines are extremely scented and elegant, fruity with real length of

flavour and a quite seductive charm. Consistently attractive wines are made here, which have been winning gold medals at tastings.

Château Maucamps
Cru Bourgeois Supérieur. Owner: Tessandier family. 30ha. 9,000 cases. CS 50%, Mer 40%, PV 10%.

This young vineyard in Macau is beginning to produce attractively fruity wines which began to take on more substance with the '98 vintage. They are sold direct by the owners' Ambrosia négociant firm as well as Sotebi.

Château Le Meynieu
Cru Bourgeois. Owner: Jacques Pédro. 19ha. 9,000 cases. CS 62%, Mer 30%, CF 8%. Second label: Château La Chône.

The energetic, meticulous Jacques Pédro is mayor of Vertheuil as well as proprietor of this *cru* and those of Lavillotte and Domaine de la Ronceray. His aim is to make typical Médocs with supple fruit, delicious for early drinking.

Château Meyre
Cru Bourgeois. Owner: Corinne Bonne. 17ha. 10,500 cases. CS 45%, Mer 30%, CF 15%, PV 10%.

This Avensan vineyard has a history going back over three centuries. It was bought by its present owner in 1998. After a good, solid '96, 2000 showed greatly improved fruit quality. A *cru* to watch.

Château du Moulin Rouge
Cru Bourgeois. Owners: Ribeiro and Pelon families. 16ha. 10,000 cases. Mer 50%, CS 45%, CF 5%. Second wine: Ch Tour de Courtebotte.

This well-known *cru* in Cissac makes rich, powerful, dense-textured wines which age well. I particularly liked the '96 and 2000.

Château Le Monteil d'Arsac
Cru Bourgeois.

See Château d'Arsac in Margaux. This bottling is the Haut-Médoc portion of the vineyard.

Château Muret
Cru Bourgeois. Owner: Philippe Boufflerd. 22ha. 15,500 cases. Mer 55%, CS 45%. Second wine: Château Tour du Mont.

The present owner acquired this old *cru* in the western part of St-Seurin de Cadourne in 1985 and has since completely renovated it. To help control yields, grass is grown between the rows of vines. I found the '96 to have a marked spicy, scented character with rich, rather extracted tannins, but undeniably attractive. The 2000 is better. As the vineyard matures, the wines can only improve.

Cave Coopérative La Paroisse
Owner: Union de Producteurs. 93ha. 36,700 cases.

The cooperative of St-Seurin was founded in 1935 and is considered to be the best in the Haut-Médoc appellation. Most of the wine is sold in bulk to négociants or under the La Paroisse brand, but a few property wines are kept separate: Châteaux La Peyregre, La Calupeyre, La Cassanet. In recent years, the cooperative has lost a number of members as new owners decide to make their own wines. These are solid, well-balanced wines which resemble the lesser St-Estèphes but usually have more flesh.

Château Paloumey V →
Cru Bourgeois Supérieur. Owner: Martine Cazeneuve. 20ha. 12,000 cases. CS 55%, Mer 40%, CF 5%. Second wine: Les Ailes de Paloumey.

This *cru* in Ludon had an excellent reputation in the 19th century but the

vineyard was finally uprooted in 1954. The present owner replanted
the vineyard in 1990. In spite of the youth of the vines I found the '96
attractively fruity and ripe for early drinking, and the 2000 is the best
yet. Watch this space!

Château Peyrabon V

Cru Bourgeois. Owner: Millésima. Administrator: Patrick Bernard.
48ha. 25,000 cases. CS 50%, Mer 26%, CF 23%, PV 1%.

This distinctive, twin-towered château has recently been bought by this
well-known négociant specializing in mail-order sales.

Prior to 1958, Peyrabon wines were relatively unknown as they were
mostly sold privately; they now have a good reputation and are classics of
the northern Médoc, with a note of terroir on the finish. The vineyards are
extensive and were supplemented by land bought from Château Liversan in
1978. They are fermented in concrete vats and matured in wood, 33 per cent
new. The '96 is attractively robust and fruity, and has good cassis notes,
while 2000 is richly exotic.

Château Pontoise-Cabarrus

Cru Bourgeois. Owner: SICA de Haut-Médoc. Administrator: François Tereygeol.
31ha. 20,000 cases. CS 55%, Mer 35%, CF 5%, PV 5%.

A modest *cru bourgeois* with an interesting history. Owned by the Cabarrus
family during "The Terror" in Bordeaux, the daughter of the house, Thereza
Cabarrus, saved many lives in her role as mistress of the notorious Tallien.
A colourful character, she was a witness at the wedding of Napoleon and
Josephine. The Tereygeols bought the château in 1960 and built up the
seven-hectare property to its current size. They produce carefully made,
solid wines with flavour, needing plenty of time to reveal their best
characteristics, but rather rustic in style.

Château Puy-Castéra

Cru Bourgeois. Owner: Marès family. 28ha. 16,600 cases. CS 50%, Mer 34%,
CF 13%, Mal 2%, PV 1%. Second label: Château Holden.

Puy-Castéra was given a new lease of life in 1973 when it was bought by Henri
Marès. At this stage, the buildings were dilapidated and the vineyards had
been returned to pasture. Replanting was gradual: 25 hectares were in
production by 1980. Winemaking was put into the hands of Bertrand de
Rozières from Château Sestignan. The vineyards are well situated and as they
mature, they yield wines of increasing quality. Attractive, early drinking wines.

Château Ramage La Batisse V

Cru Bourgeois Supérieur. Owner: MACIF. 40ha. 24,400 cases. CS 70%, Mer 23%,
CF 5%, PV 2%. Second label: Château Dutellier.

This is a combination of several properties which have been put together
since 1961. The wines are scented (I detected a smell of violets) and
extremely fruity and easy to drink. It is easy to see why these wines rapidly
gained a good reputation.

Château du Retout

Cru Bourgeois. Owner: Gérard Kopp. 30ha. 18,900 cases. CS 70%, Mer 23%,
CF 5%, PV 2%.

An old mill tower (dating from 1395) stands on this property: it was used
in the Seven Years' War (1756–63) to look out for British ships advancing up
the Gironde estuary. This is yet another example of a property where
extensive restoration has been needed. Its wines are now well-made and
sold at reasonable prices.

Château Reysson

Cru Bourgeois Supérieur. Owner: Mercian Corporation. Administrator: Jean-Pierre Angliviel de la Beaumelle. 70ha. 35,000 cases. CS 57%, Mer 33%.
Second label: Château de l'Abbaye.

Château Reysson was restored by the Mestrezat Group who bought it in 1972, subsequently selling to the Mercian Corporation (part of the Japanese Ajimoto group). Pleasant wines, suitable for drinking young, are produced at reasonable prices.

Fort du Roy

Owner: SICA des Viticulteurs de Fort-Médoc. 50ha. 32,000 cases. CS 60%, Mer 33%, CF 5%, PV 2%. Second label: Chevaliers du Roi Soleil.
Other labels: Fort-Médoc, Châteaux Les Capérans, Église Vieille, les Jacquets, Le Neurin, Le Moreau and Grand-Merrain.

Initially, this property was made up of a small group of growers who pooled their efforts in 1966 to improve their output and to market it more efficiently. Today, a négociant, Ginestet, is also involved with this group of producers based in a modern site complex, which is somewhat startling for the traveller in the Médoc countryside as it intrudes on the flat landscape en route from Lamarque to Cussac.

Some 22 members now produce wines under the label Chevaliers du Roi Soleil. They are unlike cooperative wines in that they reflect the character and personality of their château origins.

Château du Roux

Cru Bourgeois. Owner: Hélène Berand. 20ha. 10,000 cases. CS 50%, Mer 50%.
The charming 18th century château and vineyard in a single piece enjoy views over the Gironde in Cussac. Thirty per cent new oak is used. I loved the deliciously succulent fruit of the excellent 2000. A wine to watch.

Château St-Paul V

Cru Bourgeois. Owner: Boucher family. 20ha. 12,400 cases. CS 60%, Mer 35%, CF 5%.
This vineyard was created in 1979 from parcels of vineyard in St-Seurin de Cadourne belonging to two St-Estèphe properties, Le Boscq and Morin, just across the communal boundary. These are lovely, rich ample wines with good structure and fruit – yet another excellent St-Seurin de Cadourne producer.

Château Sénéjac V →

Cru Bourgeois Supérieur. Owner: Rustmann Family. 26ha. 14,400 cases. CS 60%, Mer 25%, CF 14%, PV 1%. Second label: Artique de Sénéjac. Special cuvée: Karolus.
Having belonged to the Guigné family since 1860, it was bought by the Rustmanns of Talbot fame in 1999. The wines are completely different to those of de Malleret, the other important *cru* of Pian. They are deeply coloured and perfumed, but classically austere and tannic. These wines are made to last and do last, as the older vintages show. They have a good following among many traditional English wine merchants, and it is easy to see why. In 1999 a special *cuvée*, Karolus, of 400 cases from 3.5 hectares became one of the first *garagiste* wines in the Médoc. It will be interesting to see how Sénéjac evolves under the new management.

Château Sociando-Mallet ★★ V

Owner: Jean Gautreau. 58ha. 33,000 cases. CS 55%, Mer 42%, CF 2%, PV 1%.
Second label: La Demoiselle de Sociando-Mallet.
Since buying five hectares of run-down vineyard in 1969, Jean Gautreau has created an outstanding *cru*, which not only commands the highest prices of any non-classified Médoc, but also exceeds those of a whole raft of *crus classés*.

The secret lies in an exceptional site just north of St-Estèphe, overlooking the Gironde, with certain echoes of Montrose and Latour. They never have to spray against rot and are virtually immune from frosts, as '91 proved.

The wines are characterized by massive, chewy textures combined with ripe, sweet fruit. Liquorice and chocolate, black fruits and coffee are the words that most frequently come to mind. The great vintages really begin with '82 and include '83, '85, '86, '88, '89, '90, and '91. The '93 is a stylish wine, beginning to drink well. The '94 is promising but still unevolved. The '96 seems more promising than '95. The '97 is succulent, delicious, and much more forward. The '98 will be a great wine. The '99 is very good and 2000 a great success.

Château Soudars V

Cru Bourgeois Supérieur. Owner: Eric Miailhe. 22ha. 13,900 cases. CS 44%, Mer 55%, CF 1%.

Eric Miailhe cleared 2,500 tons of stones before planting his new vineyards here in 1973. The property is near to those owned by his father and grandfather – Verdignan and Coufran – but they were discouraged from using this land by the quantity of stones and boulders covering it. Miailhe's care and attention has produced some fine wines: the '82, '83, '85, '86, '89, '90, '95, and '96 are evidence enough that this *cru* has a good future.

Château du Taillan

Cru Bourgeois Supérieur. Owner: Mme Henri-François Cruse. 26ha. 11,000 cases. Red: CS 48%, Mer 30%, CF 22%. White: Château La Dame-Blanche. 2ha. 1,000 cases. Sauv 60%, Col 40%.

This property has belonged to the Cruses since 1896. The château and the even older cellars are classified as historic monuments. The wine is kept mostly in large wooden *foudres* of 80–170 hectolitres, but 20 per cent passes through new casks of the conventional size. The aim here is to produce supple, easy-to-drink wines without much tannin.

Château La Tour-Carnet V →

4e Cru Classé. Owner: Bernard Magrez. 40ha. 20,000 cases. CS 53%, Mer 33%, CF 10%, PV 4%.

Like so much else in St-Laurent, La Tour-Carnet was on its last legs when Louis Lipschitz bought it in 1962. After he died, his daughter and her husband continued the work, yet the wines remained coarse with astringent tannins.

In the late 1980s, many changes were made and great efforts went into improving the wine; '90 seemed a big step forward, but since then, the wines have been irregular. In 1999, the château changed hands again; the new owner is also the owner of Pape-Clement. The '99 and 2000 both had riper, finer tannins and sweeter fruit. So one hopes that after a number of false starts, it has turned the corner.

Château Tour du Haut Moulin V

Cru Bourgeois Supérieur. Owner: Laurent Poitou. 32ha. 17,800 cases. CS 50%, Mer 45%, PV 5%.

The vineyards of this *cru* lie beside those of Beaumont around the village of Cussac, but the wines are different. Laurent Poitou is the fourth generation to own this property, and he makes fine, traditional wines. They are aged in wood, of which 25 per cent is new. The result is a wine of exceptional colour that is also rich in extract. Tannic and powerful but well-balanced, these wines have great character, and with ageing their real breed emerges. Consistently one of the best *crus bourgeois*.

Château Tour-du-Mirail

Cru Bourgeois. Owners: Hélène and Danielle Vialard. 18ha. 10,800 cases. CS 75%, Mer 20%, PV 5%.

This property has belonged to the daughters of Louis Vialard of neighbouring Château Cissac since 1970. Everything is quite separate from Cissac. Vinification is in stainless steel vats and the wines are matured in cask. They have a lot of flavour and a well-projected and quite perfumed bouquet. At the same time, they are fairly light in body and have a certain Cabernet Sauvignon "edge". Despite their firmness, I find these wines are at present more enjoyable when fairly young (five to seven years), before the fruit begins to fade. An honourable *cru bourgeois*, but at present, lacking the style and character of Cissac.

Château Tour St-Joseph

Cru Bourgeois. Owner: Marcel and Christian Quancard. 10ha. 5,000 cases. CS 70%, Mer 25%, CF 5%.

The owners head the family négociant business of Cheval Quancard, and also the neighbouring Cissac property of Haut-Logat. The vineyard is situated on the highest point of the commune, and the old vines produce wines with good fruit and elegance and some style.

Château Tourteran

Owner: SC du Château Ramage La Batisse. 20ha. 12,000 cases. CS 50%, Mer 50%. Second label: Château Terrey.

This château is under the same management as, and uses an adjoining vineyard to, Ramage La Batisse. Younger vines, a different name, but the same objectives.

Château Verdignan

Cru Bourgeois Supérieur. Owner: SC du Château. Administrator: Eric Miailhe. 60ha. 36,000 cases. CS 50%, Mer 45%, CF 5%. Second label: Château Plantey-de-la-Croix.

Coufran is the most northerly château in the Haut-Médoc and this is the second most northerly – both are owned by the Miailhe family. Verdignan has an attractive château with a tall turret, easily visible from the road. When Jean Miailhe bought the property in 1972, the reputation of Verdignan was not good. I remember wines of a rather tough character during the 1960s. Now Jean's son Eric is in charge of the winemaking, as he is at Coufran. The wine is fermented in stainless steel and matured in cask and, as one would expect of a wine from St-Seurin, it is solid and well-structured with a strong flavour. It also has lots of fruit, something that was lacking in the past.

Château de Villegeorge ★ V

Cru Bourgeois Supérieur. Owner: Marie-Louise Lurton. 15ha. 6,700 cases. Mer 60%, CS 40%.

Villegeorge has long enjoyed a good reputation. The soil here is extremely gravelly, resembling that of Margaux. Lucien Lurton campaigned to prevent further spoiling of his land. In 1994, he handed over the property to his daughter, Marie-Louise.

The fermentation is in stainless steel, and the wine is matured in cask, with 25 per cent new wood used. The vineyard here is particularly prone to frost damage, which often causes low and irregular yields. The high proportion of Merlot is most unusual in the Médoc. The wines of Villegeorge have always been deeply coloured, with a strong character, and they remain so under the Lurtons with the difference being that they are now rather more polished and less rustic than they sometimes were. Excellent wines were made in '82, '83, '85, '88, '89, '90, '95, '96, '98, '99, and 2000.

MÉDOC AC

The fortunes of this area have revived considerably in recent years. Between 1985 and 1996, the area under vine increased by over 50 per cent to 4,741 hectares, while between 1996 and 2000 it increased by a further six per cent to 5,040 hectares. Wine is now produced in 16 communes, of which the most important are Bégadan (by far the largest), followed in importance by Blaignan, St-Yzans, St-Germain d'Esteuil, Civrac, Valeyrac, St Christoly, Jau-Dignac-et-Loirac. Because of the heavier soils, even where there are outcrops of gravel, more Merlot is found here than in the Haut-Médoc, and there is therefore a lower proportion of Cabernet Sauvignon. The wines are pleasantly perfumed, especially when young, and develop some finesse in bottle. They are mostly light in body but well flavoured. There are plenty of good *crus bourgeois*, and 61 per cent of production is vinified in cooperatives.

Cave Pavillon Bellevue

Owner: Société Coopérative de Vinification d'Ordonnac. 240ha. 153,000 cases. Mer 50%, CS 45%, CF 5%.

The co-op at Ordonnac was founded in 1936 and has members drawn from this commune and the neighbouring one of St-Germain d'Esteuil. The cooperative is also a member of Uni-Médoc, the association of *caves coopératives* of Médoc, and supplies much wine in bulk for négociants' own brands as well as under its own *marque* of Pavillon de Bellevue. Good, dependable Médoc.

Château Blaignan

Cru Bourgeois. Owner: Cordier-Mestrezat Domaines. Administrator: Alain Duhau. 87ha. 33,000 cases. CS 50%, Mer 40%, CF 9%.
Second label: Château Prieuré-Blaignan.

A consistent, well-distributed wine run by négociants Cordier-Mestrezat. It is the largest vineyard in the commune of the same name.

Château Bournac

Cru Bourgeois Supérieur. Owner: Bruno Secret. 13.1ha. 8,500 cases. CS 65%, Mer 35%.

The Secret family arrived here in 1969 and have reconstructed this *cru* in Civrac since then. I have noted rich, sappy fruit, and good-quality tannins. These are solid, attractive wines.

Château La Cardonne

Cru Bourgeois Supérieur. Owner: Domaines CGR. 49.5ha. 30,000 cases. Mer 50%, CS 45%, CF 5%.

This large property was acquired by Domaines Rothschild in 1973, since when the vineyard has been considerably expanded, the existing buildings restored and the equipment replaced. The vineyard is well-placed on the highest plateau of the region. The wines saw no wood at all prior to 1990, when the Rothschilds sold to the present owner.

These wines are perfumed, fruity, frank, and fresh: archetypal Médoc, straightforward and easy to enjoy young. It has moved up a gear in recent years and now has more fruit and succulence – this is especially noticeable from the '88 vintage onwards. Fifty per cent new oak is usual in the maturation.

Château Castéra

Cru Bourgeois Supérieur. Owner: D. G. Tondera. 63ha. 27,500 cases. CS 45%, Mer 45%, CF 7%, PV 3%. Second label: Château Bourbon La Chapelle.

This is one of the principal *crus* of St-Germain-d'Esteuil. It is an old property which has links with the Black Prince, who besieged the original château.

It belonged to Alexis Lichine & Co, the négociants, from 1973 to 1986, when they sold to the present owners. This is a good, solid, enjoyable Médoc, developing a mellow, fruity character, full and soft when quite young. Can be enjoyed from three years onwards.

Château Chantelys V →

Cru Bourgeois. Owner: Christine Courrian Braquissac. 13.6ha. 7,500 cases. CS 55%, Mer 40%, PV 5%. Second label: Château Gauthier.

It was Jean Courrian who reconstructed this excellent vineyard in Pregnac, beginning in 1952. The present owner succeeded her father in 1982. From the mid-1980s onwards, the reputation of this *cru* has been growing. Twenty per cent new oak is used and I have been impressed by the sweet and ripe tannins in stylish, quite powerful wines.

Château La Clare V

Cru Bourgeois. Owner: Paul de Rozières. 20ha. 13,000 cases. CS 57%, Mer 36%, CF 7%. Second labels: Châteaux Laveline and du Gentilhomme.

Situated on the ridge of By, 50 per cent of La Clare's vineyards have been replanted by the present owners over the last 20 years. These are mostly mechanically harvested, but grapes for the older vines – some over 60 years old – are hand-picked. The Rozières, owners since 1969, originally came from Tunisia and used their experience as vineyard owners there to advantage, producing excellent wines that are attractive and well-made with spiciness, opulence, and plummy fruit.

Château de la Croix

Cru Bourgeois. Owner: Francesco family. 21.3ha. 13,500 cases. CS 50%, Mer 45%, CF 4%, PV 1%. Brands: Château Roc-Taillade, Château Terre-Rouge, Château Côtes de Blaignan.

This *cru* was created in 1870, and has been in the hands of the same family ever since. The domaine has gradually been increased in size, so comprises numerous parcels in Ordonnac. I found the '96 to have rich tannins and good fruit balance with an attractive and distinctive character.

Château d'Escurac V →

Cru Bourgeois Supérieur. Owner: Landureau family. Administrator: Jean-Marc Landureau. 18ha. 10,000 cases. CS 60%, Mer 40%. Second label: Chapelle d'Escurac.

This *cru* had an excellent reputation when it was mentioned in *Le Producteur* in 1839. More recently, it won the Coupe des Crus Bourgeois in 1999, no mean achievement with competition from many fine Haut-Médocs. I have noted excellent fruit character, good tannins, and real style. A wine to follow.

Château Fontis V →

Cru Bourgeois. Owner: Vincent Boivert. 10ha. 5,500 cases. CS 50%, Mer 50%.

Since Vincent Boivert bought this Ordonnac property in 1995, some notably attractive wines have been made here. The vineyard is well-placed at 38 metres (125 feet) on the highest gravel ridge in the area. Sixty-six per cent of the wine goes into cask, of which 50 per cent are new; the rest stays in vat. The clever use of new oak comes through in the form of silky, supple textures, delicious fruit and the impression of sweet, not dry, oak at the finish. The '96, '97, '98, '99, and 2000 all produced above-average expressions of these vintages.

Château Les Grands Chênes V →

Cru Bourgeois Supérieur. Owner: Bernard Magrez. 7ha. 4,400 cases. CS 65%, Mer 30%, CF 5%.

This small St-Christoly property has carved out quite a reputation for itself in recent years for its well-made concentrated wines of character that repay ageing. One-third new oak is used. In 1998, Bernard Magrez of Pape Clement bought the property. The *cuvée prestige* is a selection from certain parcels aged in 100 per cent new oak, but showing lovely sweet fruit. The standard wines have a lovely scent of violets. The '96, '98, '99, and 2000 are all excellent. A leading *cru bourgeois*.

Château Greysac

Cru Bourgeois Supérieur. Owner: Domaines Codem. Administrator: Philippe Dambrine. 75ha. 33,000 cases. CS 45%, Mer 45%, CF 5%, PV 5%.

Since the late Baron François de Gunzburg bought this château in 1973, its importance has increased. Fermentation is in stainless-steel *cuves* and the wine is aged in cask with 25 per cent new wood. I have found the wines to have an expansive, almost opulent, fruit flavour, with a rather overripe style in the best vintages. They can be drunk with pleasure when three to four years old.

Château Haut-Canteloup

Cru Bourgeois. Owner: S.C.I. du Château Haut-Canteloup. 38ha. 24,000 cases. Mer 60%, CS 30%, CF 10%. Second wine: Château les Mourlanes.

This good property in St-Christoly is now making very good wines. The '96 had rich, unctuous, expressive fruit and harmony, with elegance and persistence of flavour; a very stylish wine. Haut-Canteloup Collection is a selection of the best *cuvées* aged in new oak.

Château Lacombe-Noillac V

Owner: Jean-Michel Lapalu. 31ha. 20,000 cases. CS 58%, Mer 32%, CF 6%, PV 4%.

The vineyard was reconstructed only in 1980. The well-made, attractive wines are made with 15 per cent new oak in their maturation. The property is now under the same management as Patache d'Aux.

Château Laujac

Cru Bourgeois. Owner: Bernard Cruse. 30ha. 16,000 cases. CS 60%, Mer 30%, CF 5%, PV 5%.

A widely known château belonging to the Cruse family. This large property used to produce much more wine, of higher repute than it does now. The wines lack much of the character evident in neighbouring *crus*.

Château Les Moines V

Cru Bourgeois. Owner: Claude Pourreau. 30ha. 20,000 cases. CS 70%, Mer 30%. Other label: Château Tour St-Martin (aged in vat only).

A good *cru* in Couquèques, adjoining Les Ormes Sorbet. The grapes are mechanically harvested and matured in cask, of which 25 per cent are renewed annually. This is solid, well-made, serious wine, fruity and consistent.

Château Livran

Cru Bourgeois. Owner: Robert & Olivier Godfrin. 48ha. 30,000 cases. Mer 50%, CS 45%, CF 5%. Second label: Château La Rose-Goromey.

Once owned by the de Goth family – one of whom became Pope Clement V in 1305 – this château's history is as impressive as its appearance. It was also owned by a London wine merchant, James Denman, until the Second World War. The present proprietor is its former manager. Pleasant, well-made wines.

Château Loudenne

Cru Bourgeois Supérieur. Owner: Domaines Lafragette. 62ha. Red: 28,500 cases. CS 45%, Mer 45%, CF 7%, Mal 2%, PV 1%. White: 6,500 cases. Sauv 62%, Sém 38%.

The wines tend to be lighter in colour but have more perfume and finesse than most wines of the Médoc AC. There is a real elegance about them which becomes more noticeable as the wines mature in bottle. The '90 and especially '96 and 2000 are good here. The excellent white wine is fermented in cask of which one-third are new. It is delicious, perfumed and elegant soon after bottling in the spring, but the Sémillon lends the potential for ageing as well.

Château Lousteauneuf

Cru Bourgeois. Owner: Segond family. Administrator: Bruno Segond.
22ha. 13,000 cases. CS 54%, Mer 40%, CF 4%, PV 2%.
Second wine: Château la Rose Carbonière.

This good property in Valeyrac was bought by the Segond family in 1962, who replanted and extended the vineyard. In 1993, they left the co-op to make the wines on the property. Thirty-five per cent new oak is used. I found the '96 charmingly scented with rich, unctuous, velvety fruit, a delicious, balanced wine capable of early enjoyment. The '99 and 2000 are the same high quality.

Château de Monthil

Cru Bourgeois. Owner: Les Domaines Codem. 15ha. 8,500 cases. CS 30%,
CF 30%, Mer 30%, PV 10%.

Les Domaines Codem also owns Châteaux Greysac, Bégadan, de By and Les Bertins in the same commune. Before they bought the property in 1986, the traditionally made wines were mostly sold to restaurants within France. Now they are exported, too, and with their fine reputation – they have established a loyal following – they ought to do well. A wine to look out for.

Château Noaillac V

Cru Bourgeois. Owners: Xavier and Marc Pagès. 43ha. 28,500 cases.
CS 55%, Mer 40%, PV 5%. Second labels: Moulin de Noaillac, La Rose Noaillac,
Les Palombes de Noaillac.

Another example of *pieds noirs* enterprise (*see* La Tour de By). The Pagès family bought the property in northern Jau-Dignac-et-Loirac in 1983 and replanted the vineyard. It is now probably the leading *cru* in the commune. The wines are deeply coloured, with pronounced fruitiness and depth of flavour. Fifteen per cent new oak is used as well as *cuves* for the maturation, but the wines spend only ten months in cask, which adds dimension to the wines without drying them.

Château Les Ormes Sorbet V

Cru Bourgeois Supérieur. Owner: Jean Boivert. 21ha. 12,000 cases. CS 65%,
Mer 30%, CF 2%, PV 2%, Carmenère 1%.

The wines here are nicely perfumed and elegant, with a strong, assertive Cabernet flavour and plenty of structure. Like many wines in the Bas-Médoc, they have lots of flavour but not much body. Note the replanting of Carmenère, an important variety in the pre-phylloxera days, which virtually disappeared due to its flowering problems when grafted. In the '80s, robust, solid wines with a distinct *goût de terroir* were made, but the excellent '96 shows a more suave style, while retaining its finesse. This is an excellent example of what the Bas-Médoc can do with care and dedication.

Château Patache-d'Aux V

Cru Bourgeois Supérieur. Owner: SC du Château. Administrator: Patrice Ricard.
43ha. 26,600 cases. CS 70%, Mer 20%, CF 7%, PV 3%.
Second label: Le Relais de Patache-d'Aux.

This *cru* has had a good reputation for many years and belonged to the

Delon family (*see* Léoville-Las-Cases and Potensac) until a syndicate of *pieds noirs,* headed by Claude Lapalu, bought it in 1964. The actual château now belongs to the municipality. The fermentation is still partly in wooden *cuves* and partly in concrete and stainless-steel vats, but all the wine is matured in cask with 25 per cent new oak. The wines are finely perfumed, with clear overtones of violets and Cabernet; finely flavoured, fruity and supple, quite light in body but with a good backbone. In 2002, I tasted '89, '82, and '66 which emphasized the quality of this *cru* and its ability to age well. All were in excellent condition and of impressive quality.

Château Plagnac

Cru Bourgeois. Owner: Domaines Cordier. 30ha. 20,500 cases. CS 65%, Mer 35%.
The present owners acquired this property in Bégadan in 1972 and have brought about many changes and improvements since then: the vineyards have been adapted for mechanical harvesting, stainless-steel vats bought in for fermentation, and wooden casks for maturation. This progress has produced consistently attractive wines throughout the '80s and '90s.

Château Pontey V

Cru Bourgeois. Owner: Quancard family. 11ha. 6,500 cases. CS 45%, Mer 55%. Second label: Château Vieux Prezat.
Situated partly on the higher plateau of Blaignan, this good *cru* belongs to the family négociants Cheval Quancard. They certainly seem to know what the wine-lover looks for. New oak (one-third) is cleverly used to show off, not smother, the sweet fruit, resulting in rich, charming wines that are a joy to drink young, yet can also keep.

Château Potensac ★ V

Cru Bourgeois Exceptionnel. Owner: Delon family. Administrator: Jean-Hubert Delon. 57ha. 37,500 cases. CS 60%, Mer 25%, CF 15%.
Second labels: Châteaux Gallais-Bellevue and Lassalle, Goudy la Cardonne.
There is a good, gravelly outcrop at Potensac lying between St-Yzans and St-Germain d'Esteuil, where the Delon family (*see* Léoville-Las-Cases) owns four vineyards. Good wines have been made here for years, but in the last two decades, they seem to have gone from strength to strength. The biggest vineyard is Potensac itself, then come Lassalle, Gallais-Bellevue, and Goudy la Cardonne, and the four are effectively run together. The *cuvier* has been re-equipped with stainless-steel *cuves,* and the wines enjoy a long, slow fermentation, followed by ageing in casks, of which 20 per cent are new each year – with a further proportion from Léoville-Las-Cases. The wines are characterized by their depth of colour and a nose full of vigour, typical of the Médoc, which often has spicy or floral overtones. They have a concentrated, complex, and powerful flavour, and a rather angular structure. Usually five or six years are needed before these wines are at their best for drinking, and they last well. This is certainly one of the best wines being made today in the Médoc.

Château Preuillac

Cru Bourgeois. Owner: Yvon Mau. 30ha. 18,500 cases. Mer 44%, CS 54%, CF 2%.
Lesparre's most important *cru,* Preuillac is one of the best-kept properties in its commune. Vinification is by traditional methods, and the wines tend to be quite full-bodied and tannic. The owners are one of the most progressive négociants.

Château Ramafort V

Cru Bourgeois. Owner: Domaines CGR. 15.7ha. 10,000 cases. CS 50%, Mer 50%.

Of the three properties in Blaignan now owned by Domaines CGR, this now seems to be yielding the best results. Probably the absence of Cabernet Franc gives it the edge over La Cardonne. It recently won the Coupe de Médoc in face of competition from many leading *crus bourgeois* from the Haut-Médoc. I noted smoky, rich, ripe fruit and more personality than La Cardonne in the '95, a very harmonious, promising '97 and a '98 of real ripeness and excellent potential.

Château Rollan de By →

Cru Bourgeois Supérieur. Owner: Jean Guyon. 21.5ha. 13,500 cases. Mer 70%, CS 20%, PV 10%. Cuvée Special: Château Haut-Condessas.

This property in Bégadan really hit the headlines when its special *cuvée* performed spectacularly on the tasting circuit. The normal wine has length of flavour, supple fruit, and an attractive personality. The Condessas really pulls out all the stops, including malolactic fermentation in 100 per cent new oak. This is top new-wave wine manipulation, but very well done.

Château Roquegrave

Cru Bourgeois. Owner: M. Joannon. 30ha. 20,000 cases. CS 70%, Mer 25%, PV 5%.

A well-known and well-distributed property at Valeyrac, the most northerly of the riverside communes of the Médoc. A mixture of *cuves* and casks is used. Decent, straightforward, robust wines.

Cave Coopérative St-Jean

President: René Chaumont. 351ha. 221,900 cases. Mer 50%, CS 24%, CF 24%, PV 2%.

The Cave St-Jean, also referred to as the Cave Coopérative de Bégadan, is by far the largest cooperative in the Médoc AC. Its members come not only from this commune, but also from the neighbouring ones of Valeyrac and Civrac. The Cave is also a member of Uni-Médoc, a group of four cooperatives which store and mature the wines of the region. The external buildings have a capacity of more than 60,000 hectolitres.

The Cave has been losing numbers in recent years, as more growers take responsibility for their own wines. The produce of this cooperative has a good reputation. Much of it is supplied to négociants for their own generic blends. These wines are characteristic and attractive Médocs.

L'Elite St-Roch

Owner: Société Coopérative de Vinification de Queyrac. 155ha. 101,500 cases.

This cooperative was founded in 1939 and now has members, drawn from the communes of Queyrac, Gaillan, Jau-Dignac-et-Loirac, Vensac, Valeyrac and Vendays. The cooperative is a member of the Uni-Médoc and, apart from its own *marque*, a large proportion of the wine made here is sold in bulk to négociants for their own blends and contributes to the good overall standard of generic Médoc.

Cave Coopérative de St-Yzans-de-Médoc

Owner: Société Coopérative. 175ha. 111,000 cases. Mer 55%, CS 40%, CF 2%, PV 2%, Mal 1%.

The cooperative of St-Yzans was established in 1934. The wines are sold under the name of St-Brice or in bulk to négociants to be used for their own *marques*. The Cave has a good reputation for making fine Médocs in typical regional style. Apart from those in St-Yzans itself, St-Brice also has members in Blaignan, Couquèques and St-Christoly. There is some ageing in cask.

Château Sestignan

Cru Bourgeois. Owner: Bertrand de Rozières. 19.5ha 12,200 cases. CS 60%, Mer 25%, CF 13%, Mal 1%, PV 1%.

On the edge of the Bas-Médoc region, this château is surrounded by alluvial palus and drainage ditches. This wine has performed consistently well in a number of comparative tastings. It spends 16 months in *cuves* and four months in cask. When Bertrand de Rozières began with just a few wines in '73, he was one of the first to begin the reconstruction of the vineyards of Jau-Dignac-et-Loirac, which had been completely abandoned after the war. It is therefore a *cru* to look out for. There is a charming '96.

Château Sigognac V

Owner: SC Fermière. Administrator: Colette Bonny. 47ha. 25,000 cases. CS 33.3%, CF 33.3%, Mer 33.3%.

A Roman villa once stood on this site; some of the pottery found here may be seen at the *mairie* (town hall) at St-Yzans. This vineyard had been reduced to only four hectares of vines when Paul Grasset bought it in 1964. It was transformed, first by him and then, after his death in 1968, by his wife.

The fermentation is in concrete vats and the wine is matured partly in vat and partly in cask, with 20 per cent new oak. It has a good colour and is full and soft on the nose, with pleasant fruit and tannin on the palate: elegant, rather than powerful. If it lacks the finesse of its illustrious neighbour, Château Loudenne, it is nevertheless a pleasant, honourable Médoc of a good general standard.

Château Le Temple →

Cru Bourgeois. Owner: The Bergey family. Administrator: Jean-Pierre and Denis Bergey. 21ha. 12,000 cases. CS 60%, Mer 35%, PV 5%.

When I first tasted this wine at a *cru bourgeois* tasting for the '96 vintage, I was immediately attracted by the nostalgically scented Médoc fruit and finesse. The name comes from a domain of the Knights Templars. The Bergey family have been here since 1933. Another wine to watch.

Château La Tour de By ★ V

Cru Bourgeois Supérieur. Owner: SC (Cailloux, Lapalu, Pagès). Administrator: Marc Pagès. 73ha. 46,000 cases. CS 60%,Mer 36%, CF 4%. Second labels: Châteaux La Roque-de-By and Moulin-de-la-Roque, Cailloux de By.

This fine *cru*, on one of the highest and best gravelly ridges in the whole of the Bas-Médoc, has an attractive château; parts of the other old buildings are also pleasing. The tower, an old lighthouse, stands on high ground nearby.

Since buying the property in 1965, Marc Pagès and his partners have made many improvements. They have expanded the *chai* and installed some stainless steel (retaining the old wooden *cuves*). For those who believe mechanical harvesting and quality do not mix, the harvesting here is carried out over seven days by four machines, ensuring maximum maturity.

The wine, matured in cask with 20 per cent new oak, is deeply coloured and finely scented, and the lively, sappy fruit is often reminiscent of violets. The flavour is harmonious and attractive; it is also powerful, with real depth, and quite tannic. Other marked characteristics are elegance and length of flavour. This château certainly has a good claim to be considered as the finest wine of the Médoc appellation.

The special position of the vineyard paid off in '91, when it was much less frosted than most in the northern Médoc, and an excellent wine was made from first-generation grapes. The consistent quality can be judged by the '92 and '93, while outstanding wines were made in '95, '96, '97, '98, '99, and 2000.

Château La Tour-Haut-Caussan

Cru Bourgeois Supérieur. Owner: Philippe Courrian. 16ha. 10,000 cases. CS 50%, Mer 50%. Second label: La Landotte.

A windmill dating from 1734 stands on this property and is evidence of the polyculture that held sway in this part of the Médoc before the 19th century. The current owner comes from a family of true Médocains, whose history here is traceable to 1615. He believes in traditional methods of viticulture, and vinification is carried out with the utmost care, using high temperatures for the fermentation of his Merlots and lower temperatures for the Cabernets. The wines are then blended and matured in oak, 33 per cent of which is new. The results have been successful and won awards; the wines are in high demand from French restaurants but are also widely distributed in France and overseas.

Château La Tour-St-Bonnet

Cru Bourgeois. Owner: Jacques Merlet. 40ha. 18,000 cases. Mer 45%, CS 45%, Mal 5%, PV 5%. Second label: Château La-Fuie-St-Bonnet.

Probably the best-known *cru* in St-Christoly. The vineyard is splendidly placed on the best gravelly ridges of the commune, with its distinctive tower among the vines. The wines, typical of the Médoc, are highly coloured, vigorous, and powerful. They require some ageing to show their best.

Château Vernous

Cru Bourgeois. Owner: Châteaux en Bordeaux. Administrator: Bernard Frachet. 22.5ha. 13,000 cases. CS 63%, Mer 30%, CF 7%. Second label: La Marche de Vernous.

Deutz invested a great deal in this good Lesparre *cru* in the 1980s and the new owners continue to make good use of it. The vineyard has one of the few gravelly *croupes* (ridges) in this part of the Médoc. Forty per cent new wood is used in the maturation. This is stylish, well-made wine.

Vieux Château Landon

Cru Bourgeois. Owner: Philippe Gillet. 30ha. 20,000 cases. CS 70%, Mer 25%, Mal 5%.

This property has been in the same family for several generations. The present owner married his predecessor's daughter. It is one of a number of excellent *crus* in the commune of Bégadan and produces attractive wines with lots of fruit and plenty of Médocain character.

Château Vieux Robin V →

Cru Bourgeois Supérieur. Owner: Didier and Maryse Roba. 18ha. 11,000 cases. CS 60%, Mer 37%, CF and PV 3%.

During the last two decades, the present owners have worked hard to upgrade their wines in this old family property in Bégadan. Usually between 8,500 and 10,000 cases are sold as Vieux Robin, some 4-5,000 as Vieux Robin Bois de Lunier from a particular parcel of vines and matured with 40 per cent new oak. Then, at the summit, is Collection from the finest *cuves* and aged 100 per cent in new oak. The wines have vivid succulent Cabernet fruit and real style.

Caves Les Vieux Colombiers

Owner: Uni-Médoc. 275ha. 165,000 cases. CS 50%, Mer 40%, CF 10%.

This large cooperative, located in Prignac, collects the produce of 200 members in this commune and also those of Lesparre and St-Germain-d'Esteuil.

Château Le Vivier

Owner: Domaines C.G.R. 8ha. 5,000 cases. CS 50%, Mer 50%.

Still a very young vineyard, and because of this, the wine is kept entirely in stainless steel and bottled early. This preserves the fruit. Despite the wines still being fairly simple and on the light side, there is definitely some good potential here.

Graves

It is not easy to get to grips with this disparate region. Geographically, it is a continuation of the Médoc, but in the north, many vineyards have disappeared beneath Bordeaux's urban sprawl, and further south one can travel for miles, see nothing but trees, and believe one is already in Les Landes. This used to be a region of many mediocre whites and a few aristocratic reds, but this picture has changed significantly in the past 30 years. The changes can be gauged to an extent from the following tables comparing production figures for 1976 and 2000. Since the region is now divided into two appellations, Pessac-Léognan and Graves, I have shown these figures separately for 2000:

	1976 (hl)	2000 (hl)	Increase (hl)
Graves Rouge }	57,760	136,798	} 136,719 (+236%)
Pessac-Léognan }		57,681	
Graves Blanc }	48,243	45,272	}
Pessac-Léognan }		13,561	16,901 (+27%)
Graves Supérieur	13,708	20,019	}
	———	———	———————
	119,711	273,331	153,620 (+128%)

This demonstrates the two important trends: from white to red, and from alcoholic whites (12 per cent minimum alcohol by volume, plus some residual sugar) to drier, lighter (11 per cent) ones. The term Graves Supérieur refers to the higher alcohol level: such wines usually also have some residual sugar. Until 1975, more Graves Supérieur than Graves Sec was made. The table also shows the revival in the district as a whole, with total production up 128 per cent. Over a similar period, the areas under vine have developed as follows:

	1976 (ha)	2000 (ha)	Increase (ha)
Graves Rouge }	1,230	2,376	} 2,278 (+185%)
Pessac-Léognan }		1,122	
Graves Blanc }	1,393	792	}
Pessac-Léognan }		273	150 (+11%)
Graves Supérieur		478	}
	———	———	———————
	2,623	5,041	2,418 (+92%)

While the major expansion has been in the red-wine vineyards, there has been some increase in the white-wine vineyards, following a lengthy decline. New vineyards and better husbandry have brought much higher yields. The 1982 edition of Cocks & Féret's *Bordeaux et ses Vins* monitors the decline of the vineyards that have been caught up in the expansion of the town of Bordeaux. In the four communes most affected – Gradignan, Mérignac, Pessac, and Talence – there were 119 winemaking properties in 1908; by 1981 there were only nine. In the whole of Graves in 1981 there were 33 communes where some declarations under the Graves AC were being made (in several others entitled to the appellation, only Bordeaux or Bordeaux Supérieur was declared). Most of the wines are made in eight communes: Léognan and Martillac in the north; Portets, Illats, Cérons, St-Pierre-de-Mons, Langon, and Landiras in the south. Of these, Illats and Cérons produce both Cérons and Graves, though 80 per cent of the whites made in these communes seem to be declared as Graves, as are the reds, and the proportion is rising.

There are plenty of hopeful signs that the region is coming out of its long decline. There is the general improvement in the quality of dry white Graves through the use of cold-fermentation methods; the gospel preached by Professor Peynaud in the 1960s has been put into practice by men like André Lurton and Pierre Coste. André Lurton, for example, has reclaimed large tracts of abandoned vineyards in the best parts of the northern Graves; Pierre Coste has made delicious and inexpensive white and red wines in the southern Graves, and Denis Dubourdieu has shown how the whole gamut of modern technology, including yeast selection, can transform the quality of wines coming from even modest sites in the southern Graves. Recently there has been a strong movement back to cask fermentation, with excellent results.

Views differ as to the best *encépagement* for white wines. Traditionally Sauvignon and Sémillon are blended. Sauvignon gives the initial fruit (on the nose especially) and acidity while Sémillon provides the possibility of bottle-ageing, its bouquet gradually taking over as the Sauvignon begins to fade after one to two years in bottle. Sémillon also gives the wine body. However, in the search for freshness and fruit for early drinking, some properties have abandoned Sémillon entirely. Such wines tend to lose their charm rather quickly, and my impression is that many growers are now realizing that this grape has a role to play in giving balance.

The list of red wines available ranges from some of the greatest wines in Gironde (Haut-Brion, La Mission-Haut-Brion, Domaine de Chevalier, Haut-Bailly and Pape-Clément) to a host of modestly priced and deliciously vivid wines of individuality. All have Cabernet Sauvignon as their major grape variety, assisted by Merlot and Cabernet Franc.

It is taking time to bring the wine-drinker back to an appreciation of white Graves, so poor has its image been. But as more and more fine wines come onto the market at reasonable prices, their following is bound to grow. As far as the red wines are concerned, the special charm of those whose blend is based on Cabernet, which are quite distinct in character from their Médocain cousins, will surely win them more friends as they become more widely available.

On the quality front, growers in the north won the right to the appellation Pessac-Léognan, which came into force in 1987, with the '86 vintage the first to bear the new title. It covers Cadaujac, Canéjean, Gradignan, Léognan, Martillac, Mérignac, Pessac, St-Médard-d'Eyrans, Talence, and Villenave-d'Ornon. André Lurton, who has done so much to revive the vineyards of this area, was the driving force behind this new appellation.

The prospect of Graves taking a larger share of Bordeaux's prosperity in the future looks bright. The worldwide demand for good, dry white wines and the continuously growing market for middle-price red wines of quality must make Graves a happy hunting ground for wine-lovers.

PESSAC-LÉOGNAN

Château Baret

Owner: Mme. Lucienne Ballande. Red: 12.5ha. 10,000 cases. CS 45%, Mer 50%, CF 5%. White: 5ha. 1,000 cases. Sém 35%, Sauv 65%.

Philippe Castéja has run this property since 1981, when he took over after the death of his father-in-law, André Ballande. He commercializes the wines through the family's négociant house of Borie-Manoux.

Although Château Baret's wines have always had a good reputation, there has been a marked improvement in vintages of recent years. The reds are light but have depth and plenty of spicy fruit. The whites are stylish, classic wines.

Château Bouscaut →

Cru Classé. Owner: SA du Château Bouscaut (Sophie Lurton-Cogombles). Red: 40ha. 21,000 cases. Mer 50%, CS 45%, CF 5%, Mal 5%. White: 6ha. 3,300 cases. Sém 70%, Sauv 30%.

The only important *cru* in Cadaujac, and the Graves *cru classé* closest to the Garonne. Between 1968 and 1980 an American syndicate led by Charles Wohlstetter rescued the property from neglect by installing up-to-date equipment and restoring the 18th-century château. During this period, Jean Delmas, *régisseur* of Haut-Brion, acted as *régisseur* here. In 1980, the Americans sold to Lucien Lurton, proprietor of Brane-Cantenac and Durfort-Vivens in Margaux as well as Climens in Barsac.

The vineyards, which adjoin the Bordeaux-Toulouse road, are on gravelly ridges over limestone: perfect for natural drainage. Stainless-steel vats are used for red and white wines, and the whites are fermented at 18–20°C (64–68°F). The reds are matured in casks of which 35 per cent are new, and the whites are also cask-aged, spending six months in wood. Since Sophie Lurton and her husband, Laurent, took over from her father in 1992, there have been steady improvements in both red and white wines.

Château Brown →

Owner: Bernard Barthe. Red: 23ha. 10,000 cases. CS 60%, Mer 37%, PV 3%. White: 4ha. 2,000 cases. Sauv 70%, Sém 30%. Second label: Le Colombier (red and white).

This property takes its name from the family that owned Cantenac-Brown until the middle of the last century. Its vineyards are well-situated on two gravel ridges in the commune of Léognan. The present owner acquired the property in 1994, and has re-equipped the cellars and carried out drainage work in the vineyards. The previous owners had already worked on the vineyards and were producing attractive wines, but '94 and '95 showed a big improvement which has continued. A delicious cask-fermented white is also made.

Château Cantelys →

Owner: M & Mme Cathiard. Red: 24ha. 3,000 cases. Mer 30%, CS 70%. White: 11ha. 700 cases. Sém 50%. Sauv 50%.

Daniel Cathiard acquired this vineyard, also in Martillac, soon after he bought Smith-Haut-Lafitte. Since then, he has extended the vineyard. The red wines have appealingly vivid, ripe, red-fruit character and the white is lemony and more classically elegant than the Smith, due to its proportion of Sémillon.

Château Carbonnieux ☆

Cru Classé. Owner: Société des Grandes Graves. Administrator: Antony Perrin. Red: 45ha. 25,000 cases. CS 60%, Mer 30%, CF 7%, Mal 2%, PV 1%. White: 42ha. 20,000 cases. Sauv 65%, Sém 35%.

This famous old property first had vineyards in the 12th century, and winemaking was revived by the Bénédictine monks who took over in 1741. Marc Perrin bought and restored the property in 1956, and his son now administers the estate. The white wine is fermented in stainless steel and used to see no wood at all, but recently has been put in new oak for about three months. The reds are matured in cask, of which a third are new oak.

The more famous white Carbonnieux comes from the largest vineyard of the Graves *crus classés*. The high proportion of Sauvignon and early bottling mean that it is delicious when young (nine to 18 months), then often goes through a dull stage as the primary Sauvignon fruit fades, only to emerge again as the Sémillon begins to mature and flower (after about 2.5 years). In recent years, this has been a most consistent wine, the best of the *crus classés* available in commercial quantities. The red has been rather rustic, and is not among the top classified Graves, but determined efforts have been made in recent vintages to improve the quality.

Château Les Carmes-Haut-Brion ★

Owner: Chantecaille family. Administrator: Didier Furt. 4.7ha. 2,000 cases. Mer 50%, CF 40%, CS 10%.

The unusual combination of grape varieties yields wines that are concentrated, have deep colour and tannin, but which have been rather coarse. This may be due to the low percentage of Cabernet Sauvignon. The wine has been château-bottled only since 1985. However, since '95 the wines have more complexity and style.

Domaine de Chevalier ★★ (☆☆)

Cru Classé. Owner: Bernard family. Administrator: Olivier Bernard. Red: 33ha. 7,500 cases. CS 65%, Mer 30%, CF 5%. White: 5ha. 1,500 cases. Sauv 70%, Sém 30%.

From 1865–1983, Chevalier was the property of the Ricard family, and Claude Ricard owned it from 1948. He was obliged to sell, but the new owners, the Bernard family, contracted him to manage the *cru* for a further five years and pass on his vast experience to Olivier Bernard, who was deputed to look after the property. The red wine is fermented at a slightly higher temperature than is fashionable, 32°C (90°F), to facilitate the maximum tannin extraction from the grape skins. For the maturation in cask 50 per cent new oak is used. The white-wine fermentation takes place entirely in cask at a low temperature; the wine is then matured in oak (a small proportion of which is new) for 18 months – a traditional practice that was abandoned for a time elsewhere in Graves, but has now been revived.

The results of this meticulous winemaking are exceptional wines. The reds are deep in colour, the bouquet takes time to open and is then complex, with overtones of tobacco, while the flavour is compact and well-structured with great breed, power, and length of flavour. This wine in some years can approach the quality of Haut-Brion and La Mission. It is also a slow developer. The white wine has a different style from that of Laville or Haut-Brion, more taut and introspective. It is perfumed, firm and compact of flavour and slowly opens only after six to eight years. It has extraordinary delicacy and finesse, and can improve and last for 15–20 years.

Château Coucheroy V

Owner: André Lurton. Red: 30ha. 8000 cases. CS 50%, Mer 50%. White 6ha. 2,500 cases. Sauv 90%, Sém 10%.

The original Gascon name was *Couchéroy*, meaning "the king slept here", referring to a supposed stay by Henri IV when King of Navarre. In the 18th century, the then-owner of La Louvière purchased this vineyard, which became attached to it. When André Lurton first bought La Louvière in 1965, Coucheroy was at first run concurrently with it, before taking on an existence in its own right. The wine is still vinified at La Louvière and the vines are still young. I found the '95 red rather tannin-dominated while the '97 white had a very crisp Sauvignon character.

Château Couhins

Cru Classé. Owner: Institut National de la Recherche Agronomique.
Red: 12ha. 6,500 cases. CS 55%, Mer 40%, CF 5%.
White: 3.5ha. 1,750 cases. Sauv 70%, Sém 30%.

A curious situation exists at Couhins, which is now divided between the National Agricultural Research Institute (INRA) and André Lurton (*see* Couhins-Lurton). For many years, the Gasqueton and Hanappier families were owners and produced only white wines (this is the sole property in Graves where only the white wine is classified). Then the INRA bought the property in 1968.

The estate lies on an elevated site in Villenave-d'Ornon, with vineyards near the Garonne. The modern, low-temperature-fermented wine is fresh and elegant. Unfortunately, with the division of the property and the production of unclassified red wine, the small quantities available mean that it is hard to find.

Château Couhins-Lurton ☆ V

Cru Classé. Owner: André Lurton. White: 6ha. 3,000 cases. Sauv 100%.
Second label: Château Cantebau.

André Lurton began as *fermier* here in 1967, just before the INRA bought out Gasqueton-Hanappier, and made the wine for the whole of Couhins during most of the 1970s. The INRA then took a major part of the property into its own control and André Lurton was able to buy this part. The gravelly soil has traces of clay in the subsoil and this gives body to the wine. Unlike the INRA part, which is classically planted with both Sémillon and Sauvignon, this vineyard is 100 per cent Sauvignon. Fermentation takes place in new casks (since 1982) at 16–18°C (61–64°F), followed by ten months' ageing before bottling. Generally, these wines are at their most attractive at between two and four years due to the Sauvignon. There are plans to plant Cabernet Sauvignon and Merlot to produce red wines, and the white vineyard, already extended from 1.5 hectares, will be further enlarged.

In 1992, André Lurton bought the château and *chais* from the INRA, and he has now renovated both. Classic wines were made here in '96, '97, and '98.

Château du Cruzeau V

Owner: André Lurton. Red: 67ha. 25,000 cases. CS 55%, Mer 43%, CF 2%.
White: 30ha. 15,000 cases. Sauv 85%, Sém 15%.

Another outpost of André Lurton's viticultural empire, this is the most important St-Médard-d'Eyrans *cru* and lies on the borders of that commune and Martillac. Acquired by André Lurton in 1973, the vineyard, on deep gravel, was entirely replanted by 1974.

Harvesting of the red grapes is by machine, while the white are hand-picked. The red is vinified in lined cement tanks and stainless-steel vats at 28–30°C (82–86°F), then matured for a year in casks, of which a third are new. The white is vinified in stainless-steel and glass-lined steel vats at 16–18°C (61–64°F) and sees no new wood before bottling. The red wine is scented, full-bodied, fruity, and supple, with the capacity for ageing but is also pleasant to drink after

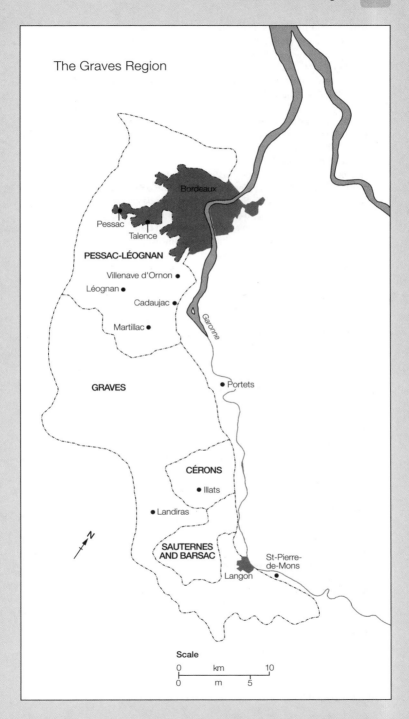

The Graves Region

Bordeaux

Pessac
Talence

PESSAC-LÉOGNAN

Villenave d'Ornon ●

Léognan ●

Cadaujac ●

Martillac ●

Garonne

GRAVES

● Portets

CÉRONS

● Illats

● Landiras

N

**SAUTERNES
AND BARSAC**

St-Pierre-
de-Mons
●

Langon

Scale

0   km   10

0   m   5

about three or four years. The white has a subtle aroma of spring blossom allied to a pleasant fruitiness of flavour. Compared with Rochemorin, the red wine here is richer and finer, while the white emphasizes its finesse.

Château Ferran

Owner: Béraud-Sadreau Family. Red: 11ha. 5,000 cases. Mer 45%, CS 45%, CF 10%. White: 4ha. 2,000 cases. Sauv 60%, Sém 40%.

This property takes its name from Robert de Ferrand, proprietor during the 17th century and member of the Parlement de Bordeaux. In 1715, it changed hands and was run by the philosopher Montesquieu. The red and white wines are long-lived and need time for their sound fruit characteristics to develop.

Château de Fieuzal ★ (☆) V

Cru Classé. Owner: Château de Fieuzal. Administrator: Gérard Gribelin. 38ha. Red: 13,000 cases.CS 60%, Mer 35%, PV 2.5%, CF 4.5%. White: 10ha. 4,000 cases. Sauv 50%, Sém 50%. Second label: l'Abeille de Fieuzal.

The transformation of this property dates from 1974, and Gérard Gribelin has been the constant factor, even after his family had to sell to the previous owner who in turn sold in 2001 to a notable Irish businessman, Lachlan Quinn. The reds are fermented in lined, steel vats equipped with an electronic temperature-control system, and are then matured in casks, of which 60 per cent are new. They are well-made: on the light side, but with elegance and a vivid fruity character. Since the '85 vintage there has been a marked filling-out, and recent wines show an extra dimension of concentration and depth of flavour that now put them in contention with those of such leading *crus* such as Haut-Bailly and Chevalier. The Graves character is there, but is not too obtrusive. The reputation of this wine has grown steadily in recent years.

The change in the white wine has been more dramatic. From 1985, it has been barrel-fermented under Denis Dubourdieu's supervision. They are intensely scented, quite rich, and fetch some of the highest prices in Graves.

Château de France

Owner: Bernard & Arnaud Thomassin. Red: 31ha. 15,000 cases. CS 60%, Mer 40%. White: 3ha. 1,100 cases. Sauv 70%, Sém 30%.

Situated just south of Léognan, this property was replanted and refurbished by Bernard Thomassin, who bought it in 1971. The white-wine vineyards are still young, but some deliciously aromatic fruity wines have been made since '93. The reds are developing well, producing good vintages from '83 onwards. This is certainly a property worth watching.

Château La Garde V →

Owner: Maison Dourthe. Red: 50ha, 11,500 cases. CS 60%, Mer 40%. White: 2ha. 1,000 cases. Sauv 100%. Second label: Château Naudin Larchay.

After belonging to Louis Eschenauer since 1926, this *cru* was sold to Dourthe in 1990. A substantial programme of development has been undertaken here in recent years. Not only has the red wine vineyard been expanded, but an elegant, pure-Sauvignon white wine has been introduced. The red wine has succulent, juicy fruit and some complexity, consistently impressive since '95.

Château Haut-Bailly ★★

Cru Classé. Owner: Robert G. Wilmers. Administrator: Véronique Sanders. Red: 28ha. 10,000 cases. CS 65%, Mer 25%, CF 10%. Second label: la Parde de Haut-Bailly.

Today, Haut-Bailly is regarded as one of the best red Graves properties, just behind Pape-Clément and often vying with Chevalier. The soil is abundant in gravel and pebbles, mixed with sand and clay.

The wine is often lighter in colour and texture than the other top red Graves, but the great feature is its harmony. It has both richness and vinosity, reminiscent of La Mission but with less tannin and power; the bouquet is strikingly similar to Pape-Clément. Thus the wines often develop quickly at first, yet keep well.

In 1998, the Sanders family sold to the present owner, an American with strong Belgian links. Happily Jean Sanders still oversees the winemaking, as he has since 1978. The '88, '89, '90, '93, '94, '95, '96, '98, '99, and 2000 are all wines of great potential.

Château Haut-Bergey V →

Owner: Mme Garcin-Cathiard. Red: 21ha. 6,000 cases. CS 65%, Mer 35%. White: 3ha. 1,000 cases. Sauv 65%, Sém 35%.

In 1991, Mme. Garcin-Cathiard, sister of Daniel Cathiard of Smith-Haut-Lafitte, bought this well placed Léognan vineyard. There has been considerable investment in the *cuvier* and *chai*. The first vintage of the new white wine was '91, and by the '94 vintage the wine, which is entirely fermented in barrel, was looking fine and distinguished. The reds now also seem more polished, with better-focused fruit and charm. This *cru* shows considerable potential for producing high-class wines.

Château Haut-Brion ★★★(☆☆☆)

1er Cru Classé 1855. Owner: Domaine Clarence Dillon. Red: 43ha. 16,000 cases. CS 45%, Mer 37%, CF 18%. White: 2.7ha. 900 cases. Sém 63%, Sauv 37%. Second label: Bahans Château Haut-Brion.

Haut-Brion is the only wine outside the Médoc to feature in the 1855 classification of red wines. In 1935, it was acquired by Clarence Dillon, the American banker. Since 1979, Clarence Dillon's granddaughter, Joan, the Duchesse de Mouchy, has been president of the company, and in 2001 her son, Prince Robert of Luxembourg, was appointed Managing Director. The much-respected Jean Delmas succeeded his father as *régisseur* in 1961 and is now technical director and assistant MD. In 1960 this was the first of the great *crus* to install stainless-steel fermentation vats.

The essence of the Haut-Brion style today can be summarized as elegance and harmony. The tannin, new oak (100 per cent each year), and fruit seem to be in balance after the first few months. This can give the wine the appearance of being ready to drink early; I remember my disbelief at the forwardness of the '75 in 1979. But, while this wine is more forward and more enjoyable than most leading wines of '75, there is also no doubting its ability to age well.

The great successes here in the 1980s are '82, '83, '85, '86, '88, '89, and '90. In the challenging 1990s, '91 is one of the few successes of the vintage, '93 is one of the best wines of the vintage, with '94 of similar quality. The '95, '96, '97, '98, '99, and 2000 are all superb. Haut-Brion seems to be on a high at the moment. The small quantity of white wine produced makes it a rarity, and most of it seems to go to the USA. It appears to show its charm more quickly than the Laville, due no doubt to the extra Sauvignon Blanc, yet it also ages well.

Château Haut-Lagrange →

Owner: François Bouterny. Red: 18.5ha. 10,500 cases. CS 55%, Mer 45%. White: 1.7ha. 1,000 cases. Sauv 50%, Sém 45%, Sauv Gris 5%.

This new vineyard in Léognan has been created by François Bouterny, after the sale of his family's neighbouring property, Larrivet-Haut-Brion. The first vintage to be commercialized was '92, and I was pleasantly surprised to find a wine with such glorious fruit flavour, with length and body, from young vines in this vintage. The white, with its interesting use of Sauvignon Gris, was aromatic and complex. An up-and-coming *cru*.

Château Larrivet-Haut-Brion ★ →

Owner: Andros. Administrator: Philippe Gervorson. Red: 43ha. 18,250 cases.
CS 50%, Mer 50%. White: 9ha. 4,000 cases. Sauv 50%, Sém 50%.

A famous old property in the central sector of Léognan, adjoining Haut-Bailly. It was called Haut-Brion-Larrivet until a lawsuit from Haut-Brion compelled a change. The Guillemaud family owned the property from 1941 and sold to the present owners in 1987.

This is a classic Graves with a fine colour and a spicy, delicate bouquet. Wines have finesse and age well. Usually they are as good or better than some of the red *crus classés*. The white wine was not of the same class until '96. The '96 vintage saw a spectacular improvement with the involvement of Jean-Michel Arcaute (*see* Château Clinet). Both red and white wines are superb and show that this property is capable of moving up a class.

Château Laville-Haut-Brion (★★★)

Cru Classé. Owner: Domaine Clarence Dillon.
White: 3.7ha. 1,100 cases. Sém 70%, Sauv 27%, Musc 3%.

The history of this tiny vineyard follows that of Château La Mission-Haut-Brion, where the wine is vinified, matured, and bottled. The soil here is richer and less stony than that of La Mission or La Tour-Haut-Brion, and this contributes to the wines' remarkable keeping powers. The vinification is in cask, in an air-conditioned cellar. From 1961, the wines were bottled in the late spring after the vintage, but since the '85 vintage, Jean Delmas has reverted to a longer cask maturation, bottling in the March of the second winter.

With Haut-Brion blanc and Chevalier, this is the great example of classic white Graves. Full-bodied, its complex flavour and character evolves only gradually. The wines differ from year to year in weight and power, so the speed at which they evolve varies. These are long-lived wines: the '34 was still superb in 1989; and "off" vintages such as '35 are a delightful surprise. After some austere vintages from '78 to '83, the wines are now richer and more harmonious; '95, '96, and '99 are exceptional.

Château La Louvière ★ (★) V

Owner: André Lurton. Red: 35ha. 18,000 cases. CS 64%, Mer 30%, CF 3%, PV 3%.
White: 13.5ha. 7,500 cases. Sauv 85%, Sém 15%. Second label: L de La Louvière.

This old property, an historical monument, has been largely restored and reconstructed by the dynamic André Lurton, who has owned it since 1965.

The white wine of Louvière has been notable for its outstanding finesse, delicacy and fruit since the '70 vintage at least. it certainly deserves to be *cru classé*. The red has made steady progress. The wines during the 1970s were vivid in colour, quite tannic but light-textured and had a tendency to be rather one-dimensional. However, the balance improved in the '80s and '90s. The '85 was better than a number of *crus classés* and the '86, more tannic but also opulent, was perhaps even finer. The '95, '96, '98, and '99 were outstandingly successful here. This is now a wine on a par with those of Pessac-Léognan's leading *crus*, and should feature in a new Graves classification.

Château Malartic-Lagravière ★ (★) →

Cru Classé. Owner: Alfred Alexandre Bonnie. 37ha. Red: 9,000 cases. CS 40%,
CF 10%, Mer 50%. White: 7ha. 2,500 cases. Sauv 80%, Sém 20%.
Second label: Le Sillage de Malartic.

This is a well-positioned vineyard on a high platform of gravelly soil, just southeast of the town of Léognan. Malartic, after remaining in the same family since 1850, was sold in 1990 to the family Champagne firm of Laurent-Perrier, then resold to the current owner in 1997. Since then major investments have been made to installations and vineyards. The red and white wines are vinified in stainless-steel vats, the white at a temperature not exceeding 18°C (64°F). The red wines are matured in casks, of which 50 per cent are new, the white in one-year-old casks for about seven months.

The red wines have a marked Graves character without a lot of weight or flesh, but with a clean, fresh flavour and good fruit. There are signs of improvement under the new regime. The white wine is one of the most attractive of white Graves with an outstanding bouquet and real individuality. It develops quickly and, for me, is at its best in its youthful phase. In the 1990s a little Sémillon was introduced into what had been a 100-per-cent Sauvignon wine, which has added complexity. Consistent.

Château La Mission-Haut-Brion ★★★

Cru Classé. Owner: Domaine Clarence Dillon. Red: 20.9ha. 7,500 cases. CS 48%, Mer 45%, CF 7%. Second label: La Chapelle de la Mission-Haut-Brion.

When the all-too-familiar problems of succession caused the Woltner heirs to put La Mission on the market in 1983, it was logical that their neighbours across the road at Haut-Brion should decide to buy. These two properties now constitute an oasis of vines surrounded by housing, much of it built on former vineyards between the two World Wars. Henri Woltner, who masterminded the vinification here from 1921 until his death in 1974, was probably the first to ferment his red wines at around 28°C (82°F) as a consistent policy, and in 1987 the old *cuvier* was replaced with the latest stainless-steel models. The wine is matured in 100 per cent new casks. The gravel in the vineyard is of exceptional depth and results in low yields and great concentration of flavour.

The wine of La Mission is rich and powerful, whereas that of Haut-Brion is all finesse and delicacy. Clearly La Mission is a *premier cru* in all but name. Its price has yearly been edging closer to that of the *premiers crus classés*, and mature wines often obtain the same prices as the firsts. The quality and individuality of this wine is outstanding. Always deep in colour, it is rich and concentrated in flavour without being uncomfortably tannic. It needs to evolve and lasts well. It also has a wonderful record for successes in "off" vintages. Classic wines were made in '81, '82, '83, '85, '86, '88, '89, and '90. The '91, '93, '94, '95, '96, '97, '98, '99, and 2000 were exceptional in these vintages. The second wine was introduced in '91.

Château Olivier (✰)

Cru Classé. Owner: GFA Château Olivier. Administrator: Jean-Jacques de Bethmann. Red: 41ha. 12,000 cases. CS 55%, Mer 35%, CF 10%.
White: 11ha. 4,500 cases. Sém 55%, Sauv 40%, Musc 5%.

For over 70 years, this famous estate was farmed by Eschenauer, the négociant, and was its monopoly. Then, in November 1981, the Bethmann family took the management back into their own hands and Jean-Jacques de Bethmann assumed responsibility for running the property. The distribution remained in Eschenauer's control until 1987, but for only part of the crop. The vineyard was radically reconstructed in the early to mid-1970s with a view to increasing the size of the red vineyard and ensuring that the grape varieties were planted on the most favourable soils. Progress has been rather disappointing and many wines seem to suffer from too much new oak for their weight.

The white wine is what Olivier has always been known for. With the high proportion of Sémillon, you must not expect the instant charm the Sauvignon gives in the first months of bottle-ageing, but the wines do become more interesting. The flavour is marked and individual with plenty of character. The '95 shows an important advance in quality.

Château le Pape
Owner: GFA du Château Le Pape. Administrator: Patrick Monjanel.
6ha. 3,000 cases. Mer 75%, CS 25%.

This property has a particularly attractive château, built in the style of the First Empire. Patrick Monjanel has been administrator since '98, and it will be interesting to see what changes he makes. An unusually small proportion of Cabernet Sauvignon is grown here. There is a rich, solid '98.

Château Pape-Clément ★★ (☆)
Cru Classé. Owner: Montagne family. Administrator: Bernard Magrez. 30ha.
Red: 7,000 cases. CS 60%, Mer 40%. White: 2.5ha. 400 cases. Sém 45%,
Sauv 45%, Musc 10%. Second label: Le Clémentin du Pape-Clément.

This vineyard has the longest continuous history of any in Bordeaux; it was first planted in 1300. It is a red-wine château, although white-wine production was expanded in the 1990s. The soil is sand and gravel, with traces of iron. After traditional vinification, wine is matured in 70–100 per cent new oak. The wines of Pape-Clément have a marvellous bouquet, intense with overtones of tobacco, and a supple, rich texture that enables them to be enjoyed relatively young. But after some wonderful vintages in the 1960s, Pape-Clément was disturbingly inconsistent for a number of years. After a good '75 came a string of small and often dilute wines. Even the '82 was disappointing. With the appointment of Bernard Pujols in 1985, however, and the completion of a new *cuvier* and re-equipped *chai*, Pape-Clément returned to its real form with the '85, and since then, '86, '88, '89, and '90 have produced wines to set beside the great vintages of the 1960s. The '93 and '94 were excellent for the years and exceptional wines were made in '95, '96, '98, '99, and 2000. In reputation, Pape-Clément has overtaken Chevalier in recent vintages.

Château Picque-Caillou
Owner: Paulin and Isabelle Calvet. 20ha. 10,500 cases. Mer 45%, CS 45%,
CF 10%. White: 1ha. 500 cases. Sém 50%, Sauv 50%.

This vineyard lies on gravelly and stony soil, surrounded by the sprawling suburbs of Bordeaux. The wines have a good reputation for being stylish, supple, and full-flavoured. They usually evolve fairly quickly and also keep well. Wines of breed. The Calvet family bought the property in '97.

Château Pontac-Monplaisir
Owner: Jean Maufras. Red: 9ha. 6,500 cases. CS 60%, Mer 40%. White: 2ha. 1,200
cases. Sauv 60%, Sém 40%. Second label: Château Limbourg.

An old *cru*, dating back to the 1600s, this property is recorded on Cassini's map produced in the 18th century. The vineyards themselves are not the original ones, as these were sold by the present owner and a supermarket now stands on their site. Much care and attention has been put into the winemaking, and the results are elegant, scented reds with the character and breed so typical of Graves; the whites are stylish, with plenty of varietal Sémillon; the Limbourg whites have more Sauvignon Blanc character.

Château de Quantin V

Owner: André Lurton. Red: 27ha. 6,000 cases. CS 50%, Mer 50%.
White: 10ha. 7,000 cases. Sauv 90%, Sém 10%.

The Beleyme map of 1770 shows that this was an extensive vineyard in the 18th century. It is on gravelly slopes in St-Médard d'Eyrans, close to its border with La Brède. But the vineyard was abandoned and the property became a stud-farm until the potential of the *terroir* was recognized by André Lurton, who had also resuscitated nearby Château Cruzeau. He bought the property in 1985. I found the '95 red had a scent of violets with real style and beautifully expressive fruit from such young vines. The only white I have seen had a strong and rather coarse Sauvignon flavour. This addition to the Lurton stable will be followed with interest.

Château de Rochemorin V

Owner: André Lurton. Red: 87ha. 30,000 cases. CS 60%, Mer 40%.
White: 18ha. 9,000 cases. Sauv 90%, Sém 10%.

The name of this château is derived from *Roche-Morine*, indicating that it was a fortified palace at the time of the Moorish incursions from Spain in the 7th and 8th centuries. The energetic André Lurton bought this old property in 1973 and began replanting the vineyards (which had been replaced by forest) in 1974. The vines are on deep gravel on the highest ridge of Martillac. As at other Lurton properties, harvesting is mechanical for the reds and manual for the whites. Fermentation is controlled at 28–30°C (82–86°F) for the reds and 16–18°C (61–64°F) for the whites. The reds are matured for a year in cask, with one-third new wood, but the whites see no wood at all.

The red wines now show quite a spicy, aromatic Graves bouquet allied to elegance and breed, and are lighter and more marked by new oak than those of nearby Cruzeau. Even from 1981, fine wines were being made here, and by the late 1980s they were filling out and moving into a higher gear. The white wine is different from that of Cruzeau. It has a less floral bouquet and more body, but is elegant, with a finish that is flinty and drier than that of Cruzeau. Now that the vineyard has gained maturity, the red wines especially have more structure and character.

Château de Rouillac

Owner: Domaines Lafragette. 16ha. 3,000 cases. CS 60%, Mer 35%, PV 5%.

Once the only *cru* left in the commune of Canéjean (it lost this distinction when Château Séguin was replanted in 1987), Rouillac has an attractive château, built by the architect Baron Haussmann in 1869. The present owners took over in '96 from the Sarthous, who had replanted the vineyard. Now that it is reaching maturity, rich, sumptuous wines of typical Graves character are being produced.

Château Le Sartre V

Owner: GFA du Château Le Sartre. Administrator: Antony Perrin. Red: 18ha.
10,000 cases. CS 65%, Mer 35%. White: 7ha. 3,000 cases. Sauv 65%, Sém 35%.

The Perrin family had to rebuild this property completely when they bought it in 1981: it had been much neglected since 1914. By the '90s very fruity stylish red wines capable of early enjoyment and delicious fresh fruity whites were being made.

Château Smith-Haut-Lafitte ★ →

Cru Classé. Owner: Daniel and Florence Cathiard. Red: 45ha. 10,000 cases. CS 55%, Mer 35%, CF 10%. White: 10ha. 2,200 cases. Sauv 90%, Sauv Gris 5%, Sém 5%.
Second label: Les Hauts-de-Smith-Haut-Lafitte.

A proprietor with the splendidly English name of George Smith bought this *cru* in 1720 and added his name to that of the place-name. The firm Louis Eschenauer owned the property from 1958 until 1991, when it sold to the Cathiard family. There has been major investment in the vineyards and buildings. In 1960, fewer than six hectares were planted, and no white wine was made. Now there are 55 hectares. A large underground cellar was built in 1974 to hold 2,000 casks, and all the vinification equipment was renewed. Half the red wine is matured in new oak.

The wines have a pronounced character, aromatic and spicy. Although there was an improvement in the the 1980s, the dramatic turnaround has been achieved under the Cathiard ownership. After the difficult vintages of the early '90s, a superb red wine was made in '95 with ripe, harmonious fruit, followed by a succession of fine vintages. For the whites, '94 proved to be a classic, one of the best of the vintage; '95 was richer and very complex, since when the introduction of Sauvignon Gris and some Sémillon have added complexity.

A lot of work has been done in the vineyards, with the emphasis on traditional methods and lower yields. Michel Rolland advises on the red wine, and Christophe Olivier on the white.

Château Le Thil Comte Clary →

Owner: Arnaud and Jean de Laître. Red: 8.5ha. 5,000 cases. Mer 70%, CS 30%. White: 3.1ha. 1,800 cases. Sém 50%. Sauv 50%.

Jean de Laître, a descendant of the Comte Clary after whom the property is named, abandoned a medical career in Paris in 1989 to recreate the vineyard here which was planted in 1990 for the red, a year later for the white. The presence of calcareous clay in part of the vineyard accounts for the unusually high level of Merlot in the vineyard. I have found the red wines to have fine fruit, charm and harmony while the whites have elegance, very fine fruit character and good balance. These are wines of real potential which can only improve as the vineyard matures.

Château La Tour-Haut-Brion ★ V

Cru Classé. Owner: Domaine Clarence Dillon.
Red: 4.9ha. 8,000 cases. CS 42%, CF 35%, Mer 23%.

This small property, adjoining La Mission, was purchased by the Woltner brothers in 1933. The wines have been vinified at La Mission since then, and under the Dewavrin administration (1975–83) were treated as second wines. One of Jean Delmas' first decisions was to restore its position as a *cru* in its own right. The result is still a fine wine, certainly better than a number of the other *crus classés* of Graves. It is full-bodied but less intense than La Mission, and matures more quickly while ageing well. Excellent wines were made in '85, '86, '88, '89, and '90. Good wines were made in '93 and '94; excellent ones in '95, '96, '98, '99, and 2000.

Château La Tour-Martillac★

Cru Classé. Owner: Kressmann Family. Red: 30ha. 10,000 cases. CS 60%, Mer 35%, CF & PV 5%. White: 10ha. 3,000 cases. Sém 55%, Sauv 40%, Musc 5%.
Second label: Château La Grave-Martillac (red) 1,000 cases.

The name comes from a 12th century tower, once the staircase of a fort, the ruins of which were used in the building of today's farm two centuries ago. In the 1870s, Edouard Kressmann, the founder of the famous old négociant house, obtained the exclusivity of this *cru*, and the family finally bought it in 1929. Ten hectares of pasture provide cattle manure for the vineyard.

The grapes from the older vines are still fermented in the traditional wooden vats at 32–33°C (90–91°F), while the production from younger vines goes into lined steel vats which are water-cooled. Maturation is in casks of which a third are new. The second wine, Château La Grave-Martillac, is made from vines less than ten years old and *vin de presse*. It is sold only direct from the château. The white wine has been vinified in cask, since Denis Dubourdieu began advising in 1987. This has given the wines an extra dimension and lifted them to the upper echelons of white Graves.

I have found the red wine to have elegant fruit on the nose and a fine flavour with breed and length, but it is rather light-textured. The white wine is elegant and fresh, with quite an original character. It has delicacy, real breed and a fine finish. This is high-class white Graves.

SOUTHERN GRAVES

Château d'Archambeau V
Owner: Jean-Philippe Dubourdieu. Red: 19ha. 10,800 cases. Mer 50%, CS 40%, CF 10%. White: 19ha. 5,500 cases. Sém 50%, Sauv 50%.
Second label: Château Mourlet, Château La Citadelle.

The commune of Illats that adjoins Barsac, like those of Cérons and Potensac, can vinify its white wines either as Cérons or as Graves Supérieur. Here at d'Archambeau only small quantities of Cérons are now made, and the emphasis is on classic, dry Graves. The Dubourdieu family has a formidable reputation as winemakers in Barsac and Graves, and Jean-Philippe, nephew of Pierre Dubourdieu of Doisy-Daëne fame, is no exception. The white wines are cold-fermented in lined metal and stainless-steel vats, and bottled in the spring. The combination of Sémillon and Sauvignon produces wines of elegance and depth of character that are delicious within months of bottling but also keep and mature well.

The red wine is a more recent development, the first commercialized vintage from young vines being the '82. The wines have vivid fruit and immediate charm, and have added a little extra roundness and depth as the vineyard has matured.

Château Ardennes
Owners: François and Bertrand Dubrey. Red: 43ha. 27,500 cases. Mer 50%, CS 40%, CF 10%. White: 17.6ha. 11,500 cases. Sém 60%, Sauv 40%.

Both red and white wines are made at Château Ardennes, the red being rather better, with a violet perfume, good structure, and the ability to age well (an unusual quality in wines of this area).

Château d'Arricaud V
Owners: Jeanine Bouyx. Red: 12ha. 6,700 cases. CS 40%, Mer 60%.
White: 11ha. 5,600 cases. Sém 65%, Sauv 30%, Musc 5%.

An old property and the most important in the commune of Landiras, Château d'Arricaud was actually built by a former president of the Parlement de Bordeaux. Its wines are well-made, the reds ideal for young drinking with a delicious fruitiness and plenty of charm; the whites elegant with good length.

Château La Blancherie and Château La Blancherie-Peyret V
Owner: Françoise Coussié-Giraud. Red: 10ha. 5,000 cases. CS 45%, Mer 50%, CF 5%. White: 11ha. 5,300 cases. Sém 50%, Sauv 45%, Musc 5%.

The commune of La Brède is famous for its château of the same name where Montesquieu, the renowned 17th century philosopher and historian, was born and lived. Today, this is the most important wine-producing château of the commune. It also has a colourful history, for its proprietors at the time of the 1789 Revolution were both guillotined!

The white wines (sold under the La Blancherie label) are fermented at low temperatures, the reds (La Blancherie-Peyret) receive a long maceration and are aged in cask. The whites are fruity and vigorous in style. The reds have an arresting bouquet, redolent of tobacco and spice, and lots of flavour and character, but are supple and powerful at the same time, so that they can be drunk young yet can also age. This is an excellent *cru* producing well-made wines.

Château Brondelle V

Owner: J. N. Belloc. Red: 25ha. 7,800 cases. CS 60%, Mer 40%. White: 15ha. 5,600 cases. Sém 60%, Sauv 35%, Musc 5%. Second label: Château La Croix-St-Pey.

Brondelle is in Langon, one of the most important winemaking communes in Graves, where the growers have profited much from the work on clonal selection carried out by the INRA. The wines produced, both the red and white, are attractive and worth looking out for.

Château Cabannieux

Owner: Régine Dudignac-Barrière. Red: 14ha. 8,000 cases. Mer 50%, CS 45%, CF 5%. White: 6ha. 3,500 cases. Sém 80%, Sauv 20%.
Second labels: Châteaux de Curcier and Haut Migot.

This property is in the highest part of the commune of Portets on well-drained, gravelly soil, with some traces of clay. It belongs to the same owners as the well-respected négociant firm of A & R Barrière. The red wines are given two to three weeks in contact with the skins for maximum extraction. Part of the crop is put in cask, and a small amount of new wood is used. For the white, there is a controlled, low-temperature fermentation at below 20°C (68°F). The aim is to produce red wines with a pronounced Graves character, full-flavoured but soft and good for early drinking. The white has a small percentage of Sauvignon to give the early bouquet. Both enjoy a good reputation.

Château de Cardaillan

Owner: Comtesse de Bournazel.
Red: 20ha. 9,000 cases. CS 50%, Mer 50%.
White: 2.8ha. 1,100 cases (sold as M de Malle).

The de Bournazel family has a large property, which is divided by the boundary between the Sauternes commune of Preignac and the Graves commune of Toulenne. The red wines of the Graves portion of the vineyard are sold as Cardaillan and the white as M de Malle. The red is early maturing, fruity, and easy, while the white has a touch of distinction with aromatic fruit flavours and a nicely balanced acidity: a really well-made wine.

Château Cazebonne

Owner: Jean-Marc Bridet. Red: 12.5ha. 7,500 cases. CS 65%, Mer 35%. White: 5ha. 3,300 cases. Sauv 60%, Sém 40%.

A property in St-Pierre-de-Mons producing red wines with plenty of fruit and colour but which are perhaps a bit firm. The whites are slightly more elegant, with a pleasant crispness.

Château de Chantegrive

Owners: Henri and Françoise Lévêque. Red: 50ha. 27,500 cases. CS 45%, Mer 45%, CF 10%. White: 38ha. 15,000 cases. Sém 50%, Sauv 45%, Musc 5%. Second label: Mayne-d'Anice.Other label: Cuvée Caroline.

The Lévêques have steadily built up this property from modest beginnings. When I first visited Chantegrive, there were only 15 hectares of vines, now there are over 80. The soil is white sand mixed with quartz pebbles.

Vinification at Chantegrive is carefully controlled at low temperatures for the whites. The white wines are fresh, delicious, fruity, aromatic, and easy to drink. The Cuvée Caroline is fermented and aged in cask, an outstanding example of new-wave aromatic Graves style. The reds are aged for 18 months in casks, of which 30 per cent are new oak, in an underground cellar. They are fruity and supple but with some depth as well, the sort of easy-to-drink wines that deserve more attention than they currently receive.

Château Chicane

Owner: Gauthier family. 5.3ha. 2,800 cases. CS 55%, Mer 30%, Mal 15%.
In 1994, François Gauthier took over from his famous uncle, Pierre Coste. Red wines are produced for drinking young – at around two to four years old. They are light-bodied with a pleasing, spicy nose and lots of fruit.

Château Coutet

Owners: Marcel and Bertrand Baly.
White: 10ha. 2,800 cases. Sém 30%, Sauv 65%, Musc 5%.
The wines of the Château Coutet can be rather confusing. Dry wines made in Sauternes and Barsac are allowed only the Bordeaux Blanc AC, and in 1977 the Baly family bought another château of the same name, the famous Barsac *cru* of Coutet, where it produces such wines. The family also owns property in Pujols-sur-Ciron, a commune with Sauternes and Barsac on three sides of it, and is selling its Pujols *cru*, formerly known as Reverdon, as "Vin Sec du Château Coutet" with the Graves AC. These wines, produced using cold fermentation, have a strong aroma of gooseberries, but they are disappointingly skeletal.

Château Ferrande

Owner: Héritiers H Delnaud. Administrators: Castel Frères. Red: 32ha. 21,000 cases. Mer 34%, CS 33%, CF 33%. White: 7ha. 3,300 cases. Sauv 50%, Sém 50%.
This is the most important *cru* in the commune of Castres. Since the Delnaud family began its partnership with Marc Teisseire in 1955, the vineyard has been expanded and the facilities improved. Concrete and stainless-steel vats are used for vinification and the red is matured in cask, with ten per cent new oak.

I have found the red deep in colour, having a lively and spicy bouquet with tobacco overtones. The flavour is frank and fresh, light-textured but full and fruity. This is an enjoyable wine which can be drunk with pleasure when three to four years old. The white has quite a pronounced Graves flavour. It is powerful and slightly earthy but fruity. It has its admirers, but for me, it has less charm and breed than the red.

Clos Floridène V

Owners: Denis and Florence Dubourdieu. Red: 5ha. 2,500 cases. CS 80%, Mer 20%. White: 12ha. 6,500 caes. Sém 50%, Sauv 30%, Musc 20%.
Second label: Château Montalivet.
Having already made a name at Château Reynon in the Premières Côtes, the Dubourdieus chose this site in Pujols/Ciron in the southern Graves to make white and red Graves. Nineteeth century editions of *Bordeaux et ses Vins* show that Puyols produced the most reputed dry white wines at a time when hardly any whites were made in Pessac-Léognan, and most other white Graves were *demi-sec*. Certainly these wines have body and breeding, with

a long flavour and a really dry finish. The reds are full of deliciously flattering, supple fruit.

Château de Gaillat V
Owner: Coste family. 12.7ha. 6,500 cases. CS 61%, Mer 30%, Mal 5%, Carmènere 4%.
The care Pierre Coste gives to vinification has resulted in some outstanding vintages. Wines are bottled in the June after the vintage to gain maximum fruit. An explosion of fruit on the nose followed by a taste of crushed fruit characterizes these wines, which are delicious within 18 months.

Château du Grand Abord
Owner: Marc and Colette Dugoua. Red: 8ha. 4,400 cases. Mer 90%, CS 10%.
White: 4ha. 2,000 cases. Sém 85%, Sauv 15%.
A property situated on the gravel soils of the plateau at Portets. The red wines are most attractive and for drinking young.

Château Landiras
Owner: SCA Adélaïde Audy. Red: 5ha. 2,600 cases. CS 50%, Mer 50%.
White: 12.5ha. 6,000 cases. Sém 70%, Sauv Gris 30%.
The château's history can be traced back to 1173; the ruins and moat of an ancient castle remain. The vineyard was replanted, mostly in the 1990s, by Peter Vinding-Diers. A new *cuvier* was completed in time for the '88 vintage and some stylish wines have been produced – the reds reflecting their Cabernet origins and the whites having plenty of classic Sémillon style and body enlivened by the spiciness of Sauvignon Gris. The property was sold in 1998, and is now distributed by Maison Sichel.

Château Magence V
Owner: Comte Jean d'Antras. Red: 26ha.13,000 cases. CS 46%, Mer 36%, CF 18%.
White: 11ha. 6,500 cases. Sauv 55%, Sém 45%.
One of the best-known properties in St-Pierre-de-Mons, the most important Graves commune lying to the southeast of Sauternes. It has been in the same family since 1800, but is fully up-to-date. Fermentation is in temperature-controlled stainless steel. This was one of the early classic modern white Graves, once entirely Sauvignon but now balanced with Sémillon: it has real finesse and style. The reds are also useful: supple yet slightly tannic.

Château Magneau V
Owner: Henri Ardurats. Red: 14ha. 6,700 cases. Mer 50%, CS 35%, CF 15%.
White: 26ha. 12,000 cases. Sauv 50%, Sém 30%, Musc 20%.
Second label: Château Guirauton.
The white wines produced at this *cru* in La Brède are particularly good: they lack the coarseness of some Graves wines and are stylish and well-made with plenty of fruit. The reds, attractive and with a distinctly pungent aroma, are mostly ready to drink when young. The Château Guirauton label is used only for white wines.

Château Millet V
Owner: de la Mette family. Red: 15ha. 8,900 cases. Mer 60%, CS 30%, CF 10%.
White: 7ha. 5,400 cases. Sém 70%, Sauv 30%.
The red, now more important than the white, is matured in cask. Wines not up to standard (such as the '77 and '80) are not bottled with the château name, but in general these are decent, fruity, early maturing wines.

Château Le Pavillon-de-Boyrein V
Owner: Société Pierre Bonnet et Fils. Red: 20ha.11,000 cases. Mer 70%, CS 30%.
White: 3ha.1,500 cases. Sém 65%, Sauv 35%.
Second label: Domaine des Lauriers.

The best *cru* in its commune of Roaillon. This château produces wines similar in quality to many *crus bourgeois* of the northern Médoc. The red wines are the more pleasant, with a hint of terroir in the form of mineral and iron overtones.

Château Rahoul

Owner: Alain Thiénot. Red: 22ha. 13,000 cases. Mer 60%, CS 40%.
White: 5ha. 2,000 cases. Sém 80%, Sauv 20%.
Second label: Château Constantin.

This old property in Portets was bought by an Australian syndicate in 1978. The Australians brought in a young Danish oenologist, Peter Vinding-Diers, and invested in stainless steel and new oak. In 1982, they sold to another Dane, who in turn sold to the present owner, a merchant from Champagne. He took over the management when Vinding-Diers left in 1988 to run his own property (*see* Château Landiras). The vineyard is not in the best position (low-lying with some drainage problems), but the expertise of the winemaker has been successful. A proportion of new oak is used for the maturation of both red and white wines after low-temperature fermentations.

The white wines are elegant and long-flavoured, lacking only the complexity and depth of the best Graves further north. The reds, full of vivid spicy fruit, are at their most delicious when young. This is what investment in expertise and the best equipment can achieve. How much room for improvement there is at many better-known and better-placed vineyards!

Château Respide-Médeville

Owner: Christian Médeville. 7.5ha. Red: 3,000 cases. CS 60%, Mer 40%.
White: 5.4ha. 2,500 cases. Sém 50%, Sauv 45%, Musc 5%.

This *cru*, on the ridge of gravelly clay in Toulenne, has been built up by Christian Médeville of Château Gilette to earn its current high reputation. The white wines develop pleasingly; the reds are charming for drinking young.

Château de Roquetaillade-La-Grange

Owner: Bruno, Dominique & Pascal Guignard. 30ha. Red:16,500 cases. Mer 30%, CS 60%, CF 8%, Mal 2%. White: 15ha. 8,200 cases. Sém 50%, Sauv 25%, Musc 25%.
Second label: Château de Carolle.

The splendid early 14th century château, built by a nephew of Pope Clement V, is regarded as the finest example of military architecture in southeastern France. The property, on the hillsides to the east of the château, is actually unconnected with the château itself, which has no important vineyards. The owners have raised the standard of the wines, winning a number of medals in Paris and a reputation as producers of one of the best red wines in southern Graves.

The consistent reds have individuality and lovely mellow fruit on nose and palate – sometimes, with an unmistakable hint of cherries, a fruit flavour unusual for Bordeaux. The white, quite full-bodied, has improved with better vinification, but is still rather unexciting.

Château St-Agrèves

Owner: Marie-Christiane Landry. Red: 12ha. 6,000 cases. CS & CF 70%, Mer 30%.
White: 4ha. 750 cases. Sauv 50%, Sém 50%.

The red wines produced at Château St-Agrèves are unusual for this region in that they benefit from longer maturation than many of their neighbours. They are attractive wines, however, and show a good balance of fruit and tannin. The whites are rather more coarse in style than those from nearby *crus*.

Château St-Jean des Graves V

Owner: Jean-Gérard David. Red: 13ha. 6000 cases. Mer 70%, CF 30%.
White 7ha. 3,300 cases. Sém 50%, Sauv 50%.

As Denis Dubourdieu has shown at Clos Floridène, the special soils of Pujols-sur-Ciron with their *sables rouges* as in Barsac, on a chalky subsoil, are ideal for producing wines of character. Here the whites are especially good, with body, fine fruit and real character; the reds show seductively lively fruit but are fairly light in spite of the Merlot.

Château St-Robert V

Owner: Foncier Vignobles. Administrator: Michel Garat. Red: 28ha.15,500 cases.
Mer 60%, CS 20%, CF 20%. White: 5ha. 2,500 cases. Sém 80%, Sauv 20%.

Another excellent property in Pujols-sur-Ciron which belongs to Crédit Foncier and is run in conjunction with their excellent Sauternes property, Bastor-Lamontagne. Its origins go back to the 17th and 18th centuries.

In recent years, these wines have consistently done well in comparative tastings. The red has real style, with lots of luscious, ripe fruit and richness, while the white has good body and character. This is one of the best properties in the Southern Graves.

Château Tourteau-Chollet

Owner: Cordier-Mestrezat Domaines. Administrator: Alain Duhau. 45ha.
Red: 12,500 cases: CS 53%, Mer 47%. White: 7ha. 2,900 cases. Sauv 100%.

The commune of Arbanat lies southeast of Portets: this is its most important property. Since taking over in 1977, the owners have steadily made improvements; now pleasant, fruity reds (gold label) and elegant, dry whites (white label) are being made. A property to watch. This is another part of the Mestrezat empire, now incorporated into Cordier (*see* Grand-Puy-Ducasse and Rayne-Vigneau).

Château Vieux Château Gaubert V →

Owner: Dominique Haverlan. Red: 20ha. 12,000 cases. CS 50%, Mer 45%, CF 5%.
White: 4ha. 2,000 cases. Sém 50%, Sauv 45%, Musc 5%.

The present owner bought Château Pessan-St-Hilaire in 1981 and has since then expanded the vineyards and enlarged the *chai*. In 1988, he bought this old property and has concentrated his efforts here since then. He is a trained oenologist and makes attractive wines. Both reds and whites show continual improvement.

Sauternes and Barsac

Sauternes is produced in five communes: Sauternes, Barsac, Fargues-de-Langon, Bommes, and Preignac. Barsac is also an AC in its own right, and producers there can label their wines Barsac or Sauternes or (as many do) Sauternes-Barsac.

Traditional Sauternes is a luxury wine, and luxury wines have to be sold at luxury prices. If an article becomes unfashionable and can no longer command its former high prices, something has to give, and that is likely to be quality. This, in a nutshell, has been the dilemma facing Sauternes since the late 1950s.

The top red growth can expect to make 40 hectolitres per hectare in a good vintage, sometimes more, and seldom fewer than 30. At Yquem, the standard-bearer for Sauternes, over the past 30 years the average yield has been nine hectolitres per hectare, in contrast with 25 allowed by the appellation. On this basis, Yquem's price would need to be around four times that of Lafite or Pétrus to produce the same income; in fact, it is in the region of two and a half times that amount. Costs are also much higher because of picking methods (*see* page 34), and there are years when frosts, hail or rain during the vintage mean that the wine is not good enough to go out under the famous label of Yquem.

The result of all this has been that only a few Sauternes properties have been able to continue to make wines in anything approaching the traditional way. Whatever short-cuts may be possible with the aid of modern technology, there can be no substitute for botrytis, or *pourriture noble* (noble rot). This is what gives Sauternes its distinctive bouquet and flavour, its complex range of fruit, flavours, and finesse. The short-cut of picking ripe but unaffected grapes and then chaptalizing can produce only unsubtle sweet wines that may be quite elegant and fresh, but will never develop into anything of interest.Fortunately, there are signs that there are now enough lovers of true Sauternes willing to pay the price for a certain quantity of this nectar, and enough dedicated proprietors with the financial strength to withstand the bad years. The 1980s and the late '90s again produced great wines and a revival of interest.

One way of helping to cover costs is to produce a proportion of dry wine, or even red. Unfortunately, however good these may be, such efforts are hampered by the appellation system which will give only a simple Bordeaux AC to such wines (or Bordeaux Supérieur in the case of red wines). Ironically, in neighbouring Cérons, the producers of this sweet wine have the right to the Graves AC for their dry whites and reds. This has so far been denied to the growers of Sauternes, apparently quite illogically.

The dividing-line between success and failure is a fine one. There are now 11 *premiers crus*. Twenty years or so ago, only five of these were making wines that were up to standard. Since then, the new owner of Guiraud has turned it around, and the Cordiers have reversed their policy at Lafaurie-Peyraguey. Most recently of all, AXA bought Suduiraut which had been underperforming and Domaines Rothschild has secured the future of one of the best properties, Rieussec.

There are 14 *deuxièmes crus*, and of these there are probably eight owners who aim to produce quality wines to some extent, and only half of these make more than 2,000 cases. On the other hand, the vines of one of the *deuxièmes crus*, Myrat, were pulled up in 1976 but, happily, replanted in 1988. Doisy-Daëne has been the *deuxième cru* most dedicated to quality over the past 30 years. Improvements also came in the 1970s, with Nairac being transformed by Tom Heeter; more recently, Pierre Perromat has leased d'Arche, and the Guignard brothers have greatly improved their part of Lamothe. There are three unclassified growths that now make wines of classified quality: Bastor-Lamontagne, Raymond-Lafon, and de Fargues.

Essentially Sauternes is a great dessert wine intended to be drunk at the end of a meal, and this clearly puts it into the special-occasions-only category. Of course, it can be drunk as an aperitif, but it is not exactly designed to put an edge on your appetite, and the Bordelais habit of drinking it with a first course of foie gras hardly has a wide application.

A more likely way forward is through the new devices for keeping open bottles under nitrogen, which make it possible for restaurant diners to order a single glass of Sauternes at the end of a meal. If this practice becomes widespread, the future of Sauternes will look brighter. But unless more people are prepared to pay more and drink Sauternes more often, then the future for even a small number of quality *crus* will remain limited.

Château d'Arche (✭)

2e Cru Classé. Owner: Bastit-St-Martin family. Administrator: Pierre Perromat.
30ha. 2,200 cases. Sém 80%, Sauv 15%, Musc 5%.
Second label: Cru de Braneyre.

This old property has a château dating from the 16th century and a reputation going back to the 18th. After a rather undistinguished period, Pierre Perromat (president of the INAO for 30 years) leased the property in 1981 and determined to make classic Sauternes again. The traditional selections are now made in the vineyard and, after fermentation in vat, the wine is matured for at least two years in casks, 40 per cent of which are new. The first wines of the new regime seem well-balanced, with attractive fruit and sweetness and a certain fineness and breed. The best vintages are '86, '88, '90, '96, '97, '98, and '99.

Château Bastor-Lamontagne (✭) V

Cru Bourgeois. Owner: Crédit Foncier de France. Administrator: Michel Garat.
50ha. 13,000 cases. Sém 78%, Sauv 17%, Musc 5%.
Second label: Les Ramparts de Bastor.

This excellent *cru* is in Preignac, adjoining Suduiraut. It has for many years consistently produced excellent wines and is on the level of the *crus classés* – indeed, better than some of them. The wines are carefully and traditionally made, with three years' cask-ageing and 25 per cent new wood. The result is rich, luscious wine with the aroma and flavour of apricots and all the stylishness of a top-rate Sauternes. Recently, '88, '89, '90, '96, '97, '98, '99, and 2001 have all been highly successful vintages.

Château Broustet

2e Cru Classé. Owner: Laulan family. Administrator: Didier Laulan.
16ha. 3,000 cases. Sém 63%, Sauv 25%, Musc 12%.
Second label: Château de Ségur.

This small property is not well known, mainly because its production is small. From 1885 it belonged to the Fournier family, although the vineyard was not replanted until 1900. Broustet was sold to its present owners in 1994.

The wine is fermented in vat but matured in casks, of which a small percentage is new. It has a fine perfume, is generous and quite rich with pleasing individuality and breed. Often seemingly clumsy when young, the wines age well. 2001 is the best wine for some years.

Château Caillou (✭)

2e Cru Classé. Owner: J-B Bravo and Marie José Pierre.
13ha. 3,300 cases. Sém 90%, Sauv 10%. Second label: Petit Mayne.

A little-known property because the wine is all sold by *vente directe* to private customers so this is a place to visit if you have your car and room in the boot! The present owner has run the property since 1969, and keeps stocks of old vintages.

The wines are carefully made, with fermentation in vat and maturation in casks, of which a small percentage is new, for up to three years. The wines have the reputation of being light, elegant, and fruity and '96 and '97 seem to mark an improvement.

Château Climens (✩✩✩)

1er Cru Classé. Owner: SCEA du Château Climens. Administrator: Bérénice Lurton. 29ha. 5,600 cases. Sém 100%. Second label: Cyprès de Climens.

For many, Climens is the region's best wine after Yquem – not that the two can really be compared. The emphasis here is on elegance, breed, and freshness: Climens does not generally attempt to compete with Yquem's lusciousness. Since 1971, the property has belonged to the Lurton family. In 1992, Lucien Lurton handed over to his two daughters: Brigitte (who ran it in the 1980s) and Bérénice, who has been in charge during the 1990s.

The soil is red sand and gravel over limestone. After settling for 24 hours in vat, the juice is fermented in casks, of which 25 per cent are new, and matured for about two years before bottling. The wines here are remarkably consistent in a region where it is not always easy to make good Sauternes. They are rather closed at first and usually need a minimum of ten years before they begin to give of their best. The qualities here are balance, freshness, elegance, and liquorousness in the great years, which make it a long-lived wine.

Since 1983, the wines seem to have moved into another gear with a succession of outstanding wines in '83, '85, '86, '88, '89, and '90, placing Climens second only to Yquem as Sauternes' quality *cru*. The '91 is one of the few good wines of this vintage, and fine wines were made in '94 and '95, great wines in '96, '97, '98, '99, and 2001.

Château Coutet (✩✩) →

1er Cru Classé. Owner: Marcel Baly. 38ha. 7,000 cases. Sém 75%, Sauv 23%, Musc 2%. Other label: Château Coutet Cuvée Madame.

The name of Coutet is always linked to that of Climens, the other great wine of Barsac. Generally, Coutet is less powerful and often a little drier than Climens, which also tends to have more finesse in the great years. For 30 years the property was well run by the Rolland-Guy family, who sold in 1977 to Marcel Baly. Production methods are traditional, with fermentation in casks, of which a third are new, and two years in cask before bottling.

The last two of the old regime were superb: '75 a classic in a year when many wines were clumsy and unbalanced; '76 is perfumed, beautifully balanced but lighter. The '79 is elegant but rather dry; '83 is better, while in '88, '89, '90, '95, '96, '97, '98, '99, and 2001 Coutet really returned to top form. Look out for the remarkable Cuvée Madame, made in minute quantities.

Château Doisy-Daëne (✩✩) V

2e Cru Classé. Owner: Pierre Dubourdieu. 15ha. 6,000 cases. Sém 100%. Second labels: Vin Sec de Doisy-Daëne, Château Cantegril.

Once the three Doisys were one, then they split up in the 19th century. The first owner of this part was an Englishman called Deane, which has become corrupted to Daëne. Its present owner, Pierre Dubourdieu, is a great innovator, being one of the first to make a dry wine in Sauternes in 1962. Denis Dubourdieu, his son and noted Professor of Oenology, took over the management in 2000, when Pierre retired.

The vinification methods here have been developed over a number of years and are special to Doisy-Daëne. Juice is fermented in vat at not more than 18°C (64°F); after 15 to 21 days, when the balance between alcohol and sugar is judged correct, the temperature is lowered to 4°C (39°F) and the wine is sterile-filtered into new casks. Arresting the fermentation in this way much reduces the amount of sulphur needed. The process is repeated for the final *assemblage* in the following March, and the wine is sterile-filtered again a year later.

All this gives Doisy-Daëne a freshness and elegance that I find delightful. The wines seem light to start with but mature and keep well, developing great finesse. The '83 is elegant, but the '86 is finer, with '88, '89, and '90 proving exceptional. Then '95, '96, '97, '98, and '99 are all excellent. This wine is finer than several *premiers crus*.

Château Doisy-Dubroca (✩)

2e Cru Classé. Owner: Louis Lurton. 3.3ha. 500 cases. Sém 100%.
Second label: La Demoiselle de Doisy.

This small property has been run in conjunction with Climens for nearly 70 years. The vinification and maturation of the wines all take place at Climens with exactly the same care as the *premier cru*. The wines, as at Climens, are remarkably consistent in quality. In style, they are light and elegant and take time to evolve in bottle, although they can also be drunk young.

Château Doisy-Védrines (✩) →

2e Cru Classé. Owner: Pierre-Antoine Castéja. 25ha. 1,500 cases. Sém 80%, Sauv 17%, Musc 3%. Second label: Château La Tour-Védrines.

This property contains the original Védrines château and *chai*. The Castéja family have inherited the property through several marriages since 1840, Pierre-Antoine also ran the négociant firm Roger Joanne. The wines are traditionally made with fermentation and maturation in casks, of which 75 per cent are new.

There is a strong contrast between this and the other Doisys, which both concentrate on elegance and delicacy. Védrines is fuller and richer, but to my mind lacks the breed and stylishness of the others. Of some good wines in the 1980s, '89 was exceptional, and '96 and '97 continued this trend. There is a red La Tour-Védrines, but another wine, Chevalier Védrines, is a Joanne brand unconnected with this property.

Château de Fargues (✩✩)

Cru Bourgeois. Owner: Comte Alexandre de Lur-Saluces. 13ha. 1,000 cases.
Sém 80%, Sauv 20%.

This tiny vineyard lies on the extremity of the commune of Fargues and of the Sauternes AC, and has belonged to the Lur-Saluces family for over 500 years. Under the present owner, Comte Alexandre de Lur-Saluces, the production of red wine has been abandoned in order to concentrate on producing the best-possible Sauternes. Winemaking is identical to that at Yquem, with fermentation and maturation in new casks.

The wines, most of which are sold in the US, combine lusciousness and elegance with great breed and finesse. The '67, '71, '75, '76, '80, '81, '83, '85, '88, '89, and '90 are all great successes here, the '76 being finer than the '75 for me. This wine is of the standard of a top *premier cru*, and the price is high – indeed higher than the *premiers crus* – at approximately half that of Yquem.

Château Filhot (☆)

2e Cru Classé. Owner: Comte Henri de Vaucelles. 60ha. 10,000 cases. Sém 50%,
Sauv 45%, Musc 5%.

There are many beautiful properties in Sauternes, and this is one of the finest,
an imposing, late 18th century mansion set among woods and fields. The wine
is fermented in glass-fibre vats and also matured in them: no wood is used. At
its best, this is a wine of individuality and great fruit but not necessarily great
sweetness, except in extraordinary years. The high proportion of Sauvignon
and the practice of keeping in vat contribute to this tendency. Yet I cannot help
feeling that the full potential here is not being realized. The '83, '86, '88, '89,
and '90 yielded raisin-like botrytized wines, more elegant wines were made in
'96, '98, and '99.

Château Gilette

Owner: Christian Médeville. 4.5ha. 500–600 cases. Sém 94%, Sauv 4%, Musc 2%.

This is a curiosity among the wines of Sauternes. Situated just outside the
village of Preignac, it belongs to the Médeville family of Château Respide-
Médeville in Graves. The soil here is sandy, with a subsoil of rocks and clay.

Between three and seven pickings are made, with the earliest being
of single berries affected by botrytis. Each picking is vinified separately
with temperatures controlled at 24–25°C (75–77°F) during the first days
of fermentation, and brought down to 20°C (68°F) for the remainder. The
result is several different *cuvées* with differing characteristics, and normally
two separate wines are made in each vintage. After the fermentation, the
wines are kept in small concrete vats, some for at least 20 years. The
theory is that the large volume gives a mature flavour and bouquet while
preserving fruit and freshness, so that the maturation process is slower
than in a bottle.

In 1985, I was able to taste the '55 and '59 bottled in 1981, and the '49
and '50 bottled only six to seven years after the vintage. I thought the
early bottlings were clearly superior to the later ones, the '55 and '59
lack the bouquet and balance of the '49 and '50. In addition, the '55 and
'59 had great sweetness and concentration but rather lacked complexity. The
'49 seemed the finest wine of all, and I preferred the '55 to the '59.
So, while this system means you can find an old vintage more easily, the
result may not be as good as that achieved by earlier and more conventional
bottlings.

Château Guiraud (☆☆) →

1er Cru Classé. Owner: SC Agricole. Administrator: Frank Narby.
100ha. 8,500 cases. Sém 65%, Sauv 35%. Dry white: Sauv 100%.
Second labels: 'G' Château Guiraud (Bordeaux Sec), Le Dauphin de
Château Guiraud (Sauternes).

This famous old property received a shot in the arm when it was bought
by the Narby family from Canada in 1981. Hamilton Narby, followed by his
father in 1988, brought in an excellent *régisseur*, Xavier Planty, in 1983 and
imposed the highest traditional standards for making classic Sauternes. A
shortage of money had reduced Guiraud to maturing its wines in vat instead
of cask, after a cask-fermentation. Now 60 per cent new wood is used for
maturation. A dry white wine is also made.

There has been a consistent programme of improvement. In 1988, a third
of the crop was barrel-fermented; in 1990, 45 per cent; and since 1992, the
whole crop. The great vintages are '88, '89, '90, '96, '97, '98, and '99. The wines

show great complexity, elegance and harmony with honeyed concentration in their best years. This is now among the greatest *crus* once more.

Château Guiteronde V

Owner: GFA du Hayot. 25ha. 6,500 cases. Sém 70%, Sauv 20%, Musc 10%.

A well-known *cru* in Barsac, where André du Hayot makes some excellent wine, with style and finesse. A wine to look out for, offering good value.

Clos Haut-Peyraguey (☆) →

1er Cru Classé. Owner: Jacques Pauly. 15ha. 2,000 cases. Sém 83%, Sauv 15%, Musc 2%. Second label: Haut-Bommes.

A single *cru* at the time of the 1855 classification, Peyraguey was divided in 1878. This is the smaller part, with just a tower built in the manner of the older, grander one at Lafaurie. Jacques Pauly has been in charge since 1969. The fermentation is in vat, then the wine spends six months in vat and about 18 months in cask. The wines are light, they can be quite fine, but can also be inconsistent. The '86 showed an improvement, the '88 and '90 are outstanding; the '94 above-average and '95, '96, '97, and '98 excellent.

Château Les Justices V

Owner: Christian Médeville. 17ha. White: 8.5ha. 2,000 cases. Sém 88%, Sauv 10%, Musc 2%. Red: (Bordeaux rouge) 5.6ha. 2,600 cases. CS 58%, Mer 42%.

This property, run by the same owners as Gilette, has belonged to the family since 1710. The harvesting and vinification are basically the same, but the wines are bottled after only four years in small vats. The wine is marketed in a more conventional manner. The '71 is superb, with a concentration of sweetness, a strong perfume and a ripe fruitiness. It was perfection at nearly 14 years of age. Good results were obtained in '88, '89, '90, and '97.

Château Lafaurie-Peyraguey (☆☆) →

1er Cru Classé. Owner: Domaines Cordier. 38.5ha. 6,000 cases. Sém 90%, Sauv 5%, Musc 5%.

After Yquem, the château is the most spectacular in Sauternes, with its 13th-century fortifications and 17th-century buildings. It has been carefully run by the Cordiers since 1913. The winemaking policy has seen changes: Sauvignon has been dropped from 30–5 per cent of the blend, and Sémillon increased from 70–90 per cent. In 1967, a new system was introduced whereby the wines were kept in glass-lined vats under nitrogen after fermentation in cask. The resulting wines became light and one-dimensional, lacking the distinction of a top Sauternes.

The winemaking has returned to more traditional ways, and wines are matured in casks, of which a third are new. Much more interesting wines were made in '79, '80, '81, and especially '83. The '84 is one of the best of the vintage. The '86 was finer than '83, with '88, '89, and '90 following the same pattern of excellence. They have a honeyed bouquet, elegant fruit and breed, and will certainly be worth waiting for. Since then '94, '95, '96, '97, '98, and '99 all produced good to excellent results.

Château Lamothe

2e Cru Classé. Owner: Guy Despujols. 7.1ha. 1,700 cases. Sém 85%, Sauv 10%, Musc 5%.

Another divided property. Lamothe used to belong to the same owners as Château d'Arche. Then, in 1961, half the property, including the château and half the cellars, was sold to the Despujols family. Now wines are fermented in tanks and matured partly in tank, partly in cask.

The result is a rather light and dryish commercial Sauternes, which is decent but no more. However, '96 marked an improvement, and '99 was the best I have seen.

Château Lamothe-Guignard (✰) V

2e Cru Classé. Owners: Philippe and Jacques Guignard. 17ha. 3,200 cases.
Sém 90%, Musc 5%, Sauv 5%.

Lamothe as a single property belonged to the owners of d'Arche. In 1961, they sold part of the property to the Despujols family and continued to sell the wines from their portion as Lamothe-Bergey. In 1981, the Guignards bought Lamothe-Bergey and substituted their name for Bergey. The same family owns Château Rolland.

The newly named château's first vintage, '81, has elegance and length and delectable fruit and moderate sweetness. This was followed by fine wines in the vintages of '83, '86, '88, '89, '90, '94, '95, '96, '97, '98, and '99 .

Château Liot V

Owner: J David. 21ha. 5,000 cases. Sém 85%, Sauv 10%, Musc 5%.

Once bottled by Harveys of Bristol, these well-made wines are sold under the château label only in good vintages – the rest is sold in bulk. The '88, '89, and '90 were particularly good vintages at this property, as were '97, '98, and '99.

Château de Malle (✰) V →

2e Cru Classé. Owner: Comtesse de Bournazel. 27ha. 4,000 cases. Sém 75%,
Sauv 23%, Musc 2%. Second labels: Château Ste-Hélène, Chevalier de Malle
(white Graves, 3,000 cases), Château de Cardaillan (red Graves, 6,000 cases).

This beautiful property has a 17th century château. The vineyard is partly in Sauternes and partly in Graves. Fermentation is in cask, with 50 per cent new, and maturation is in 30 per cent new oak.

The wine has great elegance and charm and is of a light style, only moderately liquorous. It can be drunk young (at three or four years), but in good years gradually opens up in bottle and repays keeping. The '89 and '90 vintages produced the finest wines I have ever seen here – much richer and more exotic than usual – and this pattern has continued.

Château de Myrat →

2e Cru Classé. Owner: Comte de Pontac. 22ha. Sém 88%, Sauv 8%, Musc 4%.

In 1975, the proprietor of this 17th-century château pulled up all his vines as he was no longer able to afford to run the property. Fortunately, his successor was able to begin replanting them just before the planting rights expired in 1988.

The first dry wine was made in '90, from 50 per cent Sémillon, 30 per cent Sauvignon and 20 per cent Muscadelle. The first Sauternes was made in '91, the vines yielding only three hectolitres per hectare of rich-textured, honeyed botrytized juice. After a succession of difficult vintages, '96 really showed what can be achieved here, combining opulent fruit with real finesse.

Château Nairac (✰)

2e Cru Classé. Owner: Nicole Heeter-Tari.
16ha. 1,300 cases. Sém 90%, Sauv 7%, Musc 3%.

Tom Heeter, a young American, came to work at Château Giscours to learn about wine, and in the process he carried off the daughter of the house. His father-in-law, Nicolas Tari, then spotted that Nairac, in the commune of Barsac, was for sale: the couple finally took possession in 1972.

With Professor Peynaud's guidance, Tom Heeter set out to make Barsac in a traditional way, using only wood (65 per cent new) to ferment and mature the wines. However, like Pierre Dubourdieu, he wanted to reduce the use of sulphur. He did not go to the extremes used at Doisy-Daëne, but by using vitamin C, an antioxidant, he had much success.

Following their divorce (the '86 was Tom Heeter's last vintage), Nicole has shown equal dedication and the '88, '89, and '90 are as good or better than anything that went before, and '96 and '97 continue this trend. The care of the winemaking has quickly won admirers for Nairac. The wines are not normally liquorous, but are powerful and rich under the influence of new oak. A wine to watch out for.

Château Rabaud-Promis (☆)

1er Cru Classé. Owner: GFA Rabaud-Promis. Administrator: Philippe Dejean.
33ha. 6,500 cases. Sém 80%, Sauv 18%, Musc 2%.
Second labels: Domaine de l'Estremade, Château Bequet.

Rabaud was a single property until 1903 when it was divided (*see* Sigalas-Rabaud), and this part, two-thirds of the original property, was bought by Adrien Promis. The château dates from the 18th century and is built in a fine hilltop position. The properties were reunited in 1929, but divided again in 1952. The *deuxième cru* Château Peixotto is now also incorporated into Rabaud-Promis.

The grapes, contrary to the tradition in Sauternes, are crushed before going into the presses, and the fermentation and maturation are carried out in cement vats. Improvements came with a new generation of administration, and now some casks are used. The '88 set new standards of excellence, reviving memories of past glories, and was followed by splendid wines in '89 and '90. Good, elegant wines followed in '96 and '98.

Château Raymond-Lafon (☆)

Cru Bourgeois. Owner: Marie-Françoise Meslier. Administrator: Pierre Meslier.
18ha. 1,700 cases. Sém 80%, Sauv 20%. Second label: Château Lafon-Laroze.

This property belonged to Yquem's former *régisseur*, Pierre Meslier, who has handed the running of the property to his children. Pierre Meslier gave the well-placed vineyard the same meticulous care he gave to neighbouring Yquem. The wine is matured in cask with up to a third in new oak: the results are well up to *cru classé* standards: fine, perfumed, and luscious. The wines are extremely consistent, and '88, '89, and '90 reached new heights. Very fine wines followed in '96, '97, '98, and '99.

Château Rayne-Vigneau (☆)

1er Cru Classé. Owner: Cordier-Mestrezat Domaines. Administrator: Alain Duhau.
78ha. 7,000 cases. Sém 83%, Sauv 15%, Musc 2%. Dry wine: Rayne Sec.

The wines of Rayne-Vigneau enjoyed a great reputation in the 19th and early 20th centuries. Until 1961, the property belonged to the Pontac family, which still owns the château. In 1971, it was bought by Mestrezat, which has now merged with Cordier.

The Sémillon and Sauvignon are pressed separately here, because some of the Sauvignon is also used for the dry wine (although most of this is made from less-ripe grapes picked earlier). The fermentation is in vat, then the wine goes into casks (50 per cent are new) for maturation. The property is now well run again, but the yields were too high at first and the wines tended to be correct but rather dull and uninspired – frankly commercial wines. The '76 is the best of this period, but things began to improve with the '83 and '85. The '86, '88, '89, '90, '96, '97, and '98 have maintained this progress.

Château Rieussec (✩✩✩)

1er Cru Classé. Owner: Château Rieussec. 78ha. 8,500 cases. Sém 89%,
Sauv 8%, Musc 3%. Second labels: Clos Labère, Château Mayne des Carmes,
R de Rieussec (dry).

This property is superbly placed on the highest hill in Sauternes after Yquem.
The vineyard is in the commune of Sauternes, but the estate buildings are in
Fargues. The soil here is particularly gravelly. Rieussec has always been
regarded as one of the finest *crus* in Sauternes, producing wines of great
individuality, with an outstanding bouquet and great concentration of flavour,
but also marked elegance and less lusciousness than some. In 1971, it was
acquired by Albert Vuillier, who determined to use the most traditional
methods and produced wines that have been adored by some and disliked by
others. In 1984, he sold to Domaines Rothschild and some time afterwards,
Charles Chevallier came from Lafite to run the property.

After making a classic Rieussec in 1971, Albert Vuillier mostly made heavily
botrytized wines, deep in colour, often with that dry nose and aftertaste
associated with botrytis, which, in excess, has the effect of cutting the
sweetness at the finish, owing to high volatile acidity. The '83 was Albert
Vuillier's last and best vintage.

Under the new regime, there has been an acceleration of success. A lovely
fresh, ripe '85 was followed by a concentrated '86 with real breed and finesse,
then great wines were made in the three outstanding vintages of '88, '89, and
'90, then again in '96, '97, '98, and '99.

The dry wine "R" de Rieussec was made in a rather alcoholic and heavy
style that required bottle-age, but a new lighter, fresher style, designed for
early drinking, was introduced after the '92 vintage.

Château de Rolland

Cru Bourgeois. Owners: Jean and Pierre Guignard. 16ha. 3,600 cases. Sém 80%,
Sauv 15%, Musc 5%.

This *cru* in Barsac is also a good restaurant and hotel, the only place to stay
if you want to be in the middle of the Sauternes vineyards. The owners are
also the proprietors of the excellent Château de Roquetaillade-La-Grange in
Graves. The wines enjoy a good reputation at *cru bourgeois* level. Wines are
vinified and matured in casks bought from Yquem.

Château Romer-du-Hayot

2e Cru Classé. Owner: du Hayot. 10.9ha. 3,300 cases. Sém 70%, Sauv 25%,
Musc 5%.

This *cru* deserves to be more widely known. The vineyard adjoins de Malle
on the edge of the commune of Fargues. The wine is fermented in vat and
matured in cask. The du Hayots are producing excellent wines of their sort,
with limited resources, both here and at Guiteronde in Barsac (where the
wines are actually made). There is an emphasis on fruit and freshness. Only
in years such as '76 is there much sweetness, but the wines always seem
well-balanced, if lacking real complexity '88, '89, and '99 are fruity and stylish.

Château St-Amand V

Owner: Louis Ricard and Mme Faccheti-Ricard. 19ha. 4,500 cases. Sém 85%,
Sauv 14%, Musc 1%. Second label: Château La Chartreuse.

Traditionally made and elegant, some fine *cru bourgeois* wines are produced
at this property in Preignac. They are more commonly sold in England
under the Château La Chartreuse label. The '80, '81, '83, '90, and '96 are
especially good vintages, though all are stylish and reliable.

Château Sigalas-Rabaud (★★) →

1er Cru Classé. Owner: Héritiers de la Marquise de Lambert des Granges.
Administrator: Domaines Cordier. 14ha. 2,500 cases. Sém 85%, Sauv 15%.

This *cru* formed part of the old property of Rabaud, which was divided in 1903. From 1929 to 1952 the properties were reunited. Yields are low and the traditional *trie* (selective picking of the ripest grapes) is made four or five times. Fermentation is in vat, maturation in cask with 60 per cent new.

I have found the wines to be perfumed, elegant, and quite delicate, yet liquorous and with real breeding. For me, the best and most typical vintages here have been the especially fine '67 and the '71, '75, and '81. The '83 and '86 follow the same lines.

In January 1995, the proprietors entered into a management contract with Domaines Cordier, so that the property will now benefit from the expertise which has taken its neighbour Lafaurie-Peyraguey to the top of the Sauternes hierarchy in recent vintages.

The '95, '96, '97, '98, '99, and 2001 showed that the new management can produce even more finely honed wines.

Château Suau

2e Cru Classé. Owner: Roger Biarnés. 8ha. 2,000 cases. Sém 80%, Sauv 10%, Musc 10%.

Probably the least-known of the *crus classés*. The vineyard is in Barsac, but the present owner vinifies the wine at his other property in Illats. Much of the wine is sold by *vente directe* in France. The wine is fermented in vats and then in used casks. The reputation is for rather ordinary, dull wines with an unbalanced sweetness and lacking breed, but the '88 is delicate and fine.

Château Suduiraut (★★)

1er Cru Classé. Owner: AXA-Millésimes. Administrator: Christian Seely.
86ha. 14,000 cases. Sém 80%, Sauv 20%.
Second label: Castelnau de Suduiraut.

This famous old *cru* adjoins Yquem and is partly in the commune of Sauternes and partly in that of Preignac. The Fonquernie family bought the property, with its lovely 17th century château, in 1940 and slowly nursed it back to quality and fame. In 1992, some members of the family sold a majority shareholding to AXA.

This is normally the most liquorous and intensely rich wine after Yquem, and when at its best, is also one of the best Sauternes. The juice ferments in vats after a careful selection in the vineyard, and is then matured in casks, of which 35 per cent are new. But Suduiraut did go through a bad patch when there was little or no selection and virtually no cask-ageing. This affected the vintages from '71–'75 inclusive.

The best Suduirauts are pale gold in colour, the bouquet is exquisitely perfumed and penetrating, and the flavour rich and vigorous, distinctive, honeyed, with great finesse and breed. In good years the wines usually have five degrees Baumé or more of unfermented sugar (*see* page 139, Yquem). The '70 was one of the best examples of its vintage, and '76 produced a classic wine to stand beside the '59, '62, and '67. During the 1980s the wines have generally had less residual sugar than in the great vintages of the 1950s and 1960s, so one is left with an impression of alcohol at the finish. The '83, '86, '88, '89, and '90 were the best years. The '96, '97, '98, and '99 seem closer to the classic balance of the 1960s.

Château La Tour-Blanche (✩✩✩)

1er Cru Classé. Owner: Ministère de l'Agriculture. Administrator: J-P Jausserand.
35ha. 4,400 cases. Sém 77%, Sauv 20%, Musc 3%.
Second label: Mademoiselle de St-Marc.

The *cru* was placed at the head of the *premiers crus* in 1855 and since 1910 has belonged to the state, now being run as an agricultural school. Until recently its reputation was far from what it should have been, and there were *deuxièmes crus* and, indeed, unclassified wines that were better.

The wine is fermented in vat and then matured in cask, with 25 per cent new wood. In 1988, a degree of cask-fermentation was introduced, just in time to take full advantage of the three great vintages of '88, '89, and '90 – the latter of which is one of the great wines of that year and certainly the greatest wine from this property in modern times. This is the culmination of some years of effort which is now restoring the famous *cru* to its rightful place among the finest of the *premiers crus*. Again, fine wines were made in '94, '95, '96, '97, '98, and '99.

Château d'Yquem (✩✩✩)

1er Grand Cru Classé 1855. Owner: LVHM. Administrator: Aymeric de Montault.
106ha. 6,500 cases. Sém 80%, Sauv 20%.
Second label: "Y" (Bordeaux Blanc, 2,000 cases).

In 1855, when the great sweet wines of Sauternes and Barsac were classified, Yquem was placed in a category of its own as the sole *premier grand cru*, as distinct from the *premiers crus*. Its unique position has remained unassailed ever since.

This is not only the greatest Sauternes, it is also the supreme dessert wine in the world. Since 1593, only two families have owned it. The continuity of ownership lasted for 400 years, as the Comte de Lur-Saluces married the last de Sauvage heiress in 1785. Alexandre de Lur-Saluces succeeded his uncle in 1968. In 1999, Alexandre de Lur Saluces lost his long battle to retain his independence, but remained to guide this unique *cru* into the next millennium. He officially retired from his executive duties at the end of 2003 to be succeeded by Aymeric de Montault, who has worked with the team since 2002.

The château is a superb fortress commanding fine views over the region. The vineyard is rotated, so that although there are 102 hectares under vine, only about 80 are actually producing the *grand vin*; the rest are young vines.

The picking is carefully controlled, using only skilled workers, mostly from the 57 full-time estate workers who go through the vineyard a number of times (anything from four to 11) selecting only overripe and botrytized berries. The aim is to pick at not less than 20° and not more than 22° Baumé. This produces the most balanced wines, which ferment to between 13.5 and 14 per cent, leaving between four and seven degrees Baumé unfermented sugar.

The pressing is traditional, and the musts are fermented in new oak, maturing in cask for three and a half years prior to bottling. Yquem can never be sampled, even by its buyers. A dry wine, "Y", or "Ygrec", is made in some years. It has quite a honeyed nose, and is full-bodied and fairly rich.

Yquem is the quintessence of Sauternes, with its colour turning gradually to pale gold, its intense, honeyed bouquet, and the wonderful lusciousness and elegance of the flavour itself. It is always a privilege to drink this wine.

One can begin to enjoy it when it is six or seven years old, and it has a special charm of freshness for another decade after that. In the greatest years, it can continue almost indefinitely.

Wines at their peak now are '67 (a great year), '70 (very fine), '71 (a great wine), '75, the great '76, and the lesser, but very good here, vintages of '80, '81 and '82 (exceptional for the year). The modern era in Sauternes was ushered in with the marvellously complex and balanced '83, then '86 and '88 which are even greater and look, at present, superior to '90, '84 and '87 are good lesser years. Then comes a remarkable '91, '93, '94, and '95 which are way above the level of the 1er crus. Great wines return with '96 (great succulence and breed), '97 (outstanding finesse and breed), and '98 (richer than '97 with great potential).

St-Émilion

What strikes one about St-Émilion as a district, compared to the other great regions, especially Médoc or Graves, is its small and compact nature. One can walk straight out of the cramped, medieval streets of St-Émilion and find all but one of the *premiers crus classés* of the *côtes* just a few minutes' walk away. St-Émilion covers 5,000 hectares and is divided among 1,000 different *crus*, of which only a small proportion are actually classified. The 330 members of the Union des Producteurs cooperative own 900 hectares. Another notable feature is the small size of the properties themselves. The average area of the 13 *premiers grands crus classés* is a bare 20 hectares, that of the *grands crus classés* is less than ten hectares. Compare this with the vineyard sizes in the Médoc.

A further fundamental characteristic of St-Émilion is its complex variety of soils. For practical purposes these can be divided into three groups. First, the *plateau calcaire*, or limestone plateau, and the *côtes* and *pieds de côtes*, the hillsides and lower slopes. There is also an important element of clay in these soils. This covers the area around the town of St-Émilion, where all but two of the *premiers grands crus classés* are found. The second group is the *graves et sables anciens*, an area of gravel mixed with sand, but sand of an old, wind-blown variety as distinct from the more recent alluvial kind. This is a small area near the border with Pomerol, where a succession of gravelly slopes covers about 60 hectares in a sea of sandy soils. Cheval Blanc and Figeac dominate, and nearly all the other *crus* here are classified. The third soil type is the *sables anciens*, the area of sandy soils of the type already described. There are a number of good, attractive classified *crus* in this area, which lie between the first two.

In terms of appellation and geography, divisions are as follows.

1   The *grands crus classés*: allowed by a system of classification under the control of the INAO that is subject to revision every ten years. In fact, the original system of 1954 was revised in 1969 and the second revision came in 1985. This reduced the number of classified wines from 12–11 in the *premiers grands crus classés*, and from 72–63 in the *grands crus classés*. The third revision of 1996 increased the *premiers* to 13, restoring Beau-Séjour-Bécot and promoting L'Angélus, while the *grands crus classés* were again reduced.

2   The *grands crus*: comprising some 200 *crus* that have to submit samples annually for tasting.
3   Wines bearing the simple St-Émilion appellation.

Geographically, although the best wines are to be found in the commune of St-Émilion itself, eight communes that come within the ancient jurisdiction of the Jurade de St-Émilion are also entitled to the appellation. The best wines come from St-Christophe-des-Bardes, St-Laurent-des-Combes, St-Hippolyte, and St-Étienne-de-Lisse. The remaining four – St-Pey-d'Armens, Vignonet, St-Sulpice-de-Faleyrens, and Libourne – are mostly on low-lying sandy soil or terraces of newer gravel and sand.

In the 1990s, St-Émilion stepped into the vanguard of avant-garde vinification, micro-vinification, and cult wines. Suddenly the small size of the properties became an advantage.

Château Angélus ★★ →

1er Grand Cru Classé B. Owner: de Boüard de Laforest family. Administrators: Hubert de Boüard de Laforest and Jean Bernard Gressé. 23.4ha. 8,000 cases. Mer 50%, CF 45%, CS 5%.
Second label: Carillon de L'Angélus.

This is one of the most important estates on the St-Émilion *côtes*. Before buying Angélus in 1924, the de Boüard de Laforest family owned Château Mazerat, which they later incorporated, together with several other properties, into Angélus. The apostrophe was dropped from the label with the '89 vintage. The vineyard is on the lower slopes of the *côtes*, to the west of St-Émilion. There is a large modern *chai*, and cask-maturing was introduced in 1980 – between half and two-thirds new oak is used. Before this, the wines saw no wood at all.

The wines are characterized by perfume and rich flattering fruit. '96 is one of the successes of the Right Bank wth its Cabernet Franc textures and after a delicious early drinking '97, the '98, '99, and 2000 are all excellent examples of these vintages, justifying Angélus's high reputation. Prior to 1983, many of these wines lacked concentration and needed to be drunk young. Since then, they have more solidity, but retain their crunchy fruit and richness. The '79 and '82 marked a big step forward, followed by '85 and '86. But then '89 and '90 added an extra voluptuousness, which was repeated in the '95.

My only note of caution is that the high percentage of new oak can tend to mark the wines. In 1996, efforts to upgrade the wines were rewarded by elevation to *premier cru* status. Prices have soared.

Château L'Arrosée ★

Grand Cru Classé. Owner: François Rodhain. 10ha. 4,000 cases. Mer 50%, CS 35%, CF 15%. Second label: Les Côteaux du Château L'Arrosée.

The vineyard is well-sited on the *côtes* above the cooperative and below Tertre-Daugay, southwest of the town. The name means "watered by springs". The balance of the wine comes from its position: the *haute de côte* giving body and power, the *milieu de côte* providing the richness, and the *pied de côte* contributing finesse.

This is classic St-Émilion, rich, luscious, but with great depth, flavour, and personality. Not easy to find, but well worth the effort.

Château Ausone ★★★

1er Grand Cru Classé A. Owner: Héritiers Vauthier. Administrator: Alain Vauthier. 7ha. 2,250 cases. Mer 50%, CF 50%.

Named after the Roman poet Ausonius in the 18th century, this château has the remains of a Roman villa nearby which may have belonged to the poet.

It was only in the 1890s that Ausone was recognized as the first wine of the St-Émilion *côtes*, a position previously held by its larger neighbour Belair. During the 1950s and 1960s, Ausone did not live up to its *premier cru* status, although in 1955 it had been placed alongside Cheval Blanc at the head of the new classification. In 1975, a new *régisseur*, Pascal Delbeck, arrived and took full control in 1976. Since then Ausone's reputation has soared. In 1995 a long-running battle between Mme. Dubois-Challon and the Vauthier family ended when the Vauthiers gained control of the management, and in 1996 they bought her out.

There has been a notable change of style in the '95 and '96 vintages, which are more supple, sensuous wines, due to doing the malolactic fermentation in cask. The '98 is a great wine in the making, '99 is powerful for the year, and 2000 is one of the outstanding wines of the vintage. 2001 has less weight but is very seductive, outstanding again for the vintage. The essence of Ausone is the combination of delicacy and finesse with power, so that the concentration of complex perfumes on the nose is both lively and beautiful, while the sensation of multi-layered flavours on the palate is remarkable. The wines take longer to mature than other St-Émilions and have an ability to age that is unrivalled on this side of the river.

Since the massive '75, there has been a fine '76, a great '78, a great '82 (opulent and concentrated), a softer yet exotic '83, a top-quality '85, and a complex, densely rich '86. '88 shows the quality of the Cabernet Franc, so is fresh and well-structured with lovely fruit. '89 is the star here, rather than '90, combining good structure and sweet fruit but still needing time to show its true class, while '90 has fat and glycerol with glorious sweet fruit – perfect drinking now. The best wine of the early '90s is '93,which shows harmony and elegance but should last well.

Everything seems set for Ausone to become the new Pétrus in terms of extraordinary wines produced in small quantities. Let us hope that wine-lovers as well as collectors get a look-in.

Château Balestard-la-Tonnelle ★★

Grand Cru Classé. Owner: GFA Capdemourlin. Administrator: Jacques Capdemourlin. 10.6ha. 5,000 cases. Mer 70%, CF 25%, CS 5%.
Second label: Les Tournelles de Balestard.

This estate lies at the limit of the *plateau calcaire*, to the east of St-Émilion and across the road from Soutard. Fifty per cent of the maturation is in new wood.

The wines here are consistent and most attractive, archetypal St-Émilions that are big, luscious, and full-bodied, easy to drink yet lasting longer than one might expect. The '45 is still magnificent. '88 is now drinking well but can still improve; '89 is more concentrated and youthful than either '88 or '90, which is perfect now. '94 has more charm than most wines of this year; '95 is glorious, so enjoyable now but with the structure to keep. '96 is good and charming but less complex. '97 is luscious and perfect now; '98 a fine *vin de garde* with perfect harmony. '99 has less depth but is tightly knit and needs time; 2000 is very complex and rich and promises to be exceptional.

Château Barde-Haut →

Owner: Sylviane Garcin-Cathiard. 17ha. 5,000 cases. Mer 80%, CF 20%.

This very well-placed *cru* in the commune of St Christophe-des-Bardes was bought by Sylviane Garcin-Cathiard just before the 2000 harvest. With its southerly exposure and old vines – the average is 33 years – the potential for improvement is clear. Having had considerable success at Haut-Bergey in Pessac-Léognan and following this with Clos L'Eglise in Pomerol, the new owner, together with her husband, is clearly ready for fresh challenges. Their daughter, Hélène Garcin-Lévêque, a qualified oenologist, has a charming house on the property, so this is her particular project. In 2000, two-thirds of the crop had its malolactic fermentation in new oak and showed real promise. Watch this space!

Château Beau-Séjour-Bécot ★★

1er Grand Cru Classé B. Owners: Michel, Gérard and Dominique Bécot.
16.5ha. 8,000 cases. Mer 70%, CS 15%, CF 15%.
Second label: Tournelles des Moines.

This *cru* was classified in 1955 as a *premier grand cru*, and in 1985 was demoted amid much controversy. The demotion seems to have been because Bécot added the vineyards of La Carte and Trois Moulins to the original ten hectares of Beau-Séjour which he bought in 1970, although the merger was not effected until 1979. The vineyard is on the *plateau calcaire* and the fermentation is in stainless steel; 90 per cent new wood is used. There are fine underground cellars for maturation in bottle. The style of the wines here is different from that of the other Beauséjour, more fleshy and rich, but with less tannin and style. They are attractive, easy-to-drink wines but do sometimes lack distinction. Under Gérard and Dominique's management, a great effort has been made to improve the wines and restore this *cru* to its former position. This was rewarded in the 1996 revision of the classification. Excellent wines were made in '95, '96, '97, '98, and 2000.

Château Beauséjour (Duffau-Lagarosse) ★★

1er Grand Cru Classé B. Owner: Duffau-Lagarosse. Administrator: Jean-Michel Fernandez. 7ha. 3,000 cases. Mer 60%, CF 25%, CS 15%.
Second label: Le Croix de Mazerat.

The least-known of the *premiers grands crus*, partly because about half of its tiny production is sold direct to private customers. Beauséjour was a single property until 1869, when it was divided between two daughters. One married a doctor from St-Émilion, and this part of the property now belongs to her heirs. Long vatting here gives the wine breed and stylish fruit, but perhaps rather too much tannin for wines that are light in body.

At one time, this wine owed its classification to the vineyard site and a long tradition of respectable wines, because until recently it was good but not brilliant. However, after a rich '82 with real breeding, '85 again had concentration, and the '86 was even more impressive, combining elegant fruit with rich concentrated fruit and tannins. The '88, '89, the outstanding '90, '95, '96, '98, and 2000 follow the same line of improvement. A wine of distinction.

Château Belair ★★

1er Grand Cru Classé B. Owner: Pascal Delbeck. 13ha. 5,000 cases. Mer 65%, CF 35%.

Belair adjoins Ausone, and its owner was, until 1996, also co-owner of Ausone. Pascal Delbeck, an outstanding *régisseur* has made a great difference to consistency and quality since 1976. In 2003, Madame Dubois-Challon died and left the property to Pascal Delbeck, a fitting reward for his years of passionately loyal service. The main difference between Belair and Ausone is that, while Ausone is wholly on the *côtes*, the vineyard of Belair is divided between the *côtes* and the plateau above it. Having been made and kept in the Ausone cellars for many years, the wines of Belair returned to their own cellars in 1976, and the old wooden fermentation *cuves* were replaced by stainless-steel vats after the 1980 vintage.

Today, Belair is nearly always one of the best of the *premiers grands cru* B-group. The wines tend to be a little richer and more fleshy than Ausone, without the same intensity, but with real finesse and great vigour. The wines of '82, '83, '85, and '86 are exceptional. The '89, '90, '93, '94, '95, '96, '98, and 2000 vie with each other in their dense concentration and inscrutable power.

Château Bellefont-Belcier

Grand Cru. Owner: SC BJL. Administrator: Marc Dworkin. 13ha. 5,900 cases. Mer 65%, CF 35%, CS 5%.

A good *cru* in St-Laurent-des-Combes, on the *côtes* and their lower slopes. The wines have a reputation for being robust and supple. The present owners took over in 1994.

Château Bellevue →

Grand Cru Classé. Owner: SC du Château (M. L. Horeau). Administrator: Nicolas Thienpoint. 6.5ha. 3,500 cases. Mer 85%, CF 10%, CS 5%.

The vineyard lies on the limestone plateau and *côte* just to the west of Beauséjour. It must have been one of the least known of the *grands crus classés* until Nicolas Thienpoint took charge of the management in 2000 (*see* Pavie-Macquin). It has the misfortune to have one of the commonest names in Bordeaux: there are 23 properties at present using it, several of which are in the St-Émilion region. This Château Bellevue is an old property and has belonged to the same group of connected families since the 17th century. For the '88 vintage, a proportion of new oak was used for the first time, and from being a rather anonymous pleasant wine, one began to see the breeding and style one would expect from a vineyard in this position. But this was as nothing compared with the golden opinions that greeted Nicolas Thienpoint's first vintage in 2000. This was one of the 39 *crus* of St-Émilion that represented the region at the Paris Exhibition of 1867.

Château Belregard-Figeac V

Grand Cru. Owner: Pueyo family. 5ha. 2,500 cases. Mer 68%, CF 25%, CS 7%. Second wine: Château la Fleur Garderose.

The Pueyo family has owned this small property since the late 19th century. The vineyard is partly on sandy gravel in the Libourne commune, and partly on deep sand on the Figeac plateau. This is a meticulously made wine with hints of cherries and violets, and a fresh crispness to the fruit. Not rich and showy, rather elegant and fine. The first *grand cru* vintage was the admirable '89. The '95, '96, and '97 are all good examples.

Château Bergat

Grand Cru Classé. Owner: Héritiers Castéja. Administrator: Philippe Castéja. 4.5ha. 1,500 cases. Mer 50%, CF 40%, CS 10%.

This is one of the smallest and least-known of the *grands crus classés*. It lies to the east of St-Émilion at the edge of the plateau and *côtes*. The property is farmed by Émile Castéja from nearby Trottevieille and distributed by his firm, Borie-Manoux. The '98 is rich and succulent, with plenty of style. A bottle of Bergat should always be worth investigating, if you can track it down.

Château Berliquet ★ →

Grand Cru Classé. Owners: Vicomte Patrick de Lesquen. 9ha. 3,300 cases. Mer 70%, CF 25%, CS 5%. Second label: Les Aîles de Berliquet.

An old *cru*, superbly placed on the *plateau calcaire* and the *côtes*, adjoining Magdelaine and Canon. When production moved from the cooperative here in '78 rather coarse wines were made. Then, Patrick de Lesquen called in Patrick Valette to help him, and '97 and '98 mark a great improvement. The '99 was virtually a Merlot wine due to hail, but the 2000 promises to be great. The potential is at last being unlocked.

Château Cadet-Bon ★ →

Grand Cru Classé. Owner: Société Loriene. Administrators: Marceline and Bernard Gans. 6.5ha. 2,500 cases. Mer 70%, CF 20%, CS 10%.

This small property, north of the town on the *plateau calcaire* and *côtes*, lost its status as a *cru classé* in the 1985 revision after producing poorly made wines for some years. In 1986, the present owners acquired it and determined to make wines worthy of the vineyard. The attractive new label sets the tone of the new regime.

The '88 is spicy and aromatic, a big, concentrated wine; the '89 is a classic St-Émilion with a lovely richness and lots of glycerol, power and tannin, while '90 is more supple but with gloriously concentrated fruit. The seriousness of the selection and winemaking come through in the fine '92 and lovely '97. Not surprisingly, such wines are rapidly creating a reputation for themselves and already appear on some of the best wine lists in France. These efforts were rewarded in 1996 with promotion to *grand cru classé*.

Château Cadet-Piola

Grand Cru Classé. Owner: Alain Jabiol. 7ha. 3,000 cases. Mer 51%, CS 28%, CF 18%, Mal 3%. Second label: Chevaliers de Malte.

Cadet-Piola lies to the north of St-Émilion on the *plateau calcaire* and *côtes* at their culminating northern point. The present owner bought it in 1952 and

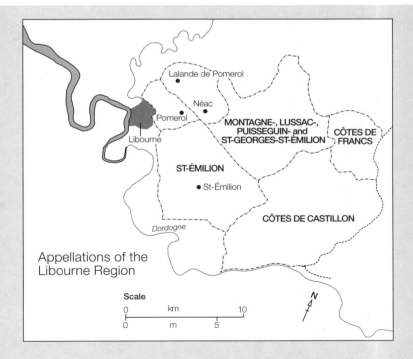

Appellations of the Libourne Region

runs it in conjunction with another *grand cru classé*, Faurie-de-Souchard. Vinification is in glass-lined vats and is carefully controlled. Maturation is in cellars quarried under the vineyard, and 50 per cent of the wood used is new.

The wines are certainly marked by their grape varieties. They need patience compared with many St-Émilions, being tightly knit and austere to start with, but with the structure and style of a wine of some distinction. However, they are rather short on charm.

Château Canon ★★

1er Grand Cru Classé B. Owner: Chanel. Administrator: John Kolasa.
21ha. 7,500 cases. Mer 60%, CF 40%.
Second label: Clos Canon.

This is a beautifully placed property, with 13 hectares of its vineyard in a walled *clos* on the plateau just outside the walls of St-Émilion, and an elegant little 18th century château. The remainder of the vineyard is on the *côtes*. The wines are matured in as much as 60 per cent new wood. The wine is classic, beautifully perfumed, with great length of flavour, and can be almost silky in texture. There is an inner concentration of tannin and rich fruit that opens out only slowly. The wine always has immense breeding, elegance, and style. It is usually one of the top St-Émilions, but one you must wait for. The '85 is compact and fruity – a lovely wine – and '86 achieves the balance of power and finesse that is the hallmark of previous owner Eric Fournier's achievements here. Sadly, in 1996 the Fournier family had to sell, fortunately to Chanel, so David Orr and John Kolasa, the highly successful Rauzan-Ségla team, promise a bright future. In 2000, they bought the neighbouring Curé-Bon and 2000 also proved their best vintage yet. This was also the first to include wines from the Curé-Bon vineyard. 2001 is also very promising, better than '99.

Château Canon-la-Gaffelière ★★ →

Grand Cru Classé. Owner: Comte von Neipperg. 20ha. 14,000 cases. Mer 55%,
CF 40%, CS 5%. Second label: Côte Mignon la Gaffelière.

This property lies on the road that runs from the Libourne–Bergerac road to St-Émilion, at the southern foot of the *côtes* on flat, sandy soil. This owner took over in 1971, but the real changes occured from 1985 onwards, when Stephan von Neipperg took over from his father. The evolution has been almost continuous, from stainless steel in '87 to a return to wooden vats (since the '97 vintage), malolactic fermentation in barrel, and *élevage* on the lees, bottling without filtration. In the late '80s and early '90s, the wines often seemed too oaky; now they are richer, denser, textured, and more harmonious. Stephan Neipperg is very much his own man and has found his own path by experimentation and experience.

Château Cap-de-Mourlin ★ →

Grand Cru Classé. Owner: Capdemourlin family. Administrator: Jacques
Capdemourlin. 14ha. 6,000 cases. Mer 65%, CF 25%, CS 10%.

During the 1970s and until after the '82 vintage, this historic property was divided between two parts of the Capdemourlin family. Generally, I found the wines vinified by Jacques Capdemourlin to be superior during this period, and he is now responsible for the reunited whole. Fifty per cent of the wood used for maturation is new. The vineyard is north of St-Émilion on the lower *côtes*. This is a classic St-Émilion, perfumed and fruity on the nose and with a generous, almost unctuous flavour, supported with a good structure. Jacques Capdemourlin made excellent wines in '82, '83, '85, '86, '88, '89, '90, '95, '96, '97, '98, '99, and 2000. The wines here offer an interesting contrast to those of Balestard, more aromatic but less intense and usually ready to drink earlier.

Château Carteau Côtes Daugay V

Grand Cru. Owner: Jacques Bertrand. 17ha. 9,000 cases. Mer 70%, CF 25%, CS 3% and Mal 2%.

A consistently reliable *grand cru*. The '95 was very perfumed, with delicious open-textured, flattering fruit at three years of age, yet with the potential to improve, as older vintages testify.

Château Le Castelot V

Grand Cru. Owner: J. Janoueix. 9.5ha. 4,000 cases. Mer 70%, CF 20%, CS 10%.

The vineyards are situated on the sandy plains of St-Sulpice-de-Faleyrens. The sand, gravel, and iron traces give these wines noticeable *terroir* with an initially strong impact that usually softens as the wine ages. Careful vinification, using 50 per cent new oak, is carried out by Paul Cazenave, *maître de chai* for all the Janoueix properties. Once matured, the wines are consistently delicious. Certainly a reliable property.

Château Chauvin ★

Grand Cru Classé. Owner: Marie-France Ferrier and Béatrice Ondet. 15ha. 6,500 cases. Mer 80%, CS 5%, CF 15%. Second label: La Borderie de Chauvin.

This *cru* lies in what misleadingly used to be called the St-Émilion Graves. It is the most southeasterly of this group of *crus*, east of Ripeau and south of Corbin. The soil is sandy, and 45 per cent of the casks for maturation are new. The wines are typical of this area near the Pomerol border: rich and dense in texture, quickly becoming mellow and unctuous in flavour. Recently, the '96 and '98 have been excellent. I have always found this to be an attractive wine.

Château Cheval Blanc ★★★

1er Grand Cru Classé A. Owner: SC du Château Cheval Blanc. Administrator: Pierre Lurton. 36ha. 12,000 cases. CF 60%, Mer 37%, Mal 2%, CS 1%. Second label: Petit Cheval.

St-Émilion's two greatest wines, Ausone and Cheval Blanc, are at opposite ends of the appellation and on quite different soils. Cheval Blanc, the most famous of all, is a large property for the region, on the border with Pomerol. Its reputation goes back to the '21 vintage, and was strengthened by the legendary '47. The soil is gravel and sand, but clay and sandstone with traces of iron are also present. The high proportion of Cabernet Franc at the expense of Merlot is an unusual feature. In 1956 the vineyard was seriously affected by the February frost and took some time to recover.

The vinification is in vat, with refrigeration available; 100 per cent new oak is used for maturation. In 1989, Jacques Hébrard retired, having successfully run the property on behalf of his wife's family since 1972. After a hiatus, the family appointed Pierre Lurton, who had been responsible for the marked improvement at Clos Fourtet. In 1998, the Fourcaud-Lussac heirs ended an ownership that had begun with the creation of the *cru* in the 1830s, by selling to Albert Frère (a Belgian businessman) and Bernard Arnault (of LVMH fame, but in his personal capacity).

The wines are famous for their powerful enveloping bouquet, which is rich and often spicy, and their full, mellow, almost unctuous flavour. It is a particular quality of this *cru* that in ripe years the wines can be drunk young. This happened with the famous '47, which was delectable when a mere six or seven years old. At this stage, the sheer animal vigour and stunning beauty of the wine is matched only by Pétrus, just across the border in Pomerol. Of course, the wines keep and develop well according to the individuality of each year, but the early exuberance is not to be missed. Cheval Blanc does not age as well as Ausone and some other wines of the *côtes*, becoming lacy and frail when over 40 years old.

Great vintages from this property are '64, '66, and '70; other major years are '75, '78, '79, and '81, all of which are delicious to drink now. Of the more recent vintages, the '82 is probably the best since '47, and the '83 is also fine. The '85 is a bull's-eye, with that opulence bordering on sweetness of the greatest years, and '86 is dense-textured, with the style to suggest a great wine. The '89 and '90 are outstanding, and '93 and '94 are elegant, stylish wines that make the best of these vintages.

The '95 is fine, classic Cheval-Blanc. The '98 promises to be a great wine, with '99 not far behind, and 2000 where the Cabernet Franc gives the wine a power and harmony seldom matched in this vintage. There is no '91 Cheval Blanc, it was sold as Petit Cheval.

Cheval Noir and "Le Fer de Cheval Noir"

Owner: Mähler-Besse. 5ha. 3,100 cases. Mer 60%, CF 20%, CS 20%.

This property hit the headlines in '98, when Bordeaux négociant Mähler-Besse selected a small parcel of old Merlot vines to carry out a micro-vinification. The yield was a mere 27hl/ha and the malolactic fermentation took place in new barrels. Only 300 cases of '98 were made, but the expectation now is to produce 500 cases in a good year.

I found the '98 delicious, with fruit that jumped out of the glass, lots of richness and glycerol, a wine of real opulence and charm. A bottle of Cheval Noir '66 drunk at lunch served to emphasize the quality of this vineyard.

Château Clos des Jacobins ★

Grand Cru Classé. Owner: Gérard Frydman. 8.4ha. 4,800 cases. Mer 70%, CF 30%.

The wines here have always been consistent and attractive, but recent vintages have been more concentrated and impressive. The '82, '83, '86, '88, '89, and '90 are excellent, with great richness and opulence, while '95 and '96 are rich and firm. This is certainly one of the best *crus* in this section of St-Émilion.

Château La Clotte

Grand Cru Classé. Owner: Héritiers Chailleau. Administrator: Mme. Nelly Moulierac. 4ha. 1,200 cases. Mer 80%, CF 15%, CS 5%.

This tiny vineyard is beautifully placed on the edge of the *plateau calcaire* and the *côtes*, just outside the walls of St-Émilion to the east. For many years the vineyard was farmed by J. P. Moueix, but in 1989 the Chailleau heirs again took over the running of the property. Fifty per cent new wood is now used. They also run a popular restaurant in St Émilion, *Logis de la Cadène*.

The wines have real finesse and delicacy, and are fresh and supple with a lovely bouquet in the best style of the *côtes* wines. But recent vintages seem more tannic and extracted.

Château La Clusière

Grand Cru Classé. Owner: M. and Mme. Gerard Perse. 2.5ha. 300 cases. Mer 100%.

This tiny vineyard forms a small enclave high on the Côte de Pavie, among the vines of Pavie and under the same ownership and management. This vineyard belonged to the Vilette family, which sold to the Perses in '97.

The wines were sound but unexciting. The '98 shows what the new ownership can do, with its plummy, sumptuous fruit.

Château Corbin

Grand Cru Classé. Owner: Blanchard & Cruse Families. Administrator: Annabelle Cruse-Bardinet. 12.7ha. 6,500 cases. Mer 80%, CF 20%.

A good example of the curse of duplicated names in St-Émilion. In this area of St-Émilion, near the Pomerol border, there are five adjoining properties, all with Corbin in their names, all *grands crus classés*, to say nothing of others in Montagne-St-Émilion and Graves.

One-third new wood is used in the maturation, and the wines have a reputation for being rich and supple, characteristic of this area of sandy soils near Pomerol.

Château Corbin-Michotte ★

Grand Cru Classé. Owner: Jean-Noël Boidron. 6.7ha. 3,000 cases. Mer 65%, CF 30%, CS 5%.

Second label: Les Abeilles.

There is a double confusion of names here. This is one of five adjoining *grands crus classés* with the name Corbin and one of two adjoining Michottes. This one lies immediately to the south of Croque-Michotte, east of La Dominique. The soil is sandy, with some clay in the subsoil, contains iron traces, and has some surface gravel. Since acquiring this property in 1959, Jean-Noël Boidron has carried out many improvements, and the *chai* was entirely rebuilt in 1980. There is 80 per cent new wood rotated, with 20 per cent in *cuves*.

I am always impressed with this wine. The rich, plummy texture, fat and full and mellow in the mouth, is typical of the best wines from this corner of St-Émilion near Pomerol.

Château Cormeil-Figeac

Grand Cru. Owner: Héritiers R. & L. Moreaud. 10ha. 5,500 cases. Mer 70%, CF 30%.

Second label: Château Haut-Cormey.

A good vineyard on the sandy soils southeast of Château Figeac. Wood maturation is carried out in 100 per cent new oak. The wines are scented, supple, and full-flavoured with vibrant fruit: delicious for early drinking.

Château Côte de Baleau →

Grand Cru. Owner: Reiffers Family. Administrator: Sophie Fourcade. 8ha. 3,300 cases. Mer 70%, CF 20%, CS 10%.

This *cru* was classified in 1969, but lost its position in 1985. It is on the lower slope of the *côtes* and on calcareous soils, north of the town, adjoining Château Laniote. In '96, a separation was made between the best terroir on *agilo-calcaire* soils, and nine hectares on sandy soil which is now sold under the name of Côte de Roches Blanches. Then, in '97, Sophie Fourcade took over the management of all three Reiffers properties (see also Grandes Murailles and Clos St. Martin) on behalf of her family. The wines are now showing a steady improvement with '99 better than '98. Sixty per cent new oak is now used.

Château La Couronne

Grand Cru. Owner: Mähler-Besse. 9ha. 5,000 cases. Mer 65%, CS 20%, CF15%.

This *cru* in St-Hippolyte was bought by the Bordeaux négociants Mähler-Besse (who are also shareholders in Château Palmer) in 1992. The improvements they have made enabled the owners to gain the *grand cru* appellation. I found the '95 deliciously ripe, with easy, flattering fruit, yet also body and depth.

Château La Couspaude ★ →

*Grand Cru Classé. Owner: Vignobles Aubert. 7ha. 3,000 cases. Mer 60%,
CF and CS 40%.*

A property on the *plateau calcaire* immediately to the east of the town,
between Villemaurine and Trottevieille. It lost its place in the classification
in 1985, but regained it in 1996. Eighty per cent new oak is used, and the
malolactic fermentation has been in barrel for much of the '90s. These are
very hedonistic wines with aromatic fruit and succulent luscious texture.

Château Couvent-des-Jacobins ★

*Grand Cru Classé. Owner: Mme. Joineau-Borde. 10ha. 4,400 cases. Mer 65%,
CF 30%, CS 5%. Second label: Beau-Mayne.*

This old property, originally belonging to the Dominican friars, was added
to the classification in 1969. The house and *chai* are in the old town of St-
Émilion, while the vineyard nestles beneath the eastern ramparts of the town
on the edge of the *plateau calcaire* and on sandy soils. Secular owners took
over in the 18th century and the present family has been here since 1902.

This is a traditionally made wine, with one-third new wood used for
the maturation. In recent vintages I have found the wines to be consistent,
well-made, with a beautiful flavour and firm finish, quite taut and well-
structured. There is a distinctive blue-black label. The wine is distributed
by Dourthe Frères.

Château Croque-Michotte

*Grand Cru. Owner: Geoffrion Family. Administrator: Robert Carle. 14ha. 6,500
cases. Mer 70%, CF 30%.*

This *cru*, on the northwest of St-Émilion, borders on Pomerol. It has been in
the same family since 1890. One-third new wood is used. The wine seems to
be consistently well-made in a robust if slightly rustic style. The wine is
average in terms of quality and consistency, and lost its classification in 1996,
partly because of its reasonable prices.

Château Curé-Bon *see* Château Canon

Château Dassault

*Grand Cru Classé. Owner: Dassault Family. Administrator: Laurence Burn-
Vergriette. 24ha. 11,000 cases. Mer 65%, CF 30%, CS 5%.*

This was one of eight *crus* added to the classification in 1969. Formerly
known as Château Couperie, it was renamed in 1955. Vinification is in
stainless steel, with maturation in wood, 90–100 per cent is new oak.

The style of the Dassault wines is uncomplicated with a combination
of oak and tannins that makes for rather lean and ungrateful wines. They
reflect careful vinification and *élevage* and are most consistent. Solid,
middle-of-the-road wines.

Le Dôme *see* Château Teyssier

Château La Dominique ★★

*Grand Cru Classé. Owner: Clément Fayat. 22.5ha. 10,000 cases. Mer 75%,
CF 15%, CS 5%, Mal 5%. Second label: St-Paul de la Dominique.*

This *cru* has always had the capacity to make exceptional wines, but was not
consistent until the present owner took over in 1969.

The wines now are an impressive blend of fruit, ripeness, and tannin
which come together to produce remarkable opulence and power-packed
flavour, placing them at the forefront of the *grands crus classés*. '82, '83, '85,
'86, '89, and '90 are all exceptional, while '93, '94, '95, '96, '97, '98, and 2000
are great successes for these vintages.

Château Faugères V →

Grand Cru Classé. Owner: Corinne Guissey. 18ha. 8,300 cases. Mer 85%, CF 10%, CS 5%.
Second label: Château Haut-Bardoulet. Special selection: Peby-Faugères.

When a new generation of the family took over in 1987, they transformed
the property with new drainage of the vineyard, replanting of vines,
installation of stainless-steel vats, selection parcel by parcel, use of 50 per
cent new oak, and château-bottling of all wine. The excellence and fame of
these new wines spread quickly and they are now widely exported. They
are rich and powerful but with unmistakable style and breed. The splendid
'90 vintage showed the potential of the property, which actually straddles
the boundary of St-Étienne-de-Lisse and St-Colombe in the Côtes de
Castillon appellation.

Château Faurie-de-Souchard

Grand Cru Classé. Owner: Jabiol-Sciard family. 11ha. 6,000 cases. Mer 65%,
CF 26%, CS 9%.

The name is not to be confused with that of the neighbouring Petit-Faurie-
de-Soutard. Previously this property also had the prefix *petit,* but this has
been dropped. The vineyard is on the plateau and *côtes* northeast of the
town. Fermentation is in concrete vats and maturation is by rotating the
wine between casks (of which one-third are new) and vats. Although there
is much more Merlot here than at Cadet-Piola, there are some similarities
of style, especially a lack of flesh and tightness of flavour. There seems to
be a lack of consistency and charm about these wines.

Château de Ferrand

Grand Cru. Owner: Baron Marcel Bich. Administrator: Jean-Pierre Palatin.
30ha. 17,800 cases. Mer 70%, CF 15%, CS 15%.

This is the most important property in St-Hippolyte, situated on the *plateau
calcaire.* Not less than 50 per cent and sometimes 100 per cent new wood is
used for the maturation. The aim is to produce rich, tannic wines that are
suitable for ageing. The '85 was impressively rich and solid wine which had
mellowed beautifully when drunk in 2003.

Château Figeac ★★

1er Grand Cru Classé B. Owner: Thierry de Manoncourt. 39ha. 17,500 cases.
CS 35%, CF 35%, Mer 30%. Second label: La Grange Neuve de Figeac.

This fine old property is the remnant of a much larger estate, which in the
18th century included Cheval Blanc and several others that now incorporate
the name of Figeac. As with Cheval Blanc, some two-thirds of the vineyard
is on gravel and the remaining third on sandy soil. A fine new *chai* with a
large underground section is the latest improvement here.

Under Thierry de Manoncourt (who was in charge from 1947 to the early
'90s), the consistency and quality of winemaking was of a high order. The
similarities and differences between Figeac and Cheval Blanc are always
fascinating. The size of the vineyards and composition of the soils are
strikingly similar, but the *encépagement* is notably different. Here, an
important role is given to Cabernet Sauvignon, while at Cheval Blanc the
Cabernet Franc reigns supreme.

As a result, for all their similarities, Figeac seldom matches Cheval Blanc
for sheer weight and opulence of flavour, although it sometimes approaches
it and occasionally (as in '53 and '55) can even surpass it. The '82, '83, '85, '86,
'88, '89, '90, '95, '98, and 2000 are superb wines. Now Thierry de
Manoncourt's son-in-law, Eric d'Aramon, manages the property.

Château La Fleur V

Grand Cru. Owner: Lily Lacoste. 6.5ha. 3,000 cases. Mer 92%, CF 8%.
This is a good vineyard northeast of Soutard on sandy soils. The owner is
better known as co-proprietor of Pétrus and owner of Latour à Pomerol.
The fleshy, rich wines are full of easy fruit and charm.

Château Fleur-Cardinale

Owner: Claude and Alain Asséo. 18ha. 4,500 cases. Mer 70%, CF 15%, CS 15%.
Situated on the clay-chalk soils of the *côte* at St-Étienne-de-Lisse, this *cru*'s
wines are traditionally vinified and matured in oak, but need time to soften
before drinking at their best.

Château Fleur-Cravignac V

*Grand Cru. Owner: Lucienne Beaupertins. 7.5ha. 3,000 cases. Mer 70%, CF 20%,
CS 10%.*
Several recent tastings have shown Fleur-Cravignac to be an excellent *grand
cru*. The '95 was rich and solid with plenty of substance, depth, and harmony.
Just what one looks for in a good St-Emilion.

Château La Fleur-Pourret

Grand Cru. Owner: Manoncourt family. 4.5ha 2,500 cases. Mer 50%, CS 50%.
A property created by the grandfather of Bruno Prats in the 19th
century, combining two *crus*: Clos Haut-Pourret and Château La Fleur.
AXA sold to the Manoncourt family (*see* Château Figeac) in 2001. The La
Fleur-Pourret wines have an unusually high proportion of Cabernet
Sauvignon in their blend.

Château Fombrauge V →

*Grand Cru. Owner: Les Montagnes & Bernard Magrez. 63ha. 32,000 cases.
Mer 70%, CF 15%, CS 15%.*
An important *cru* in St-Christophe-des-Bardes, situated partly on the *plateau
calcaire* and partly on the north-facing *côte* and its lower slopes. In 1987,
it was sold to a Danish consortium, then to the present owners in '99 (*see*
Pape Clément).
   The wines are matured in cask, with 100 per cent new oak used. This
cru has a long-established reputation in the UK for producing consistent,
reliable wines that are rich and fleshy.

Château Fonplégade

*Grand Cru Classé. Owner: Armand Moueix. 18ha. 10,000 cases. Mer 60%, CF
35%, CS 5%. Second label: Clos Goudichaud.*
These are firm rather than tannic wines that require time to show their style
and finesse. They are consistent and reliable, without the richness and
charm of some, but rewarding to keep: solid and dependable, if lacking flair.

Château Fonroque

*Grand Cru Classé. Owner: GFA Château Fonroque. Administrator: Alain Moueix.
17.6ha. 8,000 cases. Mer 87%, CF 13%.*
In 2001, Alain Moueix, son of Jean-Jacques, who is now retired from J. P.
Moueix and still lives at Trotanoy, took over the management from the J. P.
Moueix team. There is a change to a more ripe, opulent, fruit style and a
change of label as well to mark the change in management. The last vintage
of the old team is also very good, expressing the richness of the vintage.

Clos Fourtet ★★

*1er Grand Cru Classé B. Owners: Philippe Cuvelier. 20ha. 8,000 cases. Mer 72%,
CF 22%, CS 6%.*
Second label: Domaine de Martialis.

The reputation of this château was in decline until 1973, when extensive improvements were made and the proportion of Merlot increased. There are distinct similarities of style between Clos Fourtet and its neighbour, Canon. The wines tend to be tightly knit and slow to evolve, but recently richer and more open-textured than of old. In the 1980s, big improvements were made under Pierre Lurton's management. The Lurton Family sold in 2000.

The '85, '86, '88, '89, '90, '93, '95, '96, '97, '98, and 2000 are particularly good, having extra concentration and richness allied to a lovely flavour. This is a château that possesses the potential to improve its standing still further.

Château Franc-Grâce-Dieu

Grand Cru. Owner: Germain Siloret. Administrator: Daniel Fournier.
8ha. 3,500 cases. Mer 60%, CF 40%.

Until Eric Fournier from *premier grand cru* Château Canon took over the farming and management here in 1981, the property was called Guadet-Franc-Grâce-Dieu. Vinification is now in stainless steel, with maturation in cask. I found Eric Fournier's first vintage, the '81, had finesse and style with intense, vibrant young fruit – better frankly than some *crus classés* – and the improvement during the 1980s has been impressively built upon since.

Château Franc-Mayne ★

Grand Cru Classé. Owner: Georgy Fourcroy and associates. 7ha. 3,000 cases.
Mer 90%, CF 10%.

This *cru* lies northwest of St-Émilion, just off the St-Émilion–Pomerol road, and is on the *côtes*. AXA took over in 1987 and then sold in '96 to a group of Belgians headed by Belgian négociant Georgy Fourcroy. They have brought in Michel Rolland and have invested in the cellars and the vineyard. The early vintages were very heavily marked by new oak but 2000 got the balance right, as has 2001.

Château La Gaffelière ★★

1er Grand Cru Classé B. Owner: Comte Léo de Malet-Roquefort. 22ha. 10,500 cases. Mer 65%, CF 30%, CS 5%.
Second label: Clos La Gaffelière.

The reputation of La Gaffelière is mixed. It can produce marvellously perfumed, supple, rich, and fleshy wines, but in the past they have been inconsistent, lacking the backbone and breeding of some of the best *crus* on the *côtes* and plateau. In 1996, Michel Rolland was called in, so consistency and quality are much better. The '82 is reminiscent of the '47 with its dense, almost jammy concentration. The '83 is particularly successful, rich, and complex with real breeding, and the '85 and '86 have benefited from increased selection, summer pruning of bunches and longer maceration, their concentration and structure much improved – a pattern which continued with the '88, '89, '90, '94, '95, '97, '98, and 2000.

A wine of enormous charm, which perhaps needs a degree of richness to give of its best, and one to watch.

Château La Gomerie ★

Grand Cru. Owner: Gerard and Dominique Bécot. 2.5ha. 750 cases. Mer 100%.

I do not usually list properties with such a miniscule production, but this has become a trophy wine in a very short time, and is getting around. I first tasted it in Sweden! It belongs to the Bécots of neighbouring Beau-Séjour-Bécot, but sells for a higher price, due to the tiny quantities. Although this is a new-wave wine in terms of malolactic in cask and 100 per cent new oak, the old vines do give it a natural concentration which makes the '95 delicious, with rich, ripe fruit and harmony with no sign of excessive oak. Whether it is worth the money, only the buyers and the market can decide.

Château La Grâce-Dieu-Les-Menuts

Grand Cru. Owner: Audier and Pilotte families. 13ha. 6,500 cases. Mer 65%, CF 30%, CS 5%.

The name *Grâce-Dieu* comes from a Cistercian grange which was secularized in the 17th century and subsequently divided. Some new casks have been introduced for the maturation, and the reputation of this *cru* is improving. It lies northwest of St-Émilion on the Libourne road, in the sector of sandy soils. The wines tend to be light-textured – suitable for young drinking.

Château Grand-Barrail-Lamarzelle-Figeac

Owner: Parent Family. Administrator: Louis Parent. 19ha. 8,400 cases. Mer 80%, CF 20%.

The Carrère family bought the property in the disastrous year of 1956 and sold in '97 to the present owners. One-third new wood is used for the maturation and the wines have a reputation for being supple, fruity and early maturing. Given the position of the vineyard, one wonders if the full potential has yet been realized: in 1996, it lost its *grand cru* status. The château has now been converted into a luxury hotel, providing a rare opportunity to stay in a working vineyard.

Château Grand Corbin

Grand Cru. Owner: Alain Giraud. 15.5ha. 7,500 cases. Mer 68%, CF 27%, CS 5%.

The history of this property echoes that of Château Corbin, which shares the same ownership. It lies on sandy soils between Corbin and Grand-Corbin-Despagne. Maturation is in casks, of which one-third are new.

    The reputation of this *cru* is for producing wines that tend to be blander than those of Corbin.

Château Grand-Corbin-Despagne V

Grand Cru. Owner: Despagne family.
26.5ha. 12,500 cases. Mer 75%, CF 24%, CS & Mal 1%.

The wines have a reputation for being rich and fleshy, but sometimes rather dilute and rustic. *Cru classé* status was lost in 1996.

Château Grandes Murailles ★ →

Grand Cru Classé. Owner: Reiffers Family. Administrator: Sophie Fourcade.
2ha. 600 cases. Mer 95%, CF 5%.

This tiny vineyard adjoins Clos Fourtet where the *plateau calcaire* begins to fall away to the *côte*. It is easy to locate, since the high, slender Gothic church wall with its windows still discernible, marks the vineyard boundary adjoining the road from Libourne. This property lost its classification in 1985, when the wine was made in the cellars of Côte de Baleau, but regained it in 1996. A separate cellar has now been constructed in an old quarried cave in one corner of the vineyard.

    Since Sophie Fourcade (*see* Côte de Baleau) took over in 1997, the wines have become increasingly impressive with lovely sumptuous fruit and good structure, but Clos St-Martin tends to have more complexity. One hundred per cent new oak is used. 1999, 2000, and 2001 are all most impressive.

Château Grand-Mayne ★★ →

Grand Cru Classé. Owner: Nony Family. Administrator: Marie-Francoise & Jean-Antoine Nony. 19ha. 8,000 cases. Mer 72%, CF 23%, CS 5%.
Second label: Les Plants du Mayne.

This old domaine with its beautiful mansion, dating in part from the 15th century, is one of the finest buildings in the vicinity of St-Émilion. It lies on the western *côte* and its lower slopes. Stainless-steel vats replaced the traditional wooden ones in 1975. Maturation is in casks, 80 per cent of which are new.

The wines here seem to have got better and better. '85, '88, '89, and '90 have been exceptionally rich and fine, while the remarkable quality of the '92, '93, '94, '95, '96, '97, '98, '99, and 2000 confirm this improvement. A wine that seems to have moved up a notch. Sadly, Jean-Pierre Nony died in 2001, but his capable son Jean-Antoine was already involved and he, in partnership with his mother, Marie-Françoise, now runs the property. This is very much a working, lived-in family home.

Château Grand-Pontet ★
Grand Cru Classé. Owners: Bécot and Pourquet families. 14ha. 6,500 cases. Mer 75%, CF 15%, CS 10%.
This château, at the foot of the *côtes*, lies just outside St-Émilion on the Libourne road. One of the two present partners also owns nearby Beau-Séjour-Bécot. Under the present management, rich, vibrant, flattering wines of character are now being made. The '90, '95, '96, '98, and 2000 are very successful.

Château Guadet-St-Julien
Grand Cru Classé. Owner: Robert Lignac. 6ha. 2,000 cases. Mer 75%, CF 25%.
Generally, this is an attractive, supple wine, showing unmistakable class and maturing quickly. But there can also be a touch of iron in its soul.

Château Haut-Corbin ★
Grand Cru Classé. Owner: A M du Bâtiment et Travaux Publics. Administrator: Philippe Dambrine. 6ha. 3,300 cases. Mer 65%, CS 25%, CF 10%.
This small property near the border with Montagne-St-Émilion lies north and east of the other Corbin properties on sandy soil. It was the only *cru* in this part of the appellation to be upgraded to *grand cru classé* in 1969. The wines are matured in cask, with 30 per cent new oak. Since new management took over in 1986, there has been a dramatic improvement, with rich, meaty wines in '86, '88, '89, and '90. Serious wines were also made in '93, '94, and '95.

Château Haut-Pontet V
Grand Cru. Owner: Limouzin Frères. 5ha. 10,000 cases. Mer 75%, CF and CS 25%.
This small *cru* is on the lower slopes of the *côte* north of St-Émilion. The consistently well-made wine is distinctive, rich, and full-flavoured with a good backbone.

Château Haut-Sarpe ★
Grand Cru Classé. Owner: J-F Janoueix. 21ha. 5,600 cases. Mer 70%, CF 30%. Second label: Château Vieux Sarpe.
Tastings of a number of recent vintages over a period of years have confirmed this as a wine of character and breeding. The '89 and '90 are powerful and dense-textured. The '96, '98, '99 and 2000 show a more succulent style than in the past with 50 per cent new oak now used.

Château L'Hermitage ★
Owner: Veronique Gaboriaud-Bernard. 4ha. 1,000 cases. Mer 60%, CF 40%.
This tiny vineyard is contiguous with Matras, and the wine is made and matured in the same ancient chapel which serves as its *cuvier* and *chais*. The vines are old – 45 years average – malolactic is now in 100 per cent new oak. The wines show superb, complex fruit quality, aided by the freshness and power that the Cabernet Franc brings, so it is easy to see why this is now a cult wine.

Château Jean-Faure

Grand Cru. Owner: Michel Amart. 18ha. 9,000 cases. CF 60%, Mer 30%, Mal 10%.

This *cru*, lying on sandy soils between Cheval Blanc and Ripeau, belonged to Ripeau for many years, and the properties were run together until the present owner bought it in 1976. The wine is distributed by Dourthe Frères. The *cru* lost its classified status in the revision of 1985. The aim is to produce full-bodied but elegant wines. My limited experience of them is that they are either tough and ferrous or soft and lacking in personality and style.

Château Laforge *see* Château Teyssier

Château Lamarzelle →

Grand Cru Classé. Owner: Jackie Sioën. 13ha. 5,800 cases. Mer 80%, CF 20%. Second label: Prieuré Lamarzelle.

In the revision of 1996, this *cru* retained its place, while its sister *cru*, Grand-Barrail-Lamarzelle-Figeac, lost its position. Neither wine has been outstanding in recent years, but with Dourthe distributing this wine, the attention to quality may have proved decisive – and there is more gravel in the vineyard here. Fifty per cent new oak is used in the ageing. The new owner took over in 1997.

Château Laniote

Grand Cru Classé. Owner: de la Filolie family. 5ha. 2,600 cases. Mer 70%, CS 20%, CF 10%.

This is not a big, beefy St-Émilion but it has great finesse. It is perfumed and intense with a long, refined, and beautiful flavour and real breeding. It has a most enchanting texture, lush and silky, which makes the wine exciting.

Château Laplagnotte-Bellevue

Grand Cru. Owner: Henri and Claude de Labarre. 6ha. 2,500 cases. Mer 65%, CF 25%, CS 10%.

Claude de Labarie, *née* Fourcaud-Lussac, was one of the principal shareholders of Cheval Blanc, and since she and her husband bought this small property in St-Christophe-des-Bardes in the late 1980s, the reputation of the *cru* has grown. The '90 has lovely, crushed-fruit aromas with clean, crisp, fresh fruit flavours. Already delicious when three years old, it has the capacity to mature for some years.

Château Larcis-Ducasse ★

Grand Cru Classé. Owner: Jacques Olivier Gratiot. Administrator: Nicolas Thienpoint. 11ha. 5,500 cases. Mer 65%, CF 25%, CS 10%.

These wines have been noted for their breed and charm, but have sometimes been rather light. Recent vintages have shown a marked improvement in consistency and quality. Lovely, rich wines were made in '89 and '90, while the '98 and 2000 are in the same mould. In 2002, Jacques Olivier Gratiot retired from running the property, which was handed over to Nicolas Thienpoint, who has been so successful not far away at Pavie-Macquin. He believes this to be an exceptional *terroir* and it will be interesting to watch the results.

Château Larmande ★

Grand Cru Classé. Owner: Le Groupe d'Assurances Mondiale. Administrator: Claire Chenard. 25ha. 10,000 cases. Mer 65%, CF 30%, CS 5%. Second label: Le Cadet de Larmande.

This fine property lies north of St-Émilion looking towards St-Georges. It marks the end of the *côtes* and the beginning of the sandy soils. The last decade has been one of progress here. The vineyard has been enlarged, and the proportion of Merlot increased at the expense of Cabernet Franc and, to an even greater extent, Cabernet Sauvignon. A new *cuvier*, equipped with stainless-steel fermentation vats, was built in 1975. Sixty per cent new oak is now used.

This wine has won many accolades, and consistently does well in blind tastings. The bouquet tends to be perfumed, full and vibrant, the wine rich, full-flavoured, quite spicy and with depth, harmony, and style. The wines are rather heavily marked by oak in all but the most luscious years.

Château Laroque ★

Grand Cru Classé. Owner: Beaumartin family. Administrator: Bruno Sainson. 58ha. 12,500 cases. Mer 87%, CF 11%, CS 2%.
Second label: Les Tours de Laroque, Château Peymouton.

This large property is in the commune of St-Christophe-des-Bardes where it occupies an exceptional site on the *plateau calcaire* and *côte*. The château itself is one of the grandest in the St-Émilion area, built in the time of Louis XIV and having a 12th century tower as a reminder of the feudal domaine.

The improvements date from 1982, when Bruno Sainson was brought in to manage the estate. He identified 27 of the 58 hectares that could produce wines of top quality. Buildings and cellars were renovated and some plots were replanted. Yields are strictly controlled, grapes hand-picked and sorted before fermentation, and 40 per cent new oak is used for the ageing. Then there is a further strict selection for the Laroque label, the rest being sold under the Les Tours de Laroque *marque*. All this work was crowned by promotion to *grand cru classé* in 1996, the first time this has been granted to a property whose vineyards are wholly outside the St-Émilion commune. Lovely, rich, concentrated wines are now being made in years like '94, '95, '96, '97, '98, and 2000.

Château Laroze ★ V

Grand Cru Classé. Owner: Guy Meslin. 27ha. 11,000 cases. Mer 68%, CF 26%, CS 6%.

The wines here are characterized by their fresh, clean, upfront fruit. They are perfumed, supple, and easy to drink, maturing quite quickly (over three to five years) and usually at their best at around five to eight years. These are delicious, flattering, fruity wines sold at reasonable prices.

Château Magdelaine ★★

1er Grand Cru Classé B. Owner: Éts J. P. Moueix. 11ha. 5,000 cases. Mer 90%, CF 10%.

The hallmark of Magdelaine is its great delicacy, breeding, and refinement of flavour. Fine wines were made in '82, '83, '85, '86, '88, '89, '90, '94, '95, '97, '98, and 2000.

The personality of the *cru* is interesting because it is more charming than straight plateau wines such as Canon, but less fleshy and more elegant than a lower *côtes* such as La Gaffelière. For me this is certainly one of the most rewarding wines of the St-Émilion *côtes*.

Château Magnan La Gaffelière V

Grand Cru. Owner: GFA du Clos de la Madeleine. 10ha. 3,500 cases. Mer 65%, CF 25%, CS 10%.

In 1995, at a blind tasting of '45s, this wine outperformed some of the most illustrious *premiers grands crus*. We all wondered if the *cru* still existed. In fact, it was bought, along with Clos de la Madeleine, by a group of enthusiasts in 1992, and the '95 proved to be one of the outstanding wines in a large tasting organized for me by the Syndicat in 1999. This is a wine full of character and luscious Merlot fruit.

Château Matras ★

Grand Cru Classé. Owner: Mme Véronique Gaboriaud-Bernard.
8ha. 3,700 cases. Mer 60%, CF 40%.

The last decade has seen important changes here. Gone are the tanks standing in the open; the *chais* and *cuvier* are now in the old chapel of Notre Dame de Mazerat. It was only in the summer of 1989 that Francis Gaboriaud, the former husband of the owner who still runs the property, decided that to undertake the coming harvest without any cooling equipment was courting disaster, so promptly installed it.

The vineyard lies in an amphitheatre at the foot of Tertre-Daugay and Beauséjour going towards Angélus, so it is a real suntrap where the Merlot needs to be harvested rapidly once maturity arrives, and the Cabernet Franc gives a very important ingredient of freshness and spice.

The wines have opulence and richness supported by spicy tannins and show real class. In a tasting at the property in June 2001, the outstanding wines were '88, '89, '90, '95, and '98 with very good wines made in '99 (in spite of hail), '97 and '96. One does not hear much about Matras, but it certainly deserves to be better-known.

Château Monbousquet ★ →

Grand Cru. Owner: M et Mme Gérard Perse. 32ha. 17,000 cases. Mer 60%,
CF 30%, CS 10%.

When the property was run by Alain Querre, these were attractive, rich, supple wines with a distinctive character. They lacked the ultimate breed of the best St-Émilions, but were nevertheless highly enjoyable wines. Now the new owner has transformed both *chai* and wines, using the pre-fermentation cold maceration and 100 per cent new oak to make opulent, dense-textured, plummy, fruity wines, much to the new taste and quite delicious when drunk young. The first vintage was '93. Michel Rolland is the consultant oenologist.

La Mondotte ★★ →

Grand Cru. Owner: Comte Stephan von Neipperg. 4.5ha. 800 cases. Mer 80%,
CF 20%.

This small vineyard is just to the east of Troplong-Mondot, and it is only recently that Stephan von Neipperg has found that he can make more remarkable wines here than at his *grand cru classé*, Canon-la-Gaffelière. One hundred per cent new oak is now being used and a new *cuverie* with wooden vats was completed in time for the '98 crop. '96 is the first vintage of the new Mondotte, with its small yield of 30hl/ha, and '97, '98, '99, and 2000 are all superb. One finds truffles, black cherries, liquorice, together with complexity and a very special and marked character, unctuous fruit with very rich tannins. There is no doubting the quality of these wines, and demand has pushed prices to a high level.

Château Montlabert

Grand Cru. Owner: Georgy Fourcroy. 12.5ha. 5,500 cases. Mer 70%, CF 25%, CS 5%.
This property lies on sandy soils northwest of St-Émilion near Figeac. Georgy Fourcroy bought it in 1998, so improvements can be expected.

Château Moulin du Cadet V →

Grand Cru Classé. Owner: Éts J. P. Moueix. 5ha. 2,300 cases. Mer 90%, CF 10%.
A small property on the *plateau calcaire*, north of St-Émilion and adjoining the Moueix property of Fonroque. The wines bear the hallmarks of the

Château Plaisance V →

Owner: Xavier Maréschal. 17ha. 7,000 cases. Mer 85%, CS 15%.
Second label: Château La Fleur Plaisance.

This property in St-Sulpice-de-Faleyrens now uses Patrick Valette as consultant (*see* Château Berliquet). The malolactic fermentation takes place in cask with 80–100 per cent new oak. The '98 and '99 are wonderfully seductive and luscious wines with delightful fruit flavours. This really shows how lower yields (40hl/ha) and good winemaking can transform a vineyard.

Château de Pressac →

Grand Cru. Owner: Jean-François Quernin. 28.5ha. 10,000 cases. Mer 75%,
CF 20%, CS 4%, Pressac 1%.
Second label: Château Tour de Pressac.

A fine feudal château overlooks this *cru*, which is situated on the chalky soils of the plateau in St-Étienne-de-Lisse. It was here in the late 1730s that the Auxerrois, or Noir de Pressac grape, was introduced to Bordeaux. Now, it is better known as the Malbec. The new owners took over in 1997, and are clearly determined to unlock the potential here. They have now reintroduced the Pressac (or Malbec) grape variety in the vineyard. The '99 is a mouthful of a wine with more richness than most '99s, suggesting that serious, attractive wines will now be made here. One hundred per cent new oak is used. Watch this space!

Château Le Prieuré

Grand Cru Classé. Owner: Baronne Guichard. 6.3ha. 2,800 cases. Mer 60%,
CS 30%, CF 10%. Second label: Château l'Olivier.

This property on the *plateau calcaire* is on high ground, on a site set apart between Trottevieille and Troplong-Mondot. The owner also has the important property of Siaurac in Lalande de Pomerol, as well as Château Vray-Croix-de-Gay in Pomerol. Château Le Prieuré once belonged to the Franciscan house in St-Émilion, the Cordeliers. One-quarter new wood is used in the maturation. I have found the wines to be attractive, elegant, and on the light side: good breed, but not above-average.

Château Quercy

Grand Cru. Owner: Apelbaum-Pidoux. 8ha. 3,500 cases. Mer 75%, CF 20%, CS 5%.

The present owners, a Swiss famiy, bought this property in Vignonet in 1988. The combination of old vines, hand-harvesting, 30 per cent new oak, and meticulous care at every stage comes through in this attractive open-textured wine.

Château Quinault ★ →

Grand Cru. Owner: A and F Raynaud. 15ha. 6,000 cases. Mer 80%, CF 10%,
CS 5%, Mal 5%. Second label: Lafleur de Quinault.

This *cru*, now surrounded by the urban sprawl of Libourne, was saved from the developers by Dr Alain Raynaud and his wife Françoise (of Château La Croix de Gay) when they acquired it in 1997. With its old vines and special microclimate, they believe exceptional wines can be made here, and have begun auspiciously with the '97 vintage, with '98, '99, and 2000 being even better; 100 per cent new oak is used. The wine is labelled Quinault L'Enclos.

Château Ripeau ★

Grand Cru Classé. Owner: Françoise de Wilde. 15.5ha. 5,500 cases. Mer 62%,
CF 30%, CF 8%.

A fine, important *cru* on the sandy soils near the border with Pomerol, southeast of Cheval Blanc and La Dominique. Since the present owners took over in 1976 they have considerably expanded the *cuvier* and *chai*. I was impressed by the rich, powerful '90.

Château Rol Valentin

Owner: Eric and Virginie Presette. 4ha. 1,400 cases Mer 85%, CF 15%.

This *cru* was effectively created by the present owners in 1994, although it originates from the 1.6 hectares of Côtes de Rol Valentin. These are old vines and small wooden *cuves* are used for the vinification. The soil is sandy with chalky clay. One hundred per cent new oak is used. This has rapidly become a cult wine commanding high prices. I confess to having been disappointed with the '95 and '96, but there are reports of a much better 2000. Only time will determine this *cru*'s true worth.

Château Roylland V →

Owner: Chantal Vuitton Oddo and Pascal Oddo. Administrator: Bernard Oddo. 10ha. 4,500 cases. Mer 90%, CF 10%.

The vineyard here is in two parts, five hectares at Mazerat, between Angélus and Beauséjour (Duffau-Lagarosse) and 4.5 on the plateau of St-Christophe des Bardes. They started green harvesting in '89 to reduce yields. Thirty per cent new oak is used. I have found the wines well-structured with rich, attractively fruity flavours. The '95 was very good, the '98 outstanding.

Château Rozier

Grand Cru. Owner: Jean-Bernard Saby. 22ha. 12,000 cases. Mer 80%, CF 15%, CS 5%.

Rozier is a *cru* in the St-Laurent-des-Combes commune producing appealingly fruity, characterful wines which age well.

Château St-Georges-Côte-Pavie

Grand Cru Classé. Owner: Jacques Masson. 5.1ha. 2,500 cases. Mer 80%, CF 20%.

A small, well-placed *cru* on the western end of the Côte de Pavie and its lower slope. La Gaffelière is on the other side, and there are views across to Ausone. The fermentation is in stainless steel, and maturation is in cask. The wines are notable for their delicious, easy fruit and marked character and breeding. They are high-toned and flavoured and delightful to drink when four to seven years old. Though delicious when drunk young, however, they lack the concentration needed for ageing.

Clos St-Martin ★ →

Grand Cru Classé. Owner: Reiffers Family. 1.4ha. 500 cases. Mer 70%, CF 20%, CS 10%. Administrator: Sophie Fourcade.

Three *crus* – this one, Grandes Murailles and Côte de Baleau – were, until 1985, all managed together, with the wine made and kept at Côte Baleau. In 1985, however, the other two *crus* lost their *grand cru classé* status in a revision of the classification system, and since then the proprietors have made a determined effort to improve matters. Clos St-Martin now has separate facilities, and the '86 consequently showed a big step forward in quality, with a bouquet full of vivid, scented fruit; breed, elegance, and balanced tannins. Some sensational wines were made in the nineties, culminating in the 2000. They are wines which also develop real complexity.

Château Sansonnet →

Grand Cru. Owner: François d'Aulan. 7ha. 3,300 cases. Mer 70%, CF 20%, CS 10%.

This *cru* is on the *plateau calcaire* east of St-Émilion on its eastern culminating point, and just north of Trottevieille. There is clay mixed with limestone here, on rocky subsoil. In 1996, the *cru classé* status was lost. In 1999, the property was bought by François d'Aulan, former owner of

Champagne Piper Heidsieck. The '99 had malolactic fermentation in 100 per cent new oak. The 2000 is really concentrated with very ripe rich fruit and thick textures. So, without a doubt, this *cru* should soon be on the way back.

Château La Serre ★

Grand Cru Classé. Owner: Bernard d'Arfeuille. Administrator: Luc d'Arfeuille. 7ha. 3,000 cases.Mer 80%, CF 20%. Second label: Menuts de La Serre.

This is a wine with structure, depth of flavour, and a finely perfumed bouquet, a wine of individuality, highly typical of the plateau surrounding St-Émilion. La Serre is a solid, reliable *grand cru classé* of good quality: not a high-flyer but thoroughly worthy.

Château Soutard ★

Grand Cru Classé. Owners: des Ligneris Family. 22ha. 10,000 cases. Mer 70%, CF 30%. Second label: Clos de la Tonnelle.

The aim at Soutard is to make traditional, long-keeping wines, and the result is uncompromising and requires patience. My own feeling is that sometimes the fruit and natural charm of St-Émilion are unnecessarily sacrificed, and that often the wines would benefit from earlier bottling and a lighter touch – but these are matters of taste. The stylishness comes through, but the wines often seem lean and ungrateful. They are hard to judge in cask because the *assemblage* is effected shortly before bottling.

Château Tertre-Daugay ★

Grand Cru Classé. Owner: Comte Léo de Malet Roquefort. 16ha. 6,500 cases. Mer 60%, CF 40%. Second label: Château de Roquefort.

The property was in an appalling state of neglect when Comte Léo de Malet Roquefort bought it in 1978. From then until the reconstruction of the *cuvier* and *chai* in 1984, the wines had to be made and kept at La Gaffelière. This property now receives the same care and attention as the *premier grand cru*, but with 50 per cent new wood used for the maturation.

This has the potential to be one of the best of the *grands crus classés*. The wines are gloriously perfumed and spicy on the nose with a rich, ripe fruit well-matched to give a fine, powerful, complex flavour and stylish breeding.

Château Tertre Roteboeuf ★★

Owner: François Mitjavile. 5.7ha. 2,800 cases. Mer 85%, CF 15%.

The name derives from the oxen once used to plough the steep slopes: exposed to the hot sun as they worked, the oxen roasted in the heat – hence "roast beef". François Mitjavile has been the proprietor since 1978, and by late harvesting and long vatting, he aims to produce serious wines that age well. His wines have great individuality, with a lot of oak, retaining plenty of fruitiness and structure yet always harmonious, with great aromatic complexity and thick textures. '82 and '85 are still wonderfully fresh and luscious. '90 is supple and exotic with a very long finish. After a fine '95, '98 is exceptionnally muscular and long–flavoured. '97 and '99 are more elegant with lovely fruit flavours, while the low–yielding 2000 with its opulent richness, black fruit denseness and sweetness is simply superb. This is now something of a cult wine, commanding high prices.

Château Teyssier V →

Owner: Jonathan Malthus. 30ha. 12,000 cases. Mer 85%, CF 10%, CS 5%. Also vinified and matured at Château Teyssier: Château Laforge, 3ha. 1,000 cases; Mer 92%, CF 8%; Le Dôme 1.6ha. 550 cases; CF 72%, Mer 28%.

This English engineer only arrived in St-Émilion in 1994, when he bought Teyssier in Vignonet, whose flat, gravelly, sandy soils are well down the pecking

order as far as St-Émilion terroirs are concerned. The original 14 hectares have
grown and sound, well-made, fruity wines are produced here. But also to be
found in the well-ordered new *chais* are two other more recent acquisitions,
which have caused quite a stir. Laforge, bought from the daughter of the
blacksmith of St-Sulpice-de-Faleyrens in '98, consists of five separate parcels
and produces a wine rich in aromatics with a big, chocolatey richness and tannic
structure, yet preserving a lovely freshness. Le Dôme comes from a parcel of
vineyard that was part of Vieux Mazerat, lying between Angélus and Grand
Mayne and planted with a high proportion of old Cabernet Franc. The wine has
the finesse and power of Cabernet Franc in vintages such as '98 and 2000 and is
spicy and complex, with marked individuality. Both these wines get the full
avant-garde treatment – malolactic in 100 per cent new oak and no fining or
filtration – so if you cellar them for any length of time, look out for the deposit!

Château La Tour-Figeac ★ →

*Grand Cru Classé. Owner: Otto Maximilian Rettenmaïer. Administrator: Otto M.
Rettenmaïer. 14.6ha. 6,000 cases. Mer 60%, CF 40%.*

This property lies on the border with Pomerol and was part of Figeac until
1879. Three years later, the two La Tour-du-Pin-Figeacs were also hived off.
This is a powerful, yet stylish wine, rich and scented on the nose, with real
length of flavour, marked by elegant breeding. The new owners are
improving the wines yet further. Otto Maximilian, the son of the family,
took over management in 1994 and produced a delicious '95. '96, '97, '98, '99,
and 2000 have continued to enhance the reputation of this excellent *cru*.

Château La Tour-du-Pin-Figeac ★

*Grand Cru Classé. Owner: Vignobles Jean-Michel Moueix. Administrator:
Jean-Michel Moueix. 9ha. 4,000 cases. Mer 60%, CF 30%, Mal and CS 10%.*

These are powerful, robust, full-flavoured wines of style which consistently
came out well in blind tastings in the eighties. Sadly, during the second half
of the nineties, which was such an exciting time for the region as a whole,
this well-placed *cru* slipped back and is currently making rather pedestrian,
if well-priced wines.

Château La Tour-du-Pin-Figeac (Giraud-Bélivier)

*Grand Cru Classé. Owner: GFA Giraud-Bélivier. 11ha. 5,500 cases. Mer 75%,
CF 25%.*

This property is not nearly as well-known or as well-reputed as its
neighbour of the same name, owned by the Moueix family, though they
shared a common history until 1882. The Girauds bought the property
from the Béliviers in 1972, but this still hasn't resulted in wines worthy
of its excellent site.

Château Troplong-Mondot ★★

*Grand Cru Classé. Owner: Valette Family. Administrator: Christine Valette.
30ha. 11,000 cases. Mer 80%, CF 10%, CS 10%.
Second label: Mondot.*

This is one of the most important properties in St-Émilion, on the *côte* and
plateau. It should be one of the best St-Émilion *crus,* and if sites play a part,
should be challenging for a position as a *premier grand cru*. But until the
eighties the full potential was not realized in terms of consistency and quality.
Then, for the marvellous '86, 50 per cent new oak was used and all the wines
were kept in cask instead of rotating between cask and vat. Eighty per cent
new oak is now used. This vintage proved a watershed. The '88, '90, '94, '95,
'96, '97, '98, '99, and 2000 have produced wines that are increasingly on the

level of the *premiers grands crus classés*. This has all been the work of the owner's daughter, Christine Valette. Before this the best vintages were '70, '78, '79, '82, and '83.

Château Trottevieille ★

1er Grand Cru Classé B. Owner: Castéja family. Administrator: Philippe Castéja. 10ha. 3,500 cases. Mer 50%, CF 45%, CS 5%.

This is the only *premier grand cru* to be owned by a Bordeaux négociant. The vineyard is set apart from the other *premiers* on the plateau to the east of St-Émilion, somewhat below Troplong-Mondot. The soil is a mixture of limestone and clay. The very thin soil here means that the wines suffer by comparison with their Premier Grand Cru neighbours and really need time in bottle to show their class.

Philippe Castéja introduced 80 per cent new oak for the '85 vintage, and began producing much more concentrated wines. A vertical tasting held at the château in 2003 showed that the outstanding vintages here are '61, '75, '85, '89, '90, '95, '98, and 2000. The '61 and '75 showed how well this *cru* evolves in great years when yields are low; '85 has enormous charm and richness; '89 is more tannic than '90 but with wonderful blackcurrant flavours and rich textures, while '90 is more seductive. '95, '98, and 2000 follow this high standard.

Union des Producteurs de St-Émilion

Members: 360. Director: Jacques Baugier. 950ha. 550,000 cases.

There is no other cooperative in Bordeaux that produces as much high-quality wine as this one, lying just at the southern foot of the *côtes*, between the town and the Libourne–Bergerac road. In 1985, it saw one of its 330 members, Château Berliquet, become a *grand cru classé* (*see* Château Berliquet).

There are four important wines, all entitled to the *grand cru* status, which are sold under trademarks:

Royal St-Émilion This is made from properties on the plain. The wine is full, robust, and open-textured with a certain coarseness typical of its origins, but attractive.

Côtes Rocheuses As the name implies, this comes from properties in the *côtes* area. This takes longer to develop its richness, and has more power. Some 120,000 cases are made.

Haut-Quercus *Quercus* is the Latin for oak. This brand was launched in 1978, and the wine is aged in new oak. At present, 2,500 cases, all in numbered bottles, are produced annually. The wines have real intensity and are quite tannic, with a classic flavour. They take time to mature.

Cuvée Galius This is a special selection of cask-aged wines. The first vintage was '82, and it was selected at a 1984 blind tasting for the Trophée des Honneurs as one of the 12 best wines.

The quality of these branded wines is often superior to that of many small *crus* made at the property, and certainly more saleable. It is a valuable source of good, typical, sound St-Émilion. In addition, a large number of château wines are individually made and bottled under their respective labels. They are labelled *mis à la propriété*.

Château Valandraud ★★

Owner: Jean-Luc Thunevin. 8.9ha. 3,500 cases. Mer 66%, CF 33%, Mal 1%.
Second labels: Virginie de Valandraud and Clos Badon Thunevin.

Since I last commented on this *cru* of the 1990s, there have been important developments. The vineyard has grown and production has increased fivefold. However only a part of this is sold as Valandraud, the rest under two other *marques* (*see* above). The vineyard is in three parts. One-quarter clay on calcerous soil, one-quarter gravel and one-half sand on gravel.

In 2000, Valandraud itself was a selection from 3.5 hectares of 1,000 cases, 70 per cent Merlot and 30 per cent Cabernet Franc, while the Virginie represented four hectares and 1,500 cases in the same proportions of Merlot and Cabernet Franc. The wines go into new oak for their malolactic fermentation. When this is completed the wines are racked off their lees. Then they are racked every three months, but not fined or filtered prior to bottling. The wines have a lovely fruit quality, the Valandraud has rich, chunky tannins and a scent of violets, it is more structured than the supple Virginie. They are certainly seductive wines which have grown in stature, especially from '98 onwards, and it is not hard to understand their success and ability to command high prices.

Château Villemaurine
Grand Cru Classé. Owner: Robert Giraud. 8ha. 4,000 cases. Mer 70%, CS 30%.
The name is derived from *Villa Maure*, "Moorish city", the name given to the place where the Saracens camped in the 8th century. Great efforts are being made to improve the quality here, and there is certainly potential, though whether it is appropriate to have so much Cabernet Sauvignon must be open to question. After a period of over-extraction in the 1980s, the wines are lighter, with 45 per cent new oak now, but are still often coarse and sometimes dilute.

Château Yon-Figeac ★ →
Grand Cru Classé. Owner: Vignobles Germain.
25ha. 13,000 cases. Mer 80%, CF 20%.
This large vineyard lies northwest of St-Émilion on the road to Pomerol, between Laroze and Grand-Barrail-Lamarzelle-Figeac on sandy soil. The Lussiez family were owners here for four generations before selling to their distributors.

The wines have one-third new oak and have been noted for their consistency and typical attractive characteristics for many years. They tend to be scented, soft, rich, and full-flavoured, with a nice underlying firmness. Watch for significant improvements from '98 onwards.

The St-Émilion Satellites

Outside the St-Émilion appellation to the north and northeast lie the so-called St-Émilion Satellites. While they have been excluded from the straightforward St-Émilion AC, they have the right to add the name "St-Émilion" to their own communal names. Some of these wines are in fact superior to St-Émilions produced from the plain of the Dordogne, and there is a much higher proportion of large domaines than in St-Émilion and Pomerol. Many of the small owners are members of the cooperatives of Montagne, Lussac, and Puisseguin. The Satellite communes are as follows:

Montagne-St-Émilion The small communes of St-Georges and Parsac were joined to Montagne in 1972, but some growers in St-Georges continue to exercise their option of using the St-Georges-St-Émilion appellation. The AC now covers around 1,500 hectares of vineyard. The soils are *plateau calcaire* but with more clay than in St-Émilion.

Lussac-St-Émilion Here there are around 1,400 hectares of vines, on the *plateau calcaire* of the type found in St-Émilion and St-Christophe-des-Bardes. But below these are the *côtes* of *sables du Perigord* which are less favourable for viticulture. This is the most northerly of these appellations.

Puisseguin-St-Émilion This lies northeast of St-Émilion with around 700 hectares of vines. There is a large *plateau calcaire* and its *côtes*, which provide good viticultural land.

Château Beauséjour and Beauséjour "Clos L'Église" V →
Owners: Vignobles Germain 14ha. 6,000 cases. Mer 85%, CF 15%.

This good property in Montagne benefits from old vines – 53 years on average – and the dynamic management of Bernard Germain and his team. The Clos L'Eglise is a special reserve made from the oldest vines, some dating from 1903.

I have found this wine to be very rich and concentrated, with real depth and the structure to require some ageing to reach maturity. Impressive wines that show what Montagne can achieve.

Châteaux Belair-Montaiguillon and Belair St-Georges V
Owners: Nadine Pocci and Yannick Le Menn. 10ha. 5,500 cases. Mer 80%, CF and CS 20%.

This excellent *cru* is situated on one of the highest points in the commune of St-Georges, facing south towards St-Émilion on limestone and clay soils. Delicious wines are now being made here. They are full of rich, supple fruit and have a marked character – comparable to the best St-Émilion Grands Crus. Since the '88 vintage, two separate wines have been made. The Belair St-Georges is a selection from the oldest vines, aged in cask with some new oak. This wine is slower-developing, so needs longer ageing than the Belair-Montaiguillon, which sees no wood but has lots of fruit.

Château Bel-Air
Owner: Robert Adove. 16ha. 10,000 cases. Mer 80%, CF 15%, CS 5%.
A *cru* at the most northerly part of the region, in the commune of Puisseguin. Some attractive wines of good fruit and substance are produced here.

Château de Bellevue V
Owner: Chatenoud family. 12 ha. 7000 cases. Mer 95%, CF 5%.
André Chatenoud is making serious wines at this Lussac property. There are no frills, just meticulous care and 30 per cent new oak. A tasting in September 2000 of the superb '90 and '89 showed how well the wines mature, keeping their freshness and powerful flavours, while '98 and '99 were full of promise.

Château Calon V
Owner: Jean-Noël Boidron.
Montagne vineyard: 36ha. 16,500 cases. Mer 70%, CF 15%, CS 13%, Mal 2%.
St-Georges vineyard: 7.5ha. 3,500 cases. Mer 80%, CF 10%, CS 10%.
There is some cause for confusion here! This is basically one property with land in two communes: Montagne and St-Georges. The label is the same but both appellations are used. The Saint Georges portion is only 7.5 hectares, but its wines have far more depth of flavour and structure. These are reliable attractive wines. The owner also owns Château Corbin-Michotte.

Château Faizeau V
Owner: SC du Château. Administrators: Chantal Lebreton and M. Alain Raynaud. 10ha. 5,000 cases. Mer 100%.
This vineyard is in a single piece on the hill of Calon at the highest point of the Montagne appellation. The old family property has been controlled since 1983

by the administrators, who are also owners of La Croix de Gay in Pomerol. The quality of the '93, with its rich, supple, flattering fruit, the result of a selection of old vines, is exemplary, and shows that the best Montagne wines are often better than the St-Émilions from the plain.

Château de la Grenière

Owner: Jean-Pierre Dubreuil. 21ha. 12,500 cases. Mer 55%, CS 30%, CF 15%. Second label: Château les Noves.

This property in Lussac-St-Émilion makes solid, well-structured wines with plenty of rich fruit. To judge by the excellent '89 when tasted in late 1995, it may also age well.

Château Guibeau V

Owner: Bourlon family. Administrator: Henri Bourlon. 34ha. 22,000 cases. Mer 70%, CF 15%, CS 15%. Second labels: Le Vieux Château Guibeau, Châteaux La Fourvieille and Les Barrails.

The wine sold under the Guibot-La-Fourvieille label is a selection from 10 ha. Situated on the limestone plateau near Puisseguin, the wines of this large *cru* are of good quality – on a par with the St-Émilion Grands Crus even – and reflect the attention to detail shown by the Bourlon family, who have invested much in restoring and modernizing this property. The best wine in the commune.

Château Laroze-Bayard

Owner: Laporte family. 21ha. 13,000 cases. Mer 70%, CF 15%, CS 15%. Second label: Château le Tuileries-de-Bayard.

An old property in the hamlet of Bayard, which has been owned by the Laporte family since 1700. *Cuve*-matured wines, rich in colour and fruit, are produced here. They are well-structured, with good body.

Château des Laurets →

Owner: SA Château des Laurets. Administrator: Henri Bourlon. 79.5ha. 52,000 cases. Mer 70%, CF 22%, CS 8%. Second labels: Châteaux La Rochette and Maison-Rose.

This is Puisseguin's most important property and one of the largest in the St-Émilion Satellites. The vineyards are on the *plateau calcaire* and the *côtes* south of Puisseguin and in adjoining Montagne-St-Émilion, so both appellations are used. These are well-reputed, robust, and attractive wines. Since 1995, it has been run by Henri Bourlon of Château Guibeau-La-Fourvieille, so improvements can now be expected.

Château du Lyonnat V →

Owner: GFA des Vignobles Jean Milhade. 48ha. 27,000 cases. Mer 50%, CF 50%. Second label: Château La Rose-Perruchon.

This is one of the largest and best-known domaines of the St-Émilion Satellites. It lies to the east of Lussac on the *plateau calcaire*. This is reliable, fairly light-textured, stylish wine which nevertheless keeps quite well. The standard is comparable to a good St-Émilion Grand Cru. Recent vintages show more richness and definition.

Château Macquin St-Georges

Owner: Corre-Macquin. Administrator: Corre-Macquin. 13ha. 7,500 cases. Mer 70%, CF 15%, CS 15%. Second label: Château Bellonne St-Georges.

This well-known *cru* is situated on hillside sites near St-Georges. The wines are bottled and distributed by J. P. Moueix (*see also* Château Pavie-Macquin). Fine, attractive, luscious wines are made here: Macquin St-Georges wines are up to good St-Émilion Grand Cru standards.

Château Maison-Blanche V

Owners: Gérard and Nicolas Despagne. 32ha. 18,500 cases. Mer 80%, CF 20%.
Other label: Louis Rapin. Second label: Les Piliars de Maison-Blanche.

This important domaine is on the *côte* to the west of Montagne. The wines are richly perfumed and attractive for early drinking. Twenty per cent new casks are used.

Château Mayne-Blanc V

Owner: Jean Boucheau. 17ha. 11,000 cases. Mer 60%, CS 30%, CF 10%.
Other label: Cuvée St-Vincent.

One of the best *crus* in Lussac-St-Émilion, and one that has been in the same family for many generations. Only vines of eight years and older are bottled under the château name, and vines of 20 years and older are put in one-third new casks under the Cuvée St-Vincent name. The '89 Mayne-Blanc is deliciously robust with a rich, layered, fruity texture.

Château Montaiguillon V

Owner: Amart family. 26ha. 16,500 cases. Mer 40%, CS 30%, CF 30%.

One of the most reliable and attractive wines in Montagne-St-Emilion. Whenever I have found it on a wine list it has been a safe bet. Solid, fleshy, attractive wines with body and good fruit are consistently made.

Château de Musset V

Owner: Patrick Valette. 7.5ha. 4,500 cases. Mer 70%, CS 20%, CF 10%.

Situated in the commune of Parsac, now absorbed into that of Montagne, this old *cru* has attracted deserved attention since Patrick Valette, son of Jean-Paul Valette of Château Pavie, began to run the property. If he can obtain the richness and concentration allied to charm he achieved in the '92, what will he be able to do in better years? Certainly a *cru* to watch.

Château la Papeterie V

Owner: Jean-Pierre Estager. 10ha. 5,000 cases. Mer 70%, CF 30%.

This good property lies at the crossroads of four appellations: Pomerol, Lalande de Pomerol, St-Émilion, and Montagne-St-Émilion, the vineyard being in Montagne. The owner also has a well-reputed Pomerol *cru*, la Cabanne.

The '90 was most attractive in 1997, with supple fruit and good structure, and no sign of the dilution which affects some of the wines in this vintage.

Les Productions Réunies de Puisseguin et Lussac-St-Émilion

642ha. 428,000 cases. Mer 70%, CF and CS 30%.

Wines from this cooperative of 150 members are sold mostly under two separate labels, one for each of the two communes. Lussac accounts for about 75 per cent of the production and Puisseguin for the rest.

There are also 21 *crus* that are vinified here separately and marketed under their own château labels. The Cuvée Renaissance from Puisseguin is particularly good, the Lussac *cuvée* is lighter.

Château Roc de Calon V

Owner: Bernard Laydis. 20ha. 12,000 cases. Mer 75%, CF 20%, CS 5%.

This good Montagne property, with its vineyard on the Tertre de Calon, uses a combination of *cuves* (80 per cent) and casks for maturation, including some new ones.

In September 2000, the '89 especially and '90 showed how well these wines age in good vintages, while the '98 was very promising. These are good, well-made wines.

Château Rocher Corbin V

Owner: Durand family. 9.5ha. 5,000 cases. Mer 80%, CF 15%, CS 5%.

Second label: Vieux Château Rocher Corbin.

The vineyard is situtated on the west side of the *tertre de Calon*, in Montagne. The '90 has real depth and concentration of spicy fruit and is a most impressive wine.

Château de Roques V
Owner: Michel Sublett. 20ha. 13,000 cases. Mer 66%, CF 34%.
Second labels: Châteaux Vieux-Moulin, des Aubarèdes and Roc du Creuzelat.
The name comes from Jean de Roques, a former proprietor and close acquaintance of Henri IV. Some delicious wines are made, comparable to good Grand Cru St-Émilions.

Château Roudier V
Owner: Jacques Capdemourlin. 30ha. 15,000 cases. Mer 60%, CF 25%, CS 15%.
This fine and important property is on the *côte* (limestone and clay) facing south towards St-Émilion. The proprietor also manages Capdemourlin and owns Balestard-la-Tonnelle. The wines are of a high standard and have a marvellously rich, gamey flavour. Easily up to the best St-Émilion Grand Cru standard.

Château St-André-Corbin V
Owner: Robert Carré. Administrator: Alain Moueix. 19ha. 11,000 cases. Mer 77%, CF 23%.
A *cru* of comparable quality to the St-Émilion *grands crus*, producing charming wines which have spiciness, fruit, and a good, balanced structure. Management has now passed from the J. P. Moueix team to Alain Moueix.

Château St-Georges V
Owner: M Desbois-Pétrus. 50ha. 25,000 cases. Mer 60%, CS 20%, CF 20%.
Second label: Puy-St-Georges.
This is certainly one of the most spectacular properties in the whole region, with a palatial château built in 1774 by Victor Louis, architect of the Grand Théâtre, in the purest classical style. Its vineyards are on south-facing *côtes* looking towards St-Émilion. These are elegant but well-constructed wines that have a considerable life-span. Half the maturation casks used each year are of new oak. If this were in St-Émilion, it is hard to think it would not be a *grand cru classé*. As it is the wine has a great reputation, especially in France, where much is sold by mail order.

Château Teyssier
Owner: Family Durand-Teyssier. Administrator: Dourthe-Kressmann.
25ha. 13,000 cases. Mer 75%, CF and CS 25%.
Rather confusingly, this property straddles two appellations, Montagne- and Puisseguin-St-Émilion. Since 1995, Dourthe-Kressmann has been responsible for the management and commercialization of the wines. Very fruity, rich wines are now being made, but there is a tendency to over-extract.

Château Tour-du-Pas-St-Georges V
Owner: Pascal Delbeck. 15ha. 8,000 cases. Mer 50%, CF 35%, CS 15%.
This property lies on south-facing slopes of limestone and clay in St-Georges. Following the death of Mme. Dubois-Challon in 2003, the property has passed to Pascal Delbeck, who has run the vineyard for many years with such success. The results are excellent.

La Tour Mont d'Or
92ha. 72,000 cases. Mer 75%, CS 15%, CF 10%.
A cooperative of 60 members in Montagne-St-Émilion producing well-reputed wines in the classic style of the St-Émilion Satellites. Three individual labels – Châteaux Palon Grand Seigneur, La Tour Mont d'Or and Baudron – are also vinified here.

Château Vieux Bonneau

Owner: Alain Despagne. 13ha. 7,000 cases. Mer 80%, CF 10%, CS 10%.

Another good Montagne property, using 25 per cent new oak. Glorious fruit leapt from the glass of the marvellously seductive and luscious '99, which stood out in a line-up of wines from the St-Émilion satellites. Wines worth looking out for!

Château des Tours

Owner: Marne et Champagne. 52ha. 34,000 cases. Mer 34%, CF and CS 33%, Mal 33%. Second label: Château La Croix-Blanche.

This is the largest domaine in Montagne and also has the most imposing 14th century château. The vineyards are on the *côte* east of Montagne, facing St-Émilion. The *chai* is modern and well-equipped to handle the large production. There is storage capacity for over 80,000 cases. The present owners bought the property, which forms the flagship of their Bordeaux group, in 1983. Their offices are also here. Unfortunately, things have rather marked time here, but in 1998, a fresh start was made. There is the possibility, and hopefully now the will, to make very good wines here.

Pomerol

This is easily the smallest of the great red-wine districts of Bordeaux. It measures four by three kilometres and covers only about 760 hectares. It produces on average around 32,000 hectolitres of wine per year, which is roughly comparable with St-Julien in the Médoc. Yet the complexity of the Pomerol soils gives these wines an individuality and originality that sets them apart, enabling them to produce some of Bordeaux's most remarkable wines.

The best Pomerols are more intense, richer, denser, and more tannic than most St-Émilions. Although the Merlot is even more predominant here than in St-Émilion, because of the clay and generally cold soils many wines go through a stage in early maturity when they can look remarkably like Médocs, which shows how soil can change the character of grape varieties. The majority of wines become enjoyable to drink when four to seven years old, but a few top growths will take longer. The best vintages keep well. The '55, '64, and '70 are still excellent. There is no classification in Pomerol, nor will there be, since there is no desire for one locally. After Pétrus, universally acknowledged as *hors classe*, the following wines are recognized as the leading ones, in alphabetical order: Certan-de-May, La Conseillante, L'Eglise-Clinet, L'Évangile, La Fleur-Pétrus, Gazin, Lafleur, Latour à Pomerol, Petit-Village, Trotanoy, and Vieux-Château-Certan.

Château Beauregard ★ →

Owner: Crédit Foncier de France. 17.5ha. 9,000 cases. Mer 70%, CF 30%. Second label: Benjamin de Beauregard.

This counts as a large property by Pomerol standards and has a fine château dating from the 17th and 18th centuries. A replica was erected on Long Island, New York, for the Guggenheims in the 1920s – an unusual compliment for a Bordeaux château – and is called Mille-Fleurs. In 1991, the Clauzels sold to Crédit Foncier de France (*see* Bastor-Lamontagne, page 130).

The vineyard is on the high plateau of Pomerol, with some sand mixed with the gravel. This is a well-run and well-reputed *cru*; around 60 per cent new wood is used for its maturation. While not among the leading dozen *crus* of Pomerol, it is a good wine in the second flight, rich and full-flavoured. It develops quite quickly and has real breeding and charm.

Château Le Bon Pasteur ★

Owner: Dupuy-Rolland. Administrator: Michel Rolland. 7ha. 2,500 cases. Mer 80%, CF 20%.

This *cru* is right on the Pomerol–St-Émilion border in the northwest of the appellation, between Gazin and Croque-Michotte. Since the present owner took over this property, it has established quite a reputation for itself in the USA. But the wines were rich and enticing before that – I recall a splendid '70. Now 35 per cent new wood is being used for the cask-maturation. The wines are extremely attractive, supple and rich.

Château Bonalgue

Owner: Pierre Bourotte. 6.5ha. 2,500 cases. Mer 90%, CF 10%.
Second label: Château Burgrave.

This château was built in 1815 by Antoine Rabion and is situated on the sand and gravel soils of the plateau, in the south of the appellation. The Bourotte family has owned this property since 1926, and produces attractive wines. Fermentation takes place in stainless-steel vats and 50 per cent new oak is used for maturation. The wines have ample fruit and weight to balance the oak flavours, but need five to seven years before they drink at their best.

Château Bourgneuf-Vayron ★ V

Owner: Xavier Vayron. 9ha. 3,500 cases. Mer 90%, CF 10%.

A property on the western side of the high plateau of Pomerol as it slopes away in that direction. Here, the gravelly soils are mixed with sand. This is attractive, stylish, middle-weight Pomerol. The wines tend to become supple and enjoyable quite quickly and lack the concentration of the leading wines, while showing definite breed.

Château La Cabanne

Owner: Jean-Pierre Estager. 10ha. 5,000 cases. Mer 92%, CF 8%.
Second label: Domaine de Compostelle.

La Cabanne is situated on the high terrace of Pomerol, on soils of gravel and clay, which overlie a *crasse de fer*, or iron-pan. Jean-Pierre Estager bought this property in 1966 and has since modernized the *cuvier* and *chai*, installing vats of lined concrete and stainless steel. Care is taken that the grapes are fully matured and that as much tannin as possible is extracted from them to balance the high proportion of new oak used. The results are reliable wines with concentrated fruit character. They are not yet widely known but their reputation is growing.

Château Certan-de-May ★★

Owner: Mme Odette Barreau-Bader. 5ha. 2,000 cases. Mer 70%, CF 25%, CS 5%.
This minute vineyard is typical of a number of properties at the heart of Pomerol's high plateau; its size combined with the devotion of its owners creates something individual and personal. Originally part of Vieux-Château-Certan, the soil here has clay mixed with the predominant gravel. It lies in the area, close to Cheval Blanc, where nearly all the best Pomerols are to be found. In recent vintages, this *cru* has re-emerged from the shadows and has rapidly taken its place again among the leading wines of the district. Fifty per cent new oak is used for the maturation. The wines have an opulence, richness and power that are reminiscent of Trotanoy

rather than of Certan-de-May's more compact neighbour, Vieux-Château-Certan. The '82, '83, '85, '86, '88, '89, '90, '95, '98, and 2000 are splendid wines. Certainly this is a wine to snatch up when you can.

Château Clinet ★

Owner: Jean-Louis Laborde. 9ha. 4,400 cases. Mer 75%, CS 15%, CF 10%.

This *cru*, belonging to Libourne négociants Audy, is near the church of Pomerol on the high plateau with its gravelly soil mixed with sand. For years there was too much Cabernet Sauvignon in the vineyards here and the wines were tough and charmless. Then Jean-Michel Arcaute took over the management of all Audy's vineyards in the mid-1970s. Audy sold to the present owner in 1998 with Jean-Michel in charge. (Tragically, the latter was killed in an accident in 2001.)

First, Jean-Michel increased the Merlot and reduced the Cabernet, then, in 1985, in consultation with oenologist Michel Rolland, he changed his pattern of working, going for late-picking (maximum maturation), selection of grapes prior to vinification, long vatting, and the use of plenty of new oak. The difference has been dramatic, with '86 easily the best Clinet I had ever tasted, followed by the classic wines of '88, '89, and '90. These wines can be quite hard to judge in cask and need re-tasting in bottle. 1998, 2000 and 2001 are impressive. This is now one of the rising stars of Pomerol.

Clos du Clocher

Owner: Éts J-B Audy. 6ha. 2,600 cases. Mer 80%, CF 20%.
Second label: Esprit de Clocher.

Established in 1931 by Jean-Baptiste Audy, this is now well-known and reliable, its wines being vinified with much care and attention to detail. *Assemblage*, or blending, is carried out by Michel Rolland of Château Le Bon Pasteur.

Château la Conseillante ★★★

Owner: Héritiers Louis Nicolas. Administrator: Arnaud de Lamy
12ha. 5,000 cases. Mer 65%, CF 30%, Mal 5%.

This is one of the best two or three wines in Pomerol after Pétrus, year after year. Added to the consistency is the strong personality of the wine. It combines concentration and breeding on the nose with a superb flavour of real originality, an unctuous yet firm centre, and great persistence of flavour. Its neighbour, L'Évangile, is clearly from the same stable. On the other side there are similarities with Petit-Village as the wine improves. The outstanding vintages here are '79, '82, '83, '85, '86, '88, '89 and '90. Recently, '93, '94, '95, '97,'98, '99, 2000, and 2001 were all among the best Pomerols of each vintage.

Château La Croix ★

Owner: SC J Janoueix. 10ha. 5,000 cases. Mer 60%, CF 20%, CS 20%.
Second label: Château Le Gabachot.

These are well-balanced, attractive wines that are enjoyable after four or five years, yet also keep well, acquiring delicacy and spicy complexity. The '71 was keeping well and had fined down (developing a lovely flavour, mellow but with a good backbone) when 14 years old. If you can sort this château from all the others in Pomerol with *Croix* in their names, it is worth looking out for.

Château La Croix-de-Gay ★

Owner: Alain Raynaud. 13ha. 6,500 cases. Mer 80%, CS 10%, CF 10%.
Cuvée Prestige: Château La Fleur de Gay.

This property is on the northern borders of the plateau of Pomerol, where the predominantly gravelly soils mingle with sand. For the maturation, 50 per cent new wood is used. This is stylish, charmingly fruity, aromatic wine that is rich and solid in top years such as '95 and '98. Three hectares are set aside for the Fleur de Gay, which has 100 per cent new oak.

Château La Croix-du-Casse ★

Owner: GAM Audy. 9ha. 5,300 cases. Mer 70%, CF 30%.
Second label: Domaine du Casse.

La Croix-du-Casse was for years under the same management as Château Clinet, but produces wines of a totally difference style. Benefiting from the gravel soils and underlying iron pan, they are attractively perfumed, full-flavoured, and have a delicious fruit quality.

Château La Croix-St-Georges ★ →

Owner: SC J Janoueix. 5ha. 2,000 cases. Mer 95%, CF 5%.
Second label: Le Prieuré.

This property is run in conjunction with Château la Croix, the main differences in their wines being derived from the variations in the terroirs of their respective vineyards. La Croix-St-Georges is situated on the plateau and therefore is based mainly on gravel. The wines have both suppleness and finesse; 100 per cent new oak is now used.

Domaine de l'Église ★

Owners: Philippe Castéja and Mme. Peter Preben Hansen.
7ha. 3,500 cases. Mer 90%, CF 10%.

Do not look for this *cru* near the present church, it was next to a much older one, demolished in the 19th century. It is on the high plateau, where the soil is deep gravel with traces of iron deposit, which gives the wines a certain brilliance and depth of colour. The Castéjas bought the property, whose wine they had distributed for many years, in 1972. The wines tend to be light in style yet fine, perfumed, and elegant. With the '86 vintage, however, Philippe Castéja began making much more concentrated wines using a third new oak each year. This is good, second-tier Pomerol.

Clos L'Église ★ →

Owner: M and Mme Garcin-Cathiard. 6ha. 2,000 cases. Mer 57%, CF 43%.
Second label: Esprit de L'Église.

This small vineyard is on the high plateau, where the predominantly gravelly soil is mixed with sand. This well-run property (acquired in 1997 by the present owner) has undergone a transformation since the Garcin-Cathiards of Haut-Bergey bought it. Gone are the stainless-steel vats put in in 1983, replaced by small, 60hl wooden vats. In 1997, a marvellous wine of exquisite quality (23hl/ha) was the result. There is little doubt that this can be a top Pomerol.

Château L'Église-Clinet ★★ →

Owner: Denis Durantou. 6ha. 3,000 cases. Mer 80%, CF 20%.

This small vineyard has for many years been farmed by the Lasserre family of Clos René. It is next to the cemetery of the old (now demolished) church on the high plateau. The soil is mainly gravel mixed with sand. An important point here is that the vines are older than in most Pomerol domaines because they were not pulled up after the 1956 frost but left to recover, which most of them did. Wines are carefully made and 50 per cent new wood is used for the cask maturation. Their reputation has long been high among devotees. This is classic, rich, supple and fruity Pomerol, but in the last decade has become one of Pomerol's most sought-after *crus*. '90, '98, '99, and 2000 are amongst the best wines in Pomerol in those years. Unfortunately, this is a wine that takes some finding. La Petite Église comes from farmed vineyards and is therefore not a second wine.

Château L'Enclos

Owner: SC du Château L'Enclos. Administrator: Hugues Weydert.
9.5ha. 5,000 cases. Mer 82%, CF 17%, Mal 1%.

This good *cru* lies on the opposite side of the N-89 Libourne–Périgueux road from the main vineyards of the high plateau of Pomerol. The soil is mainly sandy, but there is an important gravelly outcrop here, at the neighbouring Clos René, and further away at Moulinet. Today, the style of the wines is rather similar to that of Close René: dense-textured, but coarser and less fruity.

Château L'Évangile ★★★ →

Owner: Domaines Rothschild. 14.8ha. 4,500 cases. Mer 78%, CF 32%.

This is one of the leading *crus* of Pomerol, situated near the edge of the high plateau adjoining La Conseillante and Vieux-Château-Certan. The predominantly gravelly soil is mixed with some clay and sand, the feature responsible for the unique quality of Pétrus (where the vineyard is almost entirely clay and gravel). The style of the wines most resembles that of La Conseillante, but has a different emphasis owing to the high proportion of Merlot, the presence of clay in the soil and the fact that only 20 per cent new oak was used here for the maturation until '98. The submerged cap system of vinification is used and results in high colour extraction. The wines tend to be more massive and chewy in texture, yet sometimes lack the firmness of La Conseillante.

In 1990, all the shareholders except Mme. Ducasse sold to Domaines Rothschild, which now distributes the wine, but Mme. Ducasse ran the property until 1999 using Michel Rolland as consultant oenologist. There have in the past been some inconsistencies, but the recent record is impressive. The '82 is luscious and ripe and '83 big and firm; '85 is generous and fine, and the '88 is also fine; '89 and '90 are exceptional wines; '93 was one of the outstanding wines of this vintage, and '94 is no less fine. The '95, '96, '97, '98, '99, and 2000 are exceptional, placing L'Évangile among the top *crus* in Pomerol. The wine now sells at first growth prices.

Château Feytit-Clinet ★

Owner: Ind Chasseuil. Administrator: Éts J. P. Moueix. 6.3ha. 3,000 cases.
Mer 85%, CF 15%.

A property on the northwestern edge of the plateau, where the predominantly gravelly soil is mixed with sand. It is run entirely by the highly efficient Moueix organization, presided over by Christian Moueix and his oenologist, Jean-Claude Berrouet. While the wine is all plummy fruit on the nose, the flavour is more elegant than one expects, with good length and a firm finish. An excellent second-tier Pomerol and naturally, from such a stable, most consistent.

Château La Fleur-de-Gay ★

Owner: Raynaud family. 1.75ha. 1,000 cases. Mer 100%.

The Raynaud family has set this vineyard aside for Merlot. Benefiting from deep, gravelly soils, the wines are full of flavour and concentrated fruit. Vinification is monitored by Michel Rolland and Pascal Ribéreau-Gayon and is carried out at fairly high temperatures. These special wines are of a very high quality.

Château La Fleur-Pétrus ★★ →

Owner: SC du Château. Administrator: Éts J. P. Moueix. 13.8ha. 4,500 cases. Mer 80%, CF 20%.

One of the leading *crus* of Pomerol, situated just across the road from Pétrus, but on quite different soil. Here the soil is stony with large gravel but no clay or sand. In recent years, the reputation of this wine has steadily grown, and this is now one of the flagships of the Moueix empire and almost certainly the finest Pomerol on purely gravelly soil, all the others except for Latour à Pomerol having some clay in their make-up. One-third of the wood used here for maturation is new.

The wines are gorgeous, perfumed, powerful and elegant on the nose, with great complexity, richness, and power of flavour which is so obviously of the highest quality. They are consistently good. Lovely examples were the '82, '83, '85 (quite exceptional), '86, '88, '89, '90, '95, '97, '98, '99 and 2000. Not as massive as most of the other leading *crus*, but there is no doubting the breed and beauty of this wine. In 1994, four hectares were purchased from the adjoining vineyard at Le Gay and have added an extra dimension to the wine.

Château Le Gay ★

Owner: Catherine Péré-Vergé. 6ha. 1,200 cases. Mer 65%, CF 35%.

This *cru* lies on the northern side of the high plateau on gravelly soils, near to the owner's other *cru*, Lafleur. For many years its wines have been exclusively distributed by J. P. Moueix, but the Robin sisters ran the properties themselves. However, after the death of Thérèse Robin, the Moueix team took over the management. In 2003, following the death of Marie Robin, the heirs sold to Catherine Péré-Vergé.

Le Gay has always produced big, dense, firm-textured wines that age well, as bottles of '64 and '66 still demonstrate. Now things can only get better and no doubt the wines will be polished up a little and show some consistency. In 1994, part of the vineyard was sold to neighbouring La Fleur-Pétrus.

Château Gazin ★★ →

Owner: Nicolas and Christophe de Bailliencourt. 24ha. 8,000 cases. Mer 90%, CF 7%, CS 3%.

This is the largest of the leading Pomerols, situated on the northeastern corner of the high plateau on gravelly soils. In the late 1960s, a portion of the vineyard adjoining Pétrus, with the same clay in the soil, was sold to Pétrus. Fifty per cent new oak is used for the maturation in cask.

For many years this wine underperformed, due in part to lack of investment, but from '85 onwards, greater concentration and more style have been achieved. The '85 is concentrated, rich, and firm, while the '88 has a lovely, rich aftertaste and is stylish; the '89 and '90 are both impressive. The '93 is one of the successes of the year. Excellent wines followed in '94, '95, '96, '97, '98, '99, and 2000. It is good to see this distinguished *cru* returning to proper form.

Château La Grave ★

Owner: Christian Moueix. 8.7ha. 4,000 cases. Mer 85%, CF 15%.

This small vineyard has been the personal property of Christian Moueix of J. P. Moueix since 1971. The firm owns a number of properties and farms and manages many others, with Christian Moueix heading the team. The property is on gravelly soil on the middle plateau in the northwest of Pomerol, just before the Libourne–Périgueux road. The name used to be something of a handicap, the words *Château La Grave* appearing in large characters on the label, with *Trigant de Boisset* in smaller ones underneath: now this has been simplified.

For maturation in cask, 25 per cent new oak is used. The wine is quite rich, tannic, and fine but less spectacular than that of the leading *crus*, so it is a good second-tier Pomerol. The '82, '83, '85, '86, '88, '89, '90, '94, '95, '98, '99, and 2000 are all successful here – these are beautifully made and consistent wines.

Château Hosanna ★★ →

Owner: Éts J. P. Moueix. 7.2ha. 1,500 cases. Mer 70%, CF 30%.
Second label: Certan-Marzelle

In 1999, Christian Moueix bought Certan-Giraud, sold a portion which was not on the plateau of Certan to Jean-Hubert Delon for Nenin, and then renamed the property Hosanna. In doing so, he followed in a long Pomerol tradition of using names with ecclesiastical connotations. The vineyard, of old vines averaging 35 years, adjoins Pétrus and Lafleur, and the first vintages, the '99 and 2000, have confirmed that this is destined to be one of the brightest stars in the Moueix firmament, rivalling Trotanoy and La Fleur-Pétrus. Some 3.5 hectares of younger vines are sold under the Certan-Marzelle label. It is a delicious, earlier drinking wine.

Château Lafleur ★★★

Owners: Sylvie and Jacques Guinaudeau. 4.6ha. 2,400 cases. Mer 50%, CF 50%.
Second label: Les Pensées de Lafleur.

This minute but superb property is situated on the gravelly high plateau, with some of the precious clay soils found at the best *crus* making up its vineyards. It is next to La Fleur-Pétrus, but its subsoils differ considerably, La Fleur-Pétrus having none of the clay deposits.

In 1985, the Guinaudeaus assumed responsibility and have further enhanced the already great reputation of this *cru*. In years like '82, '90, and '98 it gives Pétrus a run for its money! Unfortunately, with so little wine produced, it is rare as well as expensive. The style is all opulent charm and great finesse, and it has a lovely bouquet, but recent vintages have been slower to mature. Note the unusually high proportion of Cabernet Franc which plays a decisive rôle in giving this wine its character and longevity.

Château Lafleur Gazin ★

Owner: Mme Delfour. Administrator: Éts J. P. Moueix.
8.5ha. 3,500 cases. Mer 80%, CF 20%.

A property on the northeastern limits of the plateau next to Gazin. Here, the predominantly gravelly soil is mixed with sand.

This *cru* has come into prominence since J. P. Moueix became *fermiers* here in 1976. It is run with the meticulous care associated with the Moueix team under Christian Moueix and his oenologist, Jean-Claude Berrouet. The wine is rich and quite powerful with an underlying firmness. A serious wine worth following.

Château Lagrange ★ V

Owner: Éts J. P. Moueix. 4.7ha. 2,000 cases. Mer 95%, CF 5%.

Another Moueix property on the gravelly high plateau. Some new wood is used for the cask maturation. The wines seem to have a certain originality of flavour, a breeding allied to charm and structure, which marks them as fine wines. The vintages of the '80s and '90s are all impressive. Château Lagrange is a good second-tier Pomerol.

Château Latour à Pomerol ★★ V

Owner: Mme Lily Lacoste. Administrator: Éts J. P. Moueix. 8ha. 3,900 cases.
Mer 90%, CF 10%.

This fine property lies on the gravelly high plateau northwest of the church. Its owner is also co-proprietor of Pétrus, and it is managed and distributed by

J. P. Moueix. Cask maturation is in 25 per cent new oak. In the past there were inconsistencies, and fine bottles were interspersed with disappointments, but the property improved noticeably throughout the 1970s. More recently, the wines have been marked by a wonderful perfume and a delectable beauty of flavour, power and finesse. There is now a clear similarity of style with La Fleur-Pétrus, and with the '83 I even thought Latour the better wine. The wines since '85 have been wonderfully concentrated and impressive. Look out especially for '90, '95, '98, '99 and 2000. Now indisputably among Pomerol's leading *crus*, as well as being one of the best value for money.

Château Mazeyres ★ →

Owner: Caisse de Retraite de la Soc Générale. Administrator: Alain Moueix. 22ha. 11,000 cases. Mer 80%, CF 20%.

This property lies on the gravel and sand of the lower plateau north of Libourne and at the western extremity of the appellation. Thirty per cent new oak is now used.

Much progress has been made here since the pension fund of the Société Générale bought it in 1988, and Alain Moueix took on the management. The wines are now more concentrated without having lost their attractive style and beautifully focused fruit. Forty per cent new oak is used.

Château Moulinet ★

Owner: SC du Château. Administrator: Marie-Josée Moueix. 18ha. 10,000 cases. Mer 60%, CS 30%, CF 10%.

This relatively large property lies beyond the Libourne–Périgueux road on the gravelly sandy soils of the middle plateau and is one of Armand Moueix's well-run properties. A third of the wood used for maturation is new. The wines are scented and charming. A pleasant, widely distributed wine.

Château Nenin ★ →

Owner: J. H. Delon. 25ha. 9,000 cases. Mer 75%, CF 25%.
Second Label: Fugue de Nenin.

One of the largest and best-known Pomerol properties. It lies on lower ground northwest of the high plateau, on sandy, gravelly soils.

This important and once-famous *cru* had been an habitual under-performer until Jean-Hubert Delon from Léoville-Las-Cases bought it in 1997. In spite of some improvements in 1992–3, the wines had remained disappointing. The fact that '97 was much better than '96 showed what was possible, while '98 is really impressive. Now Nenin should soon re-establish its position as one of Pomerol's leading *crus*.

Château Petit-Village ★★

Owner: AXA-Millésimes. Administrator: Christian Seely. 11ha. 4,000 cases. Mer 82%, CF 9%, CS 9%.

A finely placed vineyard on the high plateau, with gravelly, clay soils, close to La Conseillante and St-Émilion. Previous owners, the Prats family (*see* Cos d'Estournel), sold to AXA in 1989. One problem has been that, after the '56 frost, the vineyard was largely replanted – with too much Cabernet Sauvignon. This has now been corrected and the wines are improving. A minimum of 50 per cent new wood is used, according to the year.

The style is closest to that of La Conseillante, especially since '78. The wines have a lovely aroma and are rich and deep, firm-centred with a lovely flavour and great breeding. '82 has kept its freshness and vigour, '85 is luscious and harmonious. '90 has an intense fruit character. After a fine '95, '98 is powerful and distinctive. '99 has a lovely blackcurrant fruit and thick textures while 2000 has lots of sweet fruit and glycerol; it is an outstanding success. Petit-Village is back in its rightful place among the leading *crus*.

Château Pétrus ★★★

Owners: Mme L. P. Lacoste and J. P. Moueix. Administrator: Christian Moueix. 11.4ha. 4,500 cases. Mer 95%, CF 5%.

Fifty years ago, Pétrus was unknown outside a small circle of wine-lovers in Bordeaux, but it has become one of the region's great names. Unfortunately it is more talked about than drunk, due to its price and rarity.

This is the world's greatest Merlot wine and shows what can be done with this grape when conditions are right. There is an unctuous and almost chewy quality of richness and power, which has some similarity with that of Cheval Blanc, but Pétrus tends to be more concentrated, firmer, and slower to develop.

The complexity and nuances of flavour that develop with age are astonishing. Vintages such as '67 and '71 could be enjoyed when only seven to ten years old, but then go on to surprise one with their further development. Currently '75 and '78 have matured well and '82 has acquired legendary status and prices to match. The '85 has a lovely, ripe, supple character perfect now. The '88, '89, and '90 are all massive, slow-developing wines. Then, after a great '95 and fine '96, the '98 is one of the greats, with '99 not far behind. 1997 is a delightful wine in a lighter vein which already gives pleasure, while 2000 is close to the '98 and 2001 promises much. Every wine-lover should find a way of experiencing Pétrus.

Château Le Pin ★

Owner: Thienpont family. 2ha. 700 cases. Mer 92%, CF 8%.

The wines of this tiny property have developed great prestige since the Thienpont family took over in 1979. They are attractive wines, almost Californian in style, and are sold at high prices, now in excess of Pétrus in some instances. While delicious wine, it lacks the complexity and depth of the leading *crus*.

Château Plince ★ V

Owner: Moureau family. 8.7ha. 4,300 cases. Mer 68%, CF 24%, CS 8%.

A good lesser *cru* situated on the sandy soils in the southwest of Pomerol behind Nenin. A small proportion of new oak is used for the cask maturation. This property has long had the reputation for producing deliciously fruity, supple wines. The marvellous '47 remained fresh and opulent for over 30 years. Good wines are now being made here, and they are excellent value for a *cru* on the sand. This one is making the most of its potential.

Château La Pointe ★ V

Owner: Bernard d'Arfeuille. 23ha. 11,500 cases. Mer 75%, CF 25%. Second label: La Pointe Riffat.

This large, well-known property is on the sandy, gravelly soils of the middle plateau opposite Nenin, though on slightly lower ground. For the maturation, 35 per cent new wood is used. A retrospective tasting in 1983 confirmed my suspicions that this wine is not as good as it used to be. Mostly they seem only moderate, if charming, lightweights.

A certain lightness, allied to finesse and stylishness, has long been the mark of La Pointe. After a disappointing period, '89 seems to mark a return to top form with balance and flair and this has been followed by very good wines in '95, '98, '99, 2000 and 2001.

Château Prieurs de la Commanderie

Owner: Clément Fayat. 3.5ha. 1,700 cases. Mer 80%, CF and CS 20%.

Situated on Pomerol's middle terrace, this *cru* is an amalgamation of several small plots formed in 1984 by Clément Fayat. A new *cuvier* and *chai* have been built, incorporating the most modern winemaking equipment – including automatically temperature-cooled *cuves*. There is a tendency to over-extract in some years. The '99 is excellent.

Clos René ★ V

Owner: Jean-Mari Garde. 12ha. 6,000 cases. Mer 70%, CF 20%, Mal 10%.
Other label: Château Moulinet-Lasserre.

This is a wonderfully perfumed, dense, rich, plummy Pomerol which seldom disappoints. The '86 is exceptional, with intense fruit and a lovely smell of damsons, yet it's tannic as well. The '89, '90, '95, and 2000 are also excellent vintages. This is a good second-tier Pomerol. For fiscal and family reasons, a part of the crop is sold as Château Moulinet-Lasserre. The wines are the same – this is not a second label, but an alternative one.

Château La Rose Figeac

Owner: Despagne-Rapin family. 5ha. 2,000 cases. Mer 90%, CF 10%.

This small vineyard is close to the St-Émilion–Pomerol border, and the wine is made and kept at Château Maison Blanche, the proprietor's main property. In the best years, such as '90, 100 per cent new oak is used, and the wine is concentrated with dense, chunky fruit and splendid depth and power. The '93, on the other hand, only had 80 per cent new oak, and was rich and solid for the year. These are fine, attractive, well-made wines.

Château Rouget →

Owner: Labruyère family. 18ha. 6,500 cases. Mer 85%, CF 15%.
Second label: Vieux Château des Templiers.

This is an interesting property on sandy and gravelly soils, with some clay, at the northern limit of the high plateau. The wine is traditionally made and 70 per cent of the wood used for the cask maturation is new. The present owners took over in 1992 and have undertaken a lot of work in the *chai* and vineyard.

The old wines were slow to develop and a shade rustic. The new era begins quite modestly with a pleasant '95 but then '98, '99, 2000 and 2001 really show what better selection has achieved here with some wonderful sweet fruit, richness and aromatic complexity.

Château de Sales V

Owner: GFA du Château de Sales – Héritiers de Laage. Administrator: Bruno de Lambert. 47.5ha 22,500 cases. Mer 70%, CF 15%, CS 15%.
Second label: Château Chantalouette.

This is the largest property in Pomerol by a comfortable margin and lies on sandy soils with some gravel in the northwest corner of the appellation near the Libourne–Perigord road. It has belonged to the same family for almost 400 years; Henri de Lambert's wife is a de Laage. Their son Bruno is an oenologist.

The property has an impressive 17th- and 18th-century château, set in a park. Wines are alternated between vats and used casks for maturation. There was a noticeable improvement in quality here from 1970 onwards. Wines are now scented, rich, plummy, and powerful with a pleasant stylishness, and develop quite quickly. Good, reliable Pomerol at a reasonable price.

Château du Tailhas

Owner: GFA du Tailhas. Administrator: Luc Nébout. 11ha. 5,500 cases. Mer 70%, CF 15%, CS 15%.

This property is on sandy soils in the extreme southwest corner of the appellation and near to Figeac, just the other side of the stream, which is also called Tailhas.

Fifty per cent new wood is used for the cask maturation. This is well-made and well-reputed second-tier Pomerol. The wines have a full colour, a highlighted bouquet which is most attractive, and lots of young fruit with that slightly earthy taste that occurs in some growths in Pomerol where there are iron deposits in the subsoil. There is now a pleasing degree of consistency.

Château Taillefer

Owner: Heritiers Bernard Moueix. Administrator: Catherine Moueix. 11.5ha. 5,800 cases. Mer 50%, CF 30%, CS 15%, Mal 5%.

An attractive 19th century château and park dominate this *cru*, one of the largest in Pomerol. It produces some light-bodied, fruity wines from its modern winery. The wines are elegant and quite fine.

Château Trotanoy ★★★

Owner: Éts J. P. Moueix. 7.2ha. 3,600 cases. Mer 90%, CF 10%.

This leading *cru* is on gravel and clay soils at the western edge of the high plateau. Apart from being one of the most illustrious jewels in the Moueix crown, it is also the home of Jean-Jacques Moueix, nephew of the legendary Jean-Pierre Moueix. Of course, the care of this *cru* stands high among the priorities for Christian Moueix and his oenologist Jean-Claude Berrouet. A proportion of 33 per cent new wood is used for the cask maturation.

The reputation of Trotanoy is now higher than ever before, as can be seen from the prices collectors are prepared to pay for its mature vintages at auction. The style of the wine is, for me, more reminiscent of Pétrus than any other Pomerol, with its dense colour, rich spicy enveloping bouquet, and opulent, fleshy body that develops an enchanting flavour of exceptional length.

Great and often exceptional vintages were the '75, '78, '79, '81, '82, '83, '85, '86, '89, '90, '95, '98, '99, and 2000.

Vieux-Château-Certan ★★★

Owner: Héritiers Georges Thienpont. 13.6ha. 5,000 cases. Mer 60%, CF 30%, CS 10%. Second label: Gravette de Certan.

Until the rise of Pétrus, this fine *cru* was long regarded as the leading *cru* in Pomerol. It is splendidly placed on the high plateau, with sandy clay mixed with its gravel. Pétrus, La Conseillante, and L'Évangile are neighbours, with Cheval Blanc not far away. The small but aristocratic 17th century château is the only one of note among these leading Pomerol *crus*. Until the end of the 18th century, the estate was actually much larger. It has belonged to the Belgian Thienponts since 1924, and Léon Thienpont ran the property from 1943 until his death in 1985. He was succeeded by his son, Alexandre, who had the useful experience of working at La Gaffelière from 1982 until this time. The *chai* and *cuvier* were enlarged and modernized in the early 1970s, though wooden vats were kept. A third of the wood used for the maturation is new.

This is a wine of marked individuality: perfumed, less dense in colour than other leading Pomerols, compact and firm on the palate, with a complexity, finesse and flavour that set it apart. It lacks the opulence of Trotanoy, and while it has something of the structure of La Conseillante, it lacks its unctuousness. Harmony, breeding, and finesse are the great hallmarks here. '82 with its great richness and '83 with its unusual power are two exceptional vintages, and the '85 has all the seductive charm one would hope for from this *cru* in this year. The '86 has great power and concentration and is also an exceptional wine; '88 is a classic; '89 has an amazing, overripe opulence; '90 a beautifully silky finish; '93 and '94 were successful, and '95 and '98 exceptional. '96 has evolved much better than most Pomerols, thanks to the Cabernet Franc, and '99 is fruity and delicious. 2000 is a great wine. Evolution tends to be slow; the '71 is still at its peak. For individuality, this is still one of the best Pomerols.

Château Vray-Croix-de-Gay

Owner: Olivier Guichard, 3.7ha. 1,800 cases. Mer 55%, CF 40%, CS 5%.

This small *cru* is on gravelly soils on the edge of the high plateau near Le Gay and Domaine de l'Église. Its owner also has the excellent Château Siaurac in Lalande de Pomerol. In style, the wines are closest to those of Le Gay, powerful and densely textured, needing time to show their worth. They have been inconsistent but improved from '95 onwards.

Lalande de Pomerol

This appellation of growing importance covers about 1,100 hectares of vines, of which roughly 60 per cent are in the commune of Lalande and 40 per cent in that of Néac. In Lalande, the vineyards are on relatively low-lying recent gravel and sand terraces. However, in Néac there is a high plateau with those *crus* facing south towards Pomerol being on good gravel. The best wines are close in quality to lesser Pomerols, with less power and tannin; developing quickly, but attractive, with finesse and style.

Château des Annereaux

Owner: Vignobles Jean Milhade. 22ha. 12,000 cases. Mer 70%, CF 30%.

A good *cru* on the gravel and sandy soils of the lower plateau. Very elegant, attractive wines, sometimes inclined to be dilute, but spicy and delicious in good vintages. Fifty per cent new oak is now used.

Château de Bel-Air

Owner: Jean-Pierre Musset.16ha. 8,000 cases. Mer 75%, CF 15%, Mal 5%, CS 5%.

This well-reputed *cru* is on the gravel and sand of the middle plateau, opposite Moulinet (Pomerol). It has long been considered one of the appellation's leading *crus*. These are delicious, fruity wines for early drinking.

Château La Croix-St-André

Owner: Carayon family. 16.5ha. 8,500 cases. Mer 80%, CS 10%, CF 10%.
Second label: Château La Croix-St-Louis.

One of the best *crus* in Néac, where the soil closely resembles that on the plateau of Pomerol. The vineyards and vinification are followed with meticulous attention to detail. Old vines, careful selection and the use of 25 per cent new oak completes the picture. I found the '90 had an oaky, spicy background, which, however, did not hide the lovely ripe fruit.

Château La Croix de la Chenevelle V

Owner: Bernard Lavrault. 12.3ha. 6,500 cases. Mer 90%, CF 10%.

I was deeply impressed by the '90 vintage here, with its lovely bouquet of roasted damsons and its opulent flavour of damsons macerated in chocolate – this at ten years of age! The name on the label looks like *Château La Croix*, of which there are many; the rest of the name is in small letters underneath. The property is in the commune of Lalande de Pomerol; there are old vines, and 15 per cent new oak is used in conjunction with *cuves*.

Château La Croix des Moines

Owner: Jean-Louis Trocard. 8ha. 4,400 cases. Mer 80%, CS 10%, CF 10%.

At this property on the gravel plateau of Lalande, 40 per cent new oak is used. I found the '90 scented, with delicious, upfront fruit, lacking structure perhaps, but hedonistic for early drinking.

La Fleur de Boüard V

Owner: de Boüard de Laforest family. 17ha. 8,000 cases. Mer 70%, CF 30%.
Second wine: Château La Fleur St-Georges.

When Hubert and Corinne de Boüard de Laforest of L'Angélus bought this well-sited property in Néac from AGF in '98, they decided to personalize the wine, keeping the château name for the second wine. Copybook wines had been made here under AGF since '94, but the '98 shows a real step up.

Château Grand Ormeau

Owner: Jean-Claude Beton. 11.5ha. 6,300 cases. Mer 64%, CS 18%, CF 18%.
Second label: Chevalier d'Haurange.

One of the leading *crus* of the appellation, situated in the highest part of Lalande. At a blind tasting of '90s in November 1996, it was outstanding, with delicious hedonistic fruit, great ripeness, and opulence, but also with depth and harmony, the epitome of fine Merlot-based wine. Fifty per cent new oak is used.

Château Haut-Chaigneau V →

Owner: André Chatonnet. 21ha. 10,000 cases. Mer 70%, CF 15%, CS 15%.
Second wine: Château La Croix Chaigneau.

A good *cru* in the commune of Néac. Rich, plummy, and attractive wines are made. Consistently good wines have been made here since André Chatonnet bought this old established property. There is now a *cuvée* prestige. Since Pascal Chatonnet began playing a part, better and better wines have resulted in '98, '99, 2000, and 2001. But *see also* Château Le Sergue.

Château Haut-Chatain

Owner: Héritiers Rivière. Administrator: Martine Rivière-Junquas. 10.8ha.
6,000 cases. Mer 80%, CS 10%, CF 10%.

This *cru* in Néac has passed from daughter to daughter since the family acquired it in 1912. The Rivière currently in charge is also an oenologist. The '90 has scented, ripe fruit, a supple, opulent flavour, and a delicious, silky texture: this is ripe fruit perfectly vinified.

Châteaux Les Hauts-Conseillants and Les Hauts-Tuileries V

Owners: Pierre and Monique Baurotte. 10ha. 5,500 cases. Mer 70%, CF 20%, CS 10%.

This good *cru* is in Néac. Les Hauts-Conseillants is used for *vente-directe* in France, Hauts-Tuileries for exports. One-third of the wood for the cask-maturation is new. The wines are well-made and have a marvellous, opulent, perfumed bouquet and a seductively silky texture with concentration worthy of a Pomerol. The present owners also have Château Bonalgue in Pomerol.

Château Moncets
Owner: Louis-Gabriel de Jerphanion. 18.6ha. 8,900 cases.
Second label: Château Gardour. Mer 60%, CF 30%, CS 10%.
An excellent *cru* on gravel and sand at the edge of the plateau in the best southern part of Néac. The wines are bottled in Libourne by J. P. Moueix. They are rich and velvety in texture, with style and breeding, placing them in the category of good lesser Pomerols.

Château Sergant V
Owner: Vignobles de Jean Milhade. 18ha. 8,500 cases. Mer 80%, CS 10%, CF 10%.
This excellent *cru* is on the gravelly plateau of Lalande and was the creation of the present owners. Wonderfully opulent, hedonistic wines with deliciously succulent fruit for early drinking.

Château Le Sergue V
Owner: Pascal Chatonnet. 5ha. 1,250 cases. Mer 85%, CS 10%, CS 5%.
Pascal Chatonnet is the oenologist son of André and Jeannine Chatonnet of Château Haut-Chaigneau. This *cru* is, in fact, made from a selection of different plots within the Haut-Chaigneau vineyard. After some trials in '94 and '95, '96 was the first vintage to be released. Eighty per cent new oak was used. I found the '96 had ripe, fruity highlights and vanillin with a very seductive, supple texture, a lovely fruit quality, and rich, well-integrated tannins. This was a very polished performance worthy of a *cru classé* St-Emilion or a good *cru* of Pomerol, and far superior to the Haut-Chaigneau. The '98 has a lighter texture, while the '99 is intense and concentrated, and the 2000 is better still.

Château Siaurac
Owner: Baronne Guichard. 33ha. 18,000 cases. Mer 60%, CF 35%, CS 5%.
This important *cru* is situated to the south of Néac, on gravel and sand at the edge of the plateau. One of the best-known *crus* in the appellation, consistently producing most attractive, firm, fruity wines.

Château Tournefeuille
Owner: Sautarel family. 15.5ha. 8,900 cases. Mer 75%, CF 15%, CS 10%.
One of Néac's leading *crus*, situated on the high slopes of gravel and strata of clay which form the banks of the Barbanne overlooking Pomerol. The de Belleyme map of 1765 shows that vines were already planted here at that time, when much of Pomerol was still under cereal crops. Thirty per cent new oak is used. The '90 has a good tannic backing for its attractively succulent, ripe fruit.

Château de Viaud
Owner: Soc CEH. 19ha. 8,500 cases. Mer 85%, CF 10%, CS 5%.
This is one of the oldest vineyards in the Lalande commune, appearing as it does on the Bellorme map of 1785. This is fine wine of great charm; the '90 is rich and concentrated, with more tannic structure than many wines in this appellation.

Fronsac

In the early 18th and 19th centuries, Fronsac was the most reputed of the Libournais wines, fetching higher prices than those of St-Émilion. After a long period of obscurity, it is slowly re-emerging as a quality region. There are about 1,100 hectares of vines divided between the appellations of Canon-Fronsac (27 per cent of the area) and Fronsac (73 per cent). These vineyards, like those of the St-Émilion *côtes,* are wines of the plateau and *côtes,* only more spectacularly so. The vineyards of Canon-Fronsac are on a *plateau calcaire* and on outcrops and côtes of sandstone, while those of Fronsac are mostly on a *plateau calcaire* covered with red soils similar to those of St-Christophe-des-Bardes.

The vineyards in Fronsac tend to be small, but there are some lovely buildings, such as the châteaux at La Rivière and La Dauphine. Merlot now dominates, but Cabernet Sauvignon also has an important place in some of the best vineyards. The influences of J. P. Moueix and then Michel Rolland have transformed the quality from rustic and dry to fruity and structured.

Château de Carles
Owner: Antoine Chastenet de Castaing. 20ha. 11,000 cases. Mer 65%, CF 30%, Mal 5%. Second label: Château Couperat. Prestige Cuvé: Haut Carles.
The emperor Charlemagne is said to have camped here en route to Spain, and it is to this visit that Château de Carles owes its name. Its 15th-century château is especially attractive. For some years, rather rustic wines were made here, but then improvements in both vineyard and *chai,* together with serious selection, saw dramatic improvements during the '90s.

Château Dalem V
Owner: Michel Rullier. 14.5ha. 7,000 cases. Mer 85%, CF 10%, CS 5%.
An important property on the *côte,* just southeast of Saillans, producing perfumed wines with real charm. They develop soft, ripe, fruity flavours when young, but last well: while the '78 was already pleasing when four years old, '64, '67, and '70 were still full of fruit and not drying up at all. Impressive wines were made in the '80s, and in the '90s there is more flesh and youthful charm.

Château de la Dauphine V
Owner: Domaines Jean Halley. 8.9ha. 5,000 cases. Mer 85%, CF 15%.
One of the best-known Fronsac *crus,* on the lower *côte* west of the town. The wines here at la Dauphine are well-made. Twenty per cent new wood is used, and the wines are bottled at the right time. This all leads to delicious, fruity wines with character that can be drunk young. Moueix sold this in 2000, but continues to be involved.

Château Fontenil
Owner: Michel Rolland. 8ha. 3,500 cases. Mer 90%, CS 10%.
Fontenil is in the commune of Saillans; it comprises plots from several different growers which were amalgamated by Michel Rolland to create this *cru* in 1986. A winemaker with an excellent reputation, Michel Rolland makes distinctly new-wave, intense, oaky wines at this property.

Château Gagnard
Owner: Mme Bouyge-Barthe.10ha. 5,000 cases. Mer 50%, CS 25%, CF 25%.
Wines from this *cru,* on the sandstone terrace north of Fronsac, are classics in the Fronsac style and have attractive, perfumed fruit, sound structure,

and good breeding. Also sold under the La Croix-Bertrand label.

Château Jeandeman
Owner: M. Roy-Trocard. 26ha. 13,000 cases. Mer 80%, Cab 20%.

The largest vineyard in Fronsac, on the *plateau calcaire* with red soil in the commune of St-Aignan. The wines are distinctly perfumed and have a fruitiness on the palate that makes them drinkable after three to four years.

Château Mayne-Vieil V
Owner: Sèze family. 30ha. 16,500 cases. Mer 90%, CF 10%.

An important and well-distributed *cru*. The vineyard is on sand and clay, producing attractive wines with a rich middle flavour, good structure, and character, very drinkable in three to four years.

Château Moulin Haut-Laroque V
Owner: Jean-Noël Hervé. 13ha. 5,000 cases. Mer 65%, CF 20%, CS 10%, Mal 5%.

This important Fronsac *cru* is on the *plateau calcaire* and *côte* southwest of Saillans. Wines are perfumed with more power and structure than many straight Fronsacs, and are slower to develop (four to five years) than some. Tannin and fruit are well-matched.

Château Plain-Point
Owner: Michel Aroldi. 17ha. 11,000 cases. Mer 75%, CF 10%, CS 15%.

Once an important medieval fortress, the ancient château overlooks the property and much of the surrounding Fronsac countryside. Its vineyards are on the chalky soils of the *plateau calcaire*. There is certainly the potential for these wines to do well.

Château Puyguilhem
Owner: Janine Mothes. 11ha. 7,000 cases. Mer 60%, Cab 30%, Mal 10%.

A *cru* in Saillans with vineyards on the *côte* and on the limestone plateau. The wines have a tendency to be tannic, but the high proportion of Merlot in the blend can soften this harshness in good vintages.

Château La Rivière V →
Owner: M. Peneau. 59ha. 33,000 cases. Mer 78%, CS 12%, CF 8%, Mal 2%.

A grand château, superbly sited and complete with huge underground cellars. The vineyard is on the *plateau calcaire* and *côte*. A proportion of 30–40 per cent new wood is used, and the wines are powerful and tannic and age well. The '82, '83, and '87 were the best vintages of the '80s. From 1995, M. Leprince brought extra depth and richness to the wines. In 2002, M. Leprince sadly died and has been succeeded by M. Peneau.

Château La Valade
Owner: Bernard Roux. 15.6ha. 10,000 cases. Mer 70%, CF and CS 30%.

This *cru* is on the *plateau calcaire* and *côte* of the commune of Fronsac. The wines are perfumed and vigorous, well-balanced with lots of character, and quite fine.

Château La Vieille Cure V ★ →
Owner: The Old Parsonage (C. Ferenbach, P. Sachs, B. Soulan). 20ha. 8,000 cases. Mer 80%, CF 15%, CS 5%. Second label Château Courtreau.

A *cru* with a bright future. La Vieille Cure is well-situated: its vineyards on the *plateau calcaire* and *côte* produce some luscious Merlot-based wines, full of varietal character. An American syndicate took over in 1986, and since then the winery has been thoroughly modernized. Winemaking is now controlled by Michel Rolland of Château Le Bon Pasteur, and one-third new oak casks are used for the maturation. Excellent wines with real breeding and concentrated fruit flavours have been made in the 1990s.

Château Villars

Owner: Jean-Claude Gaudrie. 28ha. 13,500 cases. Mer 73%, CF 18%, CS 9%.
This *cru* is in the commune of Saillans, on the *plateau calcaire* and *côte*.
For the maturation, one-third of the wood used is new. The wines have
a lot of fruit but tend to be rather soft and develop quickly (over about
three years).

Canon-Fronsac

The appellation Canon-Fronsac, or Côtes de Canon-Fronsac, is a small
island of about 300 hectares in the middle of the Fronsac appellation,
consisting of parts of the communes of Fronsac and St-Michel-de-Fronsac.
Although the outstanding *crus* are in Canon-Fronsac rather than Fronsac,
the two areas can, in practice, be treated as one appellation.

Château Barrabaque V →

Owner: Noël Père & Fils. 9ha. 4,500 cases. Mer 70%, CF 25%, CS 5%.
This property is on Fronsac's mid-*côte* and produces wines that have shown
dramatic improvement over recent vintages. Fine fruit flavours and plenty
of structure have been achieved at Château Barrabaque in the '90s. These
are improving wines, of some originality.

Château Canon

Owner: Jean Galland. Administrator: Éts J. P. Moueix. 1.4ha. 700 cases. Mer 100%.
The '95 and '98 were both stunning vintages from this property, full of the
breed and style expected from a *cru* such as this, on one of Fronsac's best
sites. Christian Moueix sold this property when he sold all his Fronsac
properties in 2000. However he still distributes the wine.

Château Canon

Owner: Mlle Henriette Horeau. 10ha. 6,000 cases. Mer 90%, CF 5%, CS 5%.
Château Canon is one of the leading properties in this appellation. It has
an extensive history, dating back to the early 1700s, and once belonged to
the Fontémoing family. All the wines are marketed by the Libourne
négociant firm of Horeau-Beylot.

Château Canon-de-Brem

Owner: Domaines Jean Halley. 4.7ha. 2,400 cases. Mer 65%, CF 35%.
This is one of the best-known and best-reputed of all Fronsac properties.
The wines have remarkable concentrations of fruit and flavour, and are
rich and supple with great style and character. This really reveals what the
appellation is capable of. The wines need four to five years ageing to show
at their best, and will keep well. The property was bought by J. P. Moueix
in 1985 and sold to the present owners in 2000.

Château Canon-Moueix (formerly Pichelèbre)

Owner: Domaines Jean Halley.4.1ha. 2,000 cases. Mer 90%, CF 10%.
This property belonged to the de Brem family of Canon-de-Brem fame
until sold by them to J. P. Moueix in 1985. The wines under the de Brems
were full of character, powerful, and long-keeping. The first Moueix
vintage, '85, was rich and deep-flavoured, softer and more generous early
than Canon-de-Brem and the style had been maintained. J. P. Moueix sold
the property to Domaines Jean Halley in 2000 but without the Moueix
name. It is not clear at the time of going to press how the vines will be

used in future but the last vintage under this name was 2000.

Château Cassagne-Haut-Canon

Owner: Jean-Jacques Dubois. 15ha. 7,000 cases. Mer 70%, CF 25%, CS 5%.
Second label: Haut-Canon La Truffière.

This château also produces wines under the label La Truffière, a name which is derived from the truffle oaks growing on the property. After some appealing and voluptuous wines were made at the end of the 1980s, recent vintages seem over-concentrated and rather charmless in comparison.

Château Coustolle

Owner: Alain Roux. 20ha. 11,000 cases. Mer 60%, CF 35%, Mal 5%.
Second label: Château Grand Cafour.

A fine *cru* on the *côte* north of Fronsac. For the maturation, 20 per cent new wood is used, and the result is a wine of concentration and richness which holds well and develops character and some distinction.

Château La Croix Canon V ★

Owner: Domaines Jean Halley. 12.9ha. 7,000 cases. Mer 80%, CF 20%.

Until 1993, this was Château Bodet, one of the best-placed vineyards in the appellation, on a steep slope above La Dauphine. Then Moueix acquired it and renamed it Château Charlemagne. The '94 and '95 vintages were sold under this name. Now, in response to protests from Burgundy, the name has changed again. The wines combine structure with richness of fruit. Christian Moueix believes this to be the finest site in Canon-Fronsac. It was sold to the present owner in 2000.

Château La Fleur-Cailleau

Owner: Paul Barre. 4.4ha. 2,200 cases. Mer 88%, CF 10%, Mal 2%.

Some highly individual and quite delightful wines are produced at this small property. A distinctive bouquet of wild cherries, rich tannins, and elegant fruit flavours is noticeable in good vintages. Certainly a wine to look out for.

Château La Fleur-Canon

Owner: A de Coninck. 7ha. 4,000 cases. Mer 70%, CS 30%.

A small *cru* in the commune of St-Michel, making some pleasantly fruity wines that are unusual in that they mature quickly, drinking earlier than those of their neighbours.

Château Gaby

Owner: Khayat Family. 9.5ha. 5,000 cases. Mer 85%, CF 5% CS 10%.
Second label: Château La Roche Gaby.

A fine old *cru* on the *côte* and *plateau calcaire* northwest of Fronsac. The wines are rich and powerful with lots of extract, needing time to develop, and can keep well. The '62 was still delicious when 20 years old. After a change of ownership in the 1990s, the name changed to La Roche-Gaby, but a further change in 1999 led the new owners to revert to the original name.

Château du Gazin V

Owner: Henri Robert. 25ha. 18,000 cases. Mer 70%, old vines 17%, CS 6%, CF 2%, Mal 5%.

This is the largest property in the appellation and it is situated on the limestone plateau of St-Michel. The wines it produces look set to have a promising future. Not only are they are beautifully scented with a firm structure, but they also display plenty of breeding and considerable elegance of style.

Château Grand-Renouil

Owner: J-F and M. Ponty. 6ha. 2,400 cases. Mer 85%, CF 15%.

Another *cru* in the commune of St-Michel. This property is situated on the *côte* and produces attractive wines that are certainly worth looking out for.

Château Haut-Mazeris

Owner: Mme Ubald-Bocquet. 6ha. 3,600 cases. Mer 60%, CF 20%, CS 20%.

Haut-Mazeris is on the *plateau calcaire* in the St-Michel commune. Its wines are assertive, with consistent balance and quality.

Château Junayme

Owner: Héritiers de Coninck. Administrator: René de Coninck. 16ha. 10,000 cases. Mer 80%, CF 15%, CS 5%.

This well-known *cru* is on the *côte* of Canon. Its wines are less powerful than the best *crus* today in Canon-Fronsac, but they have a wide following.

Château Lamarche-Canon V

Owner: Vignobles Germain. 5ha. 3,000 cases. Mer 90%, CS 10%.

The standard label here says *La Marche-Canon*; the prestige Candelaire with one-third new oak says *Lamarche-Canon,* so take your pick! There are old vines here and as at other Bernard Germain properties some 400-litre casks are used as well as the traditional 225-litre size. There is very aromatic fruit and rich tannins in the Candelaire, and the regular quality shows spicy herbs and also matures well.

Château Mausse

Owner: Guy Janoueix. 8ha. 4,400 cases. Mer 70%, CS 15%, CF 15%.

A good *cru* on the *plateau calcaire* northeast of St-Michel. This property produces perfumed wines with richness and concentration, which develop pleasing suppleness after four to five years.

Château Mazeris V →

Owner: Christian de Cournuaud. 17.5ha. 8,500 cases. Mer 85%, CF 15%.

This *cru* is one of the best in its appellation. Its wines have marked individuality, as was recognized by négociant J. P. Moueix, which bought the property's entire crop in '85. There is a possibility of expanding the vineyard to 20 hectares. The wines produced here have a great richness and concentration of flavour. This is one of the rising stars of the area.

Château Mazeris-Bellevue

Owner: Jacques Bussier. 11ha. 5,000 cases. Mer 45%, CS 40%, CF 15%.

A fine *cru* situated on the *plateau calcaire* and *côte*. Unusually, the Cabernet Sauvignon is in the ascendancy here, and the result is a wine of distinguished, fine flavour with lots of character and style.

Château Toumalin

Owner: Bernard d'Arfeuille. 8ha. 4,000 cases. Mer 75%, CF 25%.

This *cru* is on the *côte* above the valley of the River Isle north of Fronsac, and belongs to the well-known Libourne négociants who also own La Pointe (Pomerol) and La Serre (St-Émilion). They are vivid, fruity wines with the necessary balance to be enjoyed young.

Château Vincent

Owner: Mme. François Roux. 10.5ha. 5,600 cases AC Canon-Fronsac, 3,000 cases AC Fronsac (under the name Château Tertre de Canon). Mer 85%, CF 15%.

Rather confusingly, the Fronsac is the part of the vineyard that carries the name *Tertre de Canon,* rather than the Canon-Fronsac part.

These are well-made wines that see no wood. I have sometimes found myself preferring the more robust Tertre de Canon to the Vincent. The

'91 Tertre was a great success here, from frost-free vines; much better than the '92.

Château Vray-Canon-Boyer

Owner: Coninck family. 8.5ha. 5,000 cases. Mer 90%, CS 5%, CF 5%.

This excellently situated *cru* produces wines with elegance and finesse, and which also mature successfully. The '96 is particularly good.

Château Vrai-Canon-Bouché

Owner: Françoise Roux. 15ha. 6,500 cases. Mer 90%, CF 10%. Second label: Château Les Terrasses de Vrai-Canon-Bouché; Marque: Roc de Canon; Château Comte.

Large for a Canon-Fronsac property, this famous old *cru* is on the plateau of Canon and has very old vines. Watch out for the *cuvée prestige* here, with lovely scented fruit, structure, and harmony. This is a serious wine, which repays keeping.

Minor Appellations

The following section covers some of the appellations that do not belong to the major league of Bordeaux regions but which nevertheless produce many wines worth investigating. Wines from these appellations tend to mature earlier than the *grands crus* of the well-known appellations, which makes them useful commercially. Among them are wines of great charm and personality that it would be a pity to overlook.

CÔTES DE BOURG

The attractive, hilly, and often wooded countryside of the Côtes de Bourg has seen something of a revival in the past decade. There are now over 3,800 hectares of vines, this area having shown an increase of 26 per cent since 1985.

The region consists of a succession of three main lines of *côteaux*, running roughly parallel with the river. On the first two, the soils are mostly of limestone and clay, and gravel and clay on a limestone subsoil. The third is largely sandy on a clay base. The traditional *encépagement* was a third each of Cabernet Sauvignon, Merlot, and Malbec, but in most properties, the role of the Malbec has been reduced and that of the Merlot increased. During the last decade, an increasing number of proprietors have shown that there is the potential to follow Fronsac as the next region to produce exceptional wines, with Roc de Combes showing the way.

Château de Barbe

Owner: Richard family. 70ha. 44,000 cases. Mer 60%, CF 10 %, CS 30%.

This is one of the region's largest, finest, and best-reputed properties. Twenty per cent of the wine is in wood, 80 per cent in *cuves*. The wines are light-textured, fruity, and charming with some finesse, for drinking after two to four years.

Château Bégot V

Owner: Martine and Alain Gracia.
16ha. 9,000 cases. Mer 70%, CS 10%, CF 10%, Mal 10%.

Three distinct qualities are produced here: *cuvée prestige*, which is matured in cask, and *cuvée traditionelle*, which is kept in *cuves* – mostly these are sold direct by the owners – then Château Noirac, which is sold to négociants. This is a beautifully run property situated on the second row of *côtes* in the commune of Lausac, on clayey-calcareous soils with a southern orientation. The wines are richly scented with a touch of liquorice, firm fruit quality and richness with harmony, which age well. The '93, '96, '97, '98, and '99 all impressed during a visit in September 2000. This is in the forefront of Bourgs today.

Château Brulesécaille

Owners: Jacques Rodet and Martine Recapet. 28ha. 17,000 cases. Mer 60%, CS 30%, CF 10%.

This good property in the commune of Tauriac produces robust, earthy wines with plenty of fruit and character, which age well. The excellent Brulesécaille '88 was still improving after five years.

Château Falfas V

Owner: John and Véronique Cochran. 22ha. 9,500 cases. Mer 55%, CS 30%, Mal 10%, CF 5%.

This is one of the relatively few Bordeaux properties to be run on biodynamic lines. John Cochran, an American married to a Frenchwoman, bought the historic property situated on the second row of clayey-calcareous *côtes* facing south, in '88 and the following year set course for biodynamic viticulture. Always ranked among the best *crus* of Bourg, beautiful wines are being made here today, rich and quite powerful, very full in the mouth, needing three to four years in bottle to reach their apogee. Certainly this is in the forefront of quality in Bourg today.

Château Fougas

Owner: Jean-Yves Béchet. 11ha. 6,500 cases. Mer 50%, CF 25%, CS 25%.

Here the clay is mixed with sand instead of limestone as in much of the Côtes de Bourg. In 1993, the *cuvée* Maldoror was introduced with just 500 cases. By the '99 vintage, 2,500 cases were being made of this quality. This wine is put into 100 per cent new casks for its malolactic fermentation, the lees are stirred (*batonnage*) and the wine is not racked, so it is very much in the Libournais avant-garde mode. The wines have evolved well, with '93, '94, and '95 making very good drinking by 2000, while '98 and '99 are big-flavoured, fruity wines with a touch of liquorice on the palate. The aim is to bring all the production to this standard.

Château de la Grave V

Owner: Philippe Bassereau. 43ha. 25,000 cases. Mer 78%, CS 20%, Mal 2%.

Philippe Bassereau is the fourth generation of his family to run this important property since 1900. Basically, three wines are made on this large, well-placed *cru* on the mostly clayey-calcareous hillsides behind the town of Bourg. At the summit is Nectar, with its very modern, elegant label, which is 90 per cent Merlot, ten per cent Cabernet Sauvignon, aged in new oak, of which 1,000 cases are produced annually. The wine is harmonious, with very fresh, red-fruit aromas and clean, crisp fruit flavours and richness, very modern but not overdone. The Caractère is more traditional, with more Cabernet but less Merlot, while the second wine is called Château La Croix de Bel-Air Tradition, and adds a touch of Malbec. These are serious wines, among the leaders in the region today.

Château Guerry

Owner: Heritiers Bertrand de Rivoyre. 22ha. 14,000 cases. Mer 50%, CS 15%, Mal 20%, CF 15%.

This *cru* shows the kind of quality that Bourg is capable of. There are two distinctive features: Malbec is retained as a major variety, and this is one of the last remaining *crus* in Bourg where all the wines are matured in cask.

The result is a wine that combines richness and suppleness, power and finesse. Distribution is exclusively through GVG group.

Château Guionne

Owner: Isabelle and Alain Fabre.
20ha. 13,000 cases. Mer 50%, CF and CS 45%, Mal 5%.
This *cru* is all château-bottled and produces fruity, attractive and quite elegant wines. Ten per cent is matured in cask, 90 per cent in *cuves*.

Château Haut-Macô

Owner: Jean and Bernard Mallet. 37ha. 22,000 cases. Mer 50%, CS 40%, CF 10%.
Marque: Cuvée Jean-Bernard.
This large property is in Tauriac and has been in the Mallet family for over a century. I have found the wines have very spicy, sappy fruit and rich tannins. The '98 was very attractive in 2000, requiring another two to three years in bottle, while the '95 was beginning to drink well.

Château Macay

Owner: Bernard and Eric Latouche. 30ha. 14,500 cases. Mer 65%, CF 15%, CS 10%,
Mal 10%. Second label: Les Forges de Macay Marque: Original Château Macay.
Yes, this is a wine for Scotsmen, the original MacKay was a Scottish officer who fell in love with the region, and apparently with the Guyenne tobacco as well.

Today, the vineyard is ecologically cultivated. A special *cuvée*, Original Château Macay, comes from 80 per cent Cabernet Franc and 20 per cent Merlot, from vines over 15 years old, and matures in new oak. This is intense with lots of fat and middle richness for maturing. The production is only 1,000 cases. The regular Château Macay follows the varieties in the vineyard over 15 years old, with 25 per cent new oak producing around 6,000 cases. The wine is very fruity and pleasing for early drinking. All the production from vines under 15 years goes into the second wine. The property itself, the leading one in Samonac, is well worth a visit.

Château Mendoce

Owner: Philippe Darricarrère.
14ha. 6,000 cases. Mer 70%, CS 20%, CF 5%, PV 5%.
This is one of the best-known and best-reputed wines in this region. There is a fine château, parts of which date from the 15th century. The wines are supple, with some richness, and mature rapidly.

Château Nodez

Owner: Jean-Louis Magdeleine. 40ha. 21,000 cases. Mer 60%, CS 35%, CF 5%.
This important *cru* is one of the leading properties in Tauriac today. I found the '99 had lovely fruit flavours with hints of liquorice and good, ripe tannins. A really impressive wine with a future.

Château Peychaud V

Owner: Bernard Germain. 29ha. 17,000 cases. CS 25%, Mer 75%.
This large and well-known property was acquired by the current owners in 1971. As in other Germain properties, the Vieilles Vignes *cuvée* comes in impressively heavyweight bottles and is among the best in the region.

Château Roc de Cambes ★

Owner: François Mitjavile. 10ha. 5,000 cases. Mer 60%, CS 25%, CF 10%, Mal 5%.
The same principles of low yields, old vines, late harvesting and meticulous winemaking apply here as at the proprietor's more famous Tertre Roteboeuf in St-Émilion. The vineyard is marvellously placed on

a slope facing the river. The wine is rich, succulent, and marvellously attractive; but do not expect to pay Côte de Bourg prices. This commands the price of a St-Émilion *grand cru classé* – and is worth it.

Château Rousset

Owner: M et Mme Teisseire. Administrator: Gérard Teisseire. 23ha. 13,000 cases. Mer 47%, CS 38%, Mal 10%, CF 5%.

Situated in the commune of Samonac, this is a good Bourg. The wines have richness and length of flavour which place them above the general run of wines from this area.

Château Tayac

Owner: Saturny family. 30ha. 17,000 cases. CS 43%, Mer 51%, CF 5%, Mal 1%.

This is one of the showpieces of the Côtes de Bourg with its 1890 château in flamboyant, Renaissance style surrounded by a vineyard which commands a view over the confluence of the Dordogne and Garonne. When the present owners arrived in 1959, the property had been abandoned since 1940, so both vineyard and château needed restoration.

Three wines are produced. Le Rubis du Prince Noir, which is Merlot-dominated and matured in wooden *cuves* for drinking young; Cuvée Reserveé, which is 50:50 Cabernet and Merlot aged in casks and Le Prestige which is 80 per cent Cabernet Sauvignon from old vines and is aged in new oak. Both the Reserveé and Le Prestige are powerful, tannic wines, and some may prefer the sweet fruit of the Reserveé to the rather tannin-dominated Prestige.

PREMIÈRES CÔTES DE BLAYE

This region forms the northward extension of the Côtes de Bourg. Although it is larger than the Bourg, the parts suited to the vine are smaller. The area of vineyards has, however, more than doubled over the last 20 years, now covering over 5,500 hectares. The output consists predominantly of red wine, with only a small and unimportant production of white. The soil here is of limestone and clay, and the Merlot is more predominant than in Bourg. The prices achieved are often no more than for Bordeaux Supérieur, and some of the growers declare their wines as Bordeaux Supérieur instead of Premières Côtes de Blaye. Bernard Germain's properties show what can be done, and even make some exceptional white wines. This is a good source of fruity, easy-to-drink red Bordeaux.

Château Bourdieu

Cru Bourgeois. Owner: Domaines Scheitzer & Fils. 40ha. Red: 26,500 cases. Mer 60%, CS 40%. White: 5,000 cases. Sém 80%, Sauv and Col 20%.

A well-known and well-reputed *cru*, unusual in its high proportion of Cabernet Sauvignon. Wood maturation is used for 25 per cent, the rest is in *cuves*. The result is a wine above-average in character and quality.

Château Charron V

Owner: Vignobles Germain. 22ha. Red: 13,000 cases. Mer 90%, CS 10%. White: 4ha. 2,500 cases. Sém 75%, Sauv 25%.

This is another Germain property, using 400-litre casks. The *vieilles vignes*, Les Grappes, is very fruity with good tannins,while the exceptionally aromatic Acacia white is outstanding, and would not be out of place in Pessac-Léognan.

Château L'Escadre V
Owner: GFA L'Escadre. Administrator: Jean-Marie Carreau. 32ha. 20,000 cases.
Mer 70%, CS 20%, Mal 10%.
Second label: Château la Croix St-Pierre.
This good *cru* in the commune of Cars has acquired an excellent reputation
for consistency over the last two decades. Some wood maturation is used,
and the wines are charmingly fruity and stylish.

Château Lacaussade St Martin V
Owner: Jacques Chardat. Red: 18ha. 11,000 cases. Mer 90%, CS 10%.
White: 4ha. 2,400 cases. Sém 90%, Sauv 10%.
This fine property is managed and distributed by Vignobles Germain as
the very distinctive labels bear witness. Four-hundred-litre barrels are
used for ageing. The reds are really luscious and seductive, especially
the top-of-the-line Trois Moulins, while the delicious, richly fruity white
wine will come as a real surprise and can compete with the best dry
wines Bordeaux has to offer.

Château Maine–Gazin V
Owner: Vignobles Germain. 7.5ha. 3,000 cases. Mer 95%, CS 5%.
This small *cru* in Plassac has been owned by the Germain family since 1980
and benefits from vines with an average age of 40 years. I found the old-vine
selection Levenne had a concentrated bouquet of roasted cherries and
lovely fruit flavours with very rich tannins behind. The '98 needs another
two years. This is well above the normal level for Blaye.

Château Peyredoulle V
Owner: Vignobles Germain. 19ha. 12,000 cases. Mer 95%, PV 5%.
This is the heart of the Germain empire, host to its offices and laboratory.
Not surprisingly, the wines are impressive, especially the *vieilles vignes*
cuvée Maine Criquau. The '98 was aromatic, with firm tannins and
distinctive fruit flavours. Again, 400-litre casks are used for ageing.

Château Segonzac
Owner: Thomas Herter and Charlotte Herter-Marmet. 30ha. 20,000 cases.
Mer 60%, CS 25%, CF 10%, Mal 5%.
This *cru* in the commune of St-Genès-de-Blaye produces spicy, attractive wines
for early drinking. A third of the wine is now in wood with 25 per cent new.

ENTRE-DEUX-MERS

This huge area is the largest source of good dry white wines in Bordeaux.
There are now some 1,500 hectares benefiting from the Appellation
Contrôlée (including the small Haut-Benauge AC), considerably less
than there were fifteen years ago. This is a region of large estates, with
mechanical harvesting now widely used, and cool fermentation as the
rule. Much good red wine is also made, but this is entitled only to the
appellation Bordeaux or Bordeaux Supérieur.

Château Bonnet V
Owner: André Lurton. Red: 100ha. 50,000 cases. CS 50%, Mer 44%, CF 6%.
White: 105ha. 65,000. Sém 45%, Sauv 45%, Musc 10%.
Second label: Le Colombey. White Prestige Cuvé: Ch Bonnet Blanc Classique.
One of the most impressive properties in Entre-Deux-Mers, with an
elegant 18thcentury château and enormous vineyard. It is in Grézillac,
due south of St-Émilion. The *chai* and *cuvier* are as well-equipped

as André Lurton's prestigious Graves properties. The white wine is cold-fermented at 16–18°C (61–64°F), and some of the red is matured in cask and sold in special numbered bottles. With its interesting mixture of *cépages*, the white wine is perfumed and full of elegant, fruity flavours. This is one of the best-value and most dependable dry white wines to be found on French restaurant lists. The red grapes are mechanically harvested, and the red wines are thoroughly attractive, with quite a pronounced character.

Château Fondarzac

Owner: J. C. Barthe. White: 40ha. Sauv 40%, Sém 40%, Musc 20%. Red: 20ha. Mer 50%, CS 25%, CF 25%.

This *cru* has been owned since the 17th century by the Barthe family, whose winemaking skills have manifested themselves in more recent generations. Jean-Claude Barthe has shown himself to be a particularly talented oenologist. The wines have a delicious bouquet and plenty of fruit.

Château Fongrave

Owner: Pierre Perromat. Red: 45ha. 27,500 cases. CS 60%, Mer 40%. White: 9ha. 5,000 cases. Sém 60%, Sauv 40%.
Second label (for red wines): Château de La Sablière-Fongrave.

This *cru* at Gornac is run by Pierre Perromat, who also owns Château d'Arche and was president of the INAO for many years. The property has been in his family since the 1600s and produces some attractively scented wines, both red and white.

Château Jonqueyres V

Owner: Éts GAM Audy. Red: 38ha. 23,000 cases. Mer 80%, CS 20%. White: 3ha. 2,000 cases.

This property at St-Germain-du-Puch in the northern Entre-Deux-Mers has benefited from the winemaking capabilities of Jean-Michel Arcaute, seen to spectacular effect at Château Clinet (see page 173). Look out especially for the *vieilles vignes* selection.

Château Launay

Owner: Rémy Grèffier. Red: 25ha. 14,000 cases. Mer 63%, CS 20%, CF 17%. White: 40ha. 26,500 cases. Sém 40%, Musc 33%, Sauv 27%.
Second labels: White: Châteaux Dubory, Braidoire, La Vaillante. Red: Châteaux Haut-Castenet, Haut-Courgeaux.

This large property is at Soussac, on the road between Pellegrue and Sauveterre in the eastern Entre-Deux-Mers. All the wine is château-bottled. The wines are well-reputed.

Château Moulin-de-Launay V

Owners: Claude and Bernard Greffier. White: 75ha. 46,000 cases. Sém 45%, Sauv 35%, Musc 20%. Red: 1ha. 400 cases. CF 50%, Mer 50%.
Second labels: Châteaux Tertre-de-Launay, Plessis, La Vigerie, de Tuilerie.

This large property at Soussac, in eastern Entre-Deux-Mers between Pellegrue and Sauveterre, was devoted to the production of white wines – fruity, with elegance and length – until the planting of a hectare of red in '92.

Château de la Rose

Owner: Jean Faure. White: 8.4ha. 6,000 cases. Red: 10.5ha. 7,000 cases.

This property in the north of the region is small compared with most in Entre-Deux-Mers. The wines produced are extremely attractive with a charming bouquet, and floweriness and fruit on the palate.

Château de Sours V
Owner: Esmé Johnstone. Red: 24ha. 20,000 cases. Mer 85%, CS 5%, CF 10%.
White: 5ha. 3,500 cases. Sém 75%, Musc, Sauv, and Mer Blanc 25%.
Second label: (red) Domaine de Sours.

The owner is an Englishman who has come to Bordeaux after a career spanning banking in Hong Kong and retailing wine in the UK and California. The property is at St-Quentin de Baron, between Branne and Créon in north-central Entre-Deux-Mers. The soil is gravel and clay on limestone, and there are limestone caves under the property, now used for cask maturation.

The red wine is made with the assistance of Michel Rolland (*see* Le Bon Pasteur, page 172) and is aged for 15 months in new and second-year casks. The resulting wine is attractive for drinking when around three years old, but it will also keep and improve.

The white wine (sold as Bordeaux AC, not Entre-Deux-Mers) is made with the help of David Lowe (formerly of Rothbury in Australia's Hunter Valley) and has a pleasing middle richness combined with fruit and elegance. There is also a delicious rosé made by the *saignée* method, with free-run juice taken from the vats after 12–18 hours' skin contact. Not surprisingly, these wines have rapidly made a name for themselves.

Château Thieuley V
Owner: Francis Courselle. Red: 24ha, 8,300 cases. Mer 70%, CF 20%, CS 10%.
White: 30ha. 22,000 cases. Sauv 60%, Sém 40%.

The proprietor here is a professor of viticulture. The property is at La Sauve, near Créon in western Entre-Deux-Mers. The white wines produced have a most attractive fruit, without exaggerated acidity, and are light and fresh. Look out for the excellent prestige selections here; Réserve Courselle and Héritage de Thieuly for the red and Cuvée Courselle for the white.

Château Tour de Mirambeau V
Owner: Francis Courselle. Red: 29ha. 19,500 cases. Mer 80%, CS 20%.
White: 59ha. 35,000 cases. Sauv 50%, Sém 30%, Musc 20%.

A large property near Branne producing large quantities of consistently reliable wines: the white is particularly successful, and the red fresh and fruity for early drinking. The Bordeaux Blanc *cuvée,* Passion, is a selection from the oldest vines, harvested by hand and then fermented in new wood. The other wines are mechanically harvested.

Château de Toutigeac
Owner: Philippe Mazeau. Red: 44ha: 30,000 cases. CS 15%, Mer 25%, CF 60%.
White: 6.8ha. 4,800 cases, Sém 50%, Sauv 25%, Musc 25%.

One of the best-known properties to use the sub-appellation Entre-Deux-Mers-Haut-Benauge. The appellation can be used only for white wines. Both red and white wines here are well-reputed and all are château-bottled.

PREMIÈRES CÔTES DE BORDEAUX

This attractive area runs from the suburbs of Bordeaux southwards down the right bank of the Garonne to the sweet wine regions of Loupiac and Ste-Croix-du-Mont. It produces moderately sweet white wines and fruity, vivacious reds for early drinking. Fifteen years ago, there was a slightly greater vineyard area devoted to white than to red wine production, but today the situation is reversed, and the red vineyards have increased by over 50 per cent over the past decade to 3,100 hectares, while those covered by white vines have decreased to 600 hectares. The best whites in the south of the area carry the superior AC Cadillac, but the idea has not really caught on. The real future of the region seems to rest more with its pleasant red wines.

Château Birot

Owner: Fournier-Casteja family. Red: 17ha. 8,000 cases. Mer 69%, CF 11%, CS 20%. White: 5.9ha. 2,000 cases. Sém 58%, Sauv 35%, Musc 7%.

This *cru* in the commune of Béguey is best-known for its fresh, fruity whites, with well-balanced acidity, sweetness, and elegance. It is now run by Eve Fournier, formally of Château Canon.

Château Brethous

Owner: Denise Verdier. 13ha. 7,500 cases. Mer 67%, CF 23%, CS 5%, Mal 5%.

This good *cru* at Camblanes produces wines that are deliciously fruity and scented. They drink well when two to three years old, but can still be fresh and delicious after eight years.

Château Carsin V

Owner: Juha Berglund. Red: 21ha. 11,000 cases. Mer 27%, CF 36%, CS 37%. White: 31ha. 15,500 cases. Sém 56%, Sauv and Sauv Gris 44%.

An interesting property at Rions with an international flavour. The owner is Finnish; the winemaker, Mandy Jones, an Australian who worked previously at Château de Landiras under Peter Vinding-Diers. In addition to the vineyard belonging to the château, a further 20 hectares of pure Sémillon are leased.

The white wines have had a great success in England for several years, as well as in Juha Berglund's native Finland. The *cuvée prestige* is fermented in cask with *bâttonage*, (a stirring up of the lees before the first racking). The normal quality is fermented in stainless steel and then spends about three months in different types of oak. The attention to detail is meticulous. The normal white has zesty, lemon-like fruit and excellent acidity, the *cuvée prestige* is perfumed with oaky notes, a broader, richer flavour with clear wood influence and a distinctly New World feel to it. The '96 is outstanding. Also look out for the L'Etiquette Grise, sold without the appellation or vintage, made from the rare Sauvignon Gris, it is a real surprise. The reds are clean and fruity and need a year or two to develop.

Château Cayla

Owner: Patric Doche. 24ha. Red: 10.5ha 6,500 cases. CS 34%, CF 33%, Mer 33%. White: 6.7ha. 1,500 cases. Sém 75%, Sauv 25%. (Cadillac)

Since 1985, this property at Rions has been transformed by the present owner. The reds have varied fruit and are delicious when they are three years old; the whites are rotated through ten per cent new oak after a cool fermentation and pre-fermentation skin contact.

Château Fayau

Owner: Jean Médeville & Fils. Red: 32ha. 15,000 cases. CS 40%, Mer 35%, CF 25%. White: 26ha. 9,000 cases. Sém 50%, Sauv 40%, Musc 10%.

This excellent *cru* in Cadillac is carefully run by the Médeville family, who make a particularly good, sweet white Cadillac, with good fruit and style, that ages well.

Château Le Gardera, Château Laurétan, Château Tanesse
Owner: Domaines Cordier.

For many years, Domaines Cordier has run these adjoining properties in the Premières Côtes as a single production centre, producing several different appellations. Since 1983, the production of Château Laurétan has ceased, and this has been changed into a brand, Laurétan Rouge and Laurétan Blanc, with the simple Bordeaux appellation. The other two châteaux are as follows:

Château Le Gardera: *25ha. Red (AC Bordeaux Supérieur): 11,5000 cases. Mer 60%, CS 40%.*

Le Gardera now produces an attractive, light-bodied, Merlot-dominated red wine.

Château Tanesse: *Red (AC Premières Côtes de Bordeaux): 35ha. 12,000 cases. CS 55%, Mer 35%, CF 10%. White (AC Bordeaux Blanc): 20ha. 12,000 cases. Sauv 85%, Sém 15%.*

Tanesse makes a more Cabernet-dominated red wine, together with a flowery, fresh, Sauvignon-style white.

Château du Grand Mouëys V
Owner: SCA Les Trois Colines (Reidermeister & Ulrichs). Administrator: Carstin Bömers. Red: 59ha. 33,000 cases. Mer 50%, CS 25%, CF 25%.
White: 21ha. 10,100 cases. Sém 38%, Sauv 55%, Musc 7%.

Since the important Bremen house of Reidermeister & Ulrichs bought this large property at Capian in 1989, there has been considerable investment in the vineyard, cellar and château.

Ten hectares of the red wine vineyard are currently used to make Bordeaux Clairet; the red wine is matured for between five and ten months in cask, depending on the year. A part of the white wine is fermented in new barrels, the rest in stainless steel. Attractive white wines are already being made here, although the red wines are taking a little longer. This is clearly a property to watch.

Château de Haux V
Owners: Jorgensen brothers. Red: 22ha. 13,000 cases. Mer 42%, CS 40%, CF 18%.
White: 7ha. Sém 64%, Sauv 30%, Musc 6%.

In 1985, two brothers, wine merchants from Denmark, bought this property at Haux and have rapidly transformed it. Their red wine is rich and solid with attractive fruit and definite character. The white is exceptionally attractive, with long-flavoured, crisp fruit.

Château Lagarosse
Owner: M. Ottari. 32ha. Red: 26.7ha. 16,000 cases. Mer 80%, CS and CF 20%.
White: 5.9ha. 2,200 cases. Sém 80%, Sauv 20%.

This property at Tabanac was bought in 1987 by a Japanese importer of agricultural machinery. The red wines have intense fruit, a rich, solid flavour and a suggestion of liquorice. The whites have a big broad flavour with lots of fruit and character. In '96 and '97, excellent Cadillac was made.

Château Laroche-Bel-Air
Owner: Martine Palau. 25ha. Red: Mer 60%, CS and CF 40%.
White: Sém 60%, Sauv 40%.

This *cru* at Baurech produces stylish, fruity but quite tannic wines that need four to five years' maturation before being ready. They are matured in cask. The wine matured in vat is softer, but also robust and can be drunk earlier. It is labelled as Château Laroche. The same labelling differences are used on the white wines to distinguish those vinified in cask from those vinified in vat.

Château Lezongars V

Owner: Philip Iles Red: 39ha. 21,000 cases. Mer 60%, CS 38%, CF 2%.
White: 6ha. 3,500 cases. Sém 90%, Sauv 10%.

The Iles family, Philip, his wife Sarah and son Russell, only bought this property in 1998, but have already made their mark, assisted by an energetic and highly qualified manager. Three *cuvées* of red wine and two of white are being made. The reds are L'Enclos de Château Lezongars, an *assemblage* of their best parcels of Merlot and Cabernet, which has 20 per cent new oak, including some American oak. I found the '99 supple and elegant with rich tannins and a fine finish. 2000 is richer but also delicious. The regular Lezongars has a little more Merlot and the '99 was already better than the '98, with real character and length. Finally Château de Roques is designed for early drinking and, as with the normal *cuvée,* has 60 per cent Merlot. The '99 showed pleasingly mellow, welcoming fruit. The white is quite Sauvignon in style, intense and full flavoured. Clearly, the property is going places.

Château de Pic V

Owner: François Masson Regnault. Red: 31ha, 18,500 cases. CS 50%, Mer 45%,
CF 5%. White: 2ha. 1,100 cases. Sém 75%, Sauv 20%, Musc 5%.

This property is at Le Tourne, just outside Langoiran. Since the present owners took over in 1975, extensive improvements have been made.

There is a basic wine that is matured in vat, and delicious to drink soon after bottling, and there is a *cuvée tradition,* aged in cask, which has more structure and depth of fruit.

Château Plaisance V

Owner: Patrick Bayle. Red: 23ha. 12,000 cases. Mer 50%, CS 35%, CF 15%.
White: 1.5ha, 600 cases. Sém 100%.

Patrick Bayle left a business career to run this property at Capian in 1985. His wines have a rich, berry-like fruit that needs three or four years to show at its best maturity level. There is also a cask-fermented white wine.

Château de Plassan V

Owner: Jean Brianceau. Red: 17ha. 9,000 cases. Mer 50%, CS and CF 45%, Mal 5%.
White: 12ha. 5,000 cases. Sém 50%, Sauv 40%, Musc 10%.
Second label: Château Lamothe.

This fine property at Tabanac has one of the region's rare Palladian buildings, with château and *chai* forming a harmonious whole. The reds are concentrated and solid but with good fruit, serious wines needing time.

There is an attractive white that is vinified in vat and bottled in the spring and a *cuvée spécial* that is vinified in cask but made only in selected vintages.

Château Puy Bardens V

Owner: Yves Lamiable. 17ha. 11,000 cases. Mer 50%, CS 45%, CF 5%.

A good *cru* at Cambes, commanding fine views over the Garonne and the vineyards of Graves from its hilly position.

Two qualities are made: one matured in vat is perfumed, with structure and personality, while the *cuvée prestige* is matured in cask and has plenty of fruit and substance. A distinctly fine wine.

Château Reynon ★ V

Owner: Denis and Florence Dubourdieu. Red: 18ha. 9,500 cases. Mer 65%,
CS 30%, CF 5%. White: 23.5ha. 11,000 cases. Sauv 70%, Sém 30%.
Second labels: Le Second de Reynon (for both red and white), Le Clos de Reynon.

This well-known and well-distributed *cru* is the most important property in the commune of Béguey, near to Cadillac. The soil is gravelly with calcareous clay. Here, an excellent red wine is made, possessing the almost startling fruitiness which characterizes the area. It is aged in cask after a long maceration. In addition to the success of their red counterparts, the deliciously floral, fruity white wines have justly won a considerable reputation. They are vinified and aged in vat. In 1996, a Cadillac was made for the first time. One could have mistaken it for a Barsac, it was so fine.

STE-CROIX-DU-MONT

The two appellations of Ste-Croix-du-Mont and Loupiac are situated on some spectacular hillsides and the plateau, just across the Garonne from Sauternes and Barsac, affording a splendid panorama of the whole Graves-Sauternes region. They also provide the best sweet wines outside Sauternes. In fact, the best properties are able to make wines that can be better than the lesser Sauternes, given grapes properly affected by noble rot. They tend to be lighter and less rich than Sauternes, but are fruity and long-lived. The cooperative at Ste-Croix-du-Mont produces wines of a good standard. The area under vine is 460 hectares.

Château Coulac
Owner: Gérard Despujols. 6.4ha. 3,000 cases. Sem 80%, Sauv 10%, Musc 10%.
The Despujols produce dependable and quite rich wines that mature well.

Château Loubens
Owner: Arnaud de Sèze. 4,500 cases. Red: 7ha. 3,000 cases. Mer 45%, CS 40%, CF 15%. White: 15ha. 4,400 cases. Sém 95%, Sauv 5%.
Second labels: Château Terfort, Fleuron Blanc de Château Loubens.
This has long been one of the best *crus* of the appellation. The sweet wines have an elegant fruit and freshness about them and are well-made, with well-balanced sweetness. The vineyard is finely placed at the top of the *côte*.
  There is an attractive dry wine, sold under the name of Fleuron Blanc, and another sweet wine, Château Terfort, which also maintains an excellent standard.

Château du Pavillon
Owner: Viviane and Alain Fertal. 4.5ha. 1,700 cases. Sem 85%, Sauv 15%.
Very elegant botrytized wines of real class are being made here and at the owners' Loupiac vineyards of Les Roques.

Château La Rame V
Owner: Yves Armand. 20ha. 6,500 cases. Sem 75%, Sauv 25%.
One of the most attractive and consistent wines being made in the '90s in Ste-Croix du Mont. Elegant fruit flavours and Barsac-like breeding.

LOUPIAC

Apart from the fact that they lie in different communes, there is no useful distinction to be made between the Loupiac appellation and that of its neighbour, Ste-Croix-du-Mont. Loupiac has just over 400 hectares under vine.

Château du Cros
Owner: Michel Boyer. 38.5ha. 20,000 cases. Sem 70%, Sauv 20%, Musc 10%.
A superbly situated property with links to Richard the Lionheart in 1196. The wines have quite rich fruit with lemony acidity and are elegant and attractive.

Château Loupiac-Gaudiet V

Owner: Marc Ducau. White: 25ha. 8,900 cases. Sém 80%, Sauv 20%.

This has been one of Loupiac's best and most consistent wines for many years. The wines are mostly aged in vat. They have delicacy and finesse, with a fruity sweetness, and age well.

Château Les Roques

Owner: Viviane and Alain Fertal. 4.5ha.

See Château du Pavillon (Ste-Croix-du-Mont).

Château de Ricaud

Owner: SC Garreau-Ricard. Administrator: Alain Thienot. Red: 55ha. 12,000 cases. CS 50%, Mer 50%. White: 20ha. 10,000 cases. Sém 80%, Sauv 15%, Musc 5%.

This is the most famous *cru* in Loupiac, and many of the historic vintages (such as '29 and '47) are still superb. Unfortunately, in the last years of the previous ownership, the property was neglected and run down, but since the new owners from Champagne took over in 1980, there has been steady progress. The Loupiac is finely perfumed with finesse, real elegance and richness. Some new wood is now used for the maturation.

Fine examples were made in '81, '82, and '83, but the real breakthrough came with a gloriously botrytized '86 which could well pass for a good Barsac. There is a rather traditional Sémillon-dominated dry white with the Bordeaux AC, and a fruity, attractive red wine which has the Premières Côtes AC in the best years ('81 and '82) and otherwise the Bordeaux Supérieur AC. Again, these wines are matured in cask. The property has rapidly regained its reputation.

CÔTES DE CASTILLON

This region lies between the St-Émilionnais and the boundary of the Gironde and Dordogne departments, and used to be categorized as "St-Émilionnais" before the appellations came into force. It produces some of the best Bordeaux Supérieur, with body and some character, much of it from a good *cave coopérative*. With 2,988 hectares of vines, the area under vine in 2000 has more than doubled since 1974.

The following châteaux, among others, are worth looking out for: : Domaine de L'A (Stephane Derenoncourt's biodynamic vineyard), Domaine de l'Aiguilhe (acquired in 1998 by Stephan von Neipperg of Canon-la-Gaffelière), Joanin Bécot (a new initiative by the Beau-Séjour-Bécot family, first vintage 2001), de Belcier, Cap de Faugères, Fongaban, La Clarière-Laithwaite, Castegens (also sold as Fontenay), Chante-Grive, de Clotte, Clos L'Eglise and Ste Colombe (acquired by Gerard Perse of Pavie in 1999), L'Estang, Haut-Tuquet, Lardit, de Laussac (bought by Alain Raynaud of Château Quinault, first vintage 2001), Moulin-Rouge, Pitray, Puycarpin, Clos Puy Arnaud, Rocher-Bellevue, Roquevieille, Thibaud-Bellevue, La Treille-des-Girondiers, Veyry (very small but very beautiful!).

CÔTES DE FRANCS

This small appellation to the north of Castillon has gained a reputation in excess of its size (only 450 hectares) due to the pioneering work of the Thienpont family at Château Puygueraud, where superb red wines are being made. Other wines to look out for are Châteaux de Francs, Laclaverie, Marsau, and La Prade.

Additional Châteaux

This alphabetical listing is a directory of some 220 châteaux that
are not profiled in Part I of the book. It aims to give as broad and
useful a selection as possible within the limits of the space available.

Where possible, the following details are given, and in the
corresponding order: château name, appellation, classification
(if any), owner (*see* page 5 for types of company), size of vineyard
in hectares, colour of wine (R or W for red or white), and the
average number of cases produced annually. If a star appears after
the name, it means that the wine concerned is above-average and
worth investigating.

The appellations and classifications are abbreviated as follows:

Appellation	Abbreviation
Barsac	Bars
Blaye	Bl
Bourg	Bg
Bordeaux	Bord
Bordeaux Supérieur	Bord Sup
Canon-Fronsac	C-Fron
Cérons	Cér
Côtes de Castillon	Cast
Entre-Deux-Mers	E-D-M
Fronsac	Fron
Graves	Gr
Haut-Médoc	H-Méd
Lalande de Pomerol	L de Pom
Listrac	List
Loupiac	Loup
Lussac-St-Émilion	L-St-Ém
Margaux	Marg
Médoc	Méd
Moulis	Moul
Pauillac	Pau
Pomerol	Pom
Premières Côtes de Bordeaux	Prem Côtes
Ste-Croix-du-Mont	Ste-Cr
St-Émilion	St-Ém
St-Estèphe	St-Est
St-Julien	St-Jul
Sauternes	Saut

Classification	Abbreviation
Cru Bourgeois	CB
Grand Cru	GC
Cru Bourgeois Exceptionnel	CBE
Cru Bourgeois Supérieur	CBS

Balac H-Méd, CB, L & C Touchais, 17ha, R10,000
Barbé* Bl, Carreau, 30ha, R15,000, W3,500
Bel-Air Ste-Cr, M Méric, 12ha, W4,000
Belle-Rose Pau, CB, Bernard Jugla, 7ha, R4,000
Bellevue* Méd, CB, Lassalle et Fils, 23ha, R14,500
Bibian List, Alain Meyre, 24ha, R14,000
Le Boscq* Méd, CB Domaine Lapalu, 27ha, R16,500
du Bouilh Bord Sup, Heirs of Comte P de Feuilhade de Chauvin,
    48ha, R22,000, W1,000
du Bousquet Bg, Castel Frères, 62ha, R36,000
Bouteilley, Dom de Prem Côtes, J Guillot, 38ha, R39,000
des Brousteras Méd, CB, SCF du château, 25ha, R15,000
de Caillavet* Prem Côtes, SC, 62ha, R32,000, W5,500
le Caillou Pom, A Giraud, 7ha, R3,500
de Camarsac* E-D-M, Bérénice Lurton, 60ha, R40,000
Canet* E-D-M, B Large, 46ha, R14,000, W11,000
Carcanieux* Méd, CB, SC, 38ha, R22,000
du Cartillon* H-Méd, CB, Vignobles R Giraud, 46ha, R23,000
de Cérons* Cér, J Perromat, 12ha, W3,000
Le Châtelet St-Ém, H & P Berjal, 3.7ha, R1,700
Civrac* Bg, Vignobles Jaubert, 20ha, R10,000
La Commanderie Pom, Madame M H Dé, 5.6ha, R3,200
de la Commanderie L de Pom, Lafon, 26ha, R14,000
de Courteillac E-D-M, Dominique Menezet, 25ha, R5,500, W1,000
Crabitey* Gr, SC, 25.5ha, R13,000, W2,000
de la Croix Millorit Bg, GAEC Jaubert, 21ha, R13,000
de Cugat E-D-M, B Meyer, 53ha, R30,000, W3,300
Doms* Gr, Vignobles Parage, 17ha, R6,500, W3,500
Faubernet* Prem Côtes, Adrien Dufis, 37ha, R24,500
Ferrand* Pom, Gasparoux & Fils, 12ha, R6,500
Florimond-la Brede Bl, L Marinier, 20ha, R10,000
Fonchereau E-D-M, Mme Georges Vinot-Postry, 32ha, R15,000,
    W2,000
Fonrazade St-Ém, GC, G Balotte, 13ha, R6,000
Fort-de-Vauban H-Méd, J-N Noleau, 12ha, R4,500
La France E-D-M, La France Assurances, 72ha, R42,000, W3,500
Franquet-Grand-Poujeaux* Moul, CB, P Lambert, 8.5ha, R3,000
de Fronsac Fron, Seurin, 8ha, R4,000
Gaillard St-Ém, GC, J-J Nouvel, 20ha, R8,500
Le Gay E-D-M, R Maison, 20ha, R12,000, W2,000
Gazin-Rocquencourt Gr, Famille Michotte, 14ha, R7,500
de Goélane E-D-M, SC, 73ha, R49,000
Gombaude-Guillot* Pom, GFA, 7ha, R3,500
La Grâce-Dieu* St-Ém, GC, M Pauty, 13ha, R6,500
Grand-Duroc-Milon Pau, CB, Bernard Jugla, 6ha, R2,200
Le Grand-Enclos du Ch Cérons Cér, Lataste, 6ha, W1,000
Grand-Jour Bg, SCEA, 40ha, R25,000
Grand-Monteil Bord Sup, Jean Techenet, 113ha, R65,000,
    W8,500
Grand-Moulin H-Méd, R Gonzalvez, SC, 18ha, R11,000
de Grand-Puch E-D-M, Société Viticole, 90ha, R50,000

Grate-Cap Pom, G & M Janoueix, 10ha, R5,000

du Grava* Prem Côtes, SCI de la Rive Droite, 45ha, R30,000

Gravelines Prem Côtes, Dubourg, 10ha, W25,000, R8,500

Graville-Lacoste* Gr, Hervé Doubourdieu, 8ha, W3,500

Grimonac Prem Côtes, P Yung, 25ha, R13,000

Grolet Bl, Bömes family, 28ha, R15,000

Gros-Moulin Bg, J Arzeller, 28ha, R16,000

Gueyrot St-Ém, de la Tour du Fayet, 8ha, R4,000

Guibon E-D-M, A Lurton, 35ha, W11,000, R5,000

Haut Breton Larigaudière Marg, CB, SCEA, 13ha, R7,000

Haut-Brignon Prem Côtes, 54ha, R31,000

Haut-Lavallade* St-Ém, J. P. Chagneau, 12ha, R6,000

Haut-Lignan* Méd, Castet family, 11ha, R7,000

Haut-Maillat Pom, J. P. Estager, 5ha, R2,520

Haut Ségottes St-Ém, GC, D André, 9ha, R5,000

Hourbanon Méd, CB, SC, 13ha, R6,500

Hourtin-Ducasse* H-Méd, CB, M Marengo, 25ha, R13,000

Jacques-Blanc St-Ém, GFA, 18.8ha, R10,000

des Jaubertes* Gr, Marquis de Pontac, 31ha, R8,500, W2,000

Jean-Gervais Gr, Counilh & Fils, 39ha, R12,000, W7,500

Jean-Voisin St-Ém, GC, SC Chassagnoux, 14ha, R7,500

du Juge*, Bord Sup, (Cadillac), P Dupleich, 28ha, W10,000,
R6,000

du Juge Prem Côtes, (Haux), J Mèdeville, 28ha, R9,000,
W3,000

Le Jurat St-Ém, GC, SCA Haut Corbin, 6ha, R3,500

Justa* Prem Côtes, M Mas, 19ha, R10,000, W2,400

Laborde L de Pom, J-M Trocard, 20ha, R8,500

Lachesnaye* H-Méd, CBS, Dom Bouteiller, 20ha, R11,000

Lafite Prem Côtes, R-F Laguens, 38ha, R20,000

Lagüe* Fron, F Roux, 7.6ha, R3,500

Lalande* List, CB, Mme Darriet, 10.5ha, R6,000

Lalande St-Jul, CB, G Meffre, 32ha, R15,000

Lalibarde Bg, R Dumas, 35ha, R22,000

Lamothe Bg, M Pessonier, 23ha, R11,000

Lapelletrie St-Ém, GC, GFA, 12ha, R6,500

Larrivaux H-Méd, CB , Vicomtesse de Carheil, 23ha, R10,500

Lassègue St-Ém, GC, J P Freylon, 22.5ha, R13,000

Laurensanne Bg, D Levraud, 30ha, R15,000

Laurette Ste-Cr, F Pons, 42ha, W11,000, R8,000

Ligondras Marg, P Augeau, 10ha, R5,500

Malagar Prem Côtes, Dom Cordier, 14ha, R4,000, W4,000

Martinon E-D-M, Trollier, 44ha, W15,500, R10,000

de Martouret E-D-M, D Lurton, 40ha, R21,000, W3,000

Clos Mazeyres Pom, Laymarie & Fils, 9.7ha, R5,000

Méaume* Bord Sup, (Guitres & Coutras), A Johnson-Hill, 28ha,
R15,500

Clos des Menuts* St-Ém, GC, P Rivière, 25ha, R11,500

Mille-Sescousses* Bord Sup, P Darricarrère, 62ha, R26,000

des Moines L de Pom, H Darnazou, 17ha, R7,000

Monconseil-Gazin Bl, M Baudet, 16ha, R7,500, W600

Moulin-Pey-Labrie, C-Fron, B & G Hubau, 6.7ha, R2,500

Moulin de la Rose St-Jul, CBS, Guy Delon, 4ha, R2,000

Moulin-à-Vent* L de Pom, F-M Marret, 12ha, R6,550

Panigon* Méd, CB, J-K & J-R Leveilley, 50ha, R25,500

Pardaillan Bl, Bayle-Carreau, 15ha R8,000

Péconnet* Prem Côtes, Amiel family, 17ha, R10,000

Perenne Bl, SCA, 59ha, R38,000, W500

Pernaud* Saut, CB, Regelsperger, 15ha, W3,300

Perron L de Pom, Massonié, 15ha, R7,000

Pey-Martin Méd, CB, Jean Signoret, 10ha, R6,500

du Peyrat* Prem Côtes, SC Lambert Frères (Capian), 98ha, R44,000, W17,000

Piada Saut, CB, J & E Lalande, 9.5ha, W1,500

Pichon H-Méd, C Fayat, 23ha, R8,000

Pierredon* E-D-M, Bord Sup (Gornac), P Perromat, 18ha, R10,000

Piron* Gr, P Boyreau, 20ha, W6,000, R2,000

Plantey Pau, CB, G Meffre, 26ha, R15,000

Pontet-Chappaz Marg, Vignobles Rocher-Cap de Rive, 7.7ha, R4,500

de Portets* Gr, J-P Théron, 39ha, R12,500, W2,000

La Providence Bord Sup (Med), Bouteiller, 7ha, R3,500

Puy-Blanquet* St-Ém, GC, R Jacquet, 23ha, R10,000

Puyblanquet-Carille St-Ém, GC, J-F Carille, 12ha, R7,000

Quentin St-Ém, GC, SC, 30ha, R1,800

de Ramondon Prem Côtes, Mme van Pé, 25ha, R14,00, W9,000

du Raux H-Méd, CB, SCI, 15ha, R8,500

Raymond, E-D-M, Baron R de Montesquieu, 27ha, R28,000

de Respide Gr, Vignobles Bonnet, 40ha, R18,000, W8,000

Reynier* E-D-M, D Lurton, 75ha, R35,000, W9,000

Richelieu Fron, Y Viaud, 12.9ha, R7,500

La Rivalerie Bl, Gillibert Chauvin, 34ha, R17,500, W1,000

La Roche Prem Côtes, P Dumas, 15ha, R10,000

du Rocher St-Ém, GC, Baron de Montfort, 15ha, R7,000

La-Rose-Côte-de-Rol St-Ém, GC, Y Mirande, 9ha, R4,000

La Rose Pourret* St-Ém, GC, B Warion, 8ha, R4,000

Roumieu* Bars, Mme Craveia-Goyaud, 16ha, W3,500

Roumieu Saut, CB, R Bernadet, 20ha, W2,000

Roumieu-Lacoste* Saut, Hervé Dubourdieu, 12ha, W3,000

St-Christoly Méd, CB, Hervé Héraud, 24ha, R16,500

Ségur H-Méd, CBS, M Grazioli, 36.8ha, R24,500

Sémeillan Mazeau List, CB, SC, 17ha, R8,000

Senailhac* E-D-M, Magnat, 55ha, R29,000, W1,500

Senilhac* H-Méd, CB, L & J-L Grassin, 20.5ha, R11,500

Simon Bars, CB, J Dufour, 17ha, W4,500

Suau Prem Côtes, Monique Bonnet, 59ha, R35,000 W4,000

du Tasta* Prem Côtes, P Perret, 13ha, R6,500

Templiers, Clos des L de Pom, Vignobles Meyer, 11ha, R6,000

de Terrefort-Quancard Bord Sup, Quancard family, 65.7ha, R37,000, W1,000

de Thau Bg, Vignobles Schweitzer, 27ha, R17,000
Timberlay* Bord Sup, R Giraud, 130ha, R55,000, W11,000
Tour Blanche Méd, CB, Vignobles d'Aquitaine, 38ha, R24,000
Tour Prignac Méd, CB, SC, 140ha, R88,000
Tour-du-Roc H-Méd, CB, Philippe Robert, 12ha, R6,000
Tour-St-Pierre St-Ém, GC, J Goudineau, 12ha, R7,000
Tour-Seran Méd, CB, Jean Guyon, 18ha, R12,000
des Trois Chardons Marg, C & Y Chardon, 2.7ha R1,500
Le Tuquet* Gr, P Ragon, 54ha, R25,000, W9,500
de Tustal E-D-M, H&B d'Armaillé, 34ha, W8,500, R8,500
La Vieille France Gr, M Dugoua, 23.5ha, R10,500, W2,500
du Vieux-Moulin Loup, Mme Perromat-Dauné, 13ha,
   W3,500
La Violette Pom, Vignobles S Dumas, 4.5ha, R2,000
Virou Bl, SCEA, 68ha R45,000

Index

Profiles of châteaux and domaines are indicated by **bold** numbers.
Secondary labels are shown in *italic*.